The CLAST Review Book

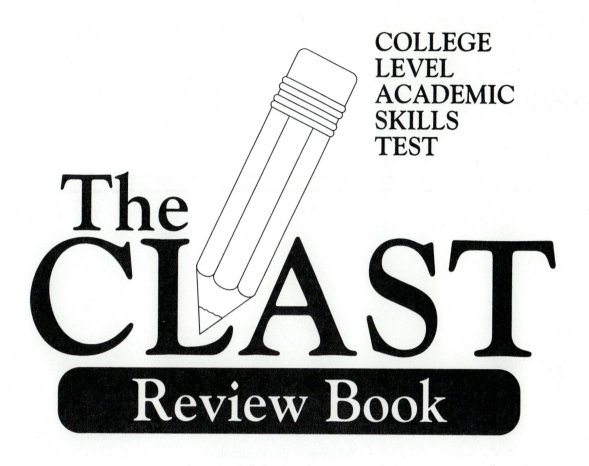

COLLEGE
LEVEL
ACADEMIC
SKILLS
TEST

The CLAST
Review Book

Elizabeth Metzger
University of South Florida
Department of English
Tampa, Florida 33620-5550

Lou Cleveland
Mathematics Department
Chipola Junior College
Mariana, Florida 32446

Jerre Kennedy
Department of English
Brevard Community College
Cocoa, Florida 32922

Harcourt Brace Jovanovich College Publishers

Fort Worth · Philadelphia · San Diego
New York · Orlando · Austin · San Antonio
Toronto · Montreal · Sydney · Tokyo

Publisher	Ted Buchholz
Acquisitions Editor	Stephen Jordan
Project Editor	Margaret Allyson
Production Manager	Cynthia Young
Design Supervisor	Terry Rasberry
Compositor	Publications Development Company of Texas

Printed in the United States of America

ISBN: 0-15-500041-1

456789012   085   9876543

The College Level Academic Skills Test (CLAST) was initiated by the Florida Legislature in the early 1970s as part of an overall program of educational accountability. Passing scores on the four subtests of the CLAST are required for all students attending Florida's public community colleges and universities who are seeking an A.A. or four-year degree. Passing the CLAST is also required for all students attending private colleges and universities who receive state financial aid and for persons who want to receive a Florida teaching certificate.

The CLAST consists of four subtests: Essay, English Language Skills, Reading Comprehension, and Mathematics. The Essay has a 60-minute time limit. The English Language Skills and Reading Comprehension Tests have a combined time limit of 80 minutes. The Mathematics Test has a time limit of 50 minutes. If students have to retake any subtest of the CLAST, they are generally allowed double the original time limit for that particular subtest.

Each subtest addresses specific basic competency academic skills that were selected by college faculty throughout the State of Florida. There are 61 mathematics skills, 12 reading skills, and 16 English language skills. The essay subtest focuses on a number of skills identified with writing (i.e., audience, purpose, coherence, support).

Each skill is assigned a specific code that identifies its subject area, its generic competency, and its broad skill category.

This text will help students prepare for the CLAST in the following ways:

1. A pre- and posttest for the math, reading, and English language skills; sample students' essays; and practice topics for the essay

2. Skills identification and commentary on the answers of the pre- and posttests for diagnosis and remediation

3. Information to help students identify incorrect and correct options

4. Helpful test-taking tips for each subtest

5. Original sample items for practice that simulate actual CLAST items

6. Instructional suggestions addressing the skills

This text can be used effectively in the classroom, in tutoring settings, and in individual preparation and review for the CLAST.

Contents

Section 1-1 Overview of the CLAST Essay Subtest   1

Section 1-2 Descriptions of Essay Ratings, Sample Student Papers, and CLAST Practice Topics   5

Section 2-1 Overview of the CLAST English Language Skills Test   21

Section 2-2 Pretest and Answer Key   23

Section 2-3 Word Choice Skills

Uses words that convey the denotative and connotative meanings required by context   35
Avoids wordiness   36

Section 2-4 Sentence Structure Skills

Places modifiers correctly   40
Coordinates and subordinates sentence elements according to their relative importance   41
Uses parallel expressions for parallel ideas   45
Makes logical comparisons   46

Section 2-5 Grammar, Spelling, Capitalization, and Punctuation Skills, Test, and Correct Passages with Answer Keys

Observes the conventions of standard American English grammar and usage   48

Section 2-6 Posttest and Answer Key   73

Section 3-1 Overview of the CLAST Reading Subtest   85

Section 3-2 Pretest and Answer Key   89

Section 3-3 Literal Comprehension Skills

Recognizes main ideas in a given passage   105
Identifies supporting details   108
Determines meaning of words on the basis of context   112

Section 3-4 Critical Comprehension Skills

Recognizes the author's purpose   115
Identifies the author's overall organizational pattern   119

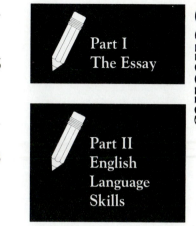

Part I
The Essay

Part II
English Language Skills

Part III
Reading

Distinguishes between statement of fact and
   statement of opinion   125
Detects bias   127
Recognizes author's tone   131
Recognizes explicit and implicit relationships
   within sentences   135
Recognizes explicit and implicit relationships
   between sentences   140
Recognizes valid arguments   143
Draws logical inferences and conclusions   152

Section 3-5   Posttest and Answer Key   156

Section 4-1   Overview of the CLAST Mathematics Subtest   169

Section 4-2   Pretest and Answer Key   171

Section 4-3   Arithmetic Skills

Adds and subtracts rational numbers   181
Multiplies and divides rational numbers   185
Adds and subtracts rational numbers in
   decimal form   188
Multiplies and divides rational numbers
   in decimal form   190
Calculates percent increase and percent
   decrease   192
Solves the sentence $a\%$ of b is c, where
   values for two variables are given   195
Recognizes the meaning of exponents   197
Recognizes the role of the base number in
   determining place value in the base-ten
   numeration system   198
Identifies equivalent forms of positive
   rational numbers involving decimals,
   percents, and fractions   201
Determines the order relation between real
   numbers   205
Identifies a reasonable estimate of a sum,
   average, or product of numbers   209
Infers relations between numbers in general
   by examining particular number pairs   213
Solves real-world problems which do not
   require the use of variables and which do
   not involve percent   217
Solves real-world problems which do require
   the use of variables and which do require
   the use of percent   219
Solves problems that involve the structure
   and logic of arithmetic   220

Part IV
Mathematics

Section 4-4   Algebra Skills

Adds and subtracts real numbers	224
Multiplies and divides real numbers	225
Applies the order-of-operations agreement to computations involving numbers and variables	227
Uses scientific notation in calculations involving very large or very small measurements	228
Solves linear equations	230
Solves linear inequalities	231
Uses given formulas to compute results, when geometric measurements are not involved	233
Finds particular values of a function	235
Factors a quadratic equation	236
Finds the roots of a quadratic equation	239
Solves a system of two linear equations in two unknowns	242
Uses properties of operations correctly	247
Determines whether a particular number is among the solutions of a given equation or inequality	251
Recognizes statements and conditions of proportionality and variation	254
Identifies regions of the coordinate plane which correspond to specified conditions and vice versa	259
Uses applicable properties to select equivalent equations and inequalities	269
Solves real-world problems involving the use of variables, aside from commonly used geometric formula	272
Solves problems that involve the structure and logic of algebra	274

Section 4-5   Geometry and Measurement Skills

Rounds measurements to the nearest given unit of the measuring device used	279
Calculates distances	282
Calculates areas	285
Calculates volumes	288
Identifies relationships between angle measures	291
Classifies simple plane figures by recognizing their properties	303
Recognizes similar triangles and their properties	308
Identifies appropriate units of measurement for geometric objects	314
Infers formulas for measuring geometric figures	317

Selects applicable formulas involving perimeters,
   areas, volumes of geometric figures   322
Solves real-world problems involving
   perimeters, areas, volumes of geometric
   figures   326
Solves real-world problems involving the
   Pythagorean property   330

Section 4-6   Statistics Skills, Including Probability

Identifies information contained in bar, line,
   and circle graphs   334
Determines the mean, median, and mode of
   a set of numbers   340
Uses the fundamental counting principle   343
Recognizes properties and interrelationships
   among the mean, median, and mode in a
   variety of distributions   347
Chooses the most appropriate procedure for
   selecting an unbiased sample from a target
   population   352
Identifies the probability of a specified
   outcome in an experiment   357
Infers relations and makes accurate
   predictions from studying statistical data   364
Interprets real-world data involving frequency
   and cumulative frequency tables   372
Solves real-world problems involving
   probabilities   380

Section 4-7   Logical Reasoning

Deduces facts of set inclusion or set
   non-inclusion from a diagram   388
Identifies statements equivalent to the
   negations of simple and compound
   statements   398
Determines equivalence or nonequivalence
   of statements   403
Draws logical conclusions from data   406
Recognizes that an argument may not be
   valid even though its conclusion is true   412
Recognizes valid reasoning patterns as
   illustrated by valid arguments in everyday
   language   415
Selects applicable rules for transforming
   statements without affecting their meaning   420
Draws logical conclusions when facts warrant
   them   422

Section 4-8   CLAST Mathematics Posttest and Answer Key   430

The CLAST requires that you write an essay on one of two topics in a 60-minute timed session. At a later date, two readers evaluate and independently score the essay holistically, not knowing what score the other reader has assigned to your essay. Presently, they use a four-point scale; each reader assigns a score for the paper reflecting the qualities of your paper as described in the rubric.

Your score on the essay is the combined score of the two readers, where scores represent "agreement" (i.e., the assignment of the same score or a contiguous score—one point away from the other score). Sometimes your essay may have been refereed, that is, read by a third reader because the two scores did not agree. In cases like this, the third reader rereads the paper, scores the paper, and discards the score that, in his or her judgment, does not reflect the quality of the paper.

The holistic evaluation procedure yields combined scores ranging from 2 (the lowest possible score) to 8 (the highest possible score), with calibrations between these. Presently, the passing score of the essay is 4 (i.e., 2/2); however, serious consideration is being given to making 5 (i.e., 3/2) the passing score beginning in the September 1991 administration of the test if the 4-point scale is retained.

In fact, during the September 1991 administration, the 6-point scale was used, and there is a strong possibility it will be used in future administrations. The combined scores of two readers range from 2 to 12, with 5 representing the passing score.

Discussions have also addressed the implementation of a 6-point rubric, offering more ranges and descriptions than the present 4-point scale. To familiarize you with both scales, this section will include papers reproduced as students actually wrote them under conditions simulating the CLAST's and scored by experienced CLAST readers according to the 4-point and the 6-point scale, sometimes offering marginal commentary to help you identify distinguishing characteristics of the essays. (However, the score that you see on the paper will be that of *one* reader, and not the combined scores of two readers.) In addition, this section includes original 4-point and 6-point scales describing overall characteristics of these particular papers to enhance the marginal commentary. Use this information carefully, however, and only as an instructional aid; evaluators are trained to read the *entire* paper quickly and impressionistically and not analytically, that is, not concentrating on the separate components of the essay.

The CLAST uses prompts (as topics) and directions that usually follow the format below:

**Part I
The Essay**

Section 1-1

Overview of the CLAST Essay Subtest

DIRECTIONS FOR ESSAY
You will have 60 minutes to plan, write, and proofread an essay on one of the topics below. READ THE TOPICS VERY CAREFULLY TO MAKE SURE YOU KNOW WHAT YOU ARE BEING ASKED TO DO.

TOPIC 1.		TOPIC 2.
The advantages/disadvantages of being a single, married, divorced, or widowed student	OR	Ways that people respond to stressful, uncomfortable, or embarrassing situations

Overview of the CLAST Essay Subtest

Read the two topics again and select the one on which you wish to write your essay. In order for your essay to be scored, it *must* be on *only one* of these topics, and it must address the entire topic.

In your essay, you should introduce the subject and then either

—explain the subject you have chosen, or

—take a position about your subject and support it.

At least two evaluators will read your essay and assign it a score. They will pay special attention to whether you

—have addressed the topic as it is written,

—have a clear thesis or main idea,

—develop your thesis logically and in sufficient detail,

—use well-formed sentences and paragraphs,

—use language appropriately and effectively, and

—follow standard practices in spelling, punctuation, capitalization, and grammar.

Take a few minutes to think about what you want to say before you start writing. Leave yourself a few minutes at the end of the period to proofread and make corrections.

You may cross out or add information as necessary. Although your handwriting will not affect your score, you should write as legibly as possible so the evaluators can easily read your essay.

You may use the following space to plan your essay. Your informal outline or plan will *not* be scored. Only what you write in your answer folder will be read.

The topics are chosen to reflect the student's general knowledge and experience, and the essay can be completed successfully in 60 minutes.

The sample student papers in this chapter address these topics. At the end of the chapter, additional CLAST topics appear to give you practice in timed, 60-minute impromptu writing. You and your instructors can compare your essays with the student essays in this chapter.

Some Tips for Writing the Essay

1. Make certain to address the topic; otherwise, your paper may not be scored because it is judged "off topic."

2. If you "freeze" during the timed writing or suffer writer's block, try to relax and get started by following one of the suggestions:

   a. Although the prompt does not specify an audience, purpose, or writer's role, try to imagine or mentally practice these for yourself. For example, you might approach the first prompt as a recently married student writing to a younger sibling, explaining the advantages or disadvantages of married life.

   b. Make a quick list of ideas to include, then organize and group the list into a loose plan for your paper.

   c. Ask journalistic questions such as who, what, where, why, and how to focus on your topic and generate ideas.

3. Try to finish your essay. Although every essay may not have a formal conclusion, try to provide some closure, even if the ending is brief.

4. Leave yourself about 10 minutes to reread, proofread, and edit your work to conform to standard edited English as closely as possible.

5. Make the essay reflect your best efforts; try to remember and demonstrate what you know about constructing a well organized and coherent piece of writing.

Remember, no *one* approach exists for addressing the topic. The evaluators are assessing how well the paper reflects the topic under the constraints of a timed writing.

Some Misconceptions about the Essay

1. Writing in pen versus pencil. Ink reproduces more easily for the raters to read, but either instrument is acceptable.

2. Skipping every other line. Students feel comfortable doing this as a practice they have used in their writing classes, but the CLAST does not require or penalize the practice.

3. Using or avoiding the first-person point of view—"I." You should select a point of view appropriate to the topic.

4. Using big, embellished words—what Ken Macrorie, author of *Telling Writing*, has called "Engfish." Let your voice, level of diction, etc., be

Overview of the CLAST Essay Subtest

natural rather than artificial. This means use the simple word or phrase if it is more appropriate than the more elaborate.

5. Copying over and scratching out. The papers are technically regarded as first drafts. Consequently, neat corrections are acceptable as long as they do not impede a smooth reading of your work.

6. Producing a five-paragraphed essay. Some students faithfully write only this type of essay during the CLAST; however, other multiparagraphed formats exist and receive passing scores from the evaluators.

What follows now are the CLAST rubrics, samples, annotated papers, additional descriptors of these papers, and practice CLAST topics.

Descriptions of the Levels of CLAST Essay Ratings (4 points)

Score of 4

Writer purposefully and effectively develops a thesis. Writer uses relevant details, including concrete examples, that clearly support generalizations. Paragraphs carefully follow an organizational plan and are fully developed and tightly controlled. A wide variety of sentences occurs, indicating that the writer has facility in the use of language; diction is distinctive. Appropriate transitional words and phrases or other techniques make the essay coherent. Few errors in syntax, mechanics, and usage occur.

Score of 3

Writer develops a thesis but may occasionally lose sight of purpose. Writer uses some relevant and specific details that adequately support generalizations. Paragraphs generally follow an organizational plan and are usually unified and developed. Sentences are often varied, and diction is usually appropriate. Some transitions are used, and parts are usually related to each other in an orderly manner. Syntactical, mechanical, and usage errors may occur but usually do not affect clarity.

Score of 2

Writer may state a thesis, but the essay shows little, if any, sense of purpose. Writer uses a limited number of details, but they often do not support generalizations. Paragraphs may relate to the thesis but often will be vague, underdeveloped, or both. Sequences lack variety and are often illogical, poorly constructed, or both. Diction is pedestrian. Transitions are used infrequently, mechanically, and erratically. Numerous errors may occur in syntax, mechanics, and usage and frequently distract from clarity.

Score of 1

Writer's thesis and organization are seldom apparent, but, if present, they are unclear, weak, or both. Writer uses generalizations for support, and details, when included, are usually ineffective. Underdeveloped, ineffective paragraphs do not support the thesis. Sentences are usually illogical, poorly constructed, or both. They usually consist of a series of subjects and verbs with an occasional complement. Diction is simplistic and frequently not idiomatic. Transitions and coherence devices, when discernible, are usually inappropriate. Syntactical, mechanical, and usage errors abound and impede communication.

Descriptions of Essay Ratings, Sample Student Papers, and CLAST Practice Topics

Descriptions of the Levels of CLAST Essay Ratings (6 points)

Score of 6

The paper presents or implies a thesis that is developed with noticeable coherence. The writer's ideas are usually substantive, sophisticated, and carefully elaborated. The writer's choice of language and structure is precise and purposeful, often to the point of being polished. Control of sentence structure, usage, and mechanics—despite an occasional flaw—contributes to the writer's ability to communicate the purpose.

Score of 5

The 5 paper presents or implies a thesis and provides convincing, specific support. The writer's ideas are usually fresh, mature, and extensively developed. The writer demonstrates a command of language and uses a variety of structures. Control of sentence structure, usage, and mechanics—despite an occasional flaw—contributes to the writer's ability to communicate the purpose.

Score of 4

The 4 paper presents a thesis and often suggests a plan of development, which is usually carried out. The writer provides enough supporting detail to accomplish the purpose of the paper. The writer makes competent use of language and sometimes varies the sentence structure. Occasional errors in sentence structure, usage, and mechanics do not interfere with the writer's ability to communicate the purpose.

Score of 3

The 3 paper presents a thesis and often suggests a plan of development, which is usually carried out. The writer provides support that tends toward generalized statements or a listing. In general, the support in a 3 paper is neither sufficient nor clear enough to be convincing. Sentence structure tends to be pedestrian and often repetitious. Errors in sentence structure, usage, and mechanics sometimes interfere with the writer's ability to communicate the purpose.

Score of 2

The 2 paper usually presents a thesis. The writer provides support that tends to be sketchy and/or illogical. Sentence structure may be simplistic and disjointed. Errors in sentence structure, usage, and mechanics frequently interfere with the writer's ability to communicate the purpose.

Score of 1

The 1 paper generally presents a thesis that is vaguely worded or weakly asserted. Support, if any, tends to be rambling and/or superficial. The writer uses language that often becomes tangled, incoherent, and thus confusing. Pervasive errors in sentence structure, usage, and mechanics frequently occur.

When I decided to return to school three and a half years ago, I was single and employed full-time. To say that my life was hectic would be an understatement, but I also knew that doing anything worthwhile is seldom easy. Fortunately, I had to keep this pace for only six months because when I married three years ago, my husband asked me to give up my job and devote my full attention to my studies. Though being a married full-time student is not always "paradise," this status does have its advantages.

First, I don't have to worry about pressure from a job competing with the abundant pressure I have from school. Keeping up with reading assignments, doing homework, writing papers, and otherwise preparing for class can be quite a task, if I do these things properly. Unless I have a few professors who have obviously conspired to give heavy assignments at the same time, I can usually juggle my work to get it all done well, and on time.

Second, and I know my unselfish husband considered this, I have time not only to do my school work, but also to spend with him. I feel that this is very important, especially because I plan to be married for longer than I plan to be a student. Though I have been married only three short years, I know my husband well. He demands a

Descriptions of Essay Ratings, Sample Student Papers, and CLAST Practice Topics

4-point scale:

4

6-point scale:

5 or **6**

—superior script; consistently witty, delightful, controlled

—superior language and diction, distinctive phrasing

—strong structure and development

Descriptions of Essay Ratings, Sample Student Papers, and CLAST Practice Topics

great deal of my time and attention, and if I were single and still working, I wouldn't even have time to date.

Another advantage is that I don't have to do all the household chores by myself. We share the work, and this frees me to have time to do fun things, too. I must admit that sharing the housework wasn't easy at first, but my investment in my husband's domestic education has really paid off.

Married life has also added an element of stability to my perspective. This is important because I think that I am far better now at analyzing things thoroughly than when I was a somewhat flighty, single person. I feel more secure, and because I feel that I have less to worry about now, I can devote more energy to truly grasping the knowledge that will help me through my new career.

Of course, I saved the best for last. My husband really supports everything I do. He proofreads papers, he argues with me when he _thinks_ I'm wrong, and he provides me with the extra push to go on when I think I can't. He's the best cheering section a person could hope for. With all of these things working in my favor, how could I fail?

There are very few incidents in life that cause one to feel pain, discomfort, embarassment, and happiness all at the same time. One of those rare and beautiful occassions is childbirth. The story that I tell is the birth of my son, Michael.

Valentine's Day had arrived and I was walking my dog, Sam, through the woods surrounding my home. God and I were having a conversation concerning the possibility that he might allow me to have the baby immediately since I was not prepared, and did not want to prepare, for a linguistics exam scheduled for the following day. I said, "God, let there be birth!" I got a cramp.

Seven hours later, I was experiencing a great deal of unbearable pain. Horror was the dominating thought that raced around the labor room. La Maze techniques were designed to occupy my mind so that I was too busy to feel the pain. I had a decision to make. Either I could pull out what little remaining hair my husband possessed or I could beg Dr. Lerner for an epidural.

Within ten minutes the anasthesiologist arrived to perform a spinal block. The pain of the contractions did little to mask the discomfort that the procedure entailed. I had to assume a tight fetal position, which is difficult to do when you have a baby in the way. My discomfort grew when the doctor missed the first opportunity to sedate me when

Descriptions of Essay Ratings, Sample Student Papers, and CLAST Practice Topics

4-point scale:
4

6-point scale:
5

—slight vagueness or inconsistent and unclear development of thesis

—some lapse in unity

—otherwise, detailed, delightful reading

—excellent choice of diction and invention

Descriptions of Essay Ratings, Sample Student Papers, and CLAST Practice Topics

my reflexes tore out the tube necessary for the solution. Once the uncomfortable procedure was completed, I was bastion of happiness. Much to the disgust of my waiting and anxious husband, I slept for the next eight hours, waking only to make sure he was still holding court in the labor room.

Embarrassment is the only word to describe many of the feelings that I experienced in the delivery room. There is no modesty allowed in a room where three people are standing between your legs wearing expressions of concentration, joy, and something that resembles nausea. I shamed myself when my first reaction to seeing Michael was to vomit. Such events in the delivery room paled in comparison to the tasks that I had to perform the next day. Nurses followed me to the bathroom, checked the episiotomy site every couple hours, and I had to learn to breastfeed my baby with my whole family watching, encouraging, and cheering.

Looking back on the birth, including the feelings of pain, discomfort, and embarrassment, I have to admit that it was one of the happiest times of my life. The birth of Michael made a family out of a couple. My son has been a source of great joy and wonder to my husband and me. I would do it all again. I would take on twice the inconveniences if it meant that I could have half the happiness that is now mine.

Descriptions of Essay Ratings, Sample Student Papers, and CLAST Practice Topics

4-point scale:

4

6-point scale:

5

The pressure placed on college students by teachers is great. The pressures placed on college students by themselves is greater. Now add the pressures placed on college students by their peers to the previously mentioned pressures, and you have one very stressed student. The single student at a college university has an unseen advantage that will benefit him or her in the long run.

Many pressures exist in the college environment that can hinder a student's performance. These pressures can be internal pressures, the normal pressure of homework and classroom competition, or external pressure, pressure from family, friends and job. The single student has the advantage of a more financially and mentally secure lifestyle that gives him or her the edge over his married peer.

All students have to deal with the pressure placed on them in the form of homework or term papers. However, a peaceful life outside of the classroom will most often lead to a peaceful life within the classroom. The single student does not have to deal with the emotional bouts of a spouse and a school assignment at the same time. He or she is the master of his or her own time and therefore can schedule his or her time for studies in a more pleasant manner. Not only does the single student have more personal time for studies, he or she usually will be financially more stable. Instead of spending money on labs, or gifts, he or she has only one person to look after. Thus, money becomes more plentiful. The more money the student has, the more options he or she has.

With the extra cash, a student could realistically cut back his or her hours from

Descriptions of Essay Ratings, Sample Student Papers, and CLAST Practice Topics

work. This would provide the student with more available time to buckle down and study. Or, if the student was on on top of his or her homework, the extra time could be spent in liesure, which in turn would help to relieve the stresses found at school. With this lessened pressure, the student would be more energetic and willing to study and learn.

Another option a single student has with the extra cash is to start a savings account. In a year or so the student will have collected a nice nest-egg that he or she could use at at his or her discretion. Perhaps the student would use the extra cash to take specialized educational courses outside of their major. Possibly a trip to Spain to learn Spanish or a trip to England to study at Cambridge. Whatever the use, the student shall be less stressed knowing that he or she is financially secure. In addition, a single student has the social advantage over the married student.

Single students can benefit from the relationships they form with their peers. They are able to socialize with students of the opposite sex without worrying about the spouse. Many late nights are spent studying with fellow students. These late nights might mean a higher grade. Most often the responsibilities of being married would prevent the married student from taking advantage of these late night study groups.

It is easy to see that the advantages offered a single student are many. School and homework affords enough pressures. The peace of mind, the financial security, and the social freedom of the single student cannot do anything but help the student enjoy school. A happy student is a good student, and the single student is both.

Ways People Respond

Depending on the type of environment a person was brought up in, reactions to stressful, embarrassing, or uncomfortable situations will undoubtedly vary. Often, the true character of a person will expose itself most honestly when forced to respond to an unpleasant or dangerous situation.

For instance, imagine that you and your girlfriend are in a restaurant or bar and an individual repeatedly pressures you to fight and/or "step outside." What you do reflects your patience, intelligence, and your ability to rationalize the specific situation. Personally, I have several times before witnessed the mentioned encounter and I am never surprised at the results. If you come from an abusive or poverty stricken family, you may react aggresively since violence is nothing new to you. If from a suburban, middle class family, mainly sheltered from occurances such as a fight seeker, you might act prematurely or unwisely because of lack of experience.

Another interesting example of varied reactions stems from public speaking of any type. Probably everyone has had knots in their stomachs in anticipation of being called upon to speak in class or for presentations of any kind. One outgoing individual might jump at the chance to grab the "spot light" while a more withdrawn person would rather take a failing grade or freeze up or even call in with a mysterious illness. Confidence comes from experience and trial upon trial of new ideas without letting one's fears inhibit progress.

Some students who "stress out" during exam time do so for several reasons. One may be that they have not studied and are

Descriptions of Essay Ratings, Sample Student Papers, and CLAST Practice Topics

4-point scale:
3

6-point scale:
4

—ample details, but somewhat mechanical and unsophisticated

—some weak or vague paragraphing

—a few infelicities of language but still rather competent

Descriptions of Essay Ratings, Sample Student Papers, and CLAST Practice Topics

unprepared to take the test or write the paper. Another student may "stress out" but still perform well under pressure because that is the only time the student will work. Still, yet another student overprepares and draws a blank on test day. Studying while fatigued or preoccupied are possible reasons for poor performance. A lousy study environment, whether avoidable or not, usually hinders a students progress.

A humorous, at least to some, happens in a crowded classroom, during silence. One student lets out an uncontrolled belch which everyone in the class can hear. The person may turn red, or could laugh with the class to relieve the tension. The more upset a person gets only magnifies the gravity of the situation. A simple "excuse me" followed by a return to studying as if nothing happened is yet another response to this situation.

Uncomfortable situations, like a room during summer with no air conditioning, bring out the worst in some people. Making things worse for everyone else, one student might complain constantly of the conditions. Another student may quietly fan his/herself and continue working whether happy or not.

The temperment or lack of temperment is directly dependant on the way you were brought up and taught to react by your parents or guardians.

"The Advantages of being a Single Student"

The transition of being a high school student into becoming an effective college level student can be an exciting road, or a vague and unsure maze. And to maintain that stability once it is achieved can be even more difficult, it may be a steady and upward climb. But no matter what, having as few obligations as possible allows for a much more managable journey. Thus, the life of a single student has many advantages.

Many of the advantages are quite obvious, Finacially, a student only has one obligation, his or herself. A prime example of this is that the single student only has to pay for themself, say for housing, food, clothing, or insurance, as oppossed to having to pay for an additional person. Another advantage may be having more time for themself. There is no need to sacrifice study time, etc. to be with a spouse. Not that being with someone else is a negative thing, but being a student requires time and dedication, and being a single student allows for ample time and dedication. And of course, being a student does not require absolutely 100% of one's time to studing, etc.

There are many free moments and sometimes a day or so. Being single would allow that student to do whatever he or she chooses to do with that free time, instead of being obligated to a marriage.

Clearly, the life of a single student has advantages, Time and money are just two examples of many advantages one may have, Of course, to be single or married is a free choice everyone has. However, during college it may be to one's advantage to remain single.

Descriptions of Essay Ratings, Sample Student Papers, and CLAST Practice Topics

4-point scale:
2

6-point scale:
2 or 3

—adequate transition and development

—errors in usage, mechanics

Descriptions of Essay Ratings, Sample Student Papers, and CLAST Practice Topics

4-point scale:
2

6-point scale:
2 or **3**

—some thoughtful ideas

—unclear thesis and paragraph development

—adequate knowledge of grammar

① The advantages & disadvantages of being a single student.

A cross-section of the students in a typical institution will probably reveal that the student body is made up primarily of young, single students who have followed the natural progression of attending a university immediately after high school. For most of them, college is just a more advanced stage of what they become used to in high school, but with more complicated courses and beurocracy. Usually, those who have take time away from the educational environment, due to careers or marriage, have to deal with a period of readjustment that can prove insurmountable.

One of the key benefits to the single status of a student is flexability. The student is able to follow whatever major they desire and school can become the focus of their lives; earning money and enduring relationships become secondary. But this very flexability can also be the cause of turmoil. Unlike a married student, there is no stable family unit to fall back on in times of crisis. Many of the friendships formed in school are transient in nature.

Single students are usually more susceptible to the fickle moods of peer pressure than those who are, or have been, married. Many seek confirmation of their acceptability from people not qualified to judge and miss the fact that they are going to school for themselves

Descriptions of Essay Ratings, Sample Student Papers, and CLAST Practice Topics

Question: The advantages or disadvantages of being a married student.

Being a Married Student

Being a married student would be difficult to explain or understand. It has many different advantages and disadvantages. In my beliefs it would be harder for the spouse than the student. The spouse may have feelings of jealousy toward the other, unless a bond of trust is built within them. Also the spouse may feel uncared for because all the student does is study. They would not spend as much time together as they intended. If the couple had a child as well, it would also be difficult. The spouse would have to tend to the child's needs all the time. That would bring up the question of family income. The fact of a child being born is unlikely, but it happens. In conclusion I would think that if you have trust and an understanding spouse you can have a successful marriage as well as being a student.

4-point scale: **1**

6-point scale: **2**

—underdeveloped, inadequately developed

—lack of focus or discernible thesis

(2) Ways people respond to stressful, uncomfortable, or embarrassing situations.

Responding to Stress

Generally people are responsive to stressful, uncomfortable, and embarrassing situations. Some responses differs from another depending on the situation. Take, for example, a stressful response. Being overstressed, people will find a way to relax themselves to the situation. Some responses are; taking certain drugs, taking time off wherever stress is generated, or even sleeping. Usually sleeping is a bad response due to the fact that stress is still present and sleeping is only temporary. Taking certain drugs can be wrong because it is also temporary and stress will build again. Drugs can also be addictive. The most successful response it to find to roots of stress and find ways to overcome it.

4-point scale: **1**

6-point scale: **1**

—inadequate development of ideas

—no paragraph development

—insufficient evidence of mastery of writing skills to assess essay

Descriptions of Essay Ratings, Sample Student Papers, and CLAST Practice Topics

If you need some additional guidance about the overall qualities of these papers, you might find the following scales written specifically for this set of papers helpful. You might also want to use the sample CLAST topics to practice writing the essay.

Topics:

1. An idea presented in modern times that has had harmful effects
2. A natural event that occurs periodically and that has beneficial effects
3. Important qualities of a friend or parent

Descriptions of Sample Student Papers (4 points)

Score of 4	The writer has a clear thesis that is very thoroughly and logically developed. The paper is virtually error-free. What distinguishes this paper more clearly from a 3 paper is the overwhelming effort to achieve a particular stylistic effect for the reader—the persuasive nature or plenitude of concrete arguments in support of the thesis, the quality of diction, variety in sentence construction, the occasional turn of phrase, and use of figures of speech, innovative organizational patterns, or transitional forms, etc.
Score of 3	The paper has organizational strength; the thesis is clear and logically and sufficiently developed. There is adequate control of the mechanics of language. There will be occasional lapses of language, which may be inconsistent because the writer is careless or has clearly failed to edit the script. Otherwise, the paper is coherent and easy to read; the writer demonstrates a satisfactory knowledge of grammar, style in sentence construction, and vocabulary.
Score of 2	The writer does have a basic notion of thesis and organization. The essay itself may sometimes be thoughtful, and the writer may even have tried to develop a stylistic approach or deploy a mature vocabulary. More often, the paper is abbreviated and not fully developed or has only an oblique or nominal relationship to the assigned topic. Some paragraph ideas may overlap or may be unclear. Where the ideas are adequately developed, the strength of the paper is usually undermined by too many obvious errors with mechanics or awkward syntax.
Score of 1	The writer has clearly not demonstrated a satisfactory knowledge of the basic principles of composition or of maturity in thinking. The paper is generally short or crowded with extraneous, unconvincing, or clichéd ideas. The writer may seem aware of paragraphing sometimes, but the supporting arguments are not sufficiently developed or are illogical and unclear. There is a general lack of clarity also because of inadequate knowledge of syntax and diction; quite often—though not always—errors in grammar, spelling, and punctuation occur.

Descriptions of Sample Student Papers (6 points)

Descriptions of Essay Ratings, Sample Student Papers, and CLAST Practice Topics

Score of 6

Paragraphs are very well developed in support of a quality thesis idea. The essay reads very well because of its superior language. The most distinctive quality of this paper is the maturity of the ideas and the deliberate and well-executed style to create a particular (poetic) effect for the reader, either through specialized diction, a specific voice, an organizational pattern, well-crafted sentences, the use of a variety of figures of speech, or innovative treatment of the topic.

Score of 5

This paper is very distinctive in terms of its thesis idea and the depth and quality of its supporting details. Organization plan is clear and strictly adhered to. The paper achieves verve through its competent diction, unobtrusive grammar, sentence variety, punctuation, etc. There may be minor errors that are invariably negligible.

Score of 4

The writer clearly understands the basic principles of composition—the thesis idea is logically developed through adequate and concrete supporting paragraphs. There are no infelicities of language to interfere with an appreciation of the writer's purpose. However, the paper may be a little on the short side, or it may have lapses in sentence construction, usage, diction, and a variety of mechanical problems that may be due to carelessness or lack of proper revision.

Score of 3

The writer has a clear thesis idea and attempts to develop it in clearly defined paragraphs. However, the ideas are not usually significant, nor are they adequately developed. The writer may attempt a deliberate style in sentence structure and diction but these are superficial, often breaking down here and there. Competence in language is generally minimal, and the longer the essay, the more obvious the weaknesses in sentence structure and mechanics manifest themselves.

Score of 2

The writer may have a notion of a thesis and its development, but the arguments are either uninspiring, predictable, illogical, or undeveloped. Language— grammar, syntax, punctuation, spelling, diction, etc.—is generally weak.

Descriptions of Essay Ratings, Sample Student Papers, and CLAST Practice Topics

Score of

1

The writer lacks knowledge of the basic principles of composition. The thesis is unclear, and paragraph ideas are extraneous, unconvincing, clichéd, or illogical. When the paper is not just too short to merit any fair assessment, it is replete with an assortment of language problems.

Introduction

The English Language Skills Test is composed of several skills. The skill descriptions with an asterisk (*) do not appear as separate discrete test items but occur in passages of approximately 250 words each. Those without an asterisk are tested separately through different formats, explained more fully in the explanatory introduction preceding these skills.

Overview of the CLAST English Language Skills Test

Word Choice Skills

B.1.a.	Uses words that convey the denotative and connotative meanings required by context
B.1.c.	Avoids wordiness

Sentence Structure Skills

B.2.a.	Places modifiers correctly
B.2.b.	Coordinates and subordinates sentence elements according to their relative importance
B.2.c.	Uses parallel expressions for parallel ideas
*B.2.d.	Avoids fragments, comma splices, and fused sentences

Grammar, Spelling, Capitalization, and Punctuation Skills

*B.4.a.	Uses standard verb forms
*B.4.b.1.	Maintains agreement between subject and verb
*B.4.b.2.	Maintains agreement between pronoun and antecedent
*B.4.c.	Uses proper case forms
*B.4.e.	Uses adjectives and adverbs correctly
*B.4.f.	Avoids inappropriate shifts in tense
B.4.g.	Makes logical comparisons
*B.5.a.	Uses standard practice for spelling
*B.5.b.	Uses standard practice for punctuation
*B.5.c.	Uses standard practice for capitalization

The Questions

The questions are multiple choice. The wrong answers will focus on various errors in grammar, usage, and mechanics. The content of the questions follows certain specified guidelines. For example, punctuation primarily focuses on commas, semicolons, colons, apostrophes, and quotation marks; proper case forms primarily focus on the nominative, objective, and possessive cases of pronouns. A general review of rules governing usage and mechanics will help you a great deal in this section.

Special Considerations

Skills tested in the passages in Part II are intended to simulate the proofreading and editing that you do in your own writing. Consequently, you will encounter the skills in the context of a whole piece of writing. Your ability to proofread and edit carefully will help you in this section of the test.

The English Language Skills Test and Reading Test have a combined time limit of 80 minutes, so use the time carefully, pacing yourself accordingly. Both tests use a number of passages to test the skills, so read attentively and efficiently at the first reading, because you may not have a great deal of time to

Overview of the CLAST English Language Skills Test

reread. The topics of the passages are of general interest and usually nontechnical, intending to appeal to a broad audience.

At the beginning and end of the section, sample pre- and posttests occur, approximating the emphasis and proportion of each item of the CLAST, to give you practice in taking the test. In addition, the test skill code occurs beside the answers so that you can review the skill independently if you need to.

Test-Taking Hints

Familiarize yourself with the format of the questions. Sometimes the passages require you to focus on three different parts of the sentence for the correct answer, and sometimes they require you to focus on one part of the sentence, offering several options from which you can choose the correct answer. The formats for the questions and items precede the skills presented in the section.

If you have time remaining during the test, recheck your answers. Usually, the position of the correct answer will vary; consequently, correct answers will occur in positions from A to D. In addition, go back and complete questions you may not have answered at first. Examine the possible answers, eliminate weak ones, and select the best remaining one.

DIRECTIONS
Some of the sentences in the following two passages contain errors.
Read the passages. Then choose the correct answer for the questions
on selected sentences from the passages.

The following pretest
simulates the types and
proportion of the items in
the College Level
Academic Skills Test.
The test is composed of
2 passages with 11
questions each.
Approximately 13
questions address the
remaining skills. In the
real test you will have
about 80 minutes total
for the English Language
Skills Test and the
Reading Test;
consequently, you might
want to practice with this
test and the Reading Test
with the time limit in
mind. In the passage
section of the test, the
answer key and corrected
passage will occur at the
end of the chapter.

Passage 1-Test Copy

At first, there was only a civilian watchman at the Tomb of the Unknown
Soldier, but since 1948 it had been guarded night and day by elite sentinels of
the 3rd Infantry Regiment, one of America's most honored military units, the
"Old Guard." Tomb guard duty is voluntary and some transfer after a year or
so, fatigued by the intensity of the job. But the rewards are unforgettable. One
is the Tomb Guard Identification Badge; issued only after six to nine months of
honorable service at the Tomb and a stringent testing of skills. So far some
2700 good men have trained as sentinels, but only about 350 has won the
coveted badge. "The greatest reward use to be to walk the post," says Sgt.
Marcus Mayville. "The men develop an emotional attachment to the
Unknowns and feel themselves priviledged to do this duty."

It is not easy. A sentinel walks. An hour at a time in winter, a half-hour in
summer—as many as eight times a day no matter the weather or distractions. He
walks on, forbidden to speak, 21 paces along the plaza, representing a 21-gun
salute; the highest military tribute. His rifle is always on the shoulder away from
the Tomb, symbolizing their readiness to defend it. Then he faces the Tomb for
21 seconds, shifts the rifle to his other shoulder, turns and walks back.

"What sets Arlington apart," says former superintendent Raymond J.
Costanzo, a D-Day veteran, "is compulsive perfection, no one around here
accepts less."

1. At first, there was only a civilian <u>watchman</u> at the Tomb of the
                                          A
   Unknown Soldier, but since 1948 it <u>had been guarded</u> night and day
                                           B
   by elite sentinels of the 3rd Infantry Regiment, one of <u>America's</u> most
                                                              C
   honored military units, the "Old Guard."

   A. watchmen
   B. has been guarded
   C. Americas'
   D. No change is necessary.

2. Tomb guard duty is <u>voluntary, and</u> some transfer after a year or so,
   fatigued by the intensity of the job.

   A. voluntarily, and
   B. voluntarily: and
   C. voluntarily; and
   D. No change is necessary.

3. One is the Tomb Guard Identification <u>Badge; issued</u> only after six to
   nine months of honorable service at the Tomb and a stringent testing
   of skills.

   A. Badge, issued
   B. Badge issued
   C. Badge. Issued
   D. No change is necessary.

4. So far some 2700 good men have trained as sentinels, but only about 350 <u>has won</u> the coveted badge.

   A. had won
   B. have won
   C. would have won
   D. No change is necessary.

5. "The <u>greatest</u> reward <u>use to be</u> to walk the <u>post</u>," says Sgt. Marcus
          A   B   C
   Mayville.

   A. greater
   B. used to be
   C. post"
   D. No change is necessary.

6. "The men develop an <u>emotional</u> <u>attachment</u> to the Unknowns and
                     A   B
   feel themselves <u>priviledged</u> to do this duty."
                  C

   A. emotionally
   B. detachment
   C. privileged
   D. No change is necessary.

7. A sentinel <u>walks. An</u> hour at a time in <u>winter,</u> a half-hour in summer—
                 A   B
   as many as eight times a day no matter <u>weather</u> or distractions.
                                   C

   A. walks an
   B. Winter a
   C. whether
   D. No change is necessary.

8. He walks <u>on, forbidden</u> to <u>speak,</u> 21 paces along the <u>plaza,</u>
                A   B
   representing a 21-gun salute; the highest military tribute.
       C

   A. on; forbidden
   B. speak: 21
   C. plaza. Representing
   D. No change is necessary.

9. His rifle is always on the shoulder away from the <u>Tomb,</u> symbolizing
                                           A
   <u>their</u> <u>readiness</u> to defend it.
    B   C

   A. Tomb symbolizing
   B. his
   C. readyness
   D. No change is necessary.

10. Then he faces the <u>Tomb</u> for 21 <u>seconds, shifts</u> the rifle to <u>his</u> other
                    A   B   C
    shoulder, turns and walks back.

    A. incorrect
    B. seconds shifts
    C. their
    D. No change is necessary.

11. "What sets Arlington apart," says former superintendent Raymond J. Costanzo, a D-Day <u>veteran</u>, "is compulsive <u>perfection, no one</u> around
                     A   B

here <u>accepts less</u>."
       C

  A. Veteran "is
  B. perfection. No one
  C. excepts less
  D. No change is necessary.

Passage 2-Test Copy

In TV's earliest days, anchors tended not to take themselves too serious, befitting people who read lines other people wrote to describe stories other people reported and pictures other people took. It was difficult getting film from the field to the studio and time-consuming to process them. Someone has to fill the gap. So anchors read headlines and, in between, would of hawked cigarettes and Chevies.

    That was more than 40 years ago. Eons in television time. And those modestly paid pitchmen bear about as much resemblance to todays pampered stars as Wilbur and Orville's first plane does to a Boeing 747.

    Modern anchors are ferried about in limousines and chartered jets; trailed by press aides, makeup artists and producers; represented by platoons of agents, attorneys and accountants; befriended by members of Congress; fawned over by admiring reporters. Their power is also reflected in their salaries—Dan Rather is reported to earn over $3 million a year, Tom Brokaw $2 million, and Peter Jennings $1.8 million.

    Network anchors enjoy more fame and power than any journalists in media history. Appearing in their usual regalia, often perched in enormous booths, they chat up pundits and pooh-bahs, and gravely emcee events. They interpret and analyze the biggest stories from hurricanes to revolutions to wars. They virtually host national elections, sometimes they even become part of the news they report.

12. In TV's earliest days, anchors <u>tended</u> not to take themselves too
                             A

   <u>serious</u> befitting people who read lines other people wrote to describe
    B

   <u>stories</u> other people reported and pictures other people took.
    C

  A. tend
  B. seriously
  C. story's
  D. No change is necessary.

13. It was <u>difficult</u> getting film from the <u>field</u> to the studio and
        A   B

   time-consuming to process <u>them</u>.
                      C

  A. difficulty
  B. feild
  C. it
  D. No change is necessary.

14. Someone <u>has</u> to fill the gap.

   A. had
   B. should of had
   C. have
   D. No change is necessary.

15. So anchors read headlines and, in between, <u>would of hawked</u> cigarettes and Chevies.

   A. would have hawked
   B. hawked
   C. would have hawk
   D. No change is necessary.

16. That was more <u>than</u> 40 <u>years</u> <u>ago. Eons</u> in television time.
                       A   B   C

   A. then
   B. year's
   C. ago, eons
   D. No change is necessary.

17. And those modestly paid pitchmen <u>bear</u> about as much <u>resemblance</u> to
                                       A   B
   <u>todays</u> pampered stars as Wilbur and Orville's first plane does to a
    C
   Boeing 747.

   A. bare
   B. resemblence
   C. today's
   D. No change is necessary.

18. Modern anchors are ferried about in limousines and chartered <u>jets;</u>
   <u>trailed</u> by press aides, makeup artists and producers; represented by
    A
   platoons of <u>agents,</u> attorneys and accountants; <u>befreinded</u> by members
                B   C
   of Congress; fawned over by admiring reporters.

   A. jets, trailed
   B. agents',
   C. befriended
   D. No change is necessary.

19. <u>Their</u> power is also reflected in their <u>salaries—Dan</u> Rather is reported
    A   B
   to earn over $3 million a year, Tom Brokaw $2 million, and Peter
   <u>Jennings</u> $1.8 million.
    C

   A. Thier
   B. salaries: Dan
   C. Jennings'
   D. No change is necessary.

20. Appearing in their usual <u>regalia, often</u> perched in enormous booths,
                              A
   they <u>chat</u> up pundits and pooh-bahs, and gravely <u>emcee</u> events.
         B   C

   A. regalia often
   B. chats

C. emsee
D. No change is necessary.

21. They interpret and analyze the biggest <u>stories from</u> hurricanes to revolutions to wars.

    A. stories, from
    B. stories: from
    C. stories; from
    D. No change is necessary.

22. They <u>virtually</u> host national <u>elections, sometimes</u> they even <u>become</u>
    　　　　A　　　　　　　　　　　B　　　　　　　　　　　C

    part of the news they report.

    A. virtual
    B. elections. Sometimes
    C. became
    D. No change is necessary.

DIRECTIONS
Choose the most effective word or phrase within the context suggested by the sentences.

---

23. One child attempted to
    A. confuse
    B. distract
    C. bewilder
    _____ the mother while the

    other child tried to swipe a couple of cookies.

24. As a student, John's greatest handicap is that he tends to
    A. omit
    B. disregard
    C. neglect
    _____ his homework at times.

DIRECTIONS
Choose the underlined and lettered portion that is unnecessary within the context of the passage.

---

25. The <u>commencement</u> speaker started delivering his remarks in a very
    　　　　A

    inaudible <u>and hard-to-hear</u> voice that frustrated some students <u>who</u>
    　　　　　　　　B

    <u>were interested</u> and bored <u>the rest</u>. Finally, someone turned on the
    　　　C　　　　　　　　　　　D

    microphone, and the speaker began <u>again</u>.
    　　　　　　　　　　　　　　　　　　E

    A. commencement
    B. and hard-to-hear
    C. who were interested
    D. the rest
    E. again

**Pretest and
Answer Key**

26. In the present world of the 1990s, people tend to buy many items they
A ——————————— B

do not need. If a new toy comes on the market, folks think they have
C

to have it. Some people even worry about whether they have the best
D

brand of a toy or whether their neighbors have better ones.
E

- A. the present world of
- B. many
- C. think they
- D. best
- E. their

DIRECTIONS
*For the underlined sentence(s), choose the answer that expresses the
meaning with the most fluency and the clearest logic within the
context.*

---

27. After the votes were counted, the excited supporters cheered. Smith
won, and he won by a landslide, but he had rigged the vote.

- A. Smith won, and he won by a landslide, but he had rigged the vote.
- B. Smith won by a landslide, but he had rigged the vote.
- C. Being that Smith won by a landslide, he had rigged the vote.
- D. Since Smith won by a landslide, he had rigged the vote.

28. Most of us expect good fortune most of the time because that is what
we get. However, the Browns no longer take good luck for granted.
Their restaurant on the harbor burned down, and they rebuilt it, and
Hurricane Hugo came through Charleston the first week it was
reopened, and Hugo blew it down again.

- A. Their restaurant on the harbor burned down, and they rebuilt it,
and Hurricane Hugo came through Charleston the first week it
was reopened, and Hugo blew it down again.
- B. After their restaurant on the harbor burned down, and they
rebuilt it, and Hurricane Hugo came through Charleston the first
week it was reopened and blew it down again.
- C. After their restaurant on the harbor burned down, they rebuilt it,
and Hurricane Hugo came through the first week it was reopened
and blew it down again.
- D. Being as their restaurant on the harbor burned down, and they
rebuilt it, and Hurricane Hugo came through Charleston the first
week it was reopened and blew it down again.

29. Unlike Wordsworth, Coleridge, who was a poet in the Romantic
period, sometimes wrote poems that are mystical. He was short and
sad, and he was an opium addict, but he was one of the best poets to
write in English.

- A. He was short and sad, and he was an opium addict, but he was one
of the best poets to write in English.
- B. He was short and sad and an opium addict, but he was one of the
best poets to write in English.

C. He was short and sad, and he was an opium addict, and he was one of the best poets to write in English.

D. A short, sad opium addict, he was one of the best poets to write in English.

DIRECTIONS
Choose the sentence that logically and correctly expresses the comparisons.

---

30. A. Sandy Lyle's golfing is better than Tom Watson's.
    B. Sandy Lyle's golfing is better than Tom Watson.
    C. The golfing of Sandy Lyle is better than Tom Watson's.

DIRECTIONS
Choose the sentence that expresses the thought most clearly and effectively and that has no errors in structure.

---

31. A. Unable to stop bleeding, the paramedic came to my rescue.
    B. Unable to stop bleeding, my rescuer was a paramedic.
    C. Unable to stop bleeding, I was rescued by a paramedic.

32. A. Discouraged by the grueling demands of boot camp, desertion seemed like a good option for Ernest.
    B. Discouraged by the grueling demands of boot camp, Ernest at first thought that desertion seemed like a good option.
    C. Discouraged by the grueling demands of boot camp, a good option for Ernest became desertion.

DIRECTIONS
Choose the sentence that expresses the thought most clearly and effectively and that has no errors in structure.

---

33. A. Cooking well requires following directions, watching the clock, and to make sure you have the necessary ingredients.
    B. Cooking well requires following directions, watching the clock, and making sure you have the necessary ingredients.
    C. Cooking well requires following directions, and also you have to watch the clock and make sure you have the necessary ingredients.

34. A. The visiting baseball team resented not only the booing but also the umpires' favoritism of the home team.
    B. Not only the booing, but the visiting baseball team also resented the umpires' favoritism of the home team.
    C. The visiting baseball team resented the booing, and also the umpires favored the home team.

35. A. Human personalities are shaped by heredity and environment.
    B. Human personalities are shaped by heredity and what type of environment we live in.
    C. Human personalities are shaped by what our heredity is and environment.

Pretest and Answer Key

Elliott, Lawrence. "This Hallowed Ground." Reader's Digest, May 1991: pp. 53–54.

Katz, Jon. "The Trouble with TV News." Reader's Digest, May 1991: p. 126.

Pretest Answer Key

Passage 1-Corrected

At first, there was only a civilian watchman at the Tomb of the Unknown Soldier, but since 1948 it has been guarded night and day by elite sentinels of the 3rd Infantry Regiment, one of America's most honored military units, the "Old Guard." Tomb guard duty is voluntary, and some transfer after a year or so, fatigued by the intensity of the job. But the rewards are unforgettable. One is the Tomb Guard Identification Badge, issued only after six to nine months of honorable service at the Tomb and a stringent testing of skills. So far some 2700 good men have trained as sentinels, but only about 350 have won the coveted badge. "The greatest reward used to be walk the post," says Sgt. Marcus Mayville. "The men develop an emotional attachment to the Unknowns and feel themselves privileged to do this duty."

It is not easy. A sentinel walks an hour at a time in winter, a half-hour in summer—as many as eight times a day no matter the weather or distractions. He walks on, forbidden to speak, 21 paces along the plaza, representing a 21-gun salute, the highest military tribute. His rifle is always on the shoulder away from the Tomb, symbolizing his readiness to defend it. Then he faces the Tomb for 21 seconds, shifts the rifle to his other shoulder, turns and walks back.

"What sets Arlington apart," says former superintendent Raymond J. Costanzo, a D-Day veteran, "is compulsive perfection. No one around here accepts less."

Passage 2-Corrected

In TV's earliest days, anchors tended not to take themselves too seriously, befitting people who read lines other people wrote to describe stories other people reported and pictures other people took. It was difficult getting film from the field to the studio and time-consuming to process it. Someone had to fill the gap. So anchors read headlines and, in between, hawked cigarettes and Chevies.

That was more than 40 years ago, eons in television time. And those modestly paid pitchmen bear about as much resemblance to today's pampered stars as Wilbur and Orville's first plane does to a Boeing 747.

Modern anchors are ferried about in limousines and chartered jets; trailed by press aides, makeup artists and producers; represented by platoons of agents, attorneys and accountants; befriended by members of Congress; fawned over by admiring reporters. Their power is also reflected in their salaries: Dan Rather is reported to earn over $3 million a year, Tom Brokaw $2 million, and Peter Jennings $1.8 million.

Network anchors enjoy more fame and power than any journalists in media history. Appearing in their usual regalia, often perched in enormous booths, they chat up pundits and pooh-bahs, and gravely emcee events. They interpret and analyze the biggest stories, from hurricanes to revolutions to wars. They virtually host national elections. Sometimes they even become part of the news they report.

Question	Answer	Skill
1. A.	is incorrect because the word is plural.	
B.	is correct because the verb tense is appropriate for the context.	III.B.4.f
C.	is incorrect because the apostrophe is in the wrong position.	
2.	A., B., and C. are incorrect because they are adverbs and the punctuation is incorrect.	
D.	is correct because no change is necessary.	III.B.4.e
3. A.	is correct because the comma is necessary.	III.B.5.b
	B. and C. are incorrect because of punctuation.	
4. B.	is correct because the verb agrees with the subject.	III.B.4.b.1
	A. and C. are incorrect because the verb tense is inappropriate.	
5. A.	is incorrect because the comparative degree is inappropriate.	
B.	is correct because it is a standard verb.	III.B.4.a
C.	is incorrect because a comma is necessary.	
6.	A. and B. are incorrect because they are the wrong words for the context.	
C.	is correct because of spelling.	III.B.5.a
7. A.	is correct because the elimination of the period eliminates a sentence fragment.	III.B.2.d
B.	is incorrect because no capital letter is necessary.	
C.	is incorrect because the word does not fit the context.	
8.	A., B., and C. are incorrect because of punctuation.	
D.	is correct because the commas are necessary.	III.B.5.b
9. A.	is incorrect because the comma is necessary.	
B.	is correct because the pronoun agrees with the antecedent.	III.B.4.b.2
C.	is incorrect because the word is misspelled.	
10. A.	is correct because no capital letter is necessary.	III.B.5.c
B.	is incorrect because a comma is necessary.	
C.	is incorrect because the pronoun is plural.	
D.	is correct because no change is necessary.	III.B.5.c III.B.5.b III.B.4.b.1

**Pretest and
Answer Key**

Question		Answer	Skill
11.	A.	is incorrect because no capital letter is necessary.	
	B.	is correct because the punctuation eliminates a comma splice.	III.B.2.d
	C.	is incorrect because the word is not appropriate for the context.	
12.	A.	is incorrect because the verb tense is inappropriate.	
	B.	is correct because an adverb is necessary.	III.B.4.e
	C.	is incorrect because the word is in the inappropriate form.	
13.	A.	is incorrect because the word is inappropriate for the context.	
	B.	is incorrect because of misspelling.	
	C.	is correct because the pronoun agrees with the antecedent.	III.B.4.b.2
14.	A.	is correct because the verb tense is appropriate.	III.B.4.f
	B.	is incorrect because the verb is nonstandard usage.	
	C.	is incorrect because the verb does not agree with the subject.	
15.	A.	is incorrect because the verb tense is inappropriate.	
	B.	is correct because the verb is a standard form and in the correct tense.	III.B.4.a
	C.	is incorrect because the verb is nonstandard usage.	
16.	A.	is incorrect because the word is inappropriate for the context.	
	B.	is incorrect because the apostrophe is inappropriate.	
	C.	is correct because the punctuation eliminates the sentence fragment.	III.B.2.d
17.	A.	is incorrect because the word is inappropriate for the context.	
	B.	is incorrect because the word is misspelled.	
	C.	is correct because the apostrophe is necessary.	III.B.5.c
18.	A.	is incorrect because the punctuation is inappropriate.	
	B.	is incorrect because the apostrophe is inappropriate.	
	C.	is correct because of spelling.	III.B.5.a

Question		Answer	Skill
19.	A.	is incorrect because the word is misspelled.	
	B.	is correct because the punctuation is appropriate.	III.B.5.b
	C.	is incorrect because the apostrophe is inappropriate.	
20.	A.	is incorrect because a comma is necessary.	
	B.	is incorrect because verb does not agree with subject.	
	C.	is incorrect because word is misspelled.	
	D.	is correct because no change is necessary.	III.B.5.b III.B.4.b.1 III.B.5.a
21.	A.	is correct because the comma is necessary.	III.B.5.b
		B. and C. are incorrect because of punctuation.	
22.	A.	is incorrect because the word is inappropriate for the context.	
	B.	is correct because the punctuation eliminates the comma splice.	III.B.2.d
	C.	is incorrect because the verb tense is inappropriate.	
23.	B.	is correct because of the context.	III.B.1.a
24.	C.	is correct because of the context.	III.B.1.a
25.	B.	is correct because the word and "inaudible" are redundant.	III.B.1.c
26.	A.	is correct because the phrase and "the 1990s" are redundant.	III.B.1.c
27.	B.	is correct because it represents the most effective embedding, in this case coordination.	III.B.2.b
28.	C.	is correct because it represents the most effective embedding, in this case subordination and coordination.	III.B.2.b
29.	D.	is correct because it represents the most effective embedding, in this case coordination of an adjective phrase.	III.B.2.b
30.	A.	is correct because the comparison is complete and logical, using possessive forms for each proper noun.	III.B.4.g
31.	C.	is correct because the phrase correctly modifies the subject.	III.B.2.a

Question	Answer	Skill
32. B.	is correct because the phrase correctly modifies the subject.	III.B.2.a
33. B.	is correct because the phrases are parallel.	III.B.2.c
34. A.	is correct because the "not only . . . but also" phrase is parallel.	III.B.2.c
35. A.	is correct because the nouns are parallel.	III.B.2.c

Denotation and Connotation

The format of the items is multiple choice, with three options. Each option should include words or phrases that are (1) emotionally loaded so as to carry highly connotative force (e.g., *The old hag*); or (2) neutral or mixed so as to carry denotative force (e.g., *mother-in-law*); or (3) precise so as to carry highly denotative force (e.g., *my spouse's mother*). The correct option is the word or phrase whose denotative and connotative meanings are appropriate within the context suggested by the sentence(s). The two incorrect options are words or phrases whose denotative or connotative meanings are inappropriate within the context suggested by the sentence(s).

Sample Items

Section 2-3

Word Choice Skills

III.B.1.a
The student uses words that convey the denotative and connotative meanings required by context.

This section requires you to select the word or phrase that has been omitted in 1 or 2 sentences not exceeding 30 words. The omitted word or phrase should be determinable from the context. The meaning, style, and level of usage should be consistent with standard written American English.

DIRECTIONS
Choose the most effective word or phrase within the context suggested by the sentences.

---

1. Adlai Stevenson, revered by many, was seen by his admirers as

   a/an   A. politician
   B. incumbent }_____, not merely an elected official.
   C. statesman

2. One personality trait people often seek to develop in themselves,

   because it is an indication of future success, is   A. assertiveness
   B. arrogance }_____.
   C. pridefulness

3. Willy Loman's   A. fickle
   B. mercurial }_____ moods frightened Linda, his wife.
   C. arbitrary

   He would frequently shift from one emotion to its opposite, even in midsentence.

4. The supervisor was chastened for having   A. antiquated
   B. ancient }_____
   C. old-fashioned

   ideas.

5. Felix and Oscar made unlikely roommates: Oscar was overly casual about cleaning and often criticized Felix for being

   A. fastidious
   B. fussy }_____.
   C. choosy

6. When we are young, we are taught to hold on tightly to our

   A. ideals
   B. illusions }_____.
   C. fallacies

7. That actress has made a success of developing a   A. childish
   B. infantile }_____
   C. childlike

   persona that is very appealing to audiences.

8. The doctor's   A. frank
   B. blunt }_____ appraisal of John's prognosis seemed
   C. candid

   almost to indicate a lack of compassion on his part.

Word Choice Skills

9. Greg didn't mind the grade he had earned; he felt it was better to earn

a/an
- A. mediocre
- B. ordinary
- C. average

____ grade after working hard than to receive an easy grade without effort.

10. His constituents praised the legislator for his persistence and

- A. resolution
- B. stubbornness
- C. obstinacy

____ in sticking to his goals.

ANSWERS: 1.C., 2.A., 3.B., 4.A., 5.B., 6.A., 7.C., 8.B., 9.C., 10.A.

III.B.1.c
The student avoids wordiness.

Wordiness

These items occur in passages of 60 words or less with 5 underlined and lettered choices. The passages contain superfluous, redundant, and/or wordy expressions. This section requires you to choose the word or word group that is unnecessary to the context without affecting the overall meaning of the passage. On the other hand, the four incorrect options serve a necessary function within the context.

Sample Items

DIRECTIONS
Choose the underlined and lettered portion that is unnecessary within the context of the passage.

---

1. After <u>we had been at</u> Dinosaur National Monument in Utah for three
   A

   days, we decided to <u>extend our vacation and</u> include a trip to Salt Lake
   B

   City, located <u>nearby</u> within a day's drive. Because both destinations
   C

   were educational <u>and exciting</u> to visit, the trip yielded memories that
   D

   lasted <u>for years.</u>
   E

   A. we had been at
   B. extend our vacation and
   C. nearby
   D. and exciting
   E. for years

2. Spelunkers, or cave explorers, face challenges <u>at every turn.</u> Not only
   A   B

   must they avoid <u>hazardous</u> formations and slippery walkways that
   C

   threaten them all along the path, they must also avoid damaging the

groups of natural outcroppings of rocks themselves. For instance, if
D

stalactites are touched even inadvertently, they could stop growing.
E

A. , or cave explorers,
B. at every turn
C. hazardous
D. groups of
E. even inadvertently

3. The International Bank for Reconstruction and Development,
otherwise known to most people as the World Bank, is the largest
A

bank in the world. It has over 150 members and an accumulated
B   C   D

income, unallocated as of 1988, of 9.2 billion dollars.
E

A. to most people
B. in the world
C. over
D. accumulated
E. as of 1988,

4. Some people choose unusual marriage ceremonies. One of the most
A   B   C

unconventional weddings of the year occurred recently near the city of
D

Clearwater, Florida. A young couple got married in a glider, hovering
2000 feet above the ground. As the best man and maid of honor
floated delicately in an adjacent glider, a notary public proclaimed the
E

marriage official.

A. people
B. unusual
C. of the most
D. the city of
E. delicately

5. In order to understand fully a written text, a student might need to
A

reread it again. Some texts are difficult and comprehension does not
B   C

come easily the first time around. Experts say, however, that the
D

increased effort will pay off in better understanding of the material.
E

A. fully
B. again
C. Some
D. , however,
E. increased

6. Patrick broke his hip in a biking mishap last weekend. Since then, his
A   B

life has completely changed. Although he has had surgery and can
C

Word Choice Skills

now walk using crutches, some of the simplest, most everyday activities present <u>inordinate</u> challenges; for example, he has difficulty
D

descending <u>down</u> a staircase.
E

A. biking
B. his
C. has had surgery and
D. inordinate
E. down

7. Carrie was an outstanding <u>softball</u> player; in fact, she was the star <u>of</u>
A

<u>the team</u>. She could play several positions <u>in the field</u> with
B   C

professionalism and spirit, but her strength was hitting the ball. When Carrie was at bat, <u>the team knew</u> it could expect a hit that was likely to
D

land outside <u>of</u> the fence.
E

A. softball
B. of the team
C. in the field
D. the team knew
E. of

8. When the phone rang <u>at midday</u> about noon, Jeff picked it up <u>quickly</u>.
A   B

He was expecting a phone call <u>from Ann</u>, and it was overdue. She had
C

told him she would call <u>when her plane arrived</u> <u>from Seattle</u>,
D   E

scheduled for an 11:30 A.M. landing.

A. at midday
B. quickly
C. from Ann
D. when her plane arrived
E. from Seattle,

9. Politicians <u>who run for political office</u> have to meet certain qualifying
A

<u>requirements</u> in order to run for specific offices. <u>Usually</u>, they have to
B   C

meet deadlines. <u>Sometimes</u> they must be in certain age ranges. For
D

some offices, they must live in <u>designated</u> precincts.
E

A. who run for political office
B. requirements
C. Usually,
D. Sometimes
E. designated

Word Choice Skills

10. Jane teaches <u>at a school</u> for <u>blind</u> children. She teaches them songs <u>to</u>
              A   B

    <u>sing</u> and games. When Jane has worked <u>with a child</u> for awhile, she
    C   D

    <u>usually</u> finds that she has gained the child's trust.
    E

    A. at a school
    B. blind
    C. to sing
    D. with a child
    E. usually

11. Many people believe that cars are <u>often</u> not as important to <u>teenage</u>
                             A   B

    females as they are to teenage males. Females certainly want cars as
    much as males <u>do</u>. The reason <u>why</u> is that females want cars mostly to
                  C   D

    have the freedom to go where they want to go when they want to go.
    Males need cars to help them protect certain images they have <u>of</u>
    <u>themselves</u>.
    E

    A. often
    B. teenage
    C. do
    D. why
    E. of themselves

ANSWERS: 1.C., 2.D., 3.A., 4.D., 5.B., 6.E., 7.E., 8.A., 9.A., 10.C., 11.D.

**Sentence
Structure Skills**

III.B.2.a
The student places
modifiers correctly.

Modifiers

This section requires you to identify the correct use of modifying words, phrases, or clauses in sentences not exceeding 30 words. The format is multiple choice, with three complete sentences that express the same general thought as the options. The correct option is the sentence that has correctly placed modifiers. Modifiers are limited to words, phrases, or clauses used as adjectives or adverbs. The two incorrect options are sentences with dangling or misplaced words, phrases, or clauses used as modifiers.

Sample Items

DIRECTIONS
Choose the sentence that expresses the thought most clearly and effectively and that has no errors in structure.

---

1. A. United States citizens are guaranteed the right to bear arms in the Constitution.
   B. The right to bear arms, in the Constitution, is guaranteed to United States citizens.
   C. In the Constitution, United States citizens are guaranteed the right to bear arms.

2. A. The parent noticed and chastened the disobedient child reading the newspaper.
   B. While reading the newspaper, the parent noticed the disobedient child and chastened him.
   C. The parent noticed the disobedient child and chastened him while he was reading the newspaper.

3. A. Jenny was so elated with her artwork she pointed it out, swelling with pride, on the wall.
   B. Jenny pointed out her artwork swelling with pride on the wall because she was so elated.
   C. Elated and swelling with pride, Jenny pointed out her artwork on the wall.

4. A. In that museum is a ring over 200 years old that was once worn by Marie Antoinette.
   B. There is a ring that was worn by Marie Antoinette in the museum that is over 200 years old.
   C. Marie Antoinette once wore the ring that is in the museum over 200 years old.

5. A. If you use that thesaurus, you may find a synonym for the word "anxiety," which is in the bookshelf.
   B. A synonym for the word "anxiety" may be found in the shelf if you use that thesaurus.
   C. In the bookshelf is a thesaurus wherein you may find a synonym for the word "anxiety."

6. A. Be ready to hang the wallpaper as soon as it is completely pasted.
   B. Be ready to hang the wallpaper as soon as completely pasted.
   C. Be ready to hang the wallpaper as soon as pasted all over completely.

Sentence Structure Skills

7. A. Torn to the ground, the contractors had to build a new hotel on the site.
   B. Torn to the ground, the hotel was replaced by another one that the contractors built on the site.
   C. The contractors, being torn to the ground, had to build a new hotel on the site.

8. A. While wondering how to work the machine, I noticed it turn on by itself.
   B. While wondering how to work the machine, it turned on by itself.
   C. The machine, while wondering how to work it, turned on by itself.

9. A. By hitting the gavel on the table, the meeting ended.
   B. By hitting the table, the meeting was ended by use of the gavel.
   C. By hitting the gavel on the table, the president ended the meeting.

10. A. Although only a little girl, the mother expected exemplary behavior.
    B. The mother expected exemplary behavior although being only a little girl.
    C. Although she was only a little girl, she knew that her mother expected exemplary behavior.

11. A. Instead of riding her bike, she read a book.
    B. Instead of riding her bike, a book was read.
    C. Instead of riding her bike, reading a book was her choice of activities.

ANSWERS: 1.C., 2.B., 3.C., 4.A., 5.C., 6.A., 7.B., 8.A., 9.C., 10.C., 11.A.

Coordination and Subordination

The format is multiple choice with four sentences that express the same general thought. The A option will replicate the form of the sentence(s) as it appears in the passage. The correct option is the sentence that logically and fluently coordinates or subordinates the ideas. The three incorrect options are sentences that employ inappropriate or ineffective coordination or subordination.

III.B.2.b
The student coordinates and subordinates sentence elements according to their relative importance.

Sample Items

DIRECTIONS
For the underlined sentence(s), choose the answer that expresses the meaning with the most fluency and clearest logic within the context.

1. Shakespeare's audiences had to use their imagination in more ways than one, when viewing a play at the Globe Theater. Since small boys whose voices had not yet changed played the female roles, women were not permitted to perform on the Elizabethan stage.

   A. Since small boys whose voices had not yet changed played the female roles, women were not permitted to perform on the Elizabethan stage.

Sentence Structure Skills

This section contains approximately 55 word passages containing 1 or 2 sentences whose logic, fluency, and effectiveness can be improved through coordination or subordination. In the test, coordination may appear as two or more independent clauses within the same sentence, or compound subjects and/or verbs. Subordination may appear as clauses that function as nouns, adjectives and adverbs, phrases (such as appositives), participial modifiers, and other embedded structures.

B. As women were not permitted to perform on the Elizabethan stage, small boys had to play the female roles, although their voices had not yet changed.

C. Because women were not permitted to perform on the Elizabethan stage, the female parts were played by small boys whose voices had not yet changed.

D. Until small boys whose voices had not yet changed were permitted to play the female roles, women were not permitted to perform on the Elizabethan stage.

2. Many of our beautiful lakes and waterways are being destroyed by acid rain, which is the result of pollutants, such as sulfates and nitrates. Since these pollutants are carried by the wind, they fall to the earth in concentration, and end up in our once-pristine lakes killing the fish.

A. Since these pollutants are carried by the wind, they fall to the earth in concentration, and end up in our once-pristine lakes killing the fish.

B. After these pollutants are carried by the wind, they fall to the earth in concentration, ending up in our once-pristine lakes and killing the fish.

C. When they end up in our once-pristine lakes killing the fish, it is because these pollutants have been carried in concentration by the wind, and have then fallen to the earth.

D. Although these pollutants end up killing the fish in our once-pristine lakes, they are concentrated when they are carried by the wind and so they fall to the earth.

3. Even though the war had not been officially declared in the spring of 1776, General Washington and General Howe spent much of the early months of that year in attempts at peaceful negotiation, through their representatives. These efforts were fruitless, however, and in August of that year, hostilities broke out and the battle was begun.

A. Even though the war had not been officially declared in the spring of 1776, General Washington and General Howe spent much of the early months of that year in attempts at peaceful negotiation, through their representatives.

B. While General Washington and General Howe spent much of the early months of that year in attempts at peaceful negotiation through their representatives, the war had not been officially declared in the spring of 1776.

C. Whereas General Washington and General Howe spent much of the early months of that year with their representatives in peaceful negotiation, the war was not officially declared in the spring of 1776.

D. After the war had not been officially declared in the spring of 1776, General Washington and General Howe spent the remaining months in attempts at peaceful negotiation with their representatives.

4. The recipe for pound cake, which is a true Southern classic, calls for simple ingredients. The complicated steps one must take to follow this recipe are also challenging, even for the most accomplished cook.

A. The complicated steps one must take to follow this recipe are also challenging, even for the most accomplished cook.

B. The complicated steps are challenging for the most accomplished cook who would try to follow this recipe.

C. While the steps are complicated, they would challenge the most accomplished cook who could follow this recipe.

D. The steps one must take to follow this recipe, however, are complicated and challenging, even for the most accomplished cook.

Sentence Structure Skills

5. Our physics professor can make a difficult but crucial lesson easy to understand. Because she is in demand, her courses are required and her classes consistently close out early during registration.

   A. Because she is in demand, her courses are required and her classes consistently close out early during registration.
   B. Although her courses are in demand, her classes are required and they consistently close out early during registration.
   C. For this reason, she is in demand; her classes, especially the required ones, consistently close out early during registration.
   D. Since she is in demand, her classes consistently close out early during registration; thus, her classes are required.

6. In *The Caine Mutiny*, the captain of the ship was judged an ineffective leader, so he was put on trial, relieved of command and he was highly embittered. The ordeal was a severe one for all concerned.

   A. In *The Caine Mutiny*, the captain of the ship was judged an ineffective leader, so he was put on trial, relieved of command and he was highly embittered.
   B. In *The Caine Mutiny*, the captain of the ship became highly embittered after he was judged incapable of effective leadership, put on trial and relieved of his command.
   C. The captain of the ship had been judged incapable of effective leadership, so he was put on trial in *The Caine Mutiny* and relieved of his command, becoming highly embittered.
   D. The trial in *The Caine Mutiny* was because the captain had become highly embittered, and so he was judged incapable of effective leadership and relieved of his command.

7. One of the most popular tourist destinations is New York City. Visitors may come for the theater, both on- and off-Broadway, or the museums, such as The Cloisters with its fabulous collection of medieval art; even the shopping attracts thousands of out-of-towners yearly.

   A. Visitors may come for the theater, both on- and off-Broadway, or the museums, such as The Cloisters with its fabulous collection of medieval art; even the shopping attracts thousands of out-of-towners yearly.
   B. Thousands of out-of-towners yearly are attracted to the theater and the museums: they come for on- or off-Broadway, the collections of medieval art, and the fabulous shopping.
   C. Out-of-towners may come because they are attracted by the thousands to the on- or off-Broadway theater as well as the shopping and museums with medieval collections of art as The Cloisters.
   D. The Theater, both on- and off-Broadway, the museums, The Cloisters, and the shopping may attract thousands of out-of-towners yearly.

Sentence Structure Skills

8. Physical challenges need not impede anyone's success or progress in life. <u>One important example would be Franklin Delano Roosevelt: he contracted polio when he was a young man, and he became President of the United States.</u>

   A. One important example would be Franklin Delano Roosevelt: he contracted polio when he was a young man, and he became President of the United States.
   B. Franklin Delano Roosevelt became President of the United States when he had contracted polio as a young man, and he would be an important example of this.
   C. Franklin Delano Roosevelt, who contracted polio as a young man but became President of the United States nevertheless, would be one important example.
   D. One important example would be a President of the United States, Franklin Delano Roosevelt, who contracted polio when he was a young man.

9. <u>Kevin Moore strutted into the room, and as he did so he tripped over the trash can.</u> Unfortunately, he frightened the cat, who promptly shredded the curtains as she tried to get out the closed window.

   A. Kevin Moore strutted into the room, and as he did so he tripped over the trash can.
   B. As Kevin Moore strutted into the room, he tripped over the trash can.
   C. Since Kevin Moore strutted into the room, he tripped over the trash can.
   D. Even though Kevin Moore strutted into the room, and he tripped over the trash can.

10. <u>Jean-Henri Dunant was a citizen of Switzerland, and he felt sorry for Austrian soldiers wounded in the Napoleonic Wars; therefore, he started an organization, and it was later named the Red Cross.</u> The Red Cross still comes to the aid of victims of war and natural disasters, such as earthquakes.

    A. Jean-Henri Dunant was a citizen of Switzerland, and he felt sorry for Austrian soldiers wounded in the Napoleonic Wars; therefore, he started an organization, and it was later named the Red Cross.
    B. Jean-Henri Dunant was a citizen of Switzerland who felt sorry for Austrian soldiers wounded in the Napoleonic Wars; therefore, he started an organization, and it was later named the Red Cross.
    C. Jean-Henri Dunant, a Swiss citizen who felt sorry for Austrian soldiers wounded in the Napoleonic Wars, started an organization, and it was later named the Red Cross.
    D. A Swiss citizen who felt sorry for Austrian soldiers wounded in the Napoleonic Wars, Jean-Henri Dunant started an organization later named the Red Cross.

ANSWERS: 1.C., 2.B., 3.A., 4.D., 5.C., 6.B., 7.A., 8.C., 9.B., 10.D.

Parallelism

This section requires you to select parallel expressions (i.e., words, phrases, clauses) for parallel ideas. The format is multiple choice, with 3 complete sentences not exceeding 30 words each that express the same general thought as options. The correct option is the sentence that contains parallel expressions for parallel ideas. The two incorrect options are sentences with nonparallel words, phrases, or clauses.

Section 2-4, cont'd

Sentence Structure Skills

III.B.2.c
The student uses parallel expressions for parallel ideas.

Sample Items

DIRECTIONS
Choose the sentence that expresses the thought most clearly and effectively and that has no errors in structure.

---

1. A. Every year, I spend several months in Colorado; I like to ski, to skate, and hiking the trails.
   B. Because I like skiing, skating, and hiking the trails, I spend several months in Colorado every year.
   C. I like skiing, skating, and to hike the trails, so I spend several months in Colorado every year.

2. A. The instructor promised his students a trip to the Keys and a day at an underwater park, if they developed expertise in diving.
   B. The instructor promised his students a trip to the Keys if they developed expertise in diving and they would also get a day at an underwater park.
   C. The instructor promised his students a trip to the Keys and that they would also get a day at an underwater park, if they developed expertise in diving.

3. A. The use of knowledge is as important as using reason.
   B. Knowledge is as important as reason.
   C. Knowledge is as important as reasoning things out.

4. A. Don is both an amateur athlete and he enjoys paleontology.
   B. Don is an amateur athlete and enjoys paleontology.
   C. Don is both an amateur athlete and a paleontologist.

5. A. In her graduation address, the valedictorian spoke eloquently and in an inspiring manner about the need for more selflessness and every member of the class contributing more.
   B. In her graduation address, the valedictorian spoke eloquently and inspiringly about the need for greater selflessness and contribution from every member of the class.
   C. The valedictorian, in her graduation address, spoke inspiring and with eloquence about the need for every member of the class to be more selfless and contribute more.

6. A. Whether drunk or when he was sober, David liked to pick fights with strangers.
   B. Whether drunk or sober, David liked to pick fights with strangers.
   C. When he was drunk or whether sober, David liked to pick fights with strangers.

7. A. Jimmy Carter is a man retired from the Navy and who was President of the United States.

**Sentence Structure
Skills**

B. Jimmy Carter is a man who retired from the Navy, and he was President of the United States.

C. Jimmy Carter is a man who retired from the Navy and who was President of the United States.

8. A. A puppy watches the way the older dogs act and how to obey the trainer.

B. A puppy watches the actions of the older dogs and also he sees how they obey the trainer.

C. A puppy watches the way the older dogs act and obey the trainer.

9. A. There are two kinds of employees: workers and those who manage.

B. There are two kinds of employees: those who work and managers.

C. There are two kinds of employees: workers and managers.

ANSWERS: 1.B., 2.A., 3.B., 4.C., 5.B., 6.B., 7.C., 8.C., 9.C.

**III.B.4.g
The student makes
logical comparisons.**

Logical Comparisons

This section requires you to select the one sentence from three choices that most logically and correctly expresses the comparison. Each sentence should not exceed 25 words. The incorrect choices may focus on incomplete comparisons (e.g., My new book is better.), ambiguous comparison (e.g., He likes Mary better than Sue.), or grammatically incorrect comparisons (e.g., We like to have a mind like Bill.).

Sample Items

DIRECTIONS
Choose the sentence that logically and correctly expresses the comparisons.

---

1. A. The new method of learning math seems to be much different than the old method.

B. The new method of learning math seems to be much different from the old method.

C. The new method of learning math, seems much more different than the old method.

2. A. Paul hit more home runs last month than any member of the team.

B. Paul hit more home runs last month than most any member of the team.

C. Paul hit more home runs last month than any other member of the team.

3. A. We had four tests in physiology this week. Which was the harder?

B. We had four tests in physiology this week. Which was the hardest?

C. We had four tests in physiology this week. Which were the harder of them all?

4. A. The new refrigerator we just bought runs more quietly and efficiently than the old one.

B. Our old refrigerator does not run quietly or efficient like the new one does.

C. Our new refrigerator we just bought runs more quietly and efficiently.

5. A. Summer Dream is the name of a rose that is more prettier than any in the garden.
   B. Summer Dream is the name of a rose that is the prettier of the others in the garden.
   C. Summer Dream is the name of a rose that is prettier than any other in the garden.

6. A. Running in the Gasparilla Distance Classic is more challenging than local sporting events.
   B. Runners in the Gasparilla Distance Classic face more of a challenge than they would in other local sporting events.
   C. Those who run in the Gasparilla Distance Classic are more challenging than runners in other local sports.

7. A. She is as friendly to her neighbors as any other person who has lived in that house, if not friendlier.
   B. She is friendly to her neighbors as any other person who has lived in that house, if not friendlier.
   C. She is equally as friendly to her neighbors, if not friendlier, than any other person who has lived in that house.

8. A. Mozart's music is more striking than the rest of his contemporaries; it has never gone out of style.
   B. Mozart's music has never gone out of style; it is more striking than that of his contemporaries.
   C. Mozart's music is the most striking of his contemporaries; it will never go out of style.

9. A. Brittany is old as, if not older than, Kelsey.
   B. Brittany is as old as, if not older than, Kelsey.
   C. Brittany is as old, if not older than, Kelsey.

10. A. Monday was warmer.
    B. Monday was warmer, as well as Tuesday.
    C. Monday was warmer than Tuesday.

11. A. Sean is taller than anybody.
    B. Sean is taller than any other boy in his class.
    C. Sean is more tall than we expected him to be.

12. A. A vacation to Mexico is cheaper than a vacation to France.
    B. A vacation to Mexico is cheaper.
    C. A Mexican vacation is cheaper than a French vacation.

ANSWERS: 1.B., 2.C., 3.B., 4.A., 5.C., 6.B., 7.A., 8.B., 9.B., 10.C., 11.B., 12.C.

Grammar, Spelling, Capitalization, and Punctuation Skills Test, and Correct Passages with Answer Keys

---

III.B.4
The student observes the conventions of standard American English grammar and usage.

Passages

This part of the test requires you to proofread and edit. Rather than the skills appearing in separate, unrelated sentences, they occur in approximately 250 word passages. Your task is to identify the correct use of the following skills appearing in the passages:

B.2.d.	a.	comma splices and fused sentences;
B.2.d.	b.	fragments;
B.4.a.	c.	standard verb forms;
B.4.b.1	d.	subject/verb agreement;
B.4.b.2	e.	pronoun/antecedent agreement;
B.4.f.	f.	verb tense;
B.5.a.	g.	spelling;
B.5.b.	h.	commas.

Any three of the following will also occur in the passages:

B.4.c.	i.	pronoun case forms;
B.4.e.	j.	adjectives and adverbs;
B.5.b.	k.	semicolons or colons;
B.5.b.	l.	apostrophes;
B.5.b.	m.	quotation marks;
B.5.c.	n.	capitalization.

Consequently, each passage will test you on a total of 11 items.

At the end of the section the skill code appears after the answer so that you may review that skill independently if you need to.

Sample items in this section follow two formats. In one format, a word or word group is underlined. The four options for answers will focus on this part of the sentence only. These questions appear like this:

> We need not blame anyone but ourselves for the mistake occurring in the <u>site</u> measurements.
>
> A. cite
> B. sight
> C. sightly
> D. No change is necessary.

In other questions, the sentence will have three underlined parts for you to analyze. The correct answer is either the one that represents usage in standard written American English, or option D., which reads "No change is necessary" or "Change all of the above."

> We need not blame <u>anyone but</u> <u>ourselves</u> for the oversight in the <u>site</u>
>   A   B   C
> measurements.
>
> A. anyone, but
> B. ourself
> C. sightly
> D. No change is necessary.

Sample Items

Grammar, Spelling, Capitalization, and Punctuation Skills Test, and Correct Passages with Answer Keys

---

DIRECTIONS
Some of the sentences in the following passages contain errors. Read the passage. Then choose the correct answer for the questions on selected sentences from this passage.

Passage 1-Test Copy

Numerous varieties of parrots exist and all can be studied through the science of Ornithology. A few of them are plane in appearance, but most of them have brilliant red, blue, green and yellow feathers. There are more than 300 species in the animal kingdom, they are native to tropical and sub-tropical forests. In fact; the parrot's body is special adopted to life in the sub-tropical forest. In this forest, there are many brightly-colored flowers and plants. The parrots colors actually help him to hide from his natural enemies. When he sits high on top of a tall tree, their colors makes him look like a simple flower, or a special fruit. In addition to coloring that is designed for a purpose, parrots also have bodies that are designed and adapted. To gathering seeds, nuts and fruit for food. Their feet have a very strong grip: two toes points forward and two backward so they can seize fruit and nuts. The bills are hooked differently because different parrots had different methods of gathering food. Some parrots are accustom to scraping seeds out of pods, and so they have bills that are pointed and very sharp.

PASSAGE 1 DIRECTIONS
Choose the correct option for each question.

---

1. <u>Numerous</u> varieties of parrots exist and all <u>can be</u> studied through the
      A   B
   science of <u>Ornithology</u>.
            C

   A. Numerus
   B. might have been
   C. ornithology
   D. Change all of the above.

2. A few of them are <u>plane</u> in <u>appearance</u>, but most of them have <u>brilliant</u>
                 A   B   C
   red, blue, green and yellow feathers.

   A. plain
   B. appearence
   C. brillient
   D. No change is necessary.

3. There are more than 300 species in the animal <u>kingdom, they</u> are native to tropical and sub-tropical forests.

   A. kingdom; They
   B. kingdom; they
   C. kingdom: they
   D. No change is necessary.

**Grammar, Spelling,
Capitalization, and
Punctuation Skills
Test, and Correct
Passages with
Answer Keys**

4. In fact; the parrot's body is <u>special</u> <u>adopted</u> to life in the sub-tropical
      <u>   </u>   B   C

forest.

  A. In fact, the
  B. specially
  C. adapted
  D. Change all of the above.

5. In this <u>forest</u>, there are many <u>brightly-colored</u> <u>flowers</u> and plants.
           A   B   C

  A. forest;
  B. brightly, colored
  C. flowers,
  D. No change is necessary.

6. The <u>parrots colors</u> actually help him to hide from his natural enemies.

  A. parrot's colors
  B. parrots' colors
  C. parrots colors'
  D. parrots color's

7. When he <u>sits</u> high on top of a tall <u>tree</u>, <u>their</u> color makes him look
          A   B C

like a simple <u>flower,</u> or a special fruit.
            D

  A. sets
  B. tree;
  C. his
  D. flower;

8. In addition to coloring that is designed for a <u>purpose</u>, parrots also have
                                          A

<u>bodies</u> that are <u>designed</u> and <u>adapted</u>. <u>To</u> gathering seeds, nuts and
  B   C   D

fruit for food.

  A. purpose:
  B. bodies'
  C. designed,
  D. adapted to

9. <u>Their</u> feet have a very strong grip: two toes <u>points</u> forward and two
  A   B

backward so they can <u>seize</u> fruit and nuts.
                  C

  A. There
  B. point
  C. sieze
  D. No change is necessary.

10. The bills are hooked <u>differently</u> because different parrots <u>had</u> different
    A   B   C

methods of gathering food.

  A. It's
  B. different
  C. have
  D. Change all of the above.

Section 2-5, cont'd

Grammar, Spelling,
Capitalization, and
Punctuation Skills
Test, and Correct
Passages with
Answer Keys

11. Some parrots are <u>accustom</u> to scraping seeds out of <u>pods, and so</u> they
                      A   B
    have <u>bills that</u> are pointed and very sharp.
         C

   A. accustomed to
   B. pods; and so
   C. bills, that
   D. Change all of the above.

Passage 2-Test Copy

Many people have a fear of snakes though this reaction may not necessarily be
based on logic. One snake, however, that has justifiably caused a response both
of fear and fasination is the rattlesnake. The rattlesnake is a deadly snake; it has
poisonous fangs that are folded back into it's mouth when not needed. When
the rattler strikes, though, those fangs came right out, ready to sink into prey.
The fangs are actually hollow, and they are connected to glands inside the
cheeks. That are full of venom. When the fangs sink in, the venom comes
quick from the glands and flows into the creature being bitten. Many people do
not realize that snakes are actually deaf they do not hear sounds. What they can
sense, however, is vibrations, and this is one of the ways the snake can find a
victim. In addition, the rattler can flicker its forked tongue in the air to pick up
scents; either from an enemy or from prey. Another way the rattler can find a
small bird or animal for prey is by sensing their body heat. This snake has two
pits on its face that are customize to help the snake "perceive" heat rays coming
from an animal's body.

PASSAGE 2 DIRECTIONS
Choose the correct option for each question.

---

1. Many people have a fear of <u>snakes though</u> this reaction may not
   necessarily be based on logic.

   A. snakes, though,
   B. snakes, though
   C. snakes; though,
   D. snakes: though

2. One snake, however, that has <u>justifiably</u> caused a <u>response</u> both of fear
                                 A   B
   and <u>fasination</u> is the rattlesnake.
       C

   A. justefiably
   B. responce
   C. fascination
   D. No change is necessary.

3. The rattlesnake is a <u>deadly snake;</u> <u>it has</u> poisonous fangs that are
                         A   B
   folded back into <u>it's mouth</u> when not needed.
                     C

   A. deadly snake,
   B. they have

Grammar, Spelling, Capitalization, and Punctuation Skills Test, and Correct Passages with Answer Keys

C. its mouth
D. Change all of the above.

4. When the rattler <u>strikes, though,</u> those fangs <u>came right</u> <u>out,</u> ready to
                 A   B   C

   <u>sink into</u> prey.
     D

   A. strikes; though,
   B. come right
   C. out: ready
   D. sink, into

5. The fangs are actually hollow, and they are connected to glands inside the <u>cheeks. That</u> are full of venom.

   A. cheeks that
   B. cheeks' that
   C. cheeks; that
   D. No change is necessary.

6. When the fangs <u>sink in</u>, the venom <u>comes</u> <u>quick</u> from the glands and
                  A   B   C

   flows <u>into</u> the creature being bitten.
       D

   A. sank in
   B. came
   C. quickly
   D. in

7. Many people do not realize that snakes are actually <u>deaf they</u> do not hear sounds.

   A. deaf; they
   B. deaf, they
   C. deaf. they
   D. No change is necessary.

8. What they can sense, <u>however,</u> <u>is</u> <u>vibrations,</u> and this sensing is one of
                        A   B   C

   the ways the snake can find a victim.

   A. ; however,
   B. are
   C. vibrations;
   D. Change all of the above.

9. In <u>addition, the</u> rattler can flicker its <u>forked</u> tongue in the air to pick
          A   B

   up <u>scents;</u> either from an enemy or from prey.
       C

   A. addition the
   B. fork
   C. scents,
   D. Change all of the above.

10. Another <u>way the</u> rattler can find a small <u>bird or</u> animal for prey is by
            A   B

   sensing <u>their</u> <u>body</u> heat.
        C   D

Section 2-5, cont'd

Grammar, Spelling,
Capitalization, and
Punctuation Skills
Test, and Correct
Passages with
Answer Keys

A. way, the
B. bird, or
C. its
D. bodies'

11. This snake has two pits on its face <u>that</u> are <u>customize</u> to help the snake
                                        A   B

    <u>"perceive"</u> heat rays coming from an <u>animal's</u> body.
        C   D

    A. who
    B. customized
    C. "Perceive"
    D. animals'

Passage 3-Test Copy

Modern technology is constantly changing; it seems every time a person turns
around, they see change. Many of these advances seem light-years away from
reality, only a few years ago. For instance, in Japan, scientists are working to
perfect a new mechanism for the telephone that will translate from one
language into another. A person speaking in one language would be able to
communicate with another person in a different country, speaking an entire
different language! Instantanously, a conversation could be translated from the
language of the speaker to the parlance of the listener. If one were to own a
telephone equipped with this special computer. One could communicate with
different people who speak different languages, and still be understood by
everyone! Experts are hopeful that by the start of the next century, through
these computerized translators, people might could be linked all over the
world. The business uses are obvious: an added advantage certainly would be
the ability to communicate with people from different cultures. The world is an
increasingly small village, a "global village," as Marshall McLuhan said. Forging
bonds of community and understanding are an essential goal for all of us.
Originally, these technological experts were seeking ways to save time and
money for the business community, they may also have done much more.

PASSAGE 3 DIRECTIONS
Choose the correct option for each question.

---

1. Modern technology is constantly changing; it seems every time a
   person turns <u>around, they see</u> change.

   A. around; they see
   B. around, one see
   C. around, he or she sees
   D. around; one sees

2. Many of these <u>advances</u> <u>seem</u> light-years away from <u>reality, only</u> a few
                    A   B   C
   years ago.

   A. advance
   B. seemed
   C. reality; only
   D. No change is necessary.

Grammar, Spelling, Capitalization, and Punctuation Skills Test, and Correct Passages with Answer Keys

3. For instance, in <u>Japan</u>, <u>scientists</u> are working to perfect a new
              A   B

   <u>mechanism</u> for the telephone that will translate from one language
     C

   into another.

   A. japan
   B. Scientists
   C. Mechanism
   D. No change is necessary.

4. A person speaking in <u>one language</u> <u>would be able to</u> communicate
                  A   B

   with another person in a different country, speaking an <u>entire</u>
   different language!   C

   A. a language
   B. might could
   C. entirely
   D. No change is necessary.

5. <u>Instantanously</u>, a conversation could be <u>translated</u> from the language
    A   B

   of the speaker to the <u>parlance</u> of the listener.
                     C

   A. Instantaneously,
   B. transslated
   C. parlence
   D. Change all of the above.

6. If <u>one were</u> to own a telephone equipped with this special <u>computer.</u>
      A   B

   <u>One</u> could communicate with different <u>people</u> who speak different
                                  C

   <u>languages, and</u> still be understood by everyone!
        D

   A. one was
   B. computer, one
   C. people, who
   D. languages: and

7. Experts <u>are hopeful</u> that by the start of the next century, through
           A

   these computerized <u>translators, people</u> <u>might could be</u> linked all over
                   B   C

   the world.

   A. were hopeful
   B. translators people
   C. could be
   D. Change all of the above.

8. The business uses are <u>obvious: an added advantage</u> certainly would be
   the ability to communicate with people from different cultures.

   A. obvious; an added advantage
   B. obvious: an added advantage,
   C. obvious; an added advantage,
   D. No change is necessary.

9. The <u>world is</u> an <u>increasingly small</u> village, a "<u>global village</u>," as
　　　 A　　　　　　　B　　　　　　　　　　　　　　　　　C

   Marshall McLuhan said.

   A. world, is
   B. increasingly, small
   C. "global village", as
   D. No change is necessary.

10. Forging <u>bonds</u> of <u>community and</u> understanding <u>are an essential</u> goal
　　　　　　 A　　　　　　 B　　　　　　　　　　　　　 C

   for all <u>of us.</u>
　　　　 D

   A. bond
   B. community, and
   C. is an essential
   D. of them.

11. <u>Originally,</u> these technological experts were seeking ways to save time
　　 A

   and <u>money for</u> the <u>business community</u> <u>,they may</u> also have done much
   more.　 B　　　　　　 C　　　　　　　　 D

   A. Originally:
   B. money, for
   C. business, community
   D. ; they <u>may</u>

Passage 4-Test Copy

One of the fastest, growing hobbies of the last decade is really a hobby that goes back to the fifties or before. Now, however, this pastime once relegated to nostalgic reminiscence is enjoying a rebirth. Collecting baseball cards has once again become one of America's favorite recreation amusements. Today, over one million people buy, sell or traded these cards. Collectors come in all ages, from todays teen-agers and pre-teens to those who were teen-agers forty and fifty years ago. Some of the earliest cards are worth more than people ever could of imagined. In fact, one of the most precious cards are part of a set produced by the American Tobacco Company around 1909, featuring Honus Wagner. Honus Wagner was a shortstop who played for the Pittsburgh Pirates, he didn't like the idea of his fans finding out that he smoked, so he supposedly had the entire printing removed from circulation before distribution. Today, these cards are so rare that one sold recently. For over $450,000! Knowledgeable collectors have a few tips for beginners: cards should be kept in mint condition, preferably in clear plastic jackets that shield them from everyday dirt: cards should be kept out of the sunlight and out of humidity as much as possible, to protect them from the elements; and cards should not be signed. As much as a collector might covet that signature of the pro, they should get the signature on another paper; cards that are in any way marked become less valuable.

PASSAGE 4 DIRECTIONS
Choose the correct option for each question.

1. One of the <u>fastest, growing</u> hobbies of the last decade <u>is really a hobby</u>
               A   B

   <u>that goes</u> back to the <u>fifties</u> or before.
      C   C

   A. fastest-growing
   B. are really hobbies that go
   C. fifty's
   D. No change is necessary.

2. Now, however, this <u>pastime</u> once <u>relegated</u> to nostalgic <u>reminiscence</u> is
                          A   B   C

   enjoying a rebirth.

   A. pasttime
   B. relagated
   C. reminescence
   D. No change is necessary.

3. Collecting <u>baseball</u> cards has once again become one of <u>America's</u>
              A   B

   favorite <u>recreation</u> <u>amusements.</u>
           C   D

   A. baseball's
   B. an American
   C. recreational
   D. amusement.

4. <u>Today,</u> over one million <u>people</u> <u>buy,</u> sell or <u>traded</u> these cards.
      A   B   C   D

   A. Today:
   B. person's
   C. bought
   D. trade

5. <u>Collectors</u> come in all ages, from <u>todays</u> teen-agers and pre-teens to
       A   B

   those who were teen-agers <u>forty and fifty</u> years ago.
                          C

   A. Collectors'
   B. today's
   C. forty, and fifty
   D. Change all of the above.

6. Some of the <u>earliest</u> cards are worth more <u>than</u> people ever could <u>of</u>
                A   B   C

   imagined.

   A. earlier
   B. then
   C. have
   D. No change is necessary.

7. In fact, one of the <u>most precious</u> cards <u>are part</u> of a set produced by
             A   B

   the American Tobacco Company around 1909, <u>featuring</u> Honus
   Wagner.   C

   A. more precious
   B. is part
   C. having featured
   D. Change all of the above.

8. Honus Wagner was a shortstop who played for the Pittsburgh <u>Pirates,</u>
                                                   A

   <u>he</u> didn't like the idea of his fans finding out that he <u>smoked, so he</u>
                                                               B

   supposedly had the entire <u>printing removed</u> from circulation before
   distribution.   C

   A. Pirates; he
   B. smoked; so he
   C. printing; removed
   D. No change is necessary.

9. Today, these cards are so <u>rare that</u> <u>one sold</u> <u>recently.</u> <u>For over $450,000!</u>
                                      A   B   C   D

   A. rare, that
   B. one had sold
   C. recently for
   D. over, $450,000!

10. Knowledgeable collectors have a few tips for <u>beginners:</u> cards should
                                                   A

    be kept in mint condition, preferably in clear plastic jackets that shield
    them from everyday <u>dirt:</u> cards should be kept out of the sunlight and
                                  B

    out of humidity as much as possible, to protect them from the
    <u>elements;</u> and cards should not be signed.
        C

    A. beginners;
    B. dirt;
    C. elements,
    D. No change is necessary.

11. As much as a collector <u>might covet</u> that signature <u>of the pro, they</u>
                                 A   B

    <u>should</u> get the signature on another <u>paper; cards</u> that are in any way
     C   D

    marked become less valuable.

    A. might have coveted
    B. pro:
    C. he or she should
    D. paper, cards

Passage 5-Test Copy

In 1986, the wedding of Sarah Margaret Ferguson to Prince Andrew, fourth in line to the British throne, had took place. For most people, a wedding is a day of joy and celebration for friends and family; for Fergie and Andrew, the day

Grammar, Spelling, Capitalization, and Punctuation Skills Test, and Correct Passages with Answer Keys

included special trained dogs and security guards out in force. The potential heir to the British throne, it seemed, is also a potential target for a terrorist attack, particularly at such a public and high-profile event. In spite of the worries. However, the event went off without a hitch. Sarah arrived at Westminster abbey in the glass coach traditionally used by Royal brides; Andrew was transported from Buckingham Palace in one of five State coaches. These coaches were drawn by exquisite grey horses and escorted by the Household Cavalry dressed in scarlet uniforms and gleaming breastplates. The bride's gown was equally ethereal: she wore an embroidered ivory satin gown with puffed medieval-type sleeves. The embroidery, most prominent on the sleeves, was patterned after Sarah's newly created coat of arms, which were replete with bees and thistles. The train, extended $17^1/_2$ feet long, it shimmered and glistened with more embroidery and beadwork. After the ceremony, the newly wedded couple rode sereenly through the streets of London in an open carriage, to the cheers of the crowd. After a wedding breakfast, Sarah and Andrew flew to the Azores to begin her honeymoon.

PASSAGE 5 DIRECTIONS
Choose the correct option.

---

1. In 1986, the wedding of Sarah Margaret Ferguson to <u>Prince Andrew,</u>
   A   B

   <u>fourth</u> in line to the British throne, <u>had took</u> place.
   C

   A. prince
   B. Andrew fourth
   C. took
   D. No change is necessary.

2. For most people, a wedding <u>is</u> a day of joy and celebration for friends
   A

   and <u>family;</u> for Fergie and Andrew, the day included <u>special</u> trained
   B   C

   dogs and security guards out in force.

   A. has been
   B. family:
   C. specially
   D. Change all of the above.

3. The potential heir to the British throne, <u>it seemed, is</u> also a potential target for a terrorist attack, particularly at such a public and high-profile event.

   A. it seems, was
   B. it seemed, was
   C. it seems, would have been
   D. it seemed, would have been

4. In spite of the <u>worries. However,</u> the event went off without a hitch.

   A. worries, however,
   B. worries; however
   C. worries: however,
   D. worries; however,

5. Sarah arrived at Westminster <u>abbey</u> in the glass coach traditionally

                                 A

used by <u>Royal</u> brides; Andrew was transported from Buckingham

       B

Palace in one of five <u>State</u> coaches.

                  C

   A. Abbey
   B. royal
   C. state
   D. Change all of the above.

6. These coaches were drawn by exquisite grey <u>horses and escorted</u> by the Household Cavalry dressed in scarlet uniforms and gleaming breastplates.

   A. horses; and, escorted
   B. horses, and, escorted
   C. horses, and escorted
   D. horses: and escorted

7. The bride's gown was equally <u>ethereal: she wore</u> an embroidered ivory satin gown with puffed medieval-type sleeves.

   A. ethereal, she wore
   B. ethereal she wore
   C. ethereal; she wore,
   D. No change is necessary.

8. The embroidery, most prominent on the sleeves, <u>was patterned</u> after

                                        A

Sarah's newly created coat of <u>arms, which</u> <u>were replete</u> with bees and thistles.

                                   B   C

   A. were patterned
   B. arms which
   C. was replete
   D. Change all of the above.

9. The train, extended 17½ feet <u>long, it shimmered</u> and glistened with more embroidery and beadwork.

   A. long; it shimmered
   B. long: it shimmered
   C. long it shimmered
   D. No change is necessary.

10. After the <u>ceremony,</u> the newly <u>wedded</u> couple rode <u>sereenly</u> through

                 A   B   C

the streets of London in an open <u>carriage,</u> to the cheers of the crowd.

                                        D

   A. ceramony
   B. weded
   C. serenely
   D. cariage

11. After a wedding breakfast, Sarah and Andrew <u>flew</u> to the <u>Azores</u> to begin <u>her</u> honeymoon.

                                        A   B

     C

   A. had flown
   B. azores
   C. their
   D. No change is necessary.

Grammar, Spelling, Capitalization, and Punctuation Skills Test, and Correct Passages with Answer Keys

Passage 6-Test Copy

If someone wanted to learn about life from television comedies today, he could choose either impeccable examples of the well-rounded, middle-class suburben family, or its opposite! An example of the former would be "Growing Pains," a show that takes place in a fairly well-to-do northern suburb. The Seaver family includes: Maggie, the mother; Jason, the father; and their children, who typically get in and out of trouble in the space of one show. The show may seem idealized, but there has been several episodes about serious issues like drunken driving, also. In contrast to "Growing Pains," the show "Rosanne" stands out from other sitcoms for their low, crude dialogue and antics. Rosanne, the central character, is anything but ideal she is hefty and frequently fights with her construction worker husband, Dan. The arguing that goes on between her and he is funny but often rude and low as well. Their children are also loud and sassy; one day the older daughter had drank too much, and her parents had to confront her with what she had done. The family survives that, however, and the problems were discussed and solved in the allotted thirty minutes. In real life. However, issues are not always solved that neatly. People, unlike characters on television need real love, understanding and communication; unfortunately, we can't always learn how to give and receive these from a half-hour television show.

PASSAGE 6 DIRECTIONS
Choose the correct option.

---

1. If someone wanted to learn about life from <u>television</u> comedies today,

A
he could choose either <u>impeccable</u> examples of the well-rounded,

B
middle-class <u>suburben</u> family, or its <u>opposite!</u>

C　　　　　　　　　　D
    A. telavision
    B. impecable
    C. suburban
    D. oppisite

2. An example of the former would be "Growing <u>Pains</u>," a show that

A
takes place in a fairly <u>well-to-do</u> northern <u>suburb</u>.

B　　　　　　　C
    A. pains
    B. well-to-so
    C. Suburb
    D. No change is necessary.

3. The Seaver family <u>includes: Maggie</u>, <u>the mother; Jason</u>, the father; and

A　　　　　　　　　　B
their <u>children, who</u> typically get in and out of trouble in the space of

C
one show.
    A. includes Maggie
    B. the mother, Jason
    C. children; who
    D. Change all of the above.

4. The show may <u>seem idealized, but</u> <u>there has been</u> several episodes
            A   B
about serious issues <u>like drunken driving,</u> also.
                            C

   A. seem idealized but
   B. there have been
   C. as drunken driving
   D. No change is necessary.

5. In contrast to "Growing Pains," the show "Rosanne" stands out from other sitcoms <u>for their low, crude</u> dialogue and antics.

   A. for its low, crude
   B. for there low-crude
   C. for it's low, crude
   D. No change is necessary.

6. Rosanne, the central <u>character, is</u> <u>anything but</u> <u>ideal she</u> is hefty and
                          A   B   C
frequently fights with her construction <u>worker husband,</u> Dan.
                                               D

   A. character is
   B. anything, but
   C. ideal; she
   D. worker, husband

7. The arguing <u>that goes on</u> between <u>her and he</u> is <u>funny but</u> often rude
                   A   B   C
and low as well.

   A. that go on
   B. her and him
   C. funny; but
   D. No change is necessary.

8. Their children <u>are also</u> loud and <u>sassy; one</u> day the older daughter had
                      A   B
<u>drank too</u> much, and her parents had to confront her with what she
    C
<u>had done.</u>
    D

   A. were also
   B. sassy, one
   C. drunk too
   D. had did.

9. The family <u>survives</u> <u>that, however,</u> and the problems were <u>discussed</u>
                  A   B   C
<u>and</u> solved in the allotted thirty minutes.

   A. survived
   B. that; however,
   C. discussed, and
   D. Change all of the above.

10. In real <u>life. However,</u> <u>issues are</u> not always solved <u>that</u> neatly.
                  A   B   C

   A. life, however,
   B. issues were

C. that neat.

D. Change all of the above.

11. People, unlike characters on television need real love, understanding
    <u>A</u>   <u>B</u>

    and communication; unfortunately, we can't always learn how to give
        <u>C</u>

    and receive these from a half-hour television show.

    A. People unlike
    B. television, need
    C. communication, unfortunately,
    D. No change is necessary.

Passage 7-Test Copy

When we see how fleeting is the respect most people accord the animal kingdom, most environmentalists want to quote William Wordsworth, the English Romantic poet: "Little we see in Nature that is ours." That is, the public may not always recognize parallels between we humans and the animal kingdom. Anyone with a backyard, however, can observe natural habitate and discern correspondences with human lifestyles. There are among the inhabitants, a scheme of balancing acts that take place, called an eco-system. Creatures depend upon each other's lifestyles for their own existence, that is, the habits of one species enable another species to exist. With respect for the environment. All can survive. Also, nearly all the creatures one could find might could teach humans a thing or two about cooperation. For example most people know that raccoons are fastidious about their food intake, carrying food to a stream to wash it well before eating. Did they also know that raccoons can actually work together to accomplish a task? Two raccoons have been known to work together to help each other reach places neither one could reach on their own. Nature apparently has many lessons for mankind, and she will teach them without a pennies worth of charge.

PASSAGE 7 DIRECTIONS
Choose the correct option.

---

1. When we see how fleeting is the respect most people accord the animal kingdom, most <u>environmentalists</u> want to quote William
   <u>A</u>

   Wordsworth, the English Romantic <u>poet:</u> "Little we see in Nature that
   <u>B</u>

   is ours."
   <u>C</u>

   A. environmentalists'
   B. poet, "Little
   C. ours".
   D. No change is necessary.

2. That is, the public may not always recognize parallels <u>between</u> <u>we</u>
   <u>A</u>   <u>B</u>

   humans and the animal kingdom.
   <u>C</u>

A. That is:
B. among
C. us humans
D. No change is necessary.

3. Anyone with a backyard, however, can observe natural <u>habitate</u> and
$$\text{A}$$
   <u>discern</u> <u>correspondences</u> with human lifestyles.
   BC

   A. habitat
   B. disern
   C. correspondances
   D. Change all of the above.

4. <u>There are</u> among the <u>inhabitants,</u> a scheme of balancing acts <u>that take</u>
   A$$B$$C
   place, called an eco-system.

   A. there is, among
   B. inhabitant,
   C. that takes
   D. No change is necessary.

5. Creatures depend upon each <u>other's</u> <u>lifestyles</u> for <u>their</u> own <u>existence,</u>
   ABCD
   <u>that</u> is, the habits of one species enable another species to exist.

   A. others'
   B. lifestyle
   C. his or her
   D. existence; that

6. With respect for the <u>environment. All</u> can survive.

   A. environment all
   B. environment, all
   C. environment; all
   D. No change is necessary.

7. Also, nearly all the creatures <u>one</u> could find <u>might could</u> teach humans
   AB
   a <u>thing or</u> <u>two about</u> cooperation.
   CD

   A. he or she
   B. could
   C. thing, or
   D. two, about

8. For <u>example</u> most people know that raccoons are fastidious about their
   A
   food <u>intake,</u> carrying food to a stream to wash it <u>well</u> before eating.
   B$$C

   A. example,
   B. intake:
   C. good
   D. Change all of the above.

Grammar, Spelling, Capitalization, and Punctuation Skills Test, and Correct Passages with Answer Keys

9. Did <u>they</u> also <u>know that raccoons</u> <u>can</u> actually work together to
      A   B   C

   accomplish a task?

   A. Do
   B. know: raccoons
   C. might could
   D. No change is necessary.

10. Two raccoons <u>have been</u> known to work <u>together to</u> help each other
                  A   B

    reach places <u>neither</u> one could reach on <u>their</u> own.
                  C   D

    A. had been
    B. together, to
    C. either
    D. its

11. Nature apparently has many lessons for mankind, and she will teach them without a <u>pennies</u> worth of charge.

    A. pennies'
    B. penny's
    C. pennys
    D. No change is necessary.

Passage 8-Test Copy

Anatoly's younger son, Ilya, missed his fathers usual good humor and gentle teasing. He could not help worrying, as he watched his father's health deteriorate week after week. "How are you feeling today, Papa?" Ilya would ask at the breakfast table.

"Not too bad, Anatoly would answer.

Both would nod. And change the subject. It was as close to complaining as Anatoly ever got.

The long hard Moscow winter blanketed the area with snow, and Anatoly grew more withdrawn. He spent much of his time bundled up at home, he bought a dog, a miniature black poodle he named Alma, and took her for walks along the city's narrow streets. Alma brought him joy, but the happy times spent with his family and friends grew less frequently.

"I sometimes feels I will never get better," he told Galina one night, "that I will always be this way."

Watching him suffer not only from his illness, but from the indignities and lies, fuels a rage inside her. In January 1987 she wrote an impassioned letter to Soviet President Mikhail Gorbachev, spelling out Anatoly's selfless duty in Chernobyl and telling of the official diagnosis that refused to link their illness to his radiation exposure.

Eventually, high-ranking physicians begun to speak more openly. As the winds of *glasnost* swept through the Soviet Union and the goverment finally put more resources into treating victims, the link between Chernobyl and illnesses suffered by scores of people involved in the rescue effort was tacitly acknowledged.

Grammar, Spelling, Capitalization, and Punctuation Skills Test, and Correct Passages with Answer Keys

PASSAGE 8 DIRECTIONS
Choose the correct option.

1. Anatoly's younger son, <u>Ilya, missed</u> his <u>fathers</u> usual good <u>humor</u> and
$\qquad\qquad\qquad\qquad$ A $\qquad\qquad$ B $\qquad\qquad\qquad$ C

gentle teasing.

   A. Ilya missed
   B. father's
   C. humer
   D. No change is necessary.

2. "Not <u>too</u> <u>bad,</u> Anatoly <u>would answer.</u>
$\qquad\quad$ A $\quad$ B $\qquad\quad$ C

   A. to
   B. bad," Anatoly
   C. would answered
   D. No change is necessary.

3. Both <u>would nod. And change</u> the <u>subject. It was</u> as close to
$\qquad\qquad\quad$ A $\qquad\qquad\qquad\qquad$ B

complaining as Anatoly ever <u>got.</u>
$\qquad\qquad\qquad\qquad\qquad\quad$ C

   A. would nod and change
   B. subject, it was as
   C. gets
   D. No change is necessary.

4. The <u>long hard</u> Moscow winter <u>blanketed</u> the area with snow, and
$\qquad$ A $\qquad\qquad\qquad\qquad$ B

Anatoly <u>grew</u> more withdrawn.
$\qquad\qquad$ C

   A. long, hard
   B. blancketed
   C. grows
   D. No change is necessary.

5. He spent much of his time bundled up at <u>home, he</u> bought a <u>dog, a</u>
$\qquad\qquad\qquad\qquad\qquad\qquad\qquad\qquad\qquad$ A

<u>miniature</u> black poodle he named Alma, and took her for walks along
$\quad$ B

the <u>city's</u> narrow streets.
$\qquad$ C

   A. home. He
   B. dog a miniature
   C. cities
   D. No change is necessary.

6. Alma <u>brought</u> him <u>joy, but</u> the happy times spent with his family and
$\qquad\quad$ A $\qquad\quad$ B

friends grew less <u>frequently.</u>
$\qquad\qquad\qquad$ C

   A. bought
   B. joy but

C. frequent

D. No change is necessary.

7. "I <u>sometimes</u> <u>feels</u> I will never get better," he told Galina one <u>night</u>,
          A   B   C

"<u>that</u> I will always be this way."

A. sometime

B. feel

C. night, that

D. No change is necessary.

8. Watching him suffer <u>not only from</u> his illness, but from the <u>indignities</u>
                            A   B

and lies, <u>fuels</u> a rage inside her.
          C

A. not only, from

B. indignaties

C. fueled

D. No change is necessary.

9. In January 1987 she wrote an impassioned letter to Soviet President Mikhail Gorbachev, spelling out <u>Anatoly's</u> selfless duty in <u>Chernobyl</u>
                                     A   B

<u>and</u> telling of the official diagnosis that refused to link <u>their</u> illness to
                                                           C

his radiation exposure.

A. Anatolys'

B. Chernobyl, and

C. his

D. No change is necessary.

10. Eventually, high-ranking <u>physicians</u> <u>begun</u> to speak more <u>openly</u>.
                                A   B   C

A. phycisians

B. began

C. open

D. No change is necessary.

11. As the winds of *glasnost* <u>swept</u> through the Soviet Union and the
                                A

<u>goverment</u> finally put more resources into treating <u>victims, the</u> link
        B   C

between Chernobyl and illnesses suffered by scores of people involved in the rescue effort was tacitly acknowledged.

A. sweeped

B. government

C. victims the

D. No change is necessary.

Grammar, Spelling, Capitalization, and Punctuation Skills Test, and Correct Passages with Answer Keys

Passage 1-Corrected

Numerous varieties of parrots exist and all can be studied through the science of ornithology. A few of them are plain in appearance, but most of them have brilliant red, blue, green, and yellow feathers. There are more than 300 species in the animal kingdom; they are native to tropical and subtropical forests. In fact, the parrot's body is specially adapted to life in the subtropical forest. In this forest, there are many brightly colored flowers and plants. The parrot's colors actually help him to hide from his natural enemies. When he sits high on top of a tall tree, his color makes him look like a simple flower, or a special fruit. In addition to coloring that is designed for a purpose, parrots also have bodies that are designed and adapted to gathering seeds, nuts, and fruit for food. Their feet have a very strong grip: two toes point forward and two backward so they can seize fruit and nuts. The bills are hooked differently because different parrots have different methods of gathering food. Some parrots are accustomed to scraping seeds out of pods, and so they have bills that are pointed and very sharp.

Passage 2-Corrected

Many people have a fear of snakes, though this reaction may not necessarily be based on logic. One snake, however, that has justifiably caused a response both of fear and fascination is the rattlesnake. The rattlesnake is a deadly snake; it has poisonous fangs that are folded back into its mouth when not needed. When the rattler strikes, though, those fangs come right out, ready to sink into prey. The fangs are actually hollow, and they are connected to glands inside the cheeks that are full of venom. When the fangs sink in, the venom comes quickly from the glands and flows into the creature being bitten. Many people do not realize that snakes are actually deaf; they do not hear sounds. What they can sense, however, are vibrations, and this is one of the ways the snake can find a victim. In addition, the rattler can flicker its forked tongue in the air to pick up scents, either from an enemy or from prey. Another way the rattler can find a small bird or animal for prey is by sensing its body heat. This snake has two pits on its face that are customized to help the snake "perceive" heat rays coming from an animal's body.

Passage 3-Corrected

Modern technology is constantly changing; it seems every time a person turns around, he or she sees change. Many of these advances seemed light-years away from reality, only a few years ago. For instance, in Japan, scientists are working to perfect a new mechanism for the telephone that will translate from one language into another. A person speaking in one language would be able to communicate with another person in a different country, speaking an entirely different language! Instantaneously, a conversation could be translated from the language of the speaker to the parlance of the listener. If one were to own a telephone equipped with this special computer, one could communicate with different people who speak different languages, and still be understood by everyone! Experts are hopeful that by the start of the next century, through these computerized translators, people could be linked all over the world. The business uses are obvious; an added advantage

Grammar, Spelling, Capitalization, and Punctuation Skills Test, and Correct Passages with Answer Keys

certainly would be the ability to communicate with people from different cultures. The world is an increasingly small village, a "global village," as Marshall McLuhan said. Forging bonds of community and understanding is an essential goal for all of us. Originally, these technological experts were seeking ways to save time and money for the business community; they may also have done much more.

Passage 4-Corrected

One of the fastest-growing hobbies of the last decade is really a hobby that goes back to the fifties or before. Now, however, this pastime once relegated to nostalgic reminiscence is enjoying a rebirth. Collecting baseball cards has once again become one of America's favorite recreational amusements. Today, over one million people buy, sell or trade these cards. Collectors come in all ages, from today's teen-agers and pre-teens to those who were teen-agers forty and fifty years ago. Some of the earliest cards are worth more than people ever could have imagined. In fact, one of the most precious cards is part of a set produced by the American Tobacco Company around 1909, featuring Honus Wagner. Honus Wagner was a shortstop who played for the Pittsburgh Pirates; he didn't like the idea of his fans finding out that he smoked, so he supposedly had the entire printing removed from circulation before distribution. Today, these cards are so rare that one sold recently for over $450,000! Knowledgeable collectors have a few tips for beginners: cards should be kept in mint condition, preferably in clear plastic jackets that shield them from everyday dirt; cards should be kept out of the sunlight and out of humidity as much as possible, to protect them from the elements; and cards should not be signed. As much as a collector might covet that signature of the pro, he or she should get the signature on another paper; cards that are in any way marked become less valuable.

Passage 5-Corrected

In 1986, the wedding of Sarah Margaret Ferguson to Prince Andrew, fourth in line to the British throne, took place. For most people, a wedding is a day of joy and celebration for friends and family; for Fergie and Andrew, the day included specially trained dogs and security guards out in force. The potential heir to the British throne, it seemed, was also a potential target for a terrorist attack, particularly at such a public and high-profile event. In spite of the worries, however, the event went off without a hitch. Sarah arrived at Westminster Abbey in the glass coach traditionally used by royal brides; Andrew was transported from Buckingham Palace in one of five state coaches. These coaches were drawn by exquisite grey horses, and escorted by the Household Cavalry dressed in scarlet uniforms and gleaming breastplates. The bride's gown was equally ethereal: she wore an embroidered ivory satin gown with puffed medieval-type sleeves. The embroidery, most prominent on the sleeves, was patterned after Sarah's newly-created coat of arms, which was replete with bees and thistles. The train, extended $17\frac{1}{2}$ feet long; it shimmered and glistened with more embroidery and beadwork. After the ceremony, the newly wedded couple rode serenely through the streets of London in an open carriage, to the cheers of the crowd. After a wedding breakfast, Sarah and Andrew flew to the Azores to begin their honeymoon.

Passage 6-Corrected

If someone wanted to learn about life from television comedies today, he could choose either impeccable examples of the well-rounded, middle-class suburban family, or its opposite! An example of the former would be "Growing Pains," a show which takes place in a fairly well-to-do northern suburb. The Seaver family includes Maggie, the mother; Jason, the father; and their children, who typically get in and out of trouble in the space of one show. The show may seem idealized, but there have been several episodes about serious issues like drunken driving, also. In contrast to "Growing Pains," the show "Rosanne" stands out from other sitcoms for its low, crude dialogue and antics. Rosanne, the central character, is anything but ideal; she is hefty and frequently fights with her construction worker husband, Dan. The arguing that goes on between her and him is funny but often rude and low as well. Their children are also loud and sassy; one day the older daughter had drunk too much, and her parents had to confront her with what she had done. The family survived that, however, and the problems were discussed and solved in the allotted thirty minutes. In real life, however, issues are not always solved that neatly. People, unlike characters on television, need real love, understanding and communication; unfortunately, we can't always learn how to give and receive these from a half-hour television show.

Passage 7-Corrected

When we see how fleeting is the respect most people accord the animal kingdom, most environmentalists want to quote William Wordsworth, the English Romantic poet: "Little we see in Nature that is ours." That is, the public may not always recognize parallels between us humans and the animal kingdom. Anyone with a backyard, however, can observe natural habitat and discern correspondences with human lifestyles. There is, among the inhabitants, a scheme of balancing acts that takes place, called an eco-system. Creatures depend upon each other's lifestyles for their own existence; that is, the habits of one species enable another species to exist. With respect for the environment, all can survive. Also, nearly all the creatures one could find could teach humans a thing or two about cooperation. For example, most people know that raccoons are fastidious about their food intake, carrying food to a stream to wash it well before eating. Do they also know that raccoons can actually work together to accomplish a task? Two raccoons have been known to work together to help each other reach places neither one could reach on its own. Nature apparently has many lessons for mankind, and she will teach them without a penny's worth of charge.

Passage 8-Corrected

Anatoly's younger son, Ilya, missed his father's usual good humor and gentle teasing. He could not help worrying, as he watched his father's health deteriorate week after week. "How are you feeling today, Papa?" Ilya would ask at the breakfast table.

"Not too bad," Anatoly would answer.

Both would nod and change the subject. It was as close to complaining as Anatoly ever got.

Grammar, Spelling, Capitalization, and Punctuation Skills Test, and Correct Passages with Answer Keys

Pekkanen, John. "The Man Who Flew into Hell." Reader's Digest, May 1991: p. 192

The long, hard Moscow winter blanketed the area with snow, and Anatoly grew more withdrawn. He spent much of his time bundled up at home. He bought a dog, a miniature black poodle he named Alma, and took her for walks along the city's narrow streets. Alma brought him joy, but the happy times spent with his family and friends grew less frequent.

"I sometimes feel I will never get better," he told Galina one night, "that I will always be this way."

Watching him suffer not only from his illness, but from the indignities and lies, fueled a rage inside her. In January 1987 she wrote an impassioned letter to Soviet President Mikhail Gorbachev, spelling out Anatoly's selfless duty in Chernobyl and telling of the official diagnosis that refused to link his illness to his radiation exposure.

Eventually, high-ranking physicians began to speak more openly. As the winds of *glasnost* swept through the Soviet Union and the government finally put more resources into treating victims, the link between Chernobyl and illnesses suffered by scores of people involved in the rescue effort was tacitly acknowledged.

Answer Key-*Passage 1*

Question	Answer	Skill
1.	C.	III.B.5.c
2.	A.	III.B.5.a
3.	B.	III.B.2.d
4.	D.	III.B.4.e
		III.B.5.b
		III.B.5.a
5.	D.	III.B.5.b
6.	A.	III.B.5.b
7.	C.	III.B.4.b.2
8.	D.	III.B.2.d
9.	B.	III.B.4.b.1
10.	C.	III.B.4.f
11.	A.	III.B.4.a

Answer Key-*Passage 2*

Question	Answer	Skill
1.	B.	III.B.5.b
2.	C.	III.B.5.a
3.	C.	III.B.5.b
4.	B.	III.B.4.f
5.	A.	III.B.2.d
6.	C.	III.B.4.e
7.	A.	III.B.2.d
8.	B.	III.B.4.b.1
9.	C.	III.B.5.b
10.	C.	III.B.4.b.2
11.	B.	III.B.4.a

Answer Key-*Passage 3*

Grammar, Spelling, Capitalization, and Punctuation Skills Test, and Correct Passages with Answer Keys

Question	Answer	Skill
1.	C.	III.B.4.b.1
		III.B.4.b.2
2.	B.	III.B.4.f
3.	D.	III.B.5.c
4.	C.	III.B.4.e
5.	A.	III.B.5.a
6.	B.	III.B.2.d
7.	C.	III.B.4.a
8.	A.	III.B.5.b
9.	D.	III.B.5.b
10.	C.	III.B.4.b.1
11.	D.	III.B.2.d

Answer Key-*Passage 4*

Question	Answer	Skill
1.	A.	III.B.5.b
2.	D.	III.B.5.a
3.	C.	III.B.4.e
4.	D.	III.B.4.f
5.	B.	III.B.5.b
6.	C.	III.B.4.a
7.	B.	III.B.4.b.1
8.	A.	III.B.2.d
9.	C.	III.B.2.d
10.	B.	III.B.5.b
11.	C.	III.B.4.b.1

Answer Key-*Passage 5*

Question	Answer	Skill
1.	C.	III.B.4.a
2.	C.	III.B.4.e
3.	B.	III.B.4.f
4.	A.	III.B.2.d
5.	D.	III.B.5.c
6.	C.	III.B.5.b
7.	D.	III.B.5.b
8.	C.	III.B.4.b.1
9.	A.	III.B.2.d
10.	C.	III.B.5.a
11.	C.	III.B.4.b.2

Grammar, Spelling, Capitalization, and Punctuation Skills Test, and Correct Passages with Answer Keys

Answer Key-*Passage 6*

Question	Answer	Skill
1.	C.	III.B.5.a
2.	D.	III.B.5.c
3.	A.	III.B.5.b
4.	B.	III.B.4.b.1
5.	A.	III.B.4.b.2
6.	C.	III.B.2.d
7.	B.	III.B.4.c
8.	C.	III.B.4.a
9.	A.	III.B.4.f
10.	A.	III.B.2.d
11.	B.	III.B.5.b

Answer Key-*Passage 7*

Question	Answer	Skill
1.	D.	III.5.B.5.b
2.	C.	III.B.4.c
3.	A.	III.B.5.a
4.	A.	III.B.4.b.1
5.	D.	III.B.2.d
6.	B.	III.B.2.d
7.	B.	III.B.4.a
8.	A.	III.B.5.b
9.	A.	III.B.4.f
10.	D.	III.B.4.b.2
11.	B.	III.B.5.b

Answer Key-*Passage 8*

Question	Answer	Skill
1.	B.	III.B.5.b
2.	B.	III.B.5.b
3.	A.	III.B.2.d
4.	A.	III.B.5.b
5.	A.	III.B.2.d
6.	C.	III.B.4.e
7.	B.	III.B.4.b.1
8.	C.	III.B.4.f
9.	C.	III.B.4.b.2
10.	B.	III.B.4.a
11.	B.	III.B.5.a

DIRECTIONS

Some of the sentences in the following two passages contain errors.
Read the passages. Then choose the correct answer for the questions
on selected sentences from the passages.

The following test
simulates the types and
proportion of the items
in the College Level
Academic Skills Test.
The test is composed of
2 passages with 11
questions each.
Approximately 13
questions address the
remaining skills. In the
real test you will have
approximately 80
minutes total for the
English Language Skills
Test and the Reading
Test; consequently, you
might want to practice
with this test and the
Reading Test with the
time limit in mind. The
answer key, skill code
and corrected passages
will occur at the end of
the test.

Passage 1-Test Copy

For the past six years, Laura Spitzer and her piano has went crisscrossing the small-town West, bringing fine music to U.S. and Canadian villages, playing almost anyplace where two or three are gathered. You might compare Laura, sowing the love of the classics in far-off nooks and crannies of North America to Johnny Appleseed.

Trained for concert performance at the prestigious Mozarteum in Salzburg, Austria, and at the Peabody Conservatory of Music in Baltimore. She has played in formal, big-city recital halls. But her missionary zeal is reserved for school Gyms and church basements.

Some of their former classmates hop from city to city to perform before black-tie audiences in places with velvet cushions. Laura perfers a truck with bed space and an ice chest, musical scores piled on the floor and wet laundry drying. She likes her listeners five feet from the piano; seated on folding chairs.

"Engaging and expert," the New York *Times'* wrote of her when she played the Big Apple. But she would rather quote the Ely, Nev., *Daily Times:* "Her ability to relate to an audience and her total piano mastery leaves an audience spellbound." Says Laura, "After all, in New York I might be the tenth pianist to perform in a week, in Duckwater I may be the first—ever."

"I am here because I followed my dream. I was a truck driver, piano mover, and pianist because I want to go to small places and play for people."

1. For the past six years, Laura Spitzer and her piano <u>has went</u> <u>crisscrossing</u> the small-town West, bringing fine music to <u>U.S.</u> and Canadian villages, playing almost anyplace where two or three are gathered.

   A. has gone crisscrossing
   B. have gone crisscrossing
   C. have went crisscrossing
   D. No change is necessary.

2. You might compare Laura, <u>sowing</u> the love of the classics in <u>far-off</u>
                           A   B

   nooks and crannies of North <u>America to</u> Johnny Appleseed.
                                     C

   A. sewing
   B. far off
   C. America, to
   D. No change is necessary.

3. Trained for concert <u>performance</u> at the prestigious Mozarteum in
                              A

   Salzburg, Austria, and at the Peabody <u>Conservatory</u> of Music in
                                               B

   <u>Baltimore. She</u> has played in formal, big-city recital halls.
                  C

**Posttest and
Answer Key**

A. performance
B. conservatory
C. Baltimore, she
D. No change is necessary.

4. But her <u>missionary</u> zeal <u>is reserved</u> for school <u>Gyms</u> and church
          A   B   C

basements.

A. missionairy
B. are reserved
C. gyms
D. No change is necessary.

5. Some of <u>their</u> <u>former</u> classmates hop from city to city to <u>perform</u>
          A   B

<u>before</u> black-tie audiences in places with velvet cushions.
 C

A. her
B. formar
C. perform, before
D. No change is necessary.

6. Laura <u>perfers</u> a truck with bed <u>space and</u> an ice chest, musical scores
          A   B

<u>piled</u> on the floor and wet laundry drying.
 C

A. prefers
B. space, and
C. piling
D. No change is necessary.

7. She likes her listeners five feet from the <u>piano; seated</u> on folding chairs.

A. piano, seated
B. piano. Seated
C. piano: seated
D. No change is necessary.

8. "Engaging and <u>expert,</u>" the New York <u>Times</u> wrote of her when she
                   A   B

played the <u>Big Apple</u>.
      C

A. expert the
B. *Times'*
C. big Apple
D. No change is necessary.

9. But she <u>would rather</u> <u>quote</u> the Ely, Nev., *Daily Times:* "Her ability to
             A   B

relate to an audience and her total piano mastery <u>leaves</u> an audience
spellbound."   C

A. would of
B. quotes
C. leave
D. No change is necessary.

10. <u>Says</u> Laura, "After all, in New York I might be the tenth pianist to
    A

    <u>perform</u> in a <u>week, in</u> Duckwater I may be the first—ever."
       B   C

    A. Say
    B. preform
    C. week. In
    D. No change is necessary.

11. I <u>was</u> a truck <u>driver, piano</u> mover, and pianist because I want to go to
       A   B

    small places and <u>play</u> for people."
                        C

    A. am
    B. driver piano
    C. played
    D. No change is necessary.

Passage 2-Test Copy

A 30-ton humpback whale was seventeen miles east of Gloucester, Mass., when it become entangled in a tough, transparent gill net. Wrapped around its body, flippers and blowhole. The net prevented the whale from moving or feeding and made breathing difficult.

In times past, the whale would have been left to parish. But on July 16, 1990, there was hope because of Charles "Stormy" Mayo, co-founder and research director of the nonprofit Center for Coastal Studies in Provincetown and head of its whale-disentanglement team.

The 47-year-old marine biologist and their crew sped the rescue boat to the site. Mayo recognized the whale as "Mallard," a frequent visitor off the coast. "Mallard is very inquisitive and playful, almost a friend," he said, "he comes up to our research vessel and looks us in the eye."

Now working in small inflatable boats, the team attached heavy buoy's to the net caught around Mallard. Fighting the extra burden, the whale soon tired enabling Mayo to maneuver his craft close to the animal, 300 times his size.

Mayo leant toward the gasping, groaning leviathan and began cutting the net with a knife. For three hours Mallard remained docile while Mayo, who admit to being scared, removed the line one strand at a time. When Mayo cut the part covering the blowhole, the 40-foot whale surged upwardly, nearly capsizing the 15-foot rubber boat. Just as abrupt, the whale calmed down, and Mayo resumed his painstaking work. Drenched by the spray, the men was relieved and cheered loudly.

12. A 30-ton humpback whale was seventeen miles <u>east</u> of Gloucester,
                                                   A

    Mass., when it <u>becomes</u> entangled in a <u>tough, transparent</u> gill net.
                      B   C

    A. East
    B. became
    C. tough transparent
    D. No change is necessary.

**Posttest and
Answer Key**

13. Wrapped around its body, flippers and <u>blowhole. The</u> net prevented
                                                    A

    the whale from <u>moving or</u> feeding and made breathing <u>difficult.</u>
                        B   C

    A. blowhole, the
    B. moving, or
    C. difficulty
    D. No change is necessary.

14. In times <u>past,</u> the whale <u>would have been left</u> to <u>parish.</u>
                   A   B   C

    A. passed
    B. would of been left
    C. perish
    D. No change is necessary.

15. But on July 16, 1990, there was hope because of Charles <u>"Stormy"</u>
                                                              A

    Mayo, co-founder and research <u>director</u> of the nonprofit Center for
                                    B

    Coastal Studies in <u>Provincetown and</u> head of its
                          C

    whale-disentanglement team.

    A. "stormy"
    B. directer
    C. Provincetown, and
    D. No change is necessary.

16. The 47-year-old marine <u>biologist</u> and <u>their</u> crew sped the rescue boat
                             A   B
    to the <u>site.</u>
            C

    A. biologists
    B. his
    C. sight
    D. No change is necessary.

17. "Mallard is very inquisitive and playful, <u>almost</u> a friend," he <u>said, "he</u>
                                                A   B

    comes up to our research vessel and <u>looks</u> us in the eye."
                                          C

    A. allmost
    B. said. "He
    C. look
    D. No change is necessary.

18. Now working in small <u>inflatable</u> <u>boats, the</u> team attaches heavy <u>buoy's</u>
                           A   B   C

    to the net caught around Mallard.

    A. inflatible
    B. boats the
    C. buoys
    D. No change is necessary.

19. Fighting the extra burden, the whale soon <u>tired enabling</u> Mayo to
    maneuver his craft close to the animal, 300 times his size.

A. tired, enabling
B. tired; enabling
C. tired. Enabling
D. No change is necessary.

20. Mayo <u>leant</u> toward the <u>gasping, groaning</u> leviathan and <u>began</u> cutting
A   B   C

the net with a knife.

A. leaned
B. gasping groaning
C. begun
D. No change is necessary.

21. Just as <u>abrupt</u>, the whale calmed <u>down, and</u> Mayo resumed <u>his</u>
A   B   C

painstaking work.

A. abruptly
B. down and
C. their
D. No change is necessary.

22. Drenched by the spray, the men <u>was</u> <u>relieved</u> and cheered <u>loudly</u>.
                                     A   B   C

A. were
B. relieved
C. loud
D. No change is necessary.

DIRECTIONS
*Choose the most effective word or phrase within the context suggested
by the sentences.*

---

23. Motorists tend to { **A. neglect** **B. boycott** **C. disregard** } _____ the stop sign at the corner of

Elm Street and Apricot Avenue and drive through it carelessly.

24. Steve left the lawn mowing { **A. incomplete** **B. partial** **C. fragmentary** } _____.

DIRECTIONS
*Choose the underlined and lettered portion that is unnecessary within
the context of the passage.*

---

25. A word that is <u>absolutely</u> impossible <u>to spell</u> is one that does not
                           A   B

follow any <u>rules</u> and does not sound like it is spelled. <u>Unfortunately,</u>
             C   D

because English has many <u>such</u> words, it is extremely difficult to learn.
                            E

A. absolutely
B. to spell

C. rules
D. Unfortunately,
E. such

26. On the campout the fathers and daughters sat around <u>the campfire</u>

                                                          A

and told <u>ghost</u> stories. A few of the <u>frightened</u> girls were afraid.
            B   C

Actually, <u>some of</u> the fathers even became nervous as they glanced
              D

toward the darkness that surrounded the group <u>huddled</u> over the fire.
                                                         E

A. the campfire
B. ghost
C. frightened
D. some of
E. huddled

DIRECTIONS
*For the underlined sentence(s), choose the answer that expresses the
meaning with the most fluency and clearest logic within the context.*

---

27. Football, America's real favorite pastime, is all excitement. <u>For example,
there are thirty seconds left to play, and Smith intercepts the pass, and
he runs downfield, and he drops the ball at the two-yard line.</u>

  A. For example, there are thirty seconds left to play, and Smith
intercepts the pass, and he runs downfield, and he drops the ball at
the two-yard line.
  B. For example, being that there are thirty seconds left to play, Smith
intercepts the pass, runs downfield, and drops the ball at the
two-yard line.
  C. For example, with thirty seconds left to play, Smith intercepts the
pass, runs downfield, and drops the ball at the two-yard line.
  D. For example, since there are thirty seconds left to play, Smith
intercepts the pass, runs downfield, and drops the ball at the
two-yard line.

28. A little-known group of heroes from World War II is the platoon of
female pilots. <u>These women were able, dedicated, and prepared, and
they transported mail and supplies in all kinds of weather and through
often grave danger.</u>

  A. These women were able, dedicated, and prepared, and they
transported mail and supplies in all kinds of weather and through
often grave danger.
  B. Able, dedicated, and prepared, they transported mail and supplies
in all kinds of weather and through often grave danger.
  C. Being as they were able, dedicated, and prepared, they transported
mail and supplies in all kinds of weather and through often grave
danger.
  D. Although they were able, dedicated, and prepared, they
transported mail and supplies in all kinds of weather and through
often grave danger.

29. Across the Thames from Shakespeare's London was Bankside. <u>The area was small, but the worst rogues in the city lived there, and so did prostitutes, and so did actors and orphans.</u>

    A. The area was small, but the worst rogues in the city lived there, and so did prostitutes, and so did actors and orphans.
    B. The area was small, and the worst rogues in the city lived there and so did prostitutes, actors, and orphans.
    C. Being that the area was small, the worst rogues in the city lived there and so did prostitutes, actors and orphans.
    D. Although the area was small, the worst rogues in the city lived there, as did prostitutes, actors, and orphans.

Posttest and Answer Key

DIRECTIONS
Choose the sentence that logically and correctly expresses the comparisons.

---

30. A. The house on Bridge Street is older.
    B. The house on Bridge Street is the oldest.
    C. The house on Bridge Street is the oldest in the neighborhood.

31. A. After sitting on the balcony awhile, it began to rain, so we went inside.
    B. After sitting on the balcony awhile, the rain made us go inside.
    C. After sitting on the balcony awhile, we went inside when the rain began.

32. A. Having taken his seat, we began to question the applicant.
    B. Having taken his seat, the questioning of the applicant began.
    C. Having taken his seat, the applicant began to answer our questions.

DIRECTIONS
Choose the sentence that expresses the thought most clearly and effectively and that has no errors in structure.

---

33. A. Most of us do not really understand what it is like to know hunger, disease, and not having enough money.
    B. Most of us do not really understand what it is like to know hunger, disease, and to be poor.
    C. Most of us do not really understand what it is like to know hunger, disease, and poverty.

34. A. We recognize our friends by what they say and their actions.
    B. We recognize our friends by their words and their actions.
    C. We recognize our friends by their words and by what they do.

35. A. Stephanie likes to swim, to watch movies, and reading books.
    B. Stephanie likes to swim, to watch movies, and to read books.
    C. Stephanie likes to swim, to watch movies, and she also likes reading books.

Posttest and Answer Key

Kiester, Edwin, Jr. "Have Steinway, Will Travel." Reader's Digest, May 1991: p. 12.

Passage 1-Corrected

For the past six years, Laura Spitzer and her piano have gone crisscrossing the small-town West, bringing fine music to U.S. and Canadian villages, playing almost anyplace where two or three are gathered. You might compare Laura, sowing the love of the classics in far-off nooks and crannies of North America, to Johnny Appleseed.

Trained for concert performance at the prestigious Mozarteum in Salzburg, Austria, and at the Peabody Conservatory of Music in Baltimore, she has played in formal, big-city recital halls. But her missionary zeal is reserved for school gyms and church basements.

Some of her former classmates hop from city to city to perform before black-tie audiences in places with velvet cushions. Laura prefers a truck with bed space and an ice chest, musical scores piled on the floor, and wet laundry drying. She likes her listeners five feet from the piano, seated on folding chairs.

"Engaging and expert," the New York *Times* wrote of her when she played the Big Apple. But she would rather quote the Ely, Nev., *Daily Times*: "Her ability to relate to an audience and her total piano mastery leave an audience spellbound." Says Laura, "After all, in New York I might be the tenth pianist to perform in a week. In Duckwater I may be the first—ever."

"I am here because I followed my dream. I am a truck driver, piano mover, and pianist because I want to go to small places and play for people."

Phillips, Christopher. "Whale of a Rescue." Reader's Digest, June 1991: pp. 154–55.

Passage 2-Corrected

A 30-ton humpback whale was seventeen miles east of Gloucester, Mass., when it became entangled in a tough, transparent gill net. Wrapped around its body, flippers, and blowhole, the net prevented the whale from moving or feeding and made breathing difficult.

In times past, the whale would have been left to perish. But on July 16, 1990, there was hope because of Charles "Stormy" Mayo, co-founder and research director of the nonprofit Center for Coastal Studies in Provincetown and head of its whale-disentanglement team.

The 47-year-old marine biologist and his crew sped the rescue boat to the site. Mayo recognized the whale as "Mallard," a frequent visitor off the coast. "Mallard is very inquisitive and playful, almost a friend," he said. "He comes up to our research vessel and looks us in the eye."

Now working in small inflatable boats, the team attached heavy buoys to the net around Mallard. Fighting the extra burden, the whale soon tired, enabling Mayo to maneuver his craft close to the animal, 300 times his size.

Mayo leaned toward the gasping, groaning leviathan and began cutting the net with a knife. For three hours Mallard remained docile while Mayo, who admits to being scared, removed the line one strand at a time. When Mayo cut the part covering the blowhole, the 40-foot whale surged upward, nearly capsizing the 15-foot rubber boat. Just as abruptly, the whale calmed down, and Mayo resumed his painstaking work. Drenched by the spray, the men were relieved and cheered loudly.

Question	Answer	Skill
1. A.	is incorrect because it does not agree in number with the subject "Laura Spitzer and her piano."	
C.	is incorrect because it is nonstandard usage.	
B.	is correct because it is a standard verb form.	III.B.4.a
2. A.	is incorrect because it is a homonym but the wrong word for the context.	
B.	is incorrect because without the hyphen, the word is not an adjective meaning distant or remote in time or space.	
C.	is correct because the comma sets off the end of the parenthetical participial phrase that occurs in the middle of the sentence.	III.B.5.b
3. A.	is incorrect because the word is misspelled.	
B.	is incorrect because the word is not a proper noun and one is needed for the context.	
C.	is correct because the comma eliminates the sentence fragment.	III.B.2.d
4. A.	is incorrect because the word is misspelled.	
B.	is incorrect because the subject and verb do not agree.	
C.	is correct because a common rather than a proper noun is needed for the context.	III.B.5.c
5. A.	is correct because the pronoun is singular and needed for the context.	III.B.4.b.2
B.	is incorrect because it is misspelled.	
C.	is incorrect because no comma is needed.	
6. A.	is correct because it is correctly spelled.	III.B.5.a
B.	is incorrect because no comma is needed.	
C.	is incorrect because it is the wrong form of the verb.	
7. A.	is correct because a comma, not a semicolon is the correct punctuation.	III.B.5.b
B.	is incorrect because a period creates a sentence fragment.	
C.	is incorrect because a colon here creates a sentence fragment.	
8. A.	is incorrect because it eliminates the needed quotation mark.	

**Posttest and
Answer Key**

Question		Answer	Skill
	B.	is incorrect because it has eliminated an unnecessary apostrophe.	III.B.5.b
	C.	is incorrect because both words should be capitalized as proper nouns.	
	D.	is correct because no change is necessary.	
9.	A.	is incorrect because it is a nonstandard verb form.	
	B.	is incorrect because it does not agree in number with the subject.	
	C.	is correct because it agrees in number with the subjects "ability and mastery."	III.B.4.b.1
10.	A.	is incorrect because it does not agree in number with the subject.	
	B.	is incorrect because it is misspelled.	
	C.	is correct because a period eliminates the comma splice.	III.B.2.d
11.	A.	is correct because the verb is in the present tense.	III.B.4.f
	B.	is incorrect because a comma is needed for the nouns in a series.	
	C.	is incorrect because the verb is in the past tense.	
12.	A.	is incorrect because "east" requires no capital letter.	
	B.	is correct because the verb is in the past tense.	III.B.4.f
	C.	is incorrect because a comma is necessary for a series.	
13.	A.	is correct because the comma eliminates the sentence fragment.	III.B.2.d
	B.	is incorrect because the comma is unnecessary.	
	C.	is incorrect because an adjective not a noun form is necessary.	
14.	A.	is incorrect because the word is misspelled.	
	B.	is incorrect because the verb is nonstandard usage.	
	C.	is correct because it is the correct spelling.	III.B.5.a
15.	A.	is incorrect because proper names require capital letters.	
	B.	is incorrect because the word is misspelled.	
	C.	is incorrect because the comma is unnecessary.	

Question		Answer	Skill
	D.	is correct because no change is necessary.	III.B.5.a III.B.5.b III.B.5.c
16.	A.	is incorrect because the word is plural.	
	B.	is correct because the pronoun agrees with the antecedent.	III.B.4.b.2
	C.	is incorrect because the word does not fit the context.	
17.	A.	is incorrect because the word is misspelled.	
	B.	is correct because the period eliminates the comma splice.	III.B.2.d
	C.	is incorrect because the verb does not agree with the subject.	
18.	A.	is incorrect because the word is misspelled.	
	B.	is incorrect because a comma is necessary (for an introductory phrase).	
	C.	is correct because no apostrophe is necessary.	III.B.5.b
19.	A.	is correct because a comma is necessary.	III.B.5.b
	B.	and C. are incorrect because the punctuation creates a sentence fragment.	
20.	A.	is correct because the verb is standard usage.	III.B.4.a
	B.	is incorrect because a comma is necessary.	
	C.	is incorrect because the verb tense does not fit the context.	
21.	A.	is correct because an adverb is necessary.	III.B.4.e
	B.	is incorrect because a comma is necessary.	
	C.	is incorrect because the pronoun is plural.	
22.	A.	is correct because the verb agrees with the subject.	III.B.4.b.1
	B.	is incorrect because the word is misspelled.	
	C.	is incorrect because the word is an adjective and not an adverb.	
23.	C.	is correct because of the context.	III.B.1.a
24.	A.	is correct because of the context.	III.B.1.a
25.	A.	is correct because the word is unnecessary to the context and upon elimination has the least effect on the passage.	III.B.1.c
26.	C.	is correct because the word is redundant of "afraid" and can be eliminated.	III.B.1.c

**Posttest and
Answer Key**

Question		Answer	Skill
27. C.		is correct because it represents the most effective embedding, in this case coordination of verbs.	III.B.2.b
28. B.		is correct because it represents the most effective embedding, in this case coordination of adjectives.	III.B.2.b
29. D.		is correct because it represents the most effective embedding, in this case subordination.	III.2.b
30. C.		is correct because the superlative form is necessary for the context.	III.B.4.g
31. C.		is correct because the phrase correctly modifies the subject.	III.B.2.a
32. C.		is correct because the phrase correctly modifies the subject.	III.B.2.a
33. C.		is correct because the verbs are parallel.	III.B.2.c
34. B.		is correct because the nouns are parallel.	III.B.2.c
35. B.		is correct because the infinitive phrases are parallel.	III.B.2.c

The Passages

The passages on the CLAST will come from one of three sources. The most common will be excerpts from college textbooks. Passages will be quoted or paraphrased from subject-area textbooks (for example, science, art, social studies, humanities, business, literature, music, physical education). Additional sources for passages may be newspapers, magazines, or public documents. And lastly, the passages may have been written specifically for the CLAST.

The passages will not contain highly technical vocabulary nor will they require specialized knowledge.

The Questions

There is a total of 44 questions on the reading subtest, with 3 or 4 questions included for each of the 12 comprehension skills; however, only 39 of these questions actually count toward your score. The other 5 questions are experimental questions being field-tested for future use, and these do not count toward your score. You will not be able to identify the experimental questions.

Of the 12 comprehension skills tested, 3 require you to read with literal comprehension. Literal comprehension means that the information required by the question is directly stated in the passage. Main idea, supporting detail, and vocabulary in context are the three skills that require you to read with literal comprehension. Literal comprehension is considered the easiest level of comprehension because it does not require an in-depth understanding of the author's thoughts and ideas. You do not have to infer or recognize unstated relationships.

The other 9 comprehension skills tested require you to read with critical comprehension, and these questions make up 75 percent of the CLAST reading subtest. Critical comprehension requires you to do much more than literally read the words. Critical comprehension requires you to comprehend what the writer did not directly say, by making inferences and by understanding unstated relationships. You must be able to follow the author's thread of thought and draw logical conclusions. You must also be able to detect the author's purpose, tone, and organizational pattern.

In this text each of these 12 comprehension skills will be examined in terms of how the question will be asked and in terms of what you should look for in choosing the correct answer while avoiding an incorrect answer. You will be given explanations and exercises that will enable you to develop and practice the specific comprehension skill being addressed.

The pre- and posttests included in this part are very similar to the actual CLAST reading test. The tests and accompanying answer keys provide opportunities for needed practice, helpful diagnosis, and remediation of errors. The end result will be improved competence in your test-taking ability.

After scoring your pretest you should be able to identify your weaknesses, and you should be ready to work through the explanations of the comprehension skills included in this text. An explanation of each comprehension skill will be followed by sample items. Finally, you will take the posttest to confirm your understanding of all the comprehension skills tested on the CLAST reading section.

Special Considerations

As mentioned earlier, some of the passages appearing on the CLAST may have been created especially for this test. These passages are sometimes written at a lower reading level than textbooks. Some students may find it upsetting to go

**Part III
Reading**

Section 3-1

Overview of the CLAST Reading Subtest

The reading subtest of the CLAST consists of passages of not more than 500 words followed by questions. Most of the passages will be comparable to material found in college textbooks. For each of 12 specific comprehension skills, 3 or 4 questions will appear on the test. One of the 12 comprehension skills, fact/opinion, will have a 2-option format; that is, the questions used to test this skill will have only 2 choices. The other 11 skills will have 4 options. The 12 skills require both literal and critical comprehension.

Overview of the CLAST Reading Subtest

from an easy passage to one with much longer sentences and a higher vocabulary level. This variation should not be a problem if you are prepared for it. The majority of the material will be equivalent to that of college textbooks.

The reading and English language sections of the CLAST are combined with a total time allotment of 80 minutes to complete both sections. You should be able to complete the reading section in 60 minutes. It is a good idea to read over the questions before reading the passage because you will more quickly identify the needed information by using the questions as a guide. Prior knowledge of the questions will encourage you to read with a purpose and thus achieve better comprehension. Also, by noting the specific kinds of questions you will need to answer on a particular passage, you will have an idea of how to adjust your reading speed for the passage.

Some of the questions will require you to return to the passage or to specific lines within the passage to note certain relationships. In short, you will be required to read analytically—that is, in a careful and thoughtful manner.

Designing a reading test where all students have equal interest in and equal background knowledge regarding the material would be impossible. These two factors are uncontrollable and yet do play a part in comprehension. We all have better comprehension of material in which we are interested and about which we know a great deal. Be assured that some of the passages you will read on the actual CLAST, and in this text, will *not* be particularly interesting to you; however, one of the signs of mature readers is that they can keep their minds on the subject and capture the critical content even when the material is uninteresting, difficult, and/or unfamiliar to them.

You will improve your comprehension if you can become more involved in the passages. Critical comprehension requires involvement and participation by the reader. With literal comprehension, you might experience a moderate level of success with a minimum level of involvement. To be successful with critical comprehension, though, you must be open-minded, receptive, and inquisitive when responding to the material.

Previously, you may have had little or no practice in dealing with some of the comprehension skills required by the CLAST. For example, you may be unfamiliar with how to determine the "tone" of the author. Most students have little knowledge regarding logical fallacies. To ensure success on the reading section of the CLAST, you should acquaint yourself with each of the 12 comprehension skills by carefully reading the explanations and by working through the samples provided in this text. These activities will enable you not only to enhance your level of proficiency in dealing with reading passages, but they will also increase your confidence in your own reading and test-taking ability.

Test-Taking Hints for the Reading Section of the CLAST

Your success on the reading subsection of the CLAST will depend on three things:

1. your ability to read and understand the passages.

2. your attitude.

3. your test-wiseness skills.

Reading Ability

You will need to read and understand the passages on the CLAST just as you have been, and will continue to be, required to read and understand your college textbooks. If you know that your reading comprehension skills are deficient, you should enroll in a college-level reading course prior to taking the CLAST.

Attitude

Second, it is important that you approach this test with a positive attitude. The purpose for taking the CLAST is to ensure that you have the necessary skills to continue in your pursuit of your academic goals. The skills needed to perform well on the CLAST have been identified as the same ones that are necessary for academic success. A positive attitude will enable you to concentrate more effectively while taking this exam and, consequently, will improve your comprehension of the reading passages. You should realize that the passages are intended to inform you, not entertain you. You should, however, make an effort to develop an interest in the reading passages. Fostering a genuine positive interest is just as easy as approaching them with a negative attitude and certainly more beneficial.

Test Wiseness

Finally, in order to perform well on the reading section of the CLAST, you should be test wise. In other words, you should be aware of how to use your knowledge and skills effectively during the testing period for optimum performance. The following hints are intended to improve your test-wiseness skills for taking the reading section of the CLAST.

1. *Look over the reading section of the test to familiarize yourself with the format and note the time.* You should have adequate time to complete this section of the test and should avoid unnecessary clock-watching; however, it is advisable to glance at the clock periodically in order to pace yourself.

2. *Read the questions prior to reading the passage.* It is not necessary to read all the alternatives, but you should carefully read the stem in order to gain a purpose for reading the passage.

3. *Read the first paragraph carefully.* Often the main idea and/or the purpose will appear here. This paragraph sets the stage for the entire passage, and you need to spend some time carefully focusing on the topic presented.

4. *Read with mental activity.* As you read, mentally predict what will come next, summarize what you have read, and visualize the situations described.

5. *Read with physical activity.* Use your pencil as a pacer. Underline any information that seems important or appears to be relevant to the questions. Physical activity encourages mental activity, which in turn increases comprehension.

6. *Attempt to answer all questions.* Guess when possible as you progress through the test. If, however, you absolutely have no idea, it is better to leave an item blank for now rather than to labor over it in lieu of answering others. Return to unanswered questions after you have completed this section of the test. You should attempt all questions, because unanswered items are counted as errors.

**Overview of the
CLAST Reading
Subtest**

7. *Attempt to answer the questions in your own words prior to looking at the options.* This procedure often eliminates confusion when you are trying to choose from several similar options.

8. *Read all the options before making your choice.* Option "a" might be a satisfactory answer, but option "d" might be the best response.

9. *Change an answer only if you are sure you are changing it for a good reason.* If, on second thought, you simply "feel" one response is better than the one previously chosen, it is usually better to leave your original answer.

10. *Do not panic if you find the passage exceedingly difficult.* Continue to read, attempting to comprehend an overview of the passage. Often these difficult passages are followed by questions that do not require thorough understanding.

11. *Read the entire passage rather than searching for answers to specific questions.* Questions, like main idea, purpose, and tone questions, require you to read and understand the entire passage.

DIRECTIONS
This pretest is similar to the reading section of the CLAST. During the actual administration of the CLAST, the English Language Skills section and the Reading section are combined for a total time allowance of 80 minutes. You should attempt to complete this practice reading test in approximately 60 minutes. Read each passage. Then choose the best answer for each item.

Passage 1-Test Copy

Altruistic behavior, in which an individual appears to behave in such a way as to benefit others rather than itself, can be observed in the more complex social groups of animals. A particularly clear case of altruistic behavior has been observed by biologists Watts and Stokes in the

5 mating of wild turkeys. Several differing groups of males, each with a dominance hierarchy, gather in a special mating territory and go through their displays of tail spreading, wing dragging, and gobbling in front of females who come to the area to copulate. One group attains dominance over other groups as a result of cooperation among the

10 males within the group. The dominant male of the dominant group then copulates frequently with the females. The males who helped establish the dominant group, but have low status within it, appear to gain nothing. Close analysis, however, has shown that members of a group are brothers from the same brood. Since they share many genes

15 with the successful male, they are indirectly perpetuating many of their genes. Altruism is closely related to kin selection, a type of natural selection where the behavior of one individual increases the likelihood of survival or reproduction of one or more genetically related individuals.

20 Kin selection may account for the evolution of the complex societies of social insects in which some individuals are specialized for reproduction while other close relatives do the chores of the colony. In the bee society, the workers are sterile females, and the queen functions vicariously as their reproductive organ. If the queen

25 successfully produces offspring, a large portion of the genes shared by the queen and workers will have passed on to the next generation, even though the workers themselves have not reproduced.

Prairie dogs are rodents that live in large colonies in which a few act as sentries. Though the sentry places its life in grave danger when

30 it exposes itself outside its burrow, it acts to protect its siblings and by so doing helps ensure that the genes they all have in common will be perpetuated in the population.

Another example of kin selection may be found among Florida jays. Here, non-reproducing individuals aid in the rearing of their

35 siblings' young. Nests tended by these additional helpers as well as parents produce more young than nests with the same number of eggs overseen only by parents. By helping to care for their siblings' children, ____, these individuals have a better chance of ensuring that at least some of their genes (the genes shared with their siblings) will be

40 maintained in future populations.

**Pretest and
Answer Key**

1. The most accurate expression of the central, or controlling, idea of this passage is

   a. altruistic behavior favors the dominant male.
   b. altruistic behavior is based on cooperation and sacrifice for species survival.
   c. kin selection affects animal reproduction, especially in bees.
   d. non-reproducing individuals share in raising the young of the species.

2. What is the meaning of the word *vicariously* as used in line 24?

   a. as a surrogate
   b. as a victim
   c. dynamically
   d. aggressively

3. The author of this passage has created a tone that could be described as

   a. evasive
   b. satirical
   c. detached
   d. incredulous

4. The passage has a word deleted on line 38. Choose the word that best completes the passage.

   a. nevertheless
   b. likewise
   c. conversely
   d. therefore

Passage 2-Test Copy

The Maya are hardly a vanished people, for they number an estimated two million souls, the largest single block of American Indians north of Peru. Most of them have resisted with remarkable tenacity the encroachments of Spanish American civilization, although in the past
5   decade these have taken an increasingly violent and repressive form. Besides their numbers and cultural integrity, the Maya are remarkable for an extraordinary cohesion. Unlike other more scattered indigenous peoples within Mexico and Central America, the Maya are confined with one exception (the Huastec) to a single, unbroken area that
10   includes all of the Yucatan Peninsula, Guatemala, Belize, parts of the Mexican states of Tabasco and Chiapas, and the Western portion of Honduras and El Salvador. Such homogeneity in the midst of such a miscellany of tongues and peoples testifies to their relative security from invasions by other native groups—the Aztec, for instance, never
15   extended their empire to include any part of Mayan territory, although they had important trading relationships with them.
   All the Mesoamerican Indians shared a number of traits which were more or less peculiar to them and absent or rare elsewhere in the New World: hieroglyphic writing, books of fig-bark paper or deerskin
20   which were folded like screens, a complex permutation calendar, knowledge of the movements of the planets (especially Venus) against the background of the stars, a game played with a rubber ball in a

25 special court, highly specialized markets, human sacrifice by head or
heart removal, an emphasis upon self-sacrifice by blood drawn from
the ears, tongue, or penis, and a highly complex, pantheistic religion
which included nature divinities as well as deities emblematic of royal
descent. Also in all Mesoamerican religions was the idea of a
multi-tiered Heaven and Underworld, and of a universe oriented to
the four directions with specific colors and gods assigned to the
30 cardinal points and to the center.

From such profound similarities one can only conclude that all
the Mesoamerican peoples must have shared a common origin, so far
back in time that it may never be brought to light by archaeology. Yet
there is some consensus among archaeologists that the Olmec of
35 southern Mexico had elaborated many of these traits beginning about
3,000 years ago, and that much of complex culture in Mesoamerica has
an Olmec origin. It is also reasonable to assume that there must have
been an active interchange of ideas and things among the
Mesoamerican elite over many centuries, a state of affairs which can be
40 documented in the terminal Classic epoch thanks to recent research;
this in itself would tend to bring about cultural homogeneity—for
example, it might explain why both the Classic Maya and the very late
Aztec held a snake-footed god to be the supernatural ruling their
respective royal houses. It was out of such a matrix of cultural
45 evolution and diffusion that Mayan civilization was born.

5. The example of the snake-footed god was used to illustrate

    a. the tenacity of the Mayan civilization.
    b. the relationship of Mayan and Aztec civilizations.
    c. that the Mayan pantheistic religion worshipped snakes.
    d. that the Mayan civilization is remarkable for its cohesion.

6. A synonym for the word *encroachments* on line 4 is

    a. instigations
    b. inflammations
    c. intrusions
    d. invitations

7. In paragraph 2 of this passage, the organizational pattern could be
   described as

    a. definition
    b. process
    c. description
    d. listing

8. If the author were delivering this passage orally, his tone of voice
   would probably be

    a. ambivalent
    b. earnest
    c. distressed
    d. obsequious

9. Which of the following arguments is valid:

    a. The Spanish encroachments into the Mayan country were not
       intentional.
    b. The Aztecs at one point successfully ruled the Mayas.

c. The Mesoamerican Indians were a peculiar group who worshipped strong gods.
d. The Mayan civilization flourished as a result of its tenacity and flexibility.

Passage 3-Test Copy

If we were to glance over the thousands of years of history of *Homo sapiens*, we might make the following generalizations: As time passed, the human way of life continually changed. The change has generally resulted from a technological advance—a new tool, a new technique, a
5 new energy source. As each technological advance broadened the base of human technological capacity, further advances become more frequent and were made in a greater number of directions, so that the rate of change has, in the course of history, continually increased.

Until modern times, the rate of change was so slow that the
10 process was unnoticeable in the course of any one person's lifetime. Mankind had the illusion, therefore, that change did not take place. When, in the face of that illusion, a change had clearly taken place, the response was to view it as something that should not have happened—as something that represented a degeneration from the
15 "good old days."

The steadily increasing rate of change reached the stage, about 1800, of becoming clearly visible to many thoughtful individuals. The Industrial Revolution was under way, and those affected by it could detect change in the course of their own lifetimes.
20 For the first time, people grew to understand that not only was change taking place but that it would continue to take place after their death. It meant there would be changes still greater than a person could live to see, changes that he would never see. This gave rise to a new curiosity—perhaps the first really new curiosity in historic
25 times—that of wondering what life on earth would be like after one was no longer alive. The literary response to that new curiosity was what we call science fiction. Science fiction can be defined as that branch of literature that deals with the reactions of human beings to changes in sciences and technology.
30 The reference can be to *any* changes, of course, and the science fiction writer chooses those that provide him with a dramatic situation out of which he can weave an exciting plot. There is usually no deliberate attempt to predict what will actually happen, but a science fiction writer is a creature of his times, and in trying to imagine a
35 change in science and technology, he is quite likely to base it on those changes he already sees in embryo.

Often this means an extrapolation of the present, an extrapolation that is so clear and obvious as to forecast something that is inevitable. When this happens, the science fiction writer does make
40 a successful prediction. Usually, this astonishes almost everyone, for mankind generally, even today, takes it for granted that things do not change.

10. The example of the Industrial Revolution was used to illustrate

a. the impact of science fiction.
b. the response of literary investigation.

    c. the new awareness of curiosity.

    d. the new awareness of change in peoples' lifetimes.

11. What is the meaning of the word *extrapolation* as used in line 37?

    a. experience

    b. exposition

    c. extension

    d. exoneration

12. What is the relationship between the sentence beginning in line 27 ("Science fiction can be defined . . . .") and the sentence beginning in line 30 ("The reference can be to *any* change . . . .")?

    a. statement and clarification

    b. generalization and example

    c. cause and effect

    d. comparison and contrast

13. Which of the following arguments is invalid?

    a. People preferred the "good old days" as they represented stability.

    b. Technology has accelerated the rate of change in our society.

    c. People dislike science fiction because they are afraid of change.

    d. People often do not bother to look into the future as it's easier to take things for granted.

Passage 4-Test Copy

The phenomenon of firewalking has become a hot topic in the popular media. For $60 or so we can take a "mind over matter" class that supposedly enables us to alter our body's chemistry. The "proof": walking on red-hot coals without feeling pain or being burned. The
5   psychological result: a newfound capacity to conquer one's fears. "If I can do something that's supposed to be impossible," says the elated firewalker, "I can do almost anything."

    Skeptical scientists have taken a cool look at firewalking (Dennett, 1985). The secret, they report, lies not in any mental power to alter the
10   senses but in the poor heat conductivity of the wood coals. Think of a cake baking in a 375° oven. Touch the aluminum cake tin and you'll get burned; touch the cake—like wood, a poor heat conductor—and you'll be okay. Of course, cakes and coals do conduct some heat, so you'd better not stay in touch with them too long or you will get
15   burned. Some have learned the hard way that, indeed, he who hesitates is lost. But the 2 seconds or less that it takes to quickstep across hot embers puts each foot in contact with the coals for only a fraction of a second, and less than a second total time per foot. Confident of these facts—and that wetting the feet before the firewalk
20   provides further insulation—skeptical scientists have themselves performed the feat without the "mind over matter" training.

14. The author reveals a biased attitude against firewalking when he says that . . . .

    a. "firewalking has become a hot topic in the popular media."

    b. ". . . so we can take a 'mind over matter' class that supposedly enables us to alter our body's chemistry."

c. "Skeptical scientists have taken a cool look at firewalking."
d. ". . . skeptical scientists have themselves performed the feat without the 'mind over matter' training."

15. The statement made by the firewalker that "If I can do something that's supposed to be impossible, I can do almost anything" is an example of what kind of faulty reasoning?

a. introduces an irrelevant point to divert attention from the main issue
b. draws conclusions not necessarily a logical result of the facts
c. asserts a truth by claiming everyone believes it
d. makes inappropriate comparison to prove a point

16. The writer of this passage probably feels that

a. firewalking is a learned talent.
b. firewalking is a case of "mind over matter."
c. firewalkers can provide proof of their ability.
d. firewalking is a fraud.

Passage 5-Test Copy

A sudden loud squeal of brakes close by, or a frightening, suspenseful movie can make your heart pound, your body perspire, and your stomach feel as though it were climbing into your throat. These various body reactions are all caused by a chemical compound that is
5   produced in a pair of hat-shaped organs called the adrenals, located on top of the kidneys. The compound is one of many chemical messengers, called hormones, that travel through the bloodstream and cause changes in body cells. This particular compound is called epinephrine, but you are probably more familiar with its common
10   name, adrenalin. Under normal conditions, small amounts of epinephrine are released into the blood to help control blood pressure and to maintain the level of sugar in the blood. But this compound is also the body's way of meeting emergencies and dealing with stress such as emotional excitement, exercise, extreme
15   temperature changes, severe hemorrhaging, and the administration of certain anesthetics.

    Epinephrine affects many parts of the body in reacting to stress. It increases the rate and strength of the heart beat, which increases the cardiac output. It raises the blood pressure by causing constriction of
20   blood vessels in all parts of the body, except for the blood vessels in such vital organs as the skeletal muscles, heart, brain, and liver. It relaxes the smooth muscles in the lungs, making epinephrine a very effective drug in the treatment of severe bronchial asthma attacks. It also increases the rate and depth of breathing, enabling more oxygen to
25   get into the lungs. Epinephrine causes an increase in blood sugar, and a general increase in the metabolic activity of the cells. It slows down the action of the digestive tract, and accelerates blood clotting. It delays the fatigue of skeletal muscles, and increases the strength of contractions of these muscles. This last property has allowed people to show
30   amazing strength under great stress; _____, after an auto accident, a man lifted his car to free his son who was trapped underneath. Each of

these changes in normal body function caused by epinephrine enables the body to meet the initial challenge of the stress. The effect lasts only a short time, because the epinephrine released into the bloodstream is
35   inactivated by the liver in about three minutes.

17. All of the following were typical epinephrine reactions to stress *except*

    a. raised blood pressure.
    b. increased rate of breathing.
    c. increased asthma attacks.
    d. increased muscle strength.

18. The author's primary purpose is to

    a. prove the value of epinephrine.
    b. explain how epinephrine works in the body.
    c. describe how hormones function.
    d. tell the story of epinephrine.

19. The organizational pattern used in this passage is

    a. time order
    b. definition
    c. classification
    d. listing

20. The passage has words deleted in line 30. Choose the word that best completes the passage.

    a. for example
    b. moreover
    c. after all
    d. in contrast

21. The author suggests that

    a. adrenalin can be dangerous.
    b. adrenalin constricts blood vessels in vital organs.
    c. adrenalin aids digestion.
    d. without adrenalin, superstrength is unlikely.

Passage 6-Test Copy

Judging by our everyday conversation, left-handedness is not all right. To be "coming from left field," or to offer a "left-handed compliment" is hardly more complimentary than to be "sinister" or "gauche" (words derived from the Latin and French for left). ____, right-handedness is
5   "right on," which any "righteous" "right-hand man" "in his right mind" usually is.

Almost 10 percent (somewhat more among males, somewhat less among females) of the human population is left-handed. Judging from cave drawings and the tools of prehistoric humans, this veer to the
10   right occurred long ago in the development of our species.

Observing 150 babies during the first 2 days after birth, George Michel (1981) found that two-thirds consistently preferred to lie with their heads turned to the right. When he restudied a sample of these babies at age 5 months, almost all of the "head right" babies reached for

15 things with their right hands, and almost all of the "head left" babies reached with their left hands. Such findings, along with the universal prevalence of right-handers, suggest that handedness is genetically influenced.

20 Tests reveal that about 95 percent of right-handers process speech primarily in the left hemisphere (Springer and Deutsch, 1985). Left-handers are more diverse. More than half process speech in the left hemisphere, just as right-handers do. About one-quarter process language in the right hemisphere; the other quarter use both hemispheres more or less equally. Such left-handers may therefore

25 require better communication between the hemispheres. This might explain the recent discovery that the corpus callosum averages 11 percent larger in left-handers (Witelson, 1985).

Left-handers are disproportionately numerous among those afflicted with reading disabilities, allergies, and migraine headaches

30 (Geschwind and Behan, 1984). But left-handedness is also more common among musicians, mathematicians, professional baseball players, architects, and artists, including such luminaries as Michelangelo, Leonardo da Vinci, and Picasso. If one can tolerate elbow-jostling at dinner parties, right-handed desks, and awkward

35 scissors, then apparently the pros and cons of being a lefty are roughly equal.

22. The main idea expressed in this passage is that

  a. left-handedness is generally misunderstood.
  b. there are advantages and disadvantages to being left-handed.
  c. many musicians, mathematicians, and artists were left-handed.
  d. that most of the population are right-handed and only 10 percent are left-handed.

23. The examples of the larger corpus callosum in left-handers was used to illustrate

  a. the larger intelligence of left-handed people.
  b. the processing that takes place in the brain's hemispheres.
  c. that better communication between the hemispheres is needed by left-handers.
  d. that right-handers process speech primarily in the left hemisphere.

24. The author's statement in the first line of this passage "Judging by our everyday conversation, . . ." is a statement of

  a. fact.
  b. opinion.

25. The passage has a word deleted in line 4. Choose the word or phrase that best completes the passage.

  a. Similarly
  b. In addition
  c. On the other hand
  d. Nevertheless

26. From this passage you could conclude that

  a. it is better to be right-handed.
  b. left-handers are likely to be female.
  c. we make negative judgment about left-handers.
  d. that most people prefer to be right-handed.

Partly because DDT does pose a serious threat to ecosystems, its use in the United States was banned in 1973. However, in the early 1980s it was still being manufactured in the United States for export to many other countries! And other countries are still manufacturing and using

5   it. Several closely-related chlorinated hydrocarbon pesticides have also been banned, but others continue to be used widely. The use of DDT is officially sanctioned by a number of international organizations because of its usefulness in checking the populations of mosquitoes that spread malaria, especially in the underdeveloped world. But even

10 without considering some of the deeper issues involved in such use, it is clear that DDT is becoming steadily less effective as a mosquito pesticide as these insects develop increasing resistance to its action.

     Although the problems connected with pesticide use are reduced somewhat when biodegradable compounds such as the carbamates or

15 organophosphates are substituted, there is no known pesticide currently in widespread use that is free from undesirable ecological consequences. The carbamate Sevin, for instance, is almost completely harmless to mammals but is instant death for bees, and bees are vital for pollination of food and wild plants. Since all pesticides kill more

20 than the pests against which they are directed, in the end pesticide problems can be solved only by avoiding their use. Yet this seems less and less likely to happen. _____, we now use more than twice the amount of pesticides used in 1962, the year Rachel Carson's famous book on the subject, *Silent Spring*, was published.

25   Unfortunately, the very characteristics of pesticides that make them ecologically dangerous make them economically attractive to agriculturalists. A broad-spectrum pesticide also kills many varieties of pests with a single application, and if it is persistent it does not need to be applied as often. On the whole (and for the short term), pesticide

30 use contributes substantially to agricultural production. There is also no reasonable doubt that public health has benefited from pesticide use, especially in underdeveloped countries.

     In the long run, _____, consequences of population growth made possible by these measures may outweigh the good that has been

35 accomplished. We can avoid using pesticides, to be realistic, only if we are content to produce less food. We can produce less food only if we have fewer mouths to feed. With fewer mouths to feed, we could, perhaps, confine human settlement to the parts of the globe that are most ecologically suited to settlement—for example, by avoiding

40 malarial swamps. Population growth and the political problems that result from it are among the most significant factors keeping us from attempting ecologically sound solutions to environmental problems.

27. The author's primary purpose is to

    a. convince us of the hazardous effects of pesticides.
    b. teach us how to avoid hazardous pesticides.
    c. tell the sequence of events surrounding pesticide use.
    d. divert attention from the problems of population growth.

28. In this passage, the author shows bias against

    a. all pesticide use.
    b. biodegradable compounds as pesticides.

c.   agricultural use of pesticides.

d.   manufacturing and selling DDT.

29. If the author were delivering this passage orally, his tone of voice
     would probably be

a.   apathetic.

b.   critical.

c.   malicious.

d.   depressed.

30. The passage has a word deleted in line 22. Choose the words that best
     completes the sentence.

a.   For instance

b.   In conclusion

c.   In fact

d.   In contrast

31. The passage has a word deleted in line 33. Choose the word or words
     that best complete the sentence.

a.   likewise

b.   for example

c.   evidently

d.   however

32. From this passage you could conclude that Rachel Carson's book,
     Silent Spring,

a.   was a best seller in 1962.

b.   condemned the use of pesticides.

c.   was popular with agriculturalists.

d.   set the appropriate usage of pesticides.

Passage 8-Test Copy

Illiteracy is not a new phenomenon in the United States. By any
standard there were many more illiterate Americans 100 years
ago—and perhaps as recently as 1960. In the past two decades, the
number of those who cannot read at all has either diminished slightly

5   or remained unchanged. It is functional illiteracy that has increased;
this is the case because this term is, in itself, a "function" of the needs
imposed upon a person by the economic and the social order. The
economy and the society have changed in every age. It is the rate of
change, and the degree to which it may outpace the literacy level of the

10 nation, that determine what part of that nation is unable to survive
and to prevail within the context of its times. The speedup in the rate
of change, especially within the past two decades, is well known.
Schools, while more inclusive, have not ceased to serve as instruments
of class selection. Those who have been left behind, assigned to lower

15 tracks throughout their education, and assigned in high school to
"vocational" or "general" curricula, can no longer meet employment
opportunities so easily as in a time when physical strength and docile
acquiescence in repetitive operations were the characteristics that could
qualify a person for a job.

20   Today, as the code words for survival in the hi-tech industries
become "retraining" and "decision making" and "decoding," the

problem becomes greater while it also grows much harder to conceal.
Corporations will be able to "retrain" only those who can participate
in training programs. Those who cannot read the training
25 manuals—persons who, in another age, could nonetheless scratch out
an income by the bending of the back and patient labor of the
hands—may find no work at all. Even if the economic situation is
improved, and opportunities for jobs expand, there will not be jobs
that can be filled by people who can read at less than ninth grade level.
30 "By the 1990s," according to Dorothy Shields, education director of
the AFL-CIO, "anyone who doesn't have at least a twelfth-grade
reading, writing, and calculating level will be absolutely lost."

33. Identify the statement that most accurately states the central idea of
paragraph 2.

   a. Illiteracy is not a new phenomenon.
   b. Functional illiteracy has grown in recent years.
   c. Corporations often have training programs to aid illiteracy.
   d. Advanced reading skills will be important for survival in the job
      market.

34. The author's primary purpose is to

   a. divert attention from the facts.
   b. explain what illiteracy really is.
   c. argue the dangers of illiteracy.
   d. prove that companies can be flexible in combating illiteracy.

35. In paragraph 2 of this passage, the organizational pattern used by the
author could be described as

   a. comparison and contrast.
   b. cause and effect.
   c. spatial/place order.
   d. order of importance.

36. The author's statement that ". . . the problem becomes greater while
it also grows much harder to conceal" (line 22) is a statement of

   a. fact.
   b. opinion.

37. The author of this passage has created a tone that could be described as

   a. satirical.
   b. arrogant.
   c. pessimistic.
   d. vindictive.

Passage 9-Test Copy

The fact that there are approximately two hundred different Native
American tribes in the United States today is evidence of the
enormous variety and diversity of American Indian culture. The tribes
were scattered over a vast geographic area, and each tribe had its own
5 way of life, its own customs and traditions; yet a fundamental belief
shared by the many Native American nations was the importance of
song and ceremony to all aspects of life. Songs were part of every act of

worship, every important ritual to mark the passing of time and the coming of death. Native American songs were also associated with the routines of daily life: hunting, praying for rain or successful harvest, coming of age, curing of ills, preparing for war, or celebrating peace.

The Native Americans believed that every living thing had power—the buffalo, the eagle, the tree, even the ant. Power also resided in the unseen things, in powerful spirits who could be called upon to help supply whatever was needed to sustain the life and health of the tribe. Songs were the means of invoking the aid of these seen and unseen beings; thus, songs were imbued with almost supernatural powers.

An important source of new songs was the "vision quest," a trancelike ritual in which a member of the tribe was "given" a new piece of music through supernatural means. He became, temporarily, a mouthpiece through which powerful beings spoke. A song revealed in a dream was always used to improve the life of the people in some way, for example to heal the sick or achieve victory in war. An interesting aspect of these dream songs was that they became the personal property of the dreamer. The singing of the song gave him power, power that would be lost if the song were sung by someone else, especially without the agreement of the owner.

Another type of individual expression was the song of praise sung to honor a powerful chieftain, a courageous warrior, or a loyal friend. A third type of song was associated with the rituals and ceremonies of the tribe. Such songs belonged to everyone and were sung during various kinds of ceremonies.

Since Native American songs had a specific function—to invoke the aid of powerful or supernatural beings in meeting the needs of the tribe—it was essential that they be performed correctly. The chants and incantations that were used to heal the sick, for example, had to be performed accurately; if they were not, the whole ceremony would be invalidated and the sick person might not recover. Thus, much Indian music was practiced again and again until a perfect rendition was virtually assured. An individual performer was not judged by the "beauty" of his voice; the "good" singer was one who could perform the song without error, thereby helping to ensure that the needs of the people would be met.

38. The author's statement that dream songs . . . became the personal property of the dreamer in line 25 is a statement of

   a. fact.
   b. opinion.

39. What is the relationship between the sentence beginning in line 36 ("The chants and incantations . . .") and the sentence beginning in line 39 ("Thus, much Indian music. . . .")?

   a. cause/effect
   b. comparison/contrast
   c. definition/classification
   d. sequence/process

The use of a few number or letter grades to assess student performance has long been criticized as being inaccurate, rigid, and unfair. Many substitutes for the grading system have been suggested, but few have gained a wide following. Among the options are pass/fail grading,

5   contract grading, and no grading. The pass/fail system is in limited use at many colleges. Contract grading means that the student and teacher agree on what kind and how much work will merit a certain grade. In systems in which no grades are given, the teacher may write lengthy evaluations for each students.

10   All of these alternatives to the usual grades assess student performance in a way that has some meaning to the students and teachers involved. The problem is how to interpret this meaning to outsiders—to colleges for high school students, for example, and to graduate schools for college students. This is a major reason why such

15   alternatives grading systems have often floundered.

In the last decade, the usual grading system in America has been attacked on another front. The charge is that grades have become "inflated." Despite a significant national decline in standardized test scores, students' grades were on average higher in the 1970s than they

20   had ever been. One university, for example, reported that it had more straight-A graduates since 1971 than it had had in its first 100 years (*The New York Times*, March 28, 1976).

Grade inflation may have stemmed originally from the campus unrest of the 1960s. During the Vietnam War, some professors gave

25   students higher grades to enable them to stay in school and avoid the draft. In addition, the general campus unrest during the 1960s encouraged those faculty members who felt the grading system was unfair or meaningless to assign higher grades to all their students. Since then, however, grade inflation seems to have been continued to

30   help students get into highly competitive graduate schools.

In the last few years, many colleges and universities have been trying to tighten their grading standards. At the same time, there is little indication that the traditional use of number or letter grades to evaluate students is being changed.

40.   In paragraph 4 of this passage, the organizational pattern used by the author could be described as

a.   time order.
b.   classification.
c.   description.
d.   definition.

41.   Which of the following statements reveals a biased attitude expressed by the author in this passage?

a.   "Many substitutes for the grading system have been suggested, but few have gained a wide following."
b.   "In systems in which no grades are given, the teacher may write a lengthy evaluation for each student."
c.   "Since then, however, grade inflation seems to have been continued to help students get into highly competitive graduate schools."
d.   "Grade inflation may have stemmed originally from the campus unrest of the 1960s."

42. What is the relationship between the sentence beginning on line 31 ("In the last few years, ...") and the sentence beginning on line 32 ("At the same time . . . .")?

    a. cause and effect
    b. comparison and contrast
    c. statement plus clarification
    d. statement plus example

43. Which of the following arguments is valid?

    a. Written evaluations are preferable to grades.
    b. Contract grading requires no guidelines for students.
    c. Pass/fail grading is fair and is widely used at many colleges.
    d. Assessment can be misinterpreted by outsiders.

44. "Knock on wood for luck" is an example of what kind of faulty reasoning? (Refer to list of fallacies.)

    a. Begging the question
    b. Hasty generalization
    c. Faulty analogy
    d. Faulty cause/effect

List of Fallacies

1. Faulty cause and effect (*post hoc, ergo propter hoc*)—falsely assumes that one event causes the second.

2. Non sequitur—conclusion not necessarily a logical result of the facts.

3. Begging the question—asserts as truth something not yet proved.

4. Circular logic—restatement of facts presented in first half of argument.

5. Hasty generalization—argument based on insufficient or unrepresentative evidence.

6. Either/or—argument limited to two extreme choices.

7. Faulty analogy—makes inappropriate comparisons to prove a point.

8. Argument to the person (often referred to as *argumentum ad hominem*, argument to the man)—attacks the opponent's character rather than the issue.

9. Argument to the people (*argumentum ad populum*)—appeals to the emotions of the audience rather than dealing with the issue.

10. Bandwagon appeal—asserts a truth by claiming everyone else believes/does it.

11. Red herring—introduces an irrelevant point to divert attention from the main issue.

**Pretest and
Answer Key**

Question	Answer	Skill
1.	b.	(I.A.1.)
2.	a.	(I.A.3.)
3.	c.	(I.B.5.)
4.	d.	(I.B.6.)
5.	b.	(I.A.2.)
6.	c.	(I.A.3.)
7.	d.	(I.B.2.)
8.	b.	(I.B.5.)
9.	d.	(I.B.8.)
10.	d.	(I.A.2.)
11.	c.	(I.A.3.)
12.	a.	(I.B.7.)
13.	c.	(I.B.8.)
14.	b.	(I.B.4.)
15.	b.	(I.B.8.)
16.	d.	(I.B.9.)
17.	c.	(I.A.2.)
18.	b.	(I.B.1.)
19.	d.	(I.B.2.)
20.	a.	(I.B.6.)
21.	d.	(I.B.9.)
22.	b.	(I.A.1.)
23.	c.	(I.A.2.)
24.	b.	(I.B.3.)
25.	c.	(I.B.7.)
26.	c.	(I.B.9.)
27.	a.	(I.B.1.)
28.	d.	(I.B.4.)
29.	b.	(I.B.5.)
30.	c.	(I.B.6.)
31.	d.	(I.B.6.)
32.	b.	(I.B.9.)
33.	d.	(I.A.1.)
34.	c.	(I.B.1.)
35.	b.	(I.B.2.)
36.	b.	(I.B.3.)
37.	c.	(I.B.5.)
38.	a.	(I.B.3.)
39.	a.	(I.B.7.)
40.	a.	(I.B.2.)
41.	c.	(I.B.4.)
42.	b.	(I.B.7.)
43.	d.	(I.B.8.)
44.	d.	(I.B.8.)

Use this table to determine which of the CLAST reading skills were most difficult for you.

**Pretest and
Answer Key**

Question Number	CLAST Skill and Code
1, 22, 33	Main idea—I.A.1
5, 10, 17, 23	Supporting detail—I.A.2
2, 6, 11	Vocabulary in context—I.A.3
18, 27, 34	Purpose—I.B.1
7, 19, 35, 40	Organizational pattern—I.B.2
24, 36, 38	Fact/opinion—I.B.3
14, 28, 41	Bias—I.B.4
3, 8, 29, 37	Tone—I.B.5
4, 20, 30, 31	Within sentences—I.B.6
12, 25, 39, 42	Between sentences—I.B.7
9, 13, 15, 43, 44	Valid arguments—I.B.8
16, 21, 26, 32	Inferences and conclusions—I.B.9

On the CLAST, the main idea is also referred to as the controlling idea or the central idea. Some authors use other terminology when referring to this idea. Regardless of the terminology used, it is the nucleus of all comprehension. If the reader has difficulty identifying the author's main idea, it is doubtful that he or she could comprehend at a higher reading level. All other comprehension skills evolve from and are related to the main idea. As you will notice when some of the critical reading comprehension skills are discussed later in this text, you can often detect the author's tone, purpose, and even the author's organizational pattern, from the main idea of the passage.

Literal Comprehension Skills

> **I.A.1**
> **The student recognizes main ideas in a given passage.**

How the Question Will Appear on the CLAST

You will be asked to identify the main idea of a passage or paragraph. The main idea may be explicitly stated within the passage or it may be implied. In either case, the question will be stated in one of the following three ways:

1. Identify the statement that most accurately states the central idea of this passage (or paragraph).

   > (4 options)

2. The main idea expressed in this passage (or paragraph) is . . . .

   > (4 options)

3. The most accurate expression of the central, or controlling, idea of the passage (or paragraph) is . . . .

   > (4 options)

Incorrect Options

Four incorrect options will be included on the CLAST to test your skill in identifying the main idea. One option may be a partial or incomplete statement of the main idea. For example, the passage may be about "active volcanoes," and the option may be written to include only "volcanoes."

Another incorrect option may be too broad; that is, it may contain information that goes beyond what was in the passage. For example, the passage may be about "active volcanoes in South America" and the incorrect option that is too broad may refer to "active volcanoes in the world."

A third incorrect option may be too narrow. This option may refer to some detail in the passage that was used to support or explain the main idea. For example, the main idea of a passage might be that volcanoes have caused monetary loss as well as loss of lives. If you were to choose an option describing the dollar amount of damage caused by volcanoes, you would be wrong. This fact was mentioned as evidence to support the main idea and therefore is a supporting detail.

The fourth possible incorrect option may simply contain incorrect information, or a gross misinterpretation of the main idea. For example, the passage may state that "volcanoes are a deadly and expensive phenomenon," and the option may state that "volcanoes are the worst disaster that nature can inflict on mankind." This statement is a misinterpretation of the main idea because it does not state or imply that volcanoes are the *worst* disaster.

How to Identify the Main Idea

Often the main idea is explicitly stated within the selection. This sentence is frequently at the beginning of the passage or paragraph, but it may also appear

Literal Comprehension Skills

in other places—within the selection, at the end of the selection, or even at the beginning and restated in a similar way at the end of the selection.

The main idea, however, is not always explicitly stated within the selection. The reader may have to infer the author's main idea based on the information provided in the supporting details. Whether the main idea is stated or implied, the details in the selection must provide relevant evidence, or they must support the author's main idea.

There are three questions you should ask in order to determine and verify the main idea regardless of whether it is stated or implied.

1. Who or what is the selection about? (This is the subject, or topic, of the selection.)

2. What is the main point the author makes about the subject? (This is the main idea of the selection.)

3. Does the majority of the information in the selection support this idea? (If yes, you have determined the main idea of the selection. If no, you have chosen a supporting detail.)

Sample Items

The following exercises will give you practice in identifying the main idea. Remember to respond to *all* of the above three questions as you work through the exercises.

DIRECTIONS
Read each passage. Then choose the best answer for each item.

---

1. Empathy is the ability to put yourself in someone else's place, and to feel sympathy for that person's motives and point of view. Lack of empathy is a primary cause of conflict in organizations. Empathy is the chief quality mediators of labor disputes must have, and successful salespersons are usually empathic to a very high degree. Empathy is an important element in leadership, and its absence can create insurmountable barriers to communication.

The main idea expressed in this paragraph is that

a. lack of empathy is a primary cause of conflict in organizations.

b. empathy is the ability to put yourself in someone else's place.

c. empathy is an important element in many areas of an organization.

d. empathy is the most important quality of a good manager.

2. Under the private enterprise system, people have the freedom to compete with others. Competition, along with profit, is the cornerstone of the private enterprise system. Competition pits one company against another in the struggle to attract and retain the consumer. Companies compete by developing better products, altering prices, developing unique advertising programs, and having the product or service where and when the consumer wants it. The benefit to the consumer: competition makes for better products and more responsiveness to consumer needs.

Identify the statement that most accurately states the central idea of this passage.

a. Under the private enterprise system, people have the freedom to compete with others.

b. Competition makes companies more responsive to consumers.

c. Competition is the cornerstone of the private enterprise system.

d. Without competition, there would be no free enterprise system.

3. Most people spend a great deal of time communicating in small groups. Our lives revolve around our families, classes, work teams, athletic teams, and committees, and this list could be extended much further. The groups that most influence peoples' behavior become their reference groups: the groups with whom values, attitudes, and beliefs are shared. Groups also provide people with opportunities to satisfy their needs for recognition and achievement. They satisfy other wishes too, such as those for dominance and autonomy.

The most accurate expression of the central, or controlling, idea of this paragraph is

a. groups help satisfy needs.

b. most people spend a great deal of time communicating in small groups.

c. groups play an important part in our lives.

d. the reference group is the group with the most influence.

4. Politics and sports usually don't mix too much, but the legacy of just such a mixture some 30 years ago has left modern America with another serious drug problem—abuse of anabolic steroids.

The Russians provided the politics in the 1950s when they gave their Olympic athletes—both men and women—a male hormone called testosterone that apparently helped the competitors build muscle. As a result, they dominated many international sports events at the time.

An American doctor, who was later to regret his action, sought to even the score in those coldest of the Cold War days by developing for our Olympic athletes a variation of a drug that was related to testosterone. The doctor came up with a form of anabolic steroid for use by weight lifters that was supposed to build muscle while minimizing masculinizing side effects. The weight lifters who found that the prescribed 5-milligram (mg) pills helped build muscle assumed immediately that 10 mg, or two pills, would add even more muscle, 15 mg more yet, and so forth. The race was on.

Today, anabolic steroids are widely used and abused by young athletes in search of bigger muscles. This drug abuse involves boys not yet in their teens; high school, college and professional athletes; and body builders of both sexes.

Identify the statement that most accurately states the central idea of this passage.

a. Anabolic steroids are the product of a Russian doctor.

b. Olympic weight lifters started using steroids 30 years ago, and an American doctor introduced them to U.S. weight lifters.

Literal Comprehension Skills

c. Today's drug problems date back to the 1950s and the Olympics.

d. The use of anabolic steroids has spread throughout the U.S. due to a conflict of politics and the Olympics.

Answers

1. The correct answer is "c." The idea that empathy is an important element in many areas of an organization was not specifically stated; however, all of the evidence (supporting details) point to it. The supporting details tell why and how empathy is important and what happens without it. Options "a." and "b." are details that are not supported by the majority of the passage. Option "d." is incorrect because empathy is not described as "the most important" quality.

2. The correct answer is "c." It is stated in the second sentence. Choice "a." is a detail that describes the relationship of competition and free enterprise. Choice "b." is also a detail that tells what competition does for the consumer. Choice "d." is an opinion not stated or even referred to in the passage.

3. The correct answer is "c." Choice "a." is a supporting detail that tells why "c." is true. Choice "b." is a detail that explains the reasons why groups are important. Choice "d." is a detail that tells about one particular group and its importance.

4. The correct answer is "d." Choice "a." is an incorrect statement, since the passage does not say that the Russian doctor produced anabolic steroids. Choice "b." lists two details that support the main idea. Choice "c." is an incorrect statement, since it refers to "drugs" in general, which is too broad for this passage.

**I.A.2
The student identifies supporting details.**

Supporting details (which may be facts, major points, and illustrations) represent the evidence used by the author to support the main idea. Supporting details are stated explicitly in the passage.

How the Question Will Appear on the CLAST

You may be asked to identify details that support the main idea of a single paragraph, or you may be asked to identify the details that support the main idea of an entire passage. This question may be stated in a number of ways. Five of the most common are the following:

1. The example of _____ was used to illustrate . . . .

   [(4 options)]

2. All of the following were factors in (or causes of) _____ EXCEPT . . . .

   [(4 options)]

3. The passage (or paragraph) compares (contrasts) _____.

   [(4 options)]

4. _____ is different from (or similar to) in that . . . .

   [(4 options)]

5. The author quotes _____ to . . . .

   [(4 options)]

Incorrect Options

Each question will be followed by four options. One of the options, of course, will be the correct answer. The other three (incorrect) options will follow these guidelines:

One of the incorrect options may be a minor or secondary detail that does not support the main idea of the passage. For example, let us assume that the correct main idea is that "Three-wheel all-terrain vehicles are unsafe."

If you were to choose as a supporting detail for this main idea an option that states, "Ten thousand were imported last year," you would be incorrect. Even though this information may have been given in the passage, it does not support the main idea, which must include the important point that these vehicles are unsafe. The fact that 10 thousand were imported last year is unrelated to their being unsafe.

Another incorrect option may be a detail, or a supporting minor idea, presented in the passage or paragraph, but it would be one that does not correctly answer this specific question. For example, if the question was "The author quotes Nixon to . . . ," the correct answer would need to be the supporting detail that specifically tells why the author quotes Nixon. The other three will contain information given in the passage; however, they will not provide evidence to support the reason why the author quotes Nixon.

The third incorrect option will be a closely related detail that is *not mentioned* in the passage or paragraph. Even though this information is not directly stated within the selection, it will be closely related to the given information. For example, the supporting details in the passage might be facts that explain why three-wheel all-terrain vehicles are unsafe. One of the options for this question might be a fact that sounds plausible and logical, but since it was not stated in the passage, it cannot be a correct option. You must answer the questions based on the information contained within the passage only rather than relying on your prior knowledge.

A negatively stated option, such as "All of the following were factors EXCEPT . . . ," are troublesome for many students, because students fail to pay attention to the word EXCEPT. In this situation, the correct response is the option containing a supporting detail that was *not* stated in the passage. The word EXCEPT will always be upper-case letters.

How to Identify a Supporting Detail

Remember that supporting details support the author's main idea. If you are able to identify the author's main idea first, you will probably be more successful in determining whether you have identified the correct supporting detail. Ask yourself, "Does this statement tell how or why what the author says is true?"

Since determining the supporting detail requires you to read with literal comprehension, the information must be explicitly stated within the lines of the passage. If you miss this question, you have chosen one of the three incorrect options previously listed. That is, you have chosen an option that was not stated in the passage, you have chosen one that incorrectly answers the specific question asked, or you have misread the question (as in the negatively stated option).

**Literal
Comprehension
Skills**

> **DIRECTIONS**
> *Read each passage. Then choose the best answer for each item.*

1. Water, although the most important component for raising fish, is often the most neglected factor. Fish are totally dependent on water: they derive oxygen from it, they ingest it, they excrete their wastes into it, they take it up and lose salts into it, and they are in perpetual contact with it. Poor water quality can cause massive fish kills and is often the major factor contributing to fish diseases. Instead of adding chemicals to the water to treat a disease outbreak, the fish culturist should first look at water quality to determine why the outbreak occurred.

Water quality does not remain constant. In ponds, it can change dramatically over a few hours. Even water from deep wells and springs can change over time. It is not a simple matter for the fish farmer or pond owner to assess water quality. The fisheries manager must use chemical tests as well as observations to detect changes.

All of the following are examples of how fish are dependent on water EXCEPT

    a. they derive oxygen from it.

    b. they excrete their waste into it.

    c. they can get diseases from it.

    d. they take it up and lose salts into it.

2. In face-to-face conversations on the job, it is important to look the other person in the eye. Engaging in direct eye contact is often interpreted as a sign of credibility. It also, apparently, can have a beneficial impact on your perceived trustworthiness. When speaking, you may be perceived as lacking confidence if you fail to maintain good eye contact with the listener. While listening, your failure to maintain good eye contact may cause the speaker to conclude that you are not interested in what he or she is saying. Interpersonal relations on the job are greatly enhanced when individuals are open and honest. Good eye contact, it should be noted, is generally perceived as a sign of openness and honesty.

All of the following were given as reasons for good eye contact EXCEPT

    a. it is a sign of credibility.

    b. it is a factor in perceived trustworthiness.

    c. it is an indication of understanding.

    d. it is a sign of openness and honesty.

3. For a young child, all the world is a plaything. Children play with their bodies, language, objects, ideas, animals, and other people. How they play

reflects the degree of their motor, cognitive, and social development. A toddler shrieks with delight at being able to roll a ball back and forth to his mother; a few years later he may hit the winning home run for his Little League team.

The example of a toddler rolling a ball was used to illustrate

a. the wide variety of things with which a child will play.

b. the complexity of a child's play at a young age.

c. the relationship between degree of development and play.

d. the age difference in relation to play.

4. Many researchers believe that both human beings and computers can be comprehended as physical systems that process meaningful symbols. People and computers do the same kinds of things: they receive information from the world, they "process" it in some way, and then they perform some action. The detailed ways in which this occurs may be very different in the two cases. Most computers have limited ways of receiving information and performing actions (for example, typewriter keyboards and television screens). Certainly the "hardware" in the two kinds of systems is very different: neurons in one case, silicon in the other. But since the same general kinds of behavior can occur in both cases, perhaps much of human thought can be analyzed in terms of how a computer might do the same thing.

A computer is different from the human mind in terms of

a. the way they "process" information.

b. the "hardware" in the two systems.

c. the fact that they are physical systems.

d. the kinds of things they do.

Answers

1. The correct answer is "c." It is the only option that is *not* an example of how fish are dependent on water. In this case all of the options were stated in the passage and were listed as benefits to fish except for option "c.," which was mentioned as an effect of poor water quality.

2. The correct answer is "c." Option "c." was not stated in the passage. It sounds logical and is closely related to the other options, but it was not given in the passage. A careless reader who misses the word EXCEPT may interpret the question as "which of the following were given as reasons for good eye contact?"

3. The correct answer is "c." Here the reader must recognize the intent of the example: to demonstrate that the degree of development is reflected in how children play. This intent is stated in the sentence preceding the example.

4. The correct answer is "b." The other three options were details stated in the passage; however, they are mentioned as ways in which the computer and human mind are similar. The question asks how they are different. Misreading the question could lead to an incorrect answer.

Literal Comprehension Skills

**I.A.3
The student determines meaning of words on the basis of context.**

Determining the meaning of words on the basis of context is the last of the three literal comprehension skills tested on the CLAST. The reader is expected to determine the meaning of a word from clues found in the sentence or passage, or through clues obtained from understanding the general sense of the passage. Since the questions require you to read with literal comprehension, the sentence or passage must be written so that the meaning of the unknown word can be determined by carefully reading the lines containing the unknown word.

How the Question Will Appear on the CLAST

You will be asked to determine the meaning of a word based on how it is used in a sentence. The question will be asked in one of the following ways:

1. In this context, the word ____ on line ____ means . . . .

   (4 options)

2. As used in line ____, the word ____ most nearly means . . . .

   (4 options)

3. What is the meaning of ____ as used in line ____ . . . ?

   (4 options)

4. A synonym (or antonym) for the word ____ is . . . .

   (4 options)

Incorrect Options

The incorrect options will be one of three types. One option might be a definition that would be correct if the word were used in a different context.

Some snakes, such as water moccasins and rattlesnakes, have a venom that is extremely *virulent*.

Even though one correct definition for *virulent* is "bitter and spiteful," it is not the correct definition for the word as it is used in this sentence. Therefore, if one of the options for *virulent* was "bitter and spiteful," it would be incorrect in the context of this sentence. In this sentence *virulent* means poisonous.

Another incorrect option could be a definition of another word that is often confused with the word being defined.

Although many adults were suspicious of the old man, the younger residents found him to be extremely *benign*.

The word benign has become synonymous with cancer and is often confused with malignant, which—in the context of cancer—does mean life threatening. If one of the options listed was "having cancer" or "cancerous," this option might look more attractive than the correct choice "warm or friendly," due to the frequent association of *benign* with cancer.

The third incorrect option could be a word or phrase that appears in the passage, but that could be mistaken for the correct definition of the word. This option simply involves misreading.

Many animals prefer to come out only at night and, therefore, they are not often seen by man. On the other hand, their *diurnal* cousins are more familiar to the average person.

If you were to choose as the definition for diurnal "Animals that come out at night," you would be wrong. It is necessary to read correctly the phrase indicating a contrast, "On the other hand." You would then realize that diurnal animals are the opposite of those animals that come out only at night.

How to Identify the Correct Meaning through Context

The writer may use synonyms within the sentence to help the reader determine the meaning of words.

His *nefarious*, or evil acts, caused his downfall.

You could determine that "evil" is a synonym for *nefarious* by recognizing the word "or" in the sentence, indicating a synonym or equivalent word is to follow.

The writer may use contrast, or an antonym, to assist the reader in determining the correct meaning.

Usually he is a very *gregarious* person, but today he seemed to avoid people and stay by himself.

Even though you might not know the meaning of the word *gregarious* in isolation, you can determine from the contrast in this sentence that *gregarious* means the opposite of avoiding people. People who are gregarious like to be around other people. Words such as "but" and "however" are often used when the writer uses contrast.

The author might give examples that the reader could use as clues to determine the meaning of the word.

Being strangers in a foreign country, we faced many *adversities*, including a different language and unusual customs.

You can determine that the meaning of *adversities* must be difficulties or hardships from the examples given in the sentence.

Finally, the reader can sometimes infer the meaning of a word from information contained within the sentence or passage.

Nita must have taken a *circuitous* route home because by the time she arrived, we had eaten and cleared the table.

From reading this passage, you can conclude that *circuitous* must mean round about or indirect.

Sample Items

DIRECTIONS
Read each passage. Then choose the best answer for each item.

---

1. The President held a *surreptitious* meeting behind closed doors with his top advisors before announcing his plan.

In this context, the word *surreptitious* means

a. quick.

b. secret.

c. illegal.

d. unorganized.

**Literal
Comprehension
Skills**

2. Bill felt that a visit to Sugar Mountain would be *anticlimactic* since we visited Mt. Hood last summer. Mt. Hood has an elevation thousands of feet higher than Sugar and is one of the most spectacular sites in the country.

As used in line 1, the word *anticlimactic* most nearly means

a. more exciting.

b. too expensive.

c. a disappointment.

d. unnecessary.

3. In doing a major research paper, it is necessary to conduct an extensive search of relevant literature. This is sometimes difficult if the topic is one that is either very new or obscure. A *dearth* of information on a topic can be very frustrating to the researcher and results in hours of fruitless effort before finding any information of value.

An antonym for the word *dearth* is

a. quality.

b. abundance.

c. scarcity.

d. obsolete.

4. Although the union wanted a salary increase, they settled for *parity* in the salary scale, knowing that equality was also an important issue.

What is the meaning of *parity* as used in line 1?

a. decrease

b. inequality

c. increase

d. equality

Answers

1. The correct answer is "b." The sentence states that the meeting was held "behind closed doors," which makes "secret" the most logical choice.

2. The correct answer is "c." In the comparison of Mt. Hood and Sugar, Mt. Hood is described in glowing terms, thus implying that a visit to Sugar would be a letdown or disappointment.

3. The correct answer is "b." If the question is misread and the reader looks for a synonym, rather than an antonym, "scarcity" might be incorrectly chosen. Based on the information in the passage, a *dearth* of research must mean scarcity.

4. The correct answer is "d." The reader may be fooled by the contrast in this statement. The union wanted an increase, but settled for parity, or a decrease; however, the passage goes on to state that equality was important. One should therefore infer that *parity* must mean equality. The hasty or careless reader might be fooled by this format.

One of the reading skills tested on the CLAST that requires you to read with critical comprehension is recognizing the author's purpose. Simply stated, the author's purpose is the *reason* or *why* the author is writing. The main idea is the primary point the author wants the reader to understand, and the author's purpose is the main reason (or why) the author wrote the passage.

Critical Comprehension Skills

I.B.1
The student recognizes the author's purpose.

On the CLAST you will be asked to identify the author's primary purpose, or intention, which may be either stated or implied. Authors of reading textbooks often differ in regard to the nomenclature used to define, or name, the purposes for writing. On the CLAST passages, however, the author's primary purpose will be one of the following:

1. To inform (to state, to teach, to explain, to clarify).

2. To persuade (to argue, to convince, to prove).

3. To narrate (to relate a sequence of events, to tell a story).

4. To describe (to appeal to the senses, to create a sensory impression).

5. To entertain (to amuse, to divert attention from reality).

Although the author's primary purpose will be one of the five listed, other words or phrases (which are similar in meaning) may be used to name these purposes. For example, "to convince" or "to argue" may be used rather than "to persuade."

How the Question Will Appear on the CLAST

An author may employ more than one purpose in a single passage. You will be asked to determine the author's primary purpose. For example, the author may describe a situation and entertain you with an amusing anecdote in an attempt to *persuade* you to adopt his or her ideas. The author's primary purpose would be to persuade, not describe or entertain. On the CLAST you will be asked to identify the author's *primary* purpose, which will be dominant in the selection. You will be asked to determine the author's purpose of either a paragraph or an entire selection.

The format for testing this skill may vary. Some of the most common are the following:

1. The author's primary purpose is to . . . .

> (4 options)

2. The author's purpose in paragraph _____ is to . . . .

> (4 options)

3. The author's primary purpose in writing this passage is to . . . .

> (4 options)

4. The author's primary purpose in this passage is to convince the reader that . . . .

> (4 options)

5. The overall purpose of this passage is to . . . .

> (4 options)

Critical Comprehension Skills

6. In this sentence, "_____," the author's primary purpose is to . . . .

(4 options)

Since identifying the author's purpose requires you to read with critical rather than literal comprehension, the information will not be directly stated in the passage. You must be able to identify the purpose by making inferences and drawing conclusions from the information stated in the selection. Often, the main idea of the selection will give an indication or a clue that can be helpful in determining the author's purpose. Additionally, the author's choice of words frequently will assist you in determining the author's purpose. If the author's purpose is to persuade, you may find words in the passage that reveal the author's opinions and/or emotions. In contrast, if the author's purpose is to inform, you will probably find words that are primarily factual and objective and generally devoid of emotional connotations.

Incorrect Options

The correct option will be a statement of the author's primary purpose, and the three incorrect options will be misstatements and/or misinterpretations of the author's primary purpose. For example, you must be able to recognize whether the writer is trying to inform you regarding some point, or if the writer is simply informing you in an effort to accomplish his or her primary purpose of persuading you.

Of the six formats that may be used to ask this type of question, only one requires you to choose an answer that is *not* one of the five identified purposes. The fourth format (The author's primary purpose in this passage is to convince the reader that . . .) indicates that the author's primary purpose is to persuade. Your task, then, is to determine the exact idea, task, concept, etc., of which the author is trying to convince you.

How to Identify the Author's Purpose

Clues within the passage should help eliminate incorrect options. Determine the author's main idea and look at the author's word choices before making your decision about the author's purpose. For example, assume that in one sample passage the author's main idea is that acid rain is dangerous. The reader can quickly eliminate "to entertain" as a possible choice for the author's purpose since there is nothing humorous or entertaining suggested by this topic. The purpose will probably be either to inform or to persuade. If the author is objective and states only the facts without opinions or emotional language, the author's purpose is most likely to inform.

The following are some additional clues that will assist you in determining the author's purpose:

1. To inform—The words will be matter-of-fact, unemotional, and straightforward, without revealing the author's opinions or bias.

2. To persuade—The author may use emotional words (with opinion) and obvious bias in an attempt to convince.

3. To narrate—The author will use factual and emotional words in an effort to relate a sequence of events, a story, or a situation. The passage may be fact or fiction.

4. To describe—Words are used that appeal to the senses. The intent is to make the events as vivid in the mind of the reader as possible by creating a sensory impression.

5. To entertain—The language may be humorous and amusing. The writer may attempt to take the reader away from reality.

Critical Comprehension Skills

Sample Items

> **DIRECTIONS**
> *Read the following passage. Then choose the best answer for each item.*

1. No Hollywood Star could be so temperamental, so hilarious, so touching, or so frightening as some of the actors that have performed their roles before my camera.

As a member of the Walt Disney wildlife camera crew, I spent two seasons filming the spectacular true-life adventure, *The Vanishing Prairie*. We followed and found our animal and bird "actors" in remote sections of the West—in the last retreats of the native wildlife of the Great Plains. My "actors" were unpredictable.

They misbehaved continually. Small ones disappeared down burrows just when I was ready to start my camera. Larger ones charged me angrily when I got too close. They wrote the script with nature as their director. My camera was merely the "invisible" intruder.

The author's primary purpose in writing this passage is to

a. inform the reader of the difficulties in filming wildlife.

b. tell a story about the author's job.

c. entertain the reader with a personal anecdote.

d. convince the reader that animals can be filmed.

2. The tropical rainstorm had stopped as suddenly as it had begun and long shafts of yellow sunlight were lancing down through the dripping trees. At the end of the long boardwalk that stretched out in the murky, sullen water of the Patuca River a half dozen curious Hondurans were assembled to watch the rapid approach of a huge *pitpan*, or native dugout canoe, as it sliced through the water like a sharp knife.

In the first sentence of this paragraph the author's primary purpose is to

a. explain how fast the rain stopped.

b. entertain the reader by comparing sunlight to lances.

c. create for the reader a vivid description of the view.

d. convince the reader of the beauty of Honduras.

3. Politics and sports usually don't mix too much, but the legacy of just such a mixture some 30 years ago has left modern America with another serious drug problem—abuse of anabolic steroids.

Critical Comprehension Skills

The Russians provided the politics in the 1950s when they gave their athletes, both men and women, a male hormone called testosterone that apparently helped the competitors build muscle. As a result, they dominated many international sports events at the time.

An American doctor, who was later to regret his action, sought to even the score in those coldest of the Cold War days by developing for our athletes a variation of a drug that was related to testosterone. The doctor came up with a form of anabolic steroid for use by weight lifters that was supposed to build muscle while minimizing masculinizing side effects. The weight lifters who found that the prescribed 5-milligram (mg) pills helped build muscle assumed immediately that 10 mg, or two pills, would add even more muscle, 15 mg more yet, and so forth. The race was on.

Today, anabolic steroids are widely used and abused by young athletes in search of bigger muscles. This drug abuse involves boys not yet in their teens; high school, college and professional athletes; and body builders of both sexes.

The author's primary purpose in writing this passage is to

   a. persuade the reader of the seriousness of the problem.

   b. inform the reader of the historical background to a serious problem.

   c. provide the reader with an entertaining historical highlight of the Olympics.

   d. describe the Russian/American relations of the 50s.

   4. The rare 1913 nickel is not the Buffalo type but is the Liberty-head type. Shortly after these were coined (only six were made), a then well-known coin dealer was detailed by the late Colonel Green to approach the mint regarding the sale. After negotiating for a short time, four of the six 1913 Liberty-head nickels were sold to him for $500 each, $2000 for the four. All were in brilliant uncirculated condition, and the fifth was kept for the United States Mint collection. No one knows what became of the sixth nickel, and this mysterious nickel is probably the reason so many noncollectors have been acquainted with the rarity of the 1913 Liberty nickel.

The author's primary purpose is to

   a. explain the mystery of the missing 1913 nickel.

   b. entertain the reader with an interesting story.

   c. tell the events leading to the popularity of the 1913 nickel.

   d. describe the popularity of the Liberty-head nickel.

Answers

   1. Choice "c." is the correct answer. The language used is light and amusing. The author is comparing the animals to people by referring to them as "actors" and telling how they misbehaved. Choice "a." is incorrect because difficulties were mentioned in a humorous way and the author did not elaborate on these difficulties. Choice "b." is incorrect because the author did not relate a sequence of events and he did more than just tell a story. Choice

"d." is incorrect because the author never made an issue of whether animals could or could not be filmed. Therefore, persuasion is not the primary purpose.

Critical Comprehension Skills

2. Choice "c." is correct. The author is trying to create a vivid impression for the reader, to make the reader see through words ("shafts," "lancing") what the author saw. The author is appealing to the senses of the reader. Choice "a." is incorrect because in this sentence the author states that the rain "stopped as fast as it had begun," but then goes on to describe what was seen. Choice "b." is incorrect; the author compares sunlight to lances and mentions dripping trees in order to create a mental picture. The primary purpose is to describe. Choice "d." is incorrect because the author does not mention Honduras in this sentence and, additionally, never refers to its beauty. It is therefore very unlikely that the author is trying to convince the reader of the beauty of Honduras.

3. Choice "b." is the correct answer. The main idea of this passage, that the mixture of politics and sports led to the anabolic steroid drug problem in America, can be concluded from the first paragraph. The main idea of this passage provides a strong clue that the author's primary purpose is to inform. Choice "a." is incorrect because the author does not go into detail giving facts or explaining the horrible effects of the drug. There is no attempt to convince or persuade the reader of any opinion. Choice "c." is incorrect because this paragraph cannot be considered amusing or humorous and is therefore not entertaining. Choice "d." is incorrect because the Russian/American relations of the 50s were not explained and were mentioned only briefly to indicate how the mixture of politics and sports served as the catalyst for the invention of anabolic steroids.

4. Choice "c." is the correct answer. The author narrates a story and, in doing so, relates the sequence of events leading to the popularity of the 1913 Liberty nickel. This sequence of events leads to the author's proposal regarding the reason for the popularity of the 1913 nickel. Choice "a." seems like a good choice; however, the author's primary purpose is not to explain the mystery of the missing nickel, but to relate the events leading to the widespread popularity of the 1913 nickel. The author does not go into detail explaining how people have searched for the missing nickel. The passage ends with the revelation of the missing nickel and the author's proposal regarding the reason for the nickel's popularity. Choice "b." is incorrect because the author makes no attempt to amuse or entertain the reader. Certainly mysteries may be entertaining, but in this passage that was not the author's primary purpose. Choice "d." is incorrect because the author makes no attempt to appeal to the senses or to create a vivid sensory impression.

It is important at this point to note the distinction made on the CLAST between the author's organizational pattern and the author's purpose. The organizational pattern deals with the technique the author uses to convey ideas: the arrangement of the material. For example, if the author wishes to inform (the author's *purpose*) the reader that acid rain is dangerous (the author's *main idea*), he or she might use any one, or a combination, of various patterns; that is, examples, comparison/contrast, cause/effect (the author's *organizational pattern*).

Authors of textbooks regarding reading may recognize a variety of organizational patterns; there is no standard list. However, you will be required to recognize the following organizational patterns on the CLAST.

definition	division/classification	example
time order	description	listing
cause/effect	spatial/place order	comparison/contrast
order of importance	sequence/process	

I.B.2
The student identifies the author's overall organizational pattern.

The author's organizational pattern refers to how the author arranges his or her thoughts and ideas to best achieve the intended purpose and to clarify the main idea.

Critical Comprehension Skills

How the Question Will Appear on the CLAST

You will be asked to identify the author's organizational pattern of a paragraph or a longer selection. The question will be asked using one of the following formats:

1. The organizational pattern used in the passage could be described as . . . .

> (4 options)

2. In paragraph _____ of this passage, the organizational pattern used by the author could be described as . . . .

> (4 options)

3. The organizational pattern used in this passage is . . . .

> (4 options)

4. For this passage, the author uses an organizational pattern that . . . .

> (4 options)

Incorrect Options

In three of the formats used on the CLAST you will be given four options that will consist of one- or two-word names of organizational patterns. The fourth format (see 4 above) will consist of a one- or two-sentence option that will describe an organizational pattern.

You will be asked to identify the author's organizational pattern from either a paragraph or from an entire passage. Only the organizational patterns listed previously will be used on the CLAST.

How to Identify the Author's Overall Organizational Pattern

Authors may use one or a combination of organizational patterns to communicate their ideas. On the CLAST, however, you will be asked to identify only the author's *dominant* organizational pattern. One of the patterns should be identified as the primary organizational pattern used by the author.

Clues to the organizational pattern used by the author lie in the words used to connect the author's ideas. These connecting words are often called transition words. For example, if the author is going to use contrast as the organizational pattern, you would be alerted by transition words such as "although," "however," or "on the other hand." Below are the organizational patterns you will be asked to identify and their respective purposes.

| DEFINITION | to show the meaning or to define something |

| EXAMPLE | to illustrate or clarify something |

| DESCRIPTION | to tell where, or how, to create a picture for the reader |

Critical Comprehension Skills

CAUSE/EFFECT	to tell how or why something happened, to indicate the reasons for an occurrence
COMPARISON/ CONTRAST	to show how one thing is different or similar to another
SEQUENCE/PROCESS	to show steps or sequence in a process or procedure
DIVISION/ CLASSIFICATION	to show exactly where or how something fits in with or is grouped with others
TIME ORDER	to show chronological order of events, or how events follow in time
LISTING	to enumerate items, ideas, or facts without regard for order
SPATIAL/ PLACE ORDER	to show location and relation in space
ORDER OF IMPORTANCE	to show priority in relation to other items, ideas, events, or facts

Below are some common transitions, words, and phrases often used with these organizational patterns.

DEFINITION	is, means, can be defined as, like
EXAMPLE	for example, for instance
DESCRIPTION	(No transitions are associated with this pattern. Figurative language is often used, as well as words intended to create a vivid mental picture for the reader.)
CAUSE/EFFECT	as a result, because, consequently, the effect, therefore, thus
COMPARISON	likewise, similarly, also

CONTRAST	on the other hand, on the contrary, however, but, conversely
SEQUENCE/PROCESS	technique, process, procedure, first step, then, next (Many of the same words as used for time order and listing are used. Sequence/process words, however, *must deal with a process or a procedure.*)
DIVISION/ CLASSIFICATION	category, group, rank, division (Any word that indicates division/classification from a discipline such as biology—i.e., kingdom, species—may be used.)
TIME ORDER	next, first, second, before, after, finally, then, now, soon (Many of the transition words used for sequence/process and for listing may be used. However, order is important. *If steps in a process, technique, or procedure are being described, it would be sequence/process rather than time order.*)
LISTING	in addition, next, first, second, finally (Order is not important in listing.)
SPATIAL/ PLACE ORDER	above, under, over, next to, below, inside, outside, behind, above, in front
ORDER OF IMPORTANCE	next, first, priority, least important, near, major, most important, first, second, third, etc. (Many of the same words used in several other patterns may be used. However, in order of importance, the words *must indicate the relationship among the items, events, or ideas about priority or importance.*)

As mentioned earlier, you will be asked to identify the author's dominant pattern in a paragraph or passage. Since some of the same terms may be used in several patterns, noting how to identify different patterns using the same clue words is important. The clue word "first" limits your options to four patterns: listing, time order, sequence/process, or order of importance. You must note the author's purpose for using this word. Is the author giving the first *step* a bill must go through to become a law (sequence/process), or is he or she mentioning the first *way* a bill can become a law (listing)? Is the author talking about the first battle in the Civil War (time order)? Presenting the first principle of good business (order of importance)?

Critical Comprehension Skills

> **DIRECTIONS**
> *Read each passage. Then choose the best answer for each item.*

1. The word *ecology* was coined in the last century from the Greek (*oikos*) meaning "house" to designate the study of organisms in their natural homes. Specifically, it means the study of the interactions of organisms with one another and with the physical and chemical environment. Although it includes the study of environmental problems such as pollution, the science of ecology also encompasses research on the natural world from many viewpoints, using many techniques. Modern ecology relies heavily on experiments, both in the laboratory and in field settings, and on mathematical models. These techniques have proven helpful in testing ecological theories and in arriving at practical decisions in the management of natural resources.

The organizational pattern used in this passage could be described as

a. description.

b. example.

c. definition.

d. listing.

2. Irrigation can change the productivity of the land. If the irrigation water contains quantities of salts and the soil does not drain well, evaporation may cause salt buildup in the soil (salination), which can stunt growth, decrease yields, and eventually kill crop plants. Improperly drained irrigated lands can also become waterlogged. Water accumulating underground gradually raises the water table close to the soil surface, saturating the soil around plant roots with toxic saline water. Salinity and waterlogging can be corrected with proper management of the water-soil system, but the economic cost is high.

The organizational pattern used in this passage is

a. division/classification.

b. comparison/contrast.

c. cause/effect.

d. sequence/process.

3. Invention helped to weld the far-flung republic into a unit. Once more we must return to 1787. The successful operation of a steamboat on the Delaware River by John Fitch while the Convention was in session was an event worthy to be chronicled with the stories of the Constitution and the Northwest Ordinance. Twenty years later Robert Fulton renewed the effort to develop steam navigation; and by 1820 river and coastal steamers were numerous. The ocean-crossing steamship was almost ready. The railroad era

Critical Comprehension Skills

began in Jackson's administration and led at once to the development of civil engineering courses and departments in academies and colleges.

For this passage, the author uses an organizational pattern that

a. lists a series of details that support a point.

b. indicates a series of events in time.

c. defines aspects of history related to a topic.

d. gives examples to support a point.

4. The most fundamental of all needs, according to Maslow, are physiological ones, such as those for food, clothing, and shelter. When these are basically satisfied, safety needs replace them. Safety needs are of two types: survival and security. Next in the hierarchy are social needs, such as the desire for friendship, affection, and acceptance. The fourth level of the hierarchy contains esteem needs, such as the need to feel important and respected. Research shows that prestige and power are two motives closely related to the esteem need, and to the degree that these motives can be satisfied, the esteem need can be met. At the top of the hierarchy are self-actualization needs.

The organizational pattern used in this passage is

a. listing.

b. order of importance.

c. definition.

d. description.

Answers

1. Choice "c." is correct. First, you should have determined the author's main idea, which in turn would provide a strong clue to the organizational pattern. The subject or topic of the passage is the word "ecology" and the point or main idea the author wants the reader to understand is the "meaning" of ecology. The author uses clue words such as "meaning," "it means," "includes," and "encompasses."

2. Choice "c." is correct. Again the main idea provides a clue to the organizational pattern. The main idea is stated in the first sentence of the passage: Irrigation can change (cause or effect) the productivity of the land. The word "causes" in the second sentence should have given you a clue. The details of the passage are examples that explain how irrigation can change the productivity of the land. The pattern of the passage is cause/effect. Irrigation is the cause and the details of the passage contain the effects.

3. Choice "b." is the correct answer. A series of events with words related to time are used throughout the passage: "1787," "twenty years later," "by 1820," "the railroad era." The author is referring to a series of inventions (events) in time "that helped to weld the far-flung republic into a unit" (main idea).

4. Choice "b." is the correct answer. The words "hierarchy," "next," "level," and "top" indicate a priority or importance in the relationship between

the items being discussed. The passage starts with "the most fundamental" and ends with the "top of the hierarchy."

How the Question Will Appear on the CLAST

You will be asked to identify whether a specific statement is fact or opinion. The question will include a quote beginning with the first few words of the statement and the specific line and/or paragraph in which the quote may be found.

1. The statement beginning on line ____ of paragraph ____ (the first few words will be quoted) is a statement of

   a. fact.
   b. opinion.

2. The author's statement that ____ (in lines ____) is a statement of

   a. fact.
   b. opinion.

How to Distinguish between Fact and Opinion

A statement is a fact if it can be proved or disproved by objective means. These objective means could be actual observation, expert opinion, official records, authoritative books, or records. It is a fact that the raccoon is classified as a member of the bear family. This statement can be verified by objective means; the accuracy of this information may be checked in an authoritative text. It is a fact that Jim was at the party last night. You can prove or disprove this statement by objective means; you could ask others who attended the party to verify this statement. It is a fact that Bill is 6'3" tall; you could measure his actual height using a tape measure.

An opinion cannot be proved or disproved by objective means. Often an opinion may sound like a fact and you might strongly support the statement, both of which might trick you into thinking that it is a fact. Statements of opinion are personal beliefs and cannot be proved to be true or false. Often value words like, "best," "worst," "prettiest," and "funniest" are used in statements of opinion.

Joe Montana is the best quarterback of all times.

You and a great many others may agree with this statement. It, however, cannot be proved by objective means and, therefore, is an opinion. The statement that movies show too much violence is an opinion. The amount that is too much is an opinion that would vary from one person to another. This type of value judgment is always an opinion.

Often opinions are disguised as facts. We may say, "That's a fact," or "It's a fact that . . ." when we feel strongly about a statement, regardless of whether or not it can be proved. The great majority of those "It's-a-fact" statements are actually opinions. (Of course, that's my opinion, not a fact.)

On the CLAST, statements whose truth or falsity can be proved by objective means are statements that deal with facts. They will be statements that deal with persons, places, objects, occurrences, or processes that actually exist or did exist.

Critical Comprehension Skills

**I.B.3
The student distinguishes between statement of fact and statement of opinion.**

Distinguishing between statements of fact and statements of opinion requires the reader to recognize the difference between a verifiable statement and one that is either a personal judgment, or just not verifiable. This is not a difficult question if you clearly understand the difference between a fact and an opinion. This question has a two-choice format; the correct answer is either fact or opinion.

Critical Comprehension Skills

Dr. Jane Perry taught that class last year.

This statement is a fact because its truth or falsity can be proved. You can call the school and ask if she taught the class last year.

A statement is a fact even if it can be proved to be false. Remember that we defined a fact as a statement that can be proved or disproved by objective means.

Three hundred runners were in the race.

This is a statement of fact even if proved to be wrong, in which case it would be an incorrect fact. Even if you knew three hundred was an incorrect number, it would be a fact because it could be proved, or verified, by objective means. The number of runners in an organized race is verifiable.

Statements that deal with evaluations, attitudes, or probabilities are statements of opinion because they cannot be proved true or false.

More people should be concerned with the environment.

Even though you may agree, and you are certain most everyone else would agree with this statement, it is an opinion in that it cannot be proved by objective means.

Statements that deal with future events are statements of opinion even when they seem very probable.

In the future, interplanetary travel will be common.

Perhaps it will, but there is no way that anything in the future can be proved or verified *now*.

Sample Items

The following exercises should give you confidence in distinguishing fact from opinion. On the CLAST, these statements will be included in passages from which four or five questions involving other comprehension skills will be asked as well. Remember, the statement will be identified in the question using one of the two formats described earlier.

DIRECTIONS
Read each passage. Then choose the best answer for each item.

---

1. If we don't stop wasting water, we will soon be without our most precious natural resource.

   a. fact
   b. opinion

2. Exercise is one of the most important components of a healthy lifestyle.

   a. fact
   b. opinion

3. A foreign language is not required for entrance to any state university.

   a. fact
   b. opinion

4. The Grand Canyon is the most spectacular site in the United States.

    a. fact
    b. opinion

Answers

    1. This statement is an opinion. Even though most people would agree with the statement, it deals with the future and cannot be proved today.

    2. This statement is a fact. It can be verified to be true or false by objective means, such as authoritative texts, by experts in the field, or by research studies.

    3. This statement is a fact. It can be proved right or wrong by objective means. One could check college catalogs or contact the state universities to verify this statement.

    4. This statement is an opinion. It involves a judgment. Perhaps the Grand Canyon is not considered the "most spectacular site" by everyone; therefore, it cannot be proved by any objective means.

For purposes of this assessment, bias may be defined as a predisposition or prejudgment that causes the author to attempt to influence the reader to like or dislike, agree or disagree with, support or refute a subject. Points to note in detecting bias would be the author's choice of words that arouse the reader's emotions and the author's presentation of material in slanted innuendos intended to ignite the reader's emotional reaction.

    Bias in writing is an attempt by the author to influence the reader to agree with or follow the author's reasoning through the use of words. To recognize bias you must be alert to the author's choice of words, and you must recognize the intent of these words.

How the Question Will Appear on the CLAST

You will be asked to identify statements revealing bias in the passage. You may also be asked to identify the object, person, action, or concept toward which bias is directed in the passage. The questions will follow one of three formats.

    1. In this passage the author shows bias in favor of (or against) . . . .

> (4 options)

    2. The author expresses (reveals, shows) a biased attitude toward (against) _____ when he says that . . . .

> (4 options)

    3. Which of the following statements shows (reveals, reflects) a biased attitude expressed by the author in this passage?

> (4 options)

Incorrect Options

The three incorrect options will follow these guidelines:

    1. a quoted or paraphrased statement that reveals a fair, unbiased attitude; and/or

Critical Comprehension Skills

**I.B.4
The student detects bias.**

This definition and explanation for bias appears in the CLAST Reading Item Specifications.

**Critical
Comprehension
Skills**

2. a statement that reveals bias not expressed in the passage; and/or

3. a statement concerning an object, person, action, or concept in the passage (or inferred from the passage) toward which bias is not directed.

In summary, the incorrect options will be either statements that are not bias, statements that are biased but that were not dealt with in the passage, or statements concerning an object, person, or action mentioned or inferred in the passage but that was not treated with bias.

Recognizing Bias

Bias will frequently be expressed on the CLAST in one of the following ways:

Stereotyping, characterized by overgeneralizations and inaccuracies

I was going to ask Bill to play ball with us. However, I remembered he is a librarian, and I figured this sport would be too rough for him.

False assumptions based on weak or inaccurate information

Real estate developments present no real threat to the environment. I have a good friend who lives next to a large one in Montana and he says it doesn't present any problems at all.

Highly emotional statements

No educated person can believe in the Adam and Eve fairy-tale theory of creation and disregard the sound scientific basis of evolution.

Name-calling

The party was great until this filthy, ignorant motorcycle bum appeared.

Contradictions

Our school system is one of the best in the nation. We are considered a leader in many areas, so why is everyone getting so excited about our high dropout rate?

Prejudgment or bias is present in the five examples above. In the example of name-calling, the choice of specific negative words clearly shows the author's bias against the motorcycle rider. In each of the other examples, the choice of specific words alone does not clearly indicate bias, but bias is evident in the way the author presents his or her ideas.

Sample Items

DIRECTIONS
Read each passage. Then choose the best answer for each item.

1. Neither rat nor man has achieved social, commercial, or economic stability. This has been, either perfectly or to some extent, achieved by ants and

by bees, by some birds, and by some of the fishes in the sea. Man and the rat are merely, so far, the most successful animals of prey. They are utterly destructive of other forms of life. Neither of them is of the slightest earthly use to any other species of living things. Bacteria nourish plants; plants nourish man and beast. Insects, in their well-organized societies, are destructive of one form of living creature but helpful to another. Most other animals are content to lead peaceful and adjusted lives, rejoicing in vigor, grateful for this gift of living, and doing the minimum of injury to obtain the things they require. Man and rat are utterly destructive. All that nature offers is taken for their own purposes, plant or beast.

In this passage the author shows bias against

a. animals of prey.

b. rats and man.

c. other animals.

d. nature.

2. Unfair and deceptive advertising—including false promises, whether spoken by a seller or packaged by an advertising agency—is illegal under the Federal Trade Commission Act. The fact that a publicly-advertised false claim is easier to establish and prosecute than the same words spoken in private is an argument for freedom in advertising. But what about general, unsupported claims that a product is superior to the alternative or that it will help one enjoy life more? Some believe that such noninformational advertising should be prohibited. They would establish a government agency to evaluate the "informativeness" of advertising. There are dangers in this approach, however. Someone would have to decide what was informative and what was not, or what was acceptable and what was not. If we could be assured that the special agency would be staffed by "regulatory saints," it would make sense to follow this course. Past experience, however, indicates that this would most likely be controlled by established business firms and advertising interests. Firms that played ball with the political bloc controlling the agency would be allowed to promote their products. Less powerful and less political rivals would be hassled. Costs would rise as a result of paperwork created by compliance procedures. If consumers are misled by slick advertisers to part with their money without good reason, might they not also be misled by a slick media campaign to support politicians and regulatory policies that are not in their interest? Why should we expect consumers to make poor decisions when they make market choices, but wise decisions when they act in the political (and regulatory) arena?

The author expresses a biased attitude against additional regulation of advertising when he says that:

a. The fact that a publicly advertised false claim is easier to prove and prosecute is an argument for freedom in advertising.

b. Some believe that such noninformational advertising should be prohibited.

c. Firms that played ball with the political bloc controlling the agency would be allowed to promote their products.

Critical Comprehension Skills

d. Someone would have to decide what was informative and what was not, or what was acceptable and what was not.

3. Our society expects us all to get married. With only rare exceptions we all do just that. Getting married is a rather complicated business. It involves mastering certain complex hustling and courtship games, the rituals and the ceremonies that celebrate the act of marriage, and finally the difficult requirements of domestic life with a husband or wife. It is an enormously elaborate round of activity, much more so than finding a job, and yet while many resolutely remain unemployed, few remain unmarried.

Now all this would not be particularly remarkable if there were no question about the advantages, the joys, and the rewards of married life, but most Americans, even young Americans, know or have heard that marriage is a hazardous affair. Of course, for all the increase in divorce, there are still young marriages that work, unions made by young men and women intelligent or fortunate enough to find the kind of mates they want, who know that they want children and how to love them when they come, or who find the artful blend between giving and receiving. It is not these marriages that concern us here, and that is not the trend in America today. We are concerned with the increasing numbers of others who, with mixed intentions and varied illusions, grope or fling themselves into marital disaster. They talk solemnly and sincerely about working to make their marriage succeed, but they are very aware of the countless marriages they have seen fail. But young people in particular do not seem to be able to relate the awesome divorce statistics to the probability of failure of their own marriage. And they rush into it, in increasing numbers, without any clear idea of the reality that underlies the myth.

Which of the following statements reflects a biased attitude expressed by the author in this passage?

a. Our society expects us all to get married.

b. It is not these marriages that concern us here, and that is not the trend in America today.

c. Americans know or have heard that marriage is a hazardous affair.

d. And they rush into it, in increasing numbers, without any clear idea of the reality that underlies the myth.

4. When critics wish to repudiate the world in which we live today, one of their familiar ways of doing it is to castigate modern man because anxiety is his chief problem. This, they say, in W. H. Auden's phrase, is the age of anxiety. That is what we have arrived at with all our vaunted progress, our great technological advances, our great wealth—everyone goes about with a burden of anxiety so enormous that, in the end, our stomachs and our arteries and our skins express the tension under which we live. Americans who have lived in Europe come back to comment on our favorite farewell which instead of the old "Good-bye" (God be with you), is now "Take it easy," each American admonishing the other not to break down from the tension and strain of modern life.

In this passage the author shows bias against

a. Americans who have lived in Europe.

b. great technological advances.

c. our modern way of life.

d. critics who repudiate the world today.

Answers

    1. The correct choice is "b." From the opening sentence the author speaks negatively about man and rats. Sentence five states that "Neither of them is of the slightest earthly use to any other species of living things."
    2. The correct choice is "c." The author reveals his or her opinion about additional regulation in option "c." The other options are facts given in the passage, but they do not show bias against regulation.
    3. The correct choice is "d." Referring to marriage as a myth reflects the author's biased attitude.
    4. The correct choice is "c." The author gives examples of the negative effects of anxiety caused by our modern way of life and mentions that we admit to the burden of this anxiety.

> *For purposes of this assessment, tone is defined as the qualities in a written passage that establish and communicate the author's attitude toward his subject matter, so that the reader recognizes a mood or feeling in the written work much as he would recognize a mood or feeling from a speaker's tone of voice.*

    Tone is an attitude expressed by the writer through the choice of words and details used in writing. As is true of the other nine skills that require comprehension skills, tone requires you to use clues and make inferences beyond the literal level.

I.B.5
The student recognizes the author's tone.

This definition and explanation for tone appears in the CLAST Reading Item Specifications.

How the Question Will Appear on the CLAST

Questions dealing with tone will most likely be asked about passages from literature, humanities, or political science textbooks. In these disciplines, the authors are more likely to be subjective and express a feeling or attitude than in other textbooks, like history or science, in which authors are generally more objective and factual in their writing. Some passages may be excerpts from newspapers and magazines or they may be written specifically for the CLAST.
    The question will be stated in one of the following ways:

1. The author of this passage has created a tone (mood, feeling) that could be described as _____.

> (4 options)

2. If the author was delivering this passage orally, his tone of voice would probably be _____.

> (4 options)

    The following words may be used to describe the author's tone:

abstruse	impassioned	ambivalent
angry	intimate	arrogant
awe	loving	comic
caustic	objective	critical
celebration	outspoken	detached

**Critical
Comprehension
Skills**

condemnation	prayerful	excited
complex	satirical	ghoulish
cynical	sympathetic	indignant
disapproval	absurd	irreverent
earnest	apathetic	mocking
ridicule	cheerful	optimistic
melancholy	condescending	pessimistic
wonder	depressed	reverent
evasive	serious	formal
gentle	uneasy	pathetic
incredulous	amused	ironic
reticent	bitter	malicious
sentimental	compassionate	obsequious
tragic	cruel	distressed
joyous	solemn	farcical
nostalgic	vindictive	hard
outraged	righteous	intense
playful	derogatory	

Incorrect Options

The three incorrect options will be words or phrases that do not accurately describe the author's tone.

How to Identify the Author's Tone

This question is more a vocabulary than a tone question for many students. They experience difficulty with the meanings of the four options and are, therefore, unable to deal with the intent of the question, to determine the author's tone. For other types of questions on the CLAST, including vocabulary questions, you may use context clues to determine the meanings of words; however, this is not possible with the questions dealing with tone. If you do not know the meaning of one or two of the four options given, and you do not feel that the choices you do recognize are correct, you must guess. It is advisable to learn the meanings of all the words previously listed since this list is often used by the CLAST writers in choosing words to describe the author's tone.

In order to determine the author's tone, it is helpful to think about how this individual would sound if he or she were speaking to you. Would the author be angry or condescending? You are trying to detect an attitude or feeling that the writer has toward what is being discussed. Choice of words and how ideas are presented are good indications of how the author feels about the topic.

The use of irony by the writer often presents a problem for students. An ironic tone is expressed in writing when authors intentionally say the opposite of what they really mean. Authors assume that you will recognize that the true intent is very different from the literal meaning of the words used when they make ironical statements.

After five straight losing hands Jim commented, "This is my lucky night."

In commenting on the exorbitant price of an object, the writer states, "Now here is a real bargain."

In both examples, the author *states* the opposite of what is meant. In situational irony, a situation or event is opposite, or different, from what we would expect to occur.

After flying two hundred combat missions and being shot down on three occasions without receiving as much as a scratch, Major Tom Swift was killed while crossing the street.

John, who has always been a math whiz, wants to pursue a career in music, whereas his sister, who composed songs at the age of six, wants to be an engineer.

Sample Items

> ## DIRECTIONS
> *Read each passage. Then choose the best answer for each item.*

1. Just to clear the air, let's note first of all that whatever an intelligence test measures it is not quite the same thing as we usually mean by intelligence. It neglects such important things as leadership and creative imagination. It takes no account of social judgment or musical or artistic or other aptitudes, to say nothing of such personality matters as diligence and emotional balance. On top of that, the tests most often given in schools are the quick-and-cheap group kind that depend a good deal upon reading facility; bright or not, the poor reader hasn't a chance.

If the author were delivering this passage orally, his tone of voice would probably be

a. outraged.

b. indignant.

c. righteous.

d. arrogant.

2. The Olympic Games, whose rules require strict verification to ascertain that no male enters a female contest and, with his masculine advantage, unfairly captures a woman's medal, formerly insisted on a visual inspection of the contestants' bodies. Science, however, has discovered that men and women are so innately different physically that their maleness/femaleness can be conclusively established by means of a simple skin test of fully clothed persons.

If sex equality were enforced in professional sports, it would mean that men could enter the women's tournaments and win most of the money. Bobby Riggs has already threatened: "I think that men 55 years and over should be allowed to play women's tournaments—like the Virginia Slims. Everybody ought to know there's no sex after 55 anyway."

Critical Comprehension Skills

The author of this passage has created a tone that could be described as

a. serious.

b. cynical.

c. amusing.

d. apathetic.

3. Once upon a time there was a small, beautiful, green and graceful country called Vietnam. It needed to be saved. (In later years no one could remember exactly what it needed to be saved from, but that is another story.) For many years Vietnam was in the process of being saved by France, but the French eventually tired of their labors and left. Then America took on the job. America was well equipped for country-saving. It was the richest and most powerful nation on earth. It had, for example, nuclear explosives on hand and ready to use equal to six tons of TNT for every man, woman, and child in the world. It had huge and very efficient factories, brilliant and dedicated scientists, and most (but not everybody) would agree, it had good intentions. Sadly, America had one fatal flaw—its inhabitants were in love with technology and thought it could do no wrong. A visitor to America during the time of this story would probably have guessed its outcome after seeing how its inhabitants were treating their own country. The air was mostly foul, the water putrid, and most of the land was either covered with concrete or garbage. But Americans were never much on introspection, and they didn't foresee the result of their loving embrace on the small country. They set out to save the small country with the same enthusiasm and determination their forefathers had displayed in conquering the frontier. They bombed. More than 3 million tons of explosives were dropped—50 percent more than the total bomb tonnage dropped in both theatres of World War II. The consequences of such a deliberate and massive ecological attack were unknown and unknowable, but that was no deterrent. Thousands of herbicide and defoliant missions were flown before anyone seriously questioned their long-range effect on humans and animals, as well as on plants. Vietnam had been saved. But the country was dead.

If the author was delivering this passage orally, his or her tone of voice would probably be

a. angry.

b. depressed.

c. sarcastic.

d. arrogant.

4. I remember vividly the last time I cried. I was twelve years old, in the seventh grade, and I had tried out for the junior high school basketball team. I walked into the gymnasium. There was a piece of paper tacked to the bulletin board.

It was a cut list. The seventh-grade coach had put it up on the board. The boys whose names were on the list were still on the team; they were welcome to keep coming to practices. The boys whose names were not on the list had been cut; their presence was no longer desired. My name was not on the list. I had not known the cut was coming that day. I stood and I stared at the list. The coach had not composed it with a great deal of subtlety; the names of the very best athletes were at the top of the sheet of paper, and the other members of the squad were listed in what appeared to be a descending order of talent. I kept looking at the bottom of the list, hoping against hope that my name would miraculously appear there if I looked hard enough.

I held myself together as I walked out of the gym and out of the school, but when I got home I began to sob. I couldn't stop. For the first time in my life, I had been told officially that I wasn't good enough.

The author of this passage has created a feeling that could be described as

   a. apathetic.

   b. ironic.

   c. nostalgic.

   d. disapproval.

Answers

   1. The correct answer is "b." The author is angered by the unfairness of intelligence tests. The author lists the virtues that intelligence tests omit and then mentions that they are unfair to poor readers.

   2. The correct answer is "c." The problem of verifying the sex of the contestants by visual inspection has a humorous tone to start with. The quote by Riggs can only be interpreted as amusing.

   3. The correct answer is "c." Through the choice of language, such as "America was well equipped for country-saving," the author creates a sarcastic tone. Even the start of the story, "Once upon a time . . ." implies sarcasm. At the end of the passage the author uses irony in a sarcastic way; the country was saved by killing it.

   4. The correct answer is "d." In this personal anecdote the author reveals his feelings and disapproval as he describes the insensitiveness of the whole procedure. The coach even subjected the boys who had made the list to public humiliation by listing them in order of worth. In the final sentence, the author explains how a seventh grader feels to be told "officially" that he wasn't good enough.

How the Question Will Appear on the CLAST

Three formats may be used in asking this question. You may be given one sentence, not to exceed 35 words. In this case you will be asked to choose from four choices the word that best describes the relationship that exists within the sentence.

   1. In each of the following sentences, a relationship between parts of the sentence can be identified. Read each sentence carefully. Then choose the word or phrase that identifies the relationship between parts of the sentence.

                      (4 options)

   2. The sentence beginning in line _____ indicates . . . .

                      (4 options)

> **I.B.6
> The student recognizes explicit and implicit relationships within sentences.**

This question involves sentence comprehension; you must recognize relationships between parts of a sentence. The relationship may be clearly expressed (explicit) or inferred (implicit).

Critical Comprehension Skills

You may be given a passage, not to exceed 500 words, with at least one blank in place of a word or phrase. Four choices for the missing word will be given.

3. The following passage has words deleted. For each blank choose the word that best completes the passage. Choices for each item are given after the passage.

Correct and Incorrect Options

If an explicit (stated) relationship exists within the sentence, the relationship will be expressed by connecting or transition words and phrases.

Tom is an excellent student; however, he failed algebra.

The transition word "however" clearly indicates a contrasting relationship within the sentence.

Tom is an excellent student; therefore, he should be considered for the award.

The transition word "therefore" clearly indicates a cause/effect relationship within the sentence.

If an implicit relationship exists within the sentence, the relationship will be implied and the main clue will be the relationship of the two parts of the sentence.

The serene stillness of the night was shattered by the earth-shaking explosion from the plant.

The descriptive phrases "stillness of the night" and "earth-shaking explosion" imply contrast without the use of connecting or transition words.

The union called a strike against the plant and forced management to close down all operations.

Although no connecting words or transitions are present, the relationship of the parts of the sentence indicates an implicit cause/effect relationship.

The passage format will require you to choose a word or phrase that best completes a sentence within the passage.

The foreign policy of this country has vacillated from one extreme to another. We are all aware of the extreme isolationist attitude of the previous administration; ____, we now see a complete reversal in that attitude.

a. also

b. however

c. because

d. since

The correct answer is "b." In this format containing a blank you are required to recognize a relationship within a sentence. Then you must choose a word that best completes the passage instead of choosing a word that describes a relationship.

How to Recognize Relationships within Sentences

Many of the words used to identify the author's organizational pattern are also used to describe relationships within sentences. Some examples of relationships and word clues that help to identify them are listed below.

Words that indicate addition

again	also	and
besides	equally important	finally
further	furthermore	in addition
last	likewise	moreover

Words that indicate clarification

as a matter of fact	clearly	evidently
in fact	in other words	obviously
of course	too	

Words that indicate comparison

also	likewise	in like manner
similarly		

Words that indicate contrast

after all	although	at the same time
however	but	conversely
for all that	in contrast	still
in spite of	nevertheless	notwithstanding
yet	on the contrary	
on the one hand . . . on the other hand		

Words that indicate example

for example	for instance	that is
thus		

Words that indicate location or spatial order

above	adjacent to	below
beyond	close by	elsewhere
inside	nearby	next to
opposite	within	without

Words to indicate cause/effect

accordingly	as a result	because
consequently	hence	in short
thus	then	therefore

Words to indicate summary

in brief	in conclusion	in short
on the whole	to sum up	to summarize

Words to indicate time

after	after a short time	afterward
at that time	before	during
immediately	of late	formerly

Critical Comprehension Skills

presently	since	shortly
thereupon	until	while
temporarily	at last	now

Sample Items

DIRECTIONS
The following exercises will provide you with additional practice. The passages have words deleted. For each blank, choose the word or phrase that best completes the passage.

1. Some extremely advanced microprocessors are capable of retaining data after power has been turned off. These chips may be used in computer-controlled machine tools, _____, automatically and constantly adjusting the tool's settings to allow for internal wear on its own gears and bearings.

    a. however

    b. thus

    c. therefore

    d. for example

2. Why do corporations desire to conduct business in the international environment? Several reasons are apparent. Compared with wages in other countries, wage rates in America are high, ____ ; it's worthwhile to take advantage of lower labor costs abroad. Some goods can be transported to another country, assembled into products, and brought back to the United States with considerable savings in expense for labor. Also, raw materials are not distributed equally around the globe, and it may be advantageous to establish a facility close to them.

    a. therefore

    b. however

    c. moreover

    d. still

3. Bail is a form of security guaranteeing that a defendant in a criminal proceeding will appear and be present in court at all times as required. Thus, bail is a guarantee: in return for being released from jail, the accused guarantees his or her future appearance by posting funds or some other form of security with the court. When the defendant appears in court as required, the security is returned; if he fails to appear, the security is forfeited.

The sentence beginning in line 1 "Bail is a . . ." indicates

    a. example.

    b. definition.

    c. clarification.

    d. classification.

4. In each of the following sentences, a relationship between parts of the sentence can be identified. Read each sentence carefully; then choose the word or phrase that identifies the relationship between parts of the sentence.

    A. The income statement and balance sheet present summarized totals and account balances, but many valuable facts are obscured by the format of the statements themselves.

        a. clarification
        b. example
        c. cause/effect
        d. compare/contrast

    B. From the end of the Mycenaean period about 1100 B.C., through the Dark Ages, and well into the eighth century B.C., Greece was the scene of tribal migrations and conquests.

        a. listing
        b. time order
        c. order of importance
        d. classification

Answers

    1. The correct answer for the blank in exercise 1 is "d." The first part of the sentence states how these chips may be used in computer-controlled machine tools and then an example of how they will work in this capacity is given. The transition "for example" correctly joins these two ideas.

    2. The correct answer for the blank in exercise 2 is "a." The statement (cause) that ". . . wage rates in America are high . . ." is followed by a result (effect), ". . . it's worthwhile to take advantage of lower labor costs abroad." The transition "therefore" indicating cause/effect joins these two ideas.

    3. The correct choice for exercise 3 is "b." The purpose or intent of this sentence is to give a definition of bail. The only clue would be the recognition of the purpose of the sentence and the use of the word "is."

    4. The correct answer for the first sentence, A., is "d." The transition word "but" joins the two ideas. The two parts of the sentence present a contrast to each other. The income and balance sheet present and obscure.

    The correct answer for the second sentence, B., is "b." The sentence presents chronologically the times when Greece was the scene of tribal migrations and conquests.

How the Question Will Appear on the CLAST

You will be given a passage of not more than 500 words, followed by questions or incomplete statements about the relationship between the sentences. Another way this skill may be tested involves presenting a passage with words or phrases deleted. You will be given four choices of words or phrases to fill the blanks correctly and complete the passage.

    1. The following passage has several words deleted. For each blank, choose the word or phrase that best completes the passage. The choices are given following the passage.

            &boxed{(4 options)}

Critical Comprehension Skills

I.B.7
The student recognizes explicit and implicit relationships between sentences.

This skill is similar to the previous skill, recognizing explicit and implicit relationships within sentences, in that the same signal words and transitions are used. In this skill, however, you are asked to recognize how one sentence relates to another sentence, rather than how one part of the sentence relates to another part of the same sentence. The relationship, as in the previous skill, may be clearly expressed using transition words (explicit) or indirectly expressed without using transition words (implicit).

2. How is sentence _____ beginning in line _____ (first three words of sentence quoted) related to sentence _____ beginning in line _____ (first three words quoted)?

> (4 options)

Correct and Incorrect Options

The correct option will be the word or phrase that best completes the passage or the statement that describes the relationship between the sentences.

The incorrect options will be words that would be incorrect if placed in the blank or statements that do not correctly describe the relationship between the sentences.

The same transitions and connecting words that were used in recognizing relationships *within* sentences are used *between* sentences; it may be helpful to refer to this list, which is found on page 137.

The Bald Eagle, our national symbol, is in danger of extinction. Therefore, it is imperative that we take every precaution to prevent this from happening.

The transition word "therefore" indicates an explicit cause/effect relationship between the two sentences.

Crime in our national parks is one of the most serious problems park management has to face. Park rangers must now be trained in everything from riot control to investigating murders.

Since there are no transition words connecting these two sentences, the relationship is not explicit; however, an implicit relationship does exist between the ideas in the two sentences. The first sentence is a statement and the second sentence further clarifies this statement.

Money spent for education is one of the best investments in the future that we can make. Almost everyone agrees with this statement as proven by numerous opinion surveys. _____, every time spending for education is put on the ballot the public votes it down.

a. thus

b. of course

c. yet

d. in fact

In a passage with a blank contained in the format you must first recognize the relationship between the sentences. Then you must choose a word or phrase that best completes the passage rather than choosing a word that describes a relationship. In this case, a relationship of contrast exists between the two sentences, and the connecting word "yet" would be the correct response for the blank.

> **DIRECTIONS**
> *Read the following passages. Then choose the best answer for each item.*

1. The availability of spiritual services to prison inmates has a long history in American correction. Solitary meditation was the theoretical basis of reform in Philadelphia's Walnut Street Jail almost two centuries ago, and penitence was encouraged by frequent visits by missionaries and local clerics. Over the years, various Christian denominations and other religious organizations have devoted their time to the spiritual needs of inmates, and many have provided ongoing programs of religious instruction.

How is sentence 2, "Solitary meditation was . . . ," beginning in line 2, related to sentence 1, "The availability of . . . ," beginning in line 1?

a. It contradicts the sentence beginning in line 1.

b. It draws a conclusion from the information in sentence 1.

c. It gives an example of what is stated in sentence 1.

d. It clarifies the information in sentence 1.

2. Before the origin of modern science, it was usually believed that all creatures were individually created to suit their special environments. Organisms were thought fixed—human beings were created as human beings, monkeys were created monkeys, and so on. But by the nineteenth century, the commonly held scientific view was that all animals did change and had developed from earlier forms of life.

What is the relationship between the sentences beginning in line 4 "But by the . . .", and the sentence beginning in line 3 "Organisms were thought . . ."?

a. comparison/contrast

b. statement/clarification

c. generalization/example

d. cause/effect

3. The visible behavior resulting from observational learning is called imitation. The ability to imitate is not as simple as it might seem. To imitate, observers must be able to recognize similarities between the model's behavior and their own and must be able to re-create that behavior. The processes of attention, retention, motivation, and reproduction are involved in even the simplest imitation. Imitation may be the earliest form of human complex learning. A 4-day-old baby can imitate the mother smiling or sticking out her tongue.

**Critical
Comprehension
Skills**

What does the sentence in line 7, "A 4-day-old . . . ," do in relation to the sentence in line 6, "Imitation may be . . ."?

a. It states an effect.

b. It gives clarification.

c. It gives an example.

d. It states a conclusion.

The following passage has several words deleted. For each blank, choose the word or phrase that best completes the passage.

4. What are the arts, and why are they important and exciting components of human life? __1__ the arts include more than the traditional visual arts of painting, sculpture, and architecture, for they include such other endeavors as drawing, printmaking, and design.

Sometimes the arts may seem a bit irrelevant in a life of practical needs and challenges. __2__, what can a painting, a poem, a song, or a speculative idea mean to those who are faced with the daily necessities of surviving, making a satisfactory living, and relating well with others? However, both daily experience and the evidence of history demonstrate the vigorous continuing roles of painting, poetry, music, and ideas to human life. It is obvious that the humanities can fulfill enduring needs of mind and spirit for persons of all ages and conditions, and in the most varied situations.

1. a. similarly
   b. for instance
   c. clearly
   d. equally important

2. a. for example
   b. after all
   c. therefore
   d. likewise

Answers

1. Choice "c." is the correct answer. The first sentence makes a statement, and the second sentence gives specific examples to verify what the first sentence states.

2. Choice "a." is the correct answer. The transition "but" indicates a change of direction or contrast to what has been stated in the previous sentence. The thought expressed in the second sentence is a contrast to the previous sentence even without the transition word.

3. Choice "c." is the correct answer. This would be more obvious if the sentence in line 2 started with "for example" or "for instance"; however, you can determine that the thought expressed in the sentence is an example of what was stated in the preceding sentence.

4. Choice "c." is the correct answer for blank 1. The second sentence is a clarification of the first sentence. It answers the question asked in the first sentence. Choice "b." is the correct answer for blank 2. The first sentence speaks of the "life of practical needs and challenges." The second sentence

presents the contrast of "a painting, a poem, a song, or a speculative idea. . . ." The transition "after all" is a more obscure connecting word that is not as obvious as the other contrast transitions on the list.

Critical Comprehension Skills

How the Question Will Appear on the CLAST

You will be asked to identify valid/invalid arguments using one of two formats. One possible format will be an argumentative/persuasive passage, not to exceed 500 words, followed by questions or incomplete statements. A second format, and the one appearing most frequently, will be statements, fallacies, or definitions of fallacies followed by questions. Examples of these formats are given below.

> **I.B.8**
> **The student recognizes valid arguments.**

You will be required to recognize valid/invalid arguments and to identify specific fallacies on the CLAST. To answer these types of questions you must be familiar with 11 key fallacies. The questions will be followed by four choices. A graphic, listing the key fallacies and definitions, will appear on the page containing a question referring specifically to these fallacies.

First Format

This example represents the first format used for this type of question. The entire passage will be argumentative or persuasive. For example, the passage could be an argument for or against gun control. Four *definitions* or four *examples* will be given as options following the passage.

The following question might follow an argumentative or persuasive passage: Which of the following does the author use in an effort to support the argument?

The options for this question may be *definitions* of fallacies. For example, one possible option for the above questions could be as follows:

Appeals to the emotions of the audience rather than dealing with the issue. (This is the definition of argument to the people. There would be three more definitions of fallacies as options.)

The options for this question may be *examples* of fallacies. For example, one possible option for the same question could be:

"Money-grabbing developers are killing the environment." (This would be an example from the passage of argument to the people. There would be three more examples from the passage as options.)

Second Format

The following examples represent the second format used for this type of question. In this first example you must determine which of four statements (arguments) is *valid* or *invalid*. There will be no listing of the key fallacies in this format since the question does not refer to the fallacies.

1. Which of the following arguments is valid (or invalid)?

a. (*statement*)

b. (*statement*)

c. (*statement*)

d. (*statement*)

The following example involves a slight variation of the previous one. As in the previous example, you are asked which of the statements is valid. Only the wording of the question is different.

2. All of the following contain fallacies EXCEPT

a. The way he dresses, he can't be much of a teacher.

b. I want those shoes; everyone in school has a pair.

c. Mr. Johnson said you can't graduate with a D in English.

d. Experience has proven that good guys finish last.

Choice "c," "Mr. Johnson said you can't graduate with a D in English," does not contain a fallacy. Choice "a" is an example of the argument to the man fallacy. Choice "b" is an example of the bandwagon fallacy, and choice "d" is an example of the hasty generalization fallacy.

Another way this question might be asked would be to require the reader to choose which fallacy or faulty reasoning is represented by a given example. This question would not be accompanied by a listing of the fallacies because the fallacies are explained in the option.

3. "Love America or leave it" is an example of what kind of faulty reasoning?

a. Making inappropriate comparisons to prove a point

b. Assuming that there are only two sides to an issue

c. Falsely assuming that one event causes another

d. Asserting as truth something not yet proved

The final way this question might be asked would be to require the reader to choose which fallacy or faulty reasoning is represented, as was the case in the above example. However, in this case a listing of fallacies is provided because no explanation is given as part of the option.

4. "Love America or leave it" is an example of what kind of faulty reasoning?

a. Faulty analogy

b. Either/or

c. Faulty cause/effect

d. Begging the question

"Love America or leave it" is an example of the either/or fallacy: assuming that there are only two sides to an issue.

List of Fallacies

The fallacies listed below will be the only ones used on the CLAST. These fallacies and their definitions will be listed on the page with any question that refers specifically to the fallacies by name. They will be listed either across the top of the page or on the side. The following list of fallacies and definitions will appear on the test page.

1. Faulty cause/effect (*post hoc, ergo propter hoc*)—falsely assumes that one event causes the second.

2. Non sequitur—conclusion not necessarily a logical result of the facts.

3. Begging the question—asserts as truth something not yet proved.

4. Circular logic—restatement of facts presented in first half of argument.

5. Hasty generalization—argument based on insufficient or unrepresentative evidence.

6. Either/or—argument limited to two extreme choices.

7. Faulty analogy—makes inappropriate comparisons to prove a point.

8. Argument to the person (often referred to as *argumentum ad hominem*, argument to the man)—attacks the opponent's character rather than the issue.

9. Argument to the people (*argumentum ad populum*)—appeals to the emotions of the audience rather than dealing with the issue.

10. Bandwagon appeal—asserts a truth claiming everyone else believes and/or does it.

11. Red herring—introduces irrelevant point to divert attention from the main issue.

Recognizing Valid Arguments

An argument, in the context of this question, involves reasons or evidence to support a conclusion or statement. The argument consists of both the reasons and the conclusion. If the evidence given to support a conclusion is logical and if it supports the conclusion, the argument is said to be valid and logical.

On the CLAST you may be asked if an argument is valid or invalid. You must ask yourself, "Is the conclusion logical?" and "Does the evidence give support and lead to the conclusion?" It is possible for the reasons or evidence given to be true and for the conclusion to be invalid. It is also possible to have a good conclusion and for the reasoning used to arrive at this conclusion to be illogical. In either case, the argument would be invalid.

As mentioned earlier, you may be asked to identify a valid or invalid argument from four choices on the CLAST. You will not, in this format, be required to tell why it is valid or invalid.

You might be asked, "Which of the following arguments is valid?" or "All of the following are invalid except . . ."

Critical Comprehension Skills

a. Don't vote for Jones; his dad was an alcoholic.

b. History proves that good guys finish last.

c. If you study hard, the test will be easier.

d. I hate abstract art because it's so unrealistic.

All of the choices above are invalid except for "c." The other choices *are* examples of fallacies; however, in this format you are not required to name them. Therefore, the list of fallacies and definitions will not appear on the test page with this format.

How do you identify the correct answer in this format? Although this example is simple, the same principles apply at all levels of difficulty. Which statement is logical from the evidence given? Even in this format, where the specific names of the fallacies are not named, knowledge of the key fallacies will help you to identify the correct answer. If you are familiar with the fallacies, you will recognize the faulty reasoning in each of the invalid statements. Choice "c" is logical. The reason, "study hard" leads logically to the conclusion, "the test will be easier." Choice "a" is an example of argument to the man. Choice "b" is an example of hasty generalization. Choice "d" is an example of circular logic.

It is possible that you have not been exposed to fallacies in your classes. The 11 fallacies used on the CLAST represent the most common fallacies listed in English and logic textbooks. With a little practice you should feel confident in recognizing these common fallacies. Study the following explanations and examples for the 11 fallacies.

1. Faulty Cause and Effect

The Latin term *post hoc, ergo propter hoc* is often used to describe this fallacy. Just because one event preceded another does not necessarily mean that it was the cause of the second event. This fallacy is sometimes stated: if A preceded B, then A caused B.

Jim became head of the department and I was fired. Jim must have been responsible for my losing my job.

There may well have been circumstances involved in his being fired other than Jim becoming the head of the department.

2. Non Sequitur

In this fallacy, the evidence may sound good but the conclusion is not necessarily true.

John really knows math; he will be an excellent math teacher.

The conclusion may not be valid. Here an inference is substituted for a logical conclusion. One cannot automatically conclude that all individuals who are good at math can effectively teach somebody else this subject.

3. Begging the Question

The point that is supposed to be proved by the argument is put forth as a truth.

All hunting is inhumane and should be outlawed.

The reader is asked (or begged) to accept as truth the statement that "hunting is inhumane" without proof. The writer presents a debatable statement as if it were a fact.

4. Circular Logic

The reason and the conclusion are the same in this type of fallacy. The writer simply restates the reason in the conclusion.

Registration is too crowded because there are too many students trying to register at the same time.

I dislike abstract art because it's unrealistic.

In these statements the same point is presented as both the reason and the conclusion, which, understandably, is called circular reasoning. In the first example the same point is made by saying that it is "too crowded" and by saying that "there are too many students." In the second example, the terms "abstract" and "unrealistic" are virtually the same.

5. Hasty Generalization

The conclusion is supported by very limited and/or inappropriate evidence in this fallacy.

I wouldn't have one of those cars; they break down all the time. Al had one and he had nothing but trouble.

Everyone is against gun control. I asked Ed and Joe from the D&K Gun Store, and they are definitely against any form of controls.

Both conclusions are invalid because the reasons are insufficient and, in the second example, also inappropriate. In the first example, one person's experience with the car is insufficient evidence on which to draw a conclusion. In the second example, one cannot logically assume that because Ed and Joe are against gun control everyone shares their opinion. It is inappropriate because one would expect those people who sell guns to be against controls.

6. Either/or

The writer offers only two viewpoints to an issue that may have many viewpoints. The reader is led to believe that no middle ground exists.

Love America or leave it.

If you don't vote, you don't deserve to live in America.

In both examples, more than two viable viewpoints exist; for example, one could continue to live in America without loving it.

7. Faulty Analogy

The writer attempts to prove an argument by comparing things or situations that are really not comparable. In conversation we sometimes counter this fallacy by saying, "You're comparing apples and oranges."

**Critical
Comprehension
Skills**

When I was your age, I walked or rode a horse to town.

If we let the government tell us where we can and can't smoke, they'll soon be telling us with whom we may socialize.

Allowing people to possess guns is like giving a bomb to a bunch of kids.

In the first example, the speaker is attempting to equate a situation to two very different times in history. Many heads would turn if one rode a horse to almost any town. In the second example, laws limiting smoking locations are intended to protect the rights and health of others, and this situation is in no way similar to deciding with whom one may socialize. And finally, allowing adults to own guns is not comparable to giving a bomb to kids.

You must be alert to these types of faulty comparisons that the writer may attempt to use as proof for an argument.

8. Argument to the Man or Person

The Latin term *argumentum ad hominem* is often used to describe this fallacy. The writer attacks a person rather than the issue.

He can't be a good teacher; it took him five years to get through four years at a second-rate college.

The senator voted for the tax increase. It's not hard to understand why when you consider that he is a millionaire and has never had to worry about money.

There may be many reasons why it took five years to finish a degree, and whether the college is second rate is debatable. In any case it is not a valid reason for not being a good teacher. In the second example, the senator's financial status and his background do not necessarily influence his vote.

9. Argument to the People

The Latin term *argumentum ad populum* is also used to name this fallacy. The writer avoids the issues by trying to arouse an emotional reaction from the reader through the use of words or by the subject matter.

A vote for gun control is a vote against a constitutional right.

Senator Smith is an advocate of socialized medicine, which is a form of communism.

In the first example, the words "constitutional right" cause the reader to make a positive emotional response and ignore the real issues surrounding gun controls. Anything against the Constitution must be bad. In the second example, the word "communism" brings a negative emotional response from the reader, and the writer avoids the real issues surrounding socialized medicine.

Every day we are subjected to this ploy by advertisers who use everything from babies to sell tires to sexually attractive men and women to sell beer.

10. Bandwagon Appeal

The writer tries to convince the reader of the validity of an issue by suggesting that everyone else believes it. Children often use this tactic on their parents by informing them that "Everyone else is doing it," or "is going," or "has one." This tactic avoids discussion of the merits of the issue itself and attempts to get the reader to accept the issue as valid simply because everyone does something.

> **We now produce the best program in existence; four thousand businesses subscribe to our program.**

> **If you don't vote for Senator Smith, you will be the only one on your block who doesn't.**

Whether or not they produce the best program should depend on more than just the number of businesses that use it. However, with this fallacy the reader is often persuaded to join the winning side by getting on the "bandwagon." Again in the second example, the idea is to avoid being left out by ignoring all other issues and simply joining the crowd.

11. Red Herring

An irrelevant point is used to draw attention away from the real issue. A smoked herring was often dragged by escaped prisoners to cover their scent and confuse the tracking dogs. As a fallacy, a red herring attempts to cover the issue and to divert the reader's attention down an irrelevant trail.

> **Latin should not be taught in school since it is not spoken anywhere in the world. All learning should have some use to be of value, and a dead language has no practical use.**

> **There is no need for additional taxes for education. Every year we throw more money into education, and all they do is hire more management and build more buildings. None of the money actually reaches the classroom or is really used for education.**

In the first example, the author diverts the reader's attention from the issue of the value of Latin with the red herring: it's a dead language. The fact that it is not spoken in the modern world is really not relevant to why Latin should be taught in schools.

In the second example, the author uses the red herring of too many buildings and management people to divert attention away from the issue of dealing with the need for money in other areas of education.

Sample Items

> **DIRECTIONS**
> *Read the following passage. Then choose the best answer for each item.*

1. The Brady bill is like a gun without a trigger. It may look good on the wall, but it doesn't work.

Even its chief congressional sponsor, the rabid anti-gun Rep. Edward Feighan, D-Ohio, has admitted publicly that he and his fellow gun grabbers

Critical Comprehension Skills

have oversold it in their effort to get passage. In his own words, "Many of us have been forced to overstate what we can get from the Brady bill."

Other overstatements, like those of *U.S.A. Today* and other anti-Second Amendment media and power-hungry politicians, are numerous.

For example, the statement that the Brady bill's seven-day wait to buy a handgun would allow police to check the background of the buyer is not true. The fact is, it does not mandate any background check of any kind.

Or that the seven-day waiting period would have stopped John Hinckley from buying the gun he used to shoot James Brady, whom the bill is named after. The fact is, Hinckley bought his gun more than five months before he used it.

Or that some states that have waiting periods, like California, Illinois, New Jersey, and Maryland, catch felons attempting to buy guns from licensed dealers. Truth is, they were caught by a background check and not a Brady-type "cooling-off period."

That's why passing the Felon Handgun Purchase Prevention Act offered by Rep. Harley Staggers, D-W.Va., instead of the shady Brady bill, makes sense. This act, unlike the Brady bill, would mandate an immediate check at the point of sale to determine whether a prospective gun buyer has a criminal record. And unlike Brady, it would provide the funds to update and computerize criminal records within six months.

But most important is the question the gun grabbers ignore: How many thousands of honest citizens will be mugged, robbed, raped and murdered each year while being forced to wait seven days to purchase a constitutionally protected means to defend their families and themselves from attack by violent criminals who get their weapons on the black market?

History shows that people who trade freedom for the promise of security end up with neither.

1. Which of the following does the author use in an effort to support the argument?

a. Asserting a truth by claiming everyone else believes it

b. Asserting as truth something not yet proved

c. Appealing to the emotions of the reader rather than dealing with the issue

d. Introducing an irrelevant point to divert attention from the main issue

2. "The Brady bill is like a gun without a trigger. It may look good on the wall, but it doesn't work." This is an example of what kind of faulty reasoning?

a. Assuming that there are only two sides to an issue

b. Making inappropriate comparisons to prove a point

c. Introducing something irrelevant to divert attention

d. Asserting as truth something not yet proved

DIRECTIONS
For the following question, refer to the list of fallacies. Then choose the correct response.

---

3. Which of the following fallacies does the author use in the statement "History shows that people who trade freedom for the promise of security end up with neither."

a. Faulty analogy

b. Red herring

c. Faulty cause and effect

d. Hasty generalization

4. Which of the following arguments is invalid?

a. This is the best movie I have seen, and it should win an Oscar.

b. Jim is the president and should conduct the meeting.

c. If you play with fire, you may get burned.

d. The college catalog has an error that should be corrected.

Answers

1. Choice "c." is the correct answer. Throughout the passage the author appeals to the emotions of the reader. The author implies that opponents to the Brady bill are against the Constitution by referring to them as "anti-Second Amendment." The author also refers to the opposition as "rabid anti-gun" and "gun grabbers." In the second-to-last paragraph the author appeals to the emotions of the reader by asking, "How many thousands of honest citizens will be mugged, robbed, raped and murdered each year . . . ?" Again the appeal is to emotion, trying to convince the reader that to be in favor of the Brady bill is to be against the Constitution and the American way of life.

2. Choice "b." is the correct answer. The author compares the Brady bill to a "gun without a trigger." It looks "good on the wall, but it doesn't work." The analogy sounds cute and humorous; however, it lacks logic. The two items being compared are not analogous, and the author's argument cannot be supported by factual evidence.

3. The correct answer is "d." The author uses a broad generalization, "History shows . . . ," without sufficient evidence. This is a situation where the author may have a valid conclusion, except for the fact that the evidence given to support the conclusion is so overstated that the conclusion loses credibility.

4. Choice "a." is the correct answer. This statement is invalid because of insufficient evidence for the conclusion. Just because one person thought the movie was the best does not mean that everyone else will. The rest of the statements are valid. The conclusions do flow logically from the evidence given.

Critical Comprehension Skills

I.B.9
The student draws logical inferences and conclusions.

The last reading comprehension skill included on the CLAST involves determining inferences and conclusions. This skill requires the reader to detect what the writer *did not* say by carefully reading what the writer *did* say. Drawing inferences and conclusions is sometimes referred to as "reading between the lines." Actually, you have been required to make inferences in answering questions on several of the reading comprehension skills discussed earlier. You were required to infer the meaning of a word from the way it was used in a sentence when you answered the vocabulary in context questions. You were required to infer the implied main ideas from details provided in the passage. In addition, you were required to infer the attitude or tone based on the author's choice of words to express his ideas. Clearly, although this is designated as a separate skill on the CLAST, drawing logical inferences and conclusions is used in all critical reading comprehension.

How the Question Will Appear on the CLAST

As with the other 11 reading comprehension skills, you will be given passages of no more than 500 words written by the test developer or quoted or paraphrased from textbooks, newspapers, magazines, or public documents. You will be asked to identify inferences and conclusions that may be logically deduced from the passage. This will be accomplished using any of the following question formats.

1. From this passage, you could infer (conclude, predict) that . . . .

    | (4 options) |

2. _____ was probably the result of (caused by) . . . .

    | (4 options) |

3. The author implies (suggests) that . . . .

    | (4 options) |

4. The writer of the passage probably is (feels, will, has never) . . . .

    | (4 options) |

The correct answer in each of the formats above will be a logical inference or conclusion that can be determined from the information given in the passage.

The three incorrect options will be either false assumptions, conclusions, or inferences that cannot be logically deduced from the information given in the passage. The incorrect option may also be a detail that was given in the passage but is unrelated to the question being asked.

Recognizing Logical Inferences and Conclusions

There is a strong relationship between making logical inferences and conclusions and recognizing valid arguments. If the evidence given to support a conclusion or argument is logical and supports the conclusion, the argument is said to be valid. If an argument is valid, it is also logical. In both instances the evidence given must support the conclusion, inference, or argument. You must ask yourself, "Can I make this inference or draw this conclusion based on the evidence given in the passage?"

The author implies and the reader infers. You cannot imply from the passage, and the author cannot infer in the passage. The sender of the message (speaker or writer) implies. The receiver of the message (listener or reader) infers. An inference is what the receiver of the message perceives the sender to be suggesting (implying) through the words and ideas presented. To answer this question correctly you must think logically and be alert for clues that suggest meanings not stated literally.

Critical Comprehension Skills

Sample Items

DIRECTIONS
Read each passage. Then choose the best answer for each item.

---

1. Some inherited traits may not show up right away, such as myopia (hereditary nearsightedness). Eye color is determined by one gene or at the most a pair of genes, but most human traits are determined by a combination of many. It is possible for a child to have nostrils like the mother's and the bridge of the nose like the father's. Some characteristics are so strong that they come to characterize a family: the Hapsburgs, the ruling family of the Austrian Empire for generations, had a characteristic lip. Some are rather inconsequential: whether you have attached or detached earlobes, whether or not you can roll your tongue, or whether your second toe is longer than your big toe.

From this passage, you could infer that

a. the Hapsburgs had many common features.

b. hair color is determined by one or two genes.

c. hereditary traits are not equal in strength.

d. eye color is a trait that may not show up right away.

2. Most Americans today seem to agree that, as a nation, we should follow an ethic of environmental stewardship. We nod our heads complacently and say, yes, we need to conserve our finite natural resources and protect our environment from becoming unfit to live in. Unfortunately, we don't live this way.

Perhaps the United States came closest to living by this ethic in 1973, the year of the Arab oil embargo. The resulting marathon gas lines and soaring heating bills left us no choice but to limit our sources. We had discovered the reality of a finite environment. Apathy, though, soon set in. A mere six years after the embargo, a Gallup poll showed that only half of Americans felt our energy situation was "fairly serious." Incredibly, 33% didn't even realize that the U.S. imports oil! Today forgetfulness seems to be running rampant. The big auto makers' marketing tests show that people again want big, soft-riding gas-guzzlers, probably because of greater gas supplies and lower prices resulting from the temporary oil glut.

The writer of the passage probably feels that

a. the government should enforce energy conservation.

b. big auto makers are only interested in profits.

c. people are too apathetic about environmental issues.

d. people were more concerned about the environment in 1979.

3. Although studies in the laboratory make clear some of the basic operations of the memory system, they shed little light on our real-life memories; lists of syllables and numbers are not important parts of our lives. The most memorable events of your life would be impossible to duplicate in the lab. When I was 6 years old I almost drowned trying to learn how to swim. I remember, as if it just happened, the blue water turning to black as I lost consciousness and the blinding light when my father pulled me out. I will never forget it. If you ask people of your parents' generation where they were when President Kennedy was shot, they will probably remember every detail. But in pursuit of scientific knowledge, we cannot deliberately create such powerful events and then check on people 20 years later to see what they remember about them.

From the passage you could conclude that

a. the author does not like to swim.

b. it is impossible to study real-life experiences in a laboratory setting.

c. most of the laboratory experiments on memory involve unimportant parts of our lives.

d. President Kennedy's death was a powerful real-life event for many people.

4. I remember vividly the last time I cried. I was twelve years old, in the seventh grade, and I had tried out for the junior high school basketball team. I walked into the gymnasium; there was a piece of paper tacked to the bulletin board.

It was a cut list. The seventh-grade coach had put it up on the board. The boys whose names were on the list were still on the team; they were welcome to keep coming to practices. The boys whose names were not on the list had been cut; their presence was no longer desired. My name was not on the list.

I had not known the cut was coming that day. I stood and I stared at the list. The coach had not composed it with a great deal of subtlety; the names of the very best athletes were at the top of the sheet of paper, and the other members of the squad were listed in what appeared to be a descending order of talent. I kept looking at the bottom of the list, hoping against hope that my name would miraculously appear there if I looked hard enough.

I held myself together as I walked out of the gym and out of the school, but when I got home I began to sob. I couldn't stop. For the first time in my life, I had been told officially that I wasn't good enough. Athletics meant everything to boys that age; if you were on the team, even as a substitute, it put you in the desirable group. If you weren't on the team, you might as well not be alive.

From this passage you could infer that

a. the coach did not have children.

b. the author expected to be on the list.

c. the author feels that the coach was a cruel man.

d. the experience made a lasting impression on the author.

Answers

1. The correct answer is "c." The passage states, "Some characteristics are so strong that they come to characterize a family." You can infer from this statement that traits are not equal in strength. The other choices require you to make inferences that are not supported by evidence in the passage.

2. The correct choice is "c." The author's main point is stated in the first paragraph. The rest of the passage gives examples to prove his point: We Americans say that we are interested in conserving, but we don't practice it. From the opening paragraph and the examples given, we can infer that the author feels that people are too apathetic. The other choices are not supported by the evidence.

3. The correct answer is choice "d." The author states that people will, ". . . probably remember every detail." Based on the author's statement about this event, it is correct to infer that it was a powerful, real-life event for many people.

4. The correct answer is choice "d." The fact that the author can recall the event so vividly and that he admits how important it was to him provides strong support for the conclusion that the experience made a lasting impression on him. The other choices are not supported by the evidence and are not logical.

DIRECTIONS
This posttest is very similar to the Reading section of the CLAST. During the actual administration of the CLAST, the English Language Skills section and the Reading section are combined for a total time allowance of 80 minutes. You should attempt to complete this practice reading test in approximately 60 minutes. Read each passage. Then choose the best answer for each item.

Passage 1-Test Copy

The phrase "I forgot" is usually associated with letting people down, failure on tests, or being unable to manage your own life. We have probably all had the experience of forgetting something at some time or another. What causes it to happen? There is no one theory, but
5   three theories may help in understanding what happens.

Fading of the Memory Trace. A common-sense theory states that information fades from the memory trace because we haven't used it in a long time. For instance, you remember your current phone number, and perhaps the last phone number you had; but do you remember
10   your first number?

This theory of fading seems logical in many cases, but it leaves some questions unanswered. Why does motor learning seem to stay with us longer than verbal learning, even when we don't use skills (such as bike riding or hitting a baseball) for years? And why do we
15   remember some inconsequential facts, events, or images from years ago, while others seem totally lost? The fading explanation can't account for these phenomena.

Repression. A second explanation is that we repress some unpleasant material, putting it out of our minds. This seems to happen
20   in some cases—as when your dental appointment slips your mind, or your parking ticket lies on your dresser for months because you keep forgetting to pay it. There are instances where anxiety, annoyance, fear, or some other negative feeling is associated with forgetting. But telephone numbers, names, and most of the things we forget usually
25   aren't negative. Thus, this theory, too, cannot explain most forgetting.

Interference. A third explanation of forgetting has become popular recently. In this theory, new information interferes with already learned material, or old information interferes with the learning of new material (Underwood, 1964). Thus, if you memorize one new phone
30   number, and then a bit later must learn another number similar to the first one, the odds are that the phone number will be lost. Or if you study Psychology of Adjustment for an hour, then switch to Sociology, the theory predicts you would confuse the two subjects, perhaps forgetting much that you learned. The more similar the subjects, the
35   more likely you would be to confuse them.

1. The author's primary purpose is to

   a. argue that the true causes of forgetting cannot be understood.
   b. describe typical memory problems of adults.
   c. describe three theories that might explain memory problems.
   d. inform readers so that their memories might improve.

2. The organizational pattern used in this passage is

   a. definition.
   b. time order.
   c. contrast.
   d. simple listing.

3. How is sentence 14, beginning in line 23 ("But telephone numbers, names . . .") related to sentence 13, beginning on line 22 ("There are instances where . . .")?

   a. Sentence 14 makes a comparison to sentence 13.
   b. Sentence 14 is a contrast to sentence 13.
   c. Sentence 14 draws a conclusion from sentence 13.
   d. Sentence 14 gives a specific example of sentence 13.

4. The first sentence of this selection ("The phrase 'I forgot' is usually associated with . . .") is a statement of

   a. fact.
   b. opinion.

5. You could infer from this passage that it would be unwise to study principles of business after studying

   a. management.
   b. literature.
   c. sociology.
   d. geology.

Passage 2-Test Copy

It's clear to see that alcohol is an American institution. What may not be so obvious are the reasons why drinking becomes a problem for so many people.

To understand this, we need to look at drinking from two levels.
5 At the first level is the glossy image of drinking that has become popularized, mostly by advertisers. Magazine ads, commercials, billboards, and many TV shows or movies show glamorous adults having a drink to celebrate one thing or another. This sophisticated image is particularly appealing, especially to teenagers who are trying to
10 act "adult." When this heavy promotion is coupled with the general availability of alcohol at most social occasions, it is easy to see why alcohol use is so widespread.

There are more personal reasons why people may drink to excess, although even the user may not always be aware of these reasons.
15 Chaftez (1970), one of the leading researchers in the field, believes there are four main reasons why people drink: because of social pressures, to combat depression, to reduce inhibitions, or as an excuse to express their feelings.

The first three of these reasons are fairly clear. The pressures to
20 drink at a party or luncheon can be great, and alcohol's ability to reduce inhibitions and to change one's psychological state is well known. But most students are surprised to hear that alcohol is also used as an excuse for acting out feelings or behaving in a certain way. Think, however, of the person who drinks too much, then lets loose
25 with a bitter tirade at her partner. Was it the drink talking, or the

person's real feelings? The same may also be true of people who overindulge, then have one-night stands with someone other than their spouse. Blaming such behaviors on alcohol may allow people to *assuage* their guilt—but perhaps they should look more closely at the
30   feelings that underline such behaviors.

Some recent research suggests that men and women may have typically different reasons for drinking. According to David McClelland and his associates (1972), men drink to enhance their sense of power—and the more a man drinks, the greater seems to be his
35   concern for the personal power and ambition our society values in men. Interestingly, Wilsack found a parallel motivation in women, who also drink to ease doubts about their sex role. Women questioned by Wilsack did not drink to feel powerful, as did the men in McClelland's study. Instead, they described their feelings after a couple of drinks as
40   "warm, loving, considerate, expressive, open, pretty, affectionate, sexy, and feminine" (1973, p. 40)—all adjectives that are associated with a sense of "enhanced womanliness."

6. Which of the following best expresses the main idea of this passage?

    a. More teenagers would abstain from drinking if they understood the reasons why people drink to excess.
    b. Excessive drinking is a serious problem in American society today.
    c. The reasons why people drink to excess are complicated and varied.
    d. Most people who drink to excess do so as either an excuse to express their feelings or to reduce social inhibitions.

7. The sentence beginning in line 10 ("When this heavy promotion . . .") is a statement of

    a. fact.
    b. opinion.

8. The author's tone in this selection could be described as

    a. critical.
    b. matter-of-fact.
    c. sympathetic.
    d. concerned.

9. As used in line 29, the word *assuage* most nearly means

    a. explain.
    b. understand.
    c. enhance.
    d. relieve.

10. The dominant pattern of organization in the last paragraph of this selection is

    a. cause/effect.
    b. contrast.
    c. classification.
    d. simple listing.

11. For the following question, refer to the List of Fallacies on page 145. Which fallacy does the author of the following statement use? "The real reason behind most marital infidelity is the use of too much alcohol."

a. circular logic
b. argument to the person
c. faulty cause and effect
d. bandwagon appeal

Passage 3-Test Copy

Beer is the most popular alcoholic beverage in the United States and an integral part of the American economy—an $11 billion a year industry in 1982. Americans consume about 24 gallons of beer annually per capita, a total of almost 180 million barrels in 1985.

5   Serious beer drinkers are aware that beer has changed in the past several years. There are fewer independent brands to choose from, though there are many new labels and new kinds of brew, such as the light beers. To many drinkers, the different beers seem to taste more and more alike. And beer, like nearly everything else, costs more than

10   it used to.

Behind these changes lies a drastic reorganization of the beer industry that has had even deeper consequences for those who work in the industry itself. The beer business, once a classic example of a small, family-based enterprise, has become an arena in which a handful

15   of giant, aggressive corporations are battling tooth and nail for shares of the national beer market. In the process thousands of independent businesses have been wiped out, along with tens of thousands of good, skilled jobs and a good part of the economic base of many communities. The beer industry, in short, is a kind of microcosm of

20   the wider trend toward concentration in the American economy, and it tells us a lot about the social impact of the trend.

The beer industry in the United States grew during the nineteenth century, largely through the efforts of European (especially German) immigrants who brought with them long-established,

25   sometimes centuries-old brewing skills. The small breweries they built catered mainly to local markets, and they took great pride in producing a small (by current standards) number of barrels of high-quality, distinctive beer. In 1880, there were 2,741 independent breweries in the United States.

30   But the industry began to change rapidly by the early part of this century. By 1935 there were 750 brewers; by 1967, 125; and by 1979, only 40. Concentration of the industry is continuing so rapidly that some beer industry experts expect as few as 5 or 6 large brewers to survive within the next few years. In 1986 the two largest brewers

35   alone, Anheuser-Busch and Miller, were estimated to share about 60 percent of the market—up from 43 percent just eight years earlier.

12. In this passage, the authors express a bias against

    a. family-based businesses.
    b. large beer companies.
    c. against independent brands.
    d. against consumption of alcohol.

13. The sentence beginning in line 25, "The small breweries they built . . ." indicates

    a. contrast.
    b. comparison.

**Posttest and
Answer Key**

    c. addition.
    d. cause/effect.

14. The sentence beginning in line 11 ("Behind these changes lies . . .")
is a statement of

    a. fact.
    b. opinion.

Passage 4-Test Copy

Another common element in stress is conflict. Conflict occurs when
people are faced with two or more alternatives and must choose
between them. We are called upon to make hundreds of decisions
daily, and while we *negotiate* many of them easily, the cumulative
5   effects can be great.
    Kurt Lewin (1951) described three different types of conflict, each
of which produces stress. These are the approach-approach situation,
the avoidance-avoidance conflict, and the approach-avoidance situation.
    Approach-Approach Conflict. In the approach-approach situation,
10   the person must choose between two pleasant situations. Should you
treat yourself to the éclair on the menu, or to the world-renowned
mousse au chocolate? Or, let's see, a vacation in Tahiti, or should it be
the French Riviera this year? Such decisions tend to be rather
delightful, and therefore we may not take them very seriously. They
15   can be stressful, however, since only one alternative can be chosen.
This is one reason why many marital arguments center around the
issue of how money is to be spent.
    Avoidance-Avoidance Conflict. Far more conflict is likely to arise
when both alternatives are unpleasant. The proverbial "frying pan or
20   the fire" situation is the classic example of the avoidance-avoidance
situation, but it takes form in many everyday choices. Should you stay
home alone during the holidays, or spend them with people you don't
like? Should you study for your math test or do your household
chores? In either case, a decision has to be made . . . even though
25   there is a tendency to avoid the moment of truth until the very last
minute. At that point, things are no easier, however—for the greater
the time pressure, the more stressful are decisions.
    Approach-Avoidance Conflict. It is unusual for alternatives to be
either completely positive or completely negative. More often, they are
30   a combination of both. These situations, called approach-avoidance
situations, cause us quite a bit of consternation, and that is because this
type of conflict includes a new element that is not present in the other
two conflict situations. The same goal has both positive and negative
qualities, and that makes the decision even more difficult.
35   Should you take a job in the photography studio? On the one
hand, it's just what you've always wanted to do, and you think it will
help you get a start toward your career. On the other hand, the pay is
pretty bad, and the hours are inconvenient. Should you ask your
friend for a cigarette? You want one so desperately you can taste
40   it—yet you've resolved to quit smoking and you haven't had a cigarette
for a week. In cases like this last one, the battle may be almost visible as
your hand starts to reach out for the pack, then is consciously
withdrawn.

15. The main idea in this selection is that

    a. conflict is easier to manage if we accept that it is inevitable in life.
    b. conflict most frequently includes some aspect of avoidance.
    c. conflict according to Lewin consists of three different types.
    d. conflict is a common element in human stress reactions.

16. As used in line 4, *negotiate* most nearly means

    a. manage.
    b. sidestep.
    c. avoid.
    d. negate.

17. The author's tone in the third paragraph might best be described as

    a. informal and light.
    b. ironic yet amused.
    c. formal and reserved.
    d. jovial and unconcerned.

18. The dominant pattern of organization in this passage is one of

    a. description.
    b. classification.
    c. time order.
    d. comparison.

Passage 5-Test Copy

As well may be imagined, the same agents that are responsible for socialization in general are also responsible for socialization into sex roles. The family is the most important agent of socialization into sex roles, though it is certainly far from being the only one. Peers,
5   teachers, and the media reinforce the message first learned within the family. Children's books, from the picture books given to the smallest toddler to textbooks used in school, have, up to very recent times, presented wholly stereotyped images of male and female roles. One team of researchers found that the ratio of male to female pictures in
10   children's books ran heavily in favor of males, and a majority of the books were entirely about boys (Weitzman and Eifler, 1972). In these books, girls were represented as engaged in domestic chores, playing with dolls, helping their mothers, or being subservient to the male heroes. Little boys were depicted as specialists or professionals and
15   were busy with such dramatic adventures as saving little girls' lives or rescuing animals from death. Most showed complete and intact families where fathers were handed pipes and slippers when they came home and mothers were shown puttering in the kitchen, wearing aprons. Working mothers and divorced parents were almost totally absent in
20   such books, an obvious distortion of truth in a society in which nine out of ten married women work outside the home sometime during their lifetime and one out of three marriages ends in divorce. In recent years, an attempt has been made by publishers and textbook authors to eradicate the most flagrant stereotypes.
25   In addition to sex stereotypes found in books, schools stress traditional sex roles by segregating boys and girls in a number of activities. In sports, extracurricular activities, and even academic

30   subjects, boys and girls are pushed onto different paths. Again,
awareness of the situation has prompted steps to remedy it, but by the
time a child reaches school age, traits such as competitiveness,
independence, self-reliance, and emotional expressiveness are already
largely established; thus, even if girls are allowed to play football and
take shop, they will probably not benefit from an unbiased approach to
sex roles.

35   The mass media, especially women's magazines and television, are
perhaps most responsible for reinforcing traditional stereotypes. Not
only in the content of articles and programs, but especially in the
advertising that precedes, follows, and constantly interrupts them,
women are presented as housecleaners, child-careers, and husband

40   pamperers. In addition, the subject of women's conversations is
represented as revolving around rings around the collars of their
husbands' shirts, mud on their sons' pants, and the difficulty of
maintaining shiny kitchen floors. Women are also used as sex objects
to sell products to males. In this function, young, beautiful women are

45   shown seductively caressing automobiles, being thrilled by the aroma
of an after-shave lotion, or succumbing to the man who drinks a
particular brand of whiskey.

19. The author's primary purpose in this selection is to

    a. describe the various sources of sex-role socialization.
    b. explain the effects of sex-role stereotypes.
    c. persuade parents to treat children of both sexes alike.
    d. persuade that the mass media is the most powerful agent on
        sex-role socialization.

20. In the passage, the authors show a bias against

    a. girls' participation in extracurricular sports.
    b. working women.
    c. authors of textbooks and children's books.
    d. women's magazines.

21. According to this passage, the source most responsible for reinforcing
    traditional stereotypes is

    a. the family
    b. same sexed peers
    c. the mass media
    d. teachers and schools

22. The writer of this passage probably feels

    a. more concerned about the sex-role development of boys.
    b. girls are at a distinct disadvantage in overcoming stereotyping.
    c. women's magazines are more biased than men's magazines.
    d. sex-role stereotyping is stronger today than in the previous decade.

23. In the last paragraph, what is the relationship of the sentence
    beginning in line 43 ("Women are also used . . . ") to the preceding
    sentence in the paragraph?

    a. cause/effect
    b. contrast
    c. addition
    d. comparison

24. The author's main idea in this passage is that

    a. a variety of forces work together to maintain and reinforce sex-role socialization.

    b. the mass media need to present more responsible representations of women's roles.

    c. parents should take a greater role in their children's sex-role socialization.

    d. schools should combat traditional sex-role stereotyping.

Passage 6-Test Copy

Few people enter a marriage with the idea that they will somehow end it if it doesn't work out. Hilsdale (1962) found that four out of five couples entering marriage do not even consider the possibility of divorce. What happens?

5   In some cases, the cards already seem to be stacked, at least in terms of statistical likelihood. We know, for instance, that couples who marry at a very young age are likely to have more problems. In addition, both the level of education and income status are linked to the divorce rate. The lower the income and education level, the greater

10 the chances seem to be for a divorce. Divorce is also more common for people who marry as a means of escape, among children of unhappy or divorced parents, and among couples who married because the bride was expecting a child (Duvall, 1971).

    Such factors can make divorce more likely; but more immediate

15 causes are the relationship problems that develop. Landis and Landis (1973) found a number of common problem areas that are most frequently listed as causes of divorce.

    Money Problems. One of the most common sources of marital stress is economic problems. A couple who are unable to pay bills or to

20 maintain a comfortable standard of living are likely to feel a great deal of pressure, and it is easy to blame one's spouse for not being a good enough provider or not knowing how to budget what money there is.

    Sexual Problems. A second frequent contributor to divorce is sexual problems. Such problems run the spectrum from an inability to

25 feel satisfied with sexual interactions in the relationship, to a desire for variety. In addition, higher expectations of marriage lead couples to look for more from their spouses, in terms of sexual as well as emotional satisfaction. When one or both partners feel that the couple's sexual needs are not compatible, then the entire relationship

30 can be affected.

    Child-Related Problems. A number of marital problems revolve around children. These include jealousy of one spouse's relationship with a child and disagreements on how to raise children.

    In-Law Problems. Our social heritage includes a number of

35 standard in-law jokes, and sometimes not without reason. Meddling in-laws, or excessive loyalty of one spouse to his or her parents, can be a source of considerable stress. If a partner can't learn to balance loyalties between a spouse and parents, the other partner is put into a difficult position, with marital stress as a result.

40   *Blocked Communication.* "We just don't talk to each other any more. There just doesn't seem to be anything to say." Statements such as these are signals of marital problems. Even when a couple remain

close, there is, after a time, a tendency to expect a spouse to know
what we are thinking and to communicate less directly. Assuming that
45 someone else knows how we feel can be a mistake. Whether there are
immediate problems or not, both partners need to keep making the
effort to communicate.

25. According to this passage, a couple is more likely to divorce if

    a. they have a low income, marry young, and had divorced parents.
    b. they have a low income and marry later in life.
    c. the bride was expecting and the couple had a moderate income.
    d. there is a disparity in ages and financial problems occur.

26. The author's tone in this selection can best be described as

    a. judgmental and moralistic
    b. philosophical
    c. optimistic
    d. objective yet concerned

27. The author's purpose in this selection is to

    a. inform readers about the primary causes of divorce.
    b. inform readers about potential solutions to marital problems.
    c. argue that marital problems could be avoided if couples received
       guidance prior to marriage.
    d. persuade readers that most divorces could be avoided through
       better communication.

28. The sentence beginning in line 28, "When one or both partners feel
    that . . . ," indicates

    a. clarification
    b. comparison
    c. cause/effect
    d. time order

29. Which of the following statements reflects a biased attitude expressed
    in this passage?

    a. Higher expectations of marriage lead couples to look for more
       from their spouses in terms of emotional satisfaction.
    b. One of the most common sources of marital stress is economic
       problems.
    c. Few people enter a marriage with the idea that they will somehow
       end it if it doesn't work out.
    d. Our social heritage includes a number of standard in-law jokes, and
       sometimes not without reason.

30. *(For the following question, refer to the List of Fallacies on page 145.)*
    If the author of this selection had argued that either unhappy couples
    seek professional help or their marriages will end in divorce, which
    fallacy would this be an example of?

    a. begging the question
    b. either/or
    c. faulty analogy
    d. hasty generalization

**Posttest and
Answer Key**

In the United States, considered to be the most affluent of the
societies of the world, poverty has different faces. The United States
government defines poverty as the level of income at which a person is
incapable of providing such basics as food, clothing, and shelter. The
5   Census Bureau lists 32.5 million Americans as officially poor. This
figure is based on a poverty index that the Social Security
Administration developed in 1964 establishing a range of income levels
according to factors such as family size, sex and age of the family head,
number of children under 18, and urban or farm residence. Every year,
10 revisions of price levels are based on changes in the consumer price
index. For example, in the year 1986 an urban family of four that
averaged $11,203 in income was considered to be at poverty level. The
average family income for that year was slightly more than three times
the official poverty level (Pear, 1988).

15   Obviously, then, poverty in this society means a condition of
having less income than the average. Thus, we are not dealing with
absolute deprivation, or not having enough income to provide the
barest necessities for survival. We are dealing with *relative deprivation*,
a condition in which people are deprived compared with others in
20 their own society at a particular time and place.

Poverty occurs more frequently among some groups than among
others. It is chronic, for instance, in families with a female householder
in which no husband is present. Unfortunately, because of the increase
in illegitimate births and greater rates of dissolution of marital and
25 nonmarital unions, single parenthood is reaching epidemic
proportions. Currently, half of all black families with children are
headed by a single parent, and approximately 60 percent of black births
are out of wedlock. By comparison, 15.7 percent of white children
under 18 lived with their mother only and 2.5 percent lived with their
30 father only in 1986 (U.S. Bureau of the Census 1988, p. 38). American
teenagers have the highest pregnancy and abortion rates in the
Western world: in 1983, 86 percent of black and nearly 40 percent of
white babies born to girls under age 19 were illegitimate. These
"children of children" add to the rolls of the poor. Whereas children
35 make up only 27 percent of the nation's residents, they make up 40
percent of the people in poverty (Moynihan 1986).

Even though in numerical terms more whites are below the
poverty level than any minority groups, in proportion to their
percentage of the total population, more blacks and persons of
40 Hispanic origin are in that category. In 1987, for instance, 10.5 percent
of white Americans were poor, compared with 33.1 of black Americans
and 28.2 percent of Hispanic Americans (Tochin 1988).

31. The author's primary purpose in this selection is to

    a. persuade the reader that more should be done to help the poor.
    b. describe the type, extent, and correlates of poverty in America.
    c. explain the causes of world poverty.
    d. inform the reader of the contribution of promiscuity to poverty.

32. The author's tone in this selection is

    a. indignant
    b. sympathetic

**Posttest and
Answer Key**

c. matter-of-fact

d. bitter

33. In the following sentence, a relationship between parts of the sentence can be identified. Choose the word or phrase that identifies the relationship between parts of the sentence:

"Unfortunately, because of the increase in illegitimate births and greater rates of dissolution of marital and nonmarital unions, single parenthood is reaching epidemic proportions."

a. cause/effect

b. contrast

c. addition

d. comparison

34. In the last paragraph, what is the relationship between the sentence beginning in line 40 ("In 1987, for instance . . .") to the sentence in line 37 ("Even though . . .")?

a. cause/effect

b. comparison/contrast

c. illustration

d. summary

35. The writer of this passage probably feels that

a. the American poor are worse off than the poor of the Third World.

b. the American poor are not responsible for their plight.

c. less affluent teenagers are more promiscuous than affluent teens.

d. the roles of the poor could be reduced through better sex education of American youth.

Passage 8-Test Copy

In its simplest definition, a *status* is a position in a social group—a mother in a family group, a teacher in a school group, a plumber in a work group, or a violinist in an orchestra group. A *role* is the carrying out of the status, its dynamic aspect, or what the mother, the teacher,

5 the plumber, and the violinist *do*. Statuses are ranked; that is, they are value rated according to the prevailing values of the group. In American society, the teacher has a higher status than a plumber, and both have a lower status than the famous violinist Itzhak Perlman.

A person who occupies a specific status is expected to behave in a

10 way befitting that status. We do not expect the plumber to give us a lecture on the English literature of the Middle Ages, nor do we expect the teacher to fix our leaking faucets. (But, as an <u>avocation</u>, the teacher may in fact be able to fix faucets, just as the plumber may be an expert in literature.) In an earlier example, we saw that we would allow a

15 college instructor to tell us what to do in a classroom situation but we would not give our kid brother this privilege.

Statuses and roles evolve out of the need of each group to perform its tasks efficiently. In a society, a great many functions must be performed each day if the society is to operate well. Food must be

20 produced and made available for consumption, shelter must be built, the sick must be healed, children must be educated, and so on. In time and through experience, it became clear that efficiency is much

improved when tasks are allocated to particular individuals who
specialize in performing them. Such an allocation of tasks is what we
25 call *division of labor*, which is the origin of most, though not all,
statuses (some statuses are allocated on the basis of gender or age).

   Statuses and roles that grow out of them are not static. They are
continually subject to change, growth, and replacement. Change
within each group and change in society, as well as daily interaction,
30 constantly redefine statuses and roles.

36. The organizational pattern used by the author in the first paragraph
    could be described as

    a. time order
    b. cause/effect
    c. comparison and contrast
    d. definition

37. A synonym for <u>avocation</u> as used in paragraph 2, line 12, is a/an

    a. refuge
    b. hobby
    c. substitution
    d. preference

38. From this passage, you could infer that

    a. a nurse would occupy a higher status than a teacher.
    b. plumbers are not valued by American society.
    c. an individual might occupy more than one status.
    d. all statuses should be equal.

Passage 9-Test Copy

   Most people equate deviance with crime, but of course the two are not
the same. Everyone is deviant to some extent or other, at one time or
another, but not everyone is a criminal. Criminals, in fact, represent
only a small minority of people in society, but the acts they perpetrate
5 are very damaging, so that crime and criminals are very much on the
public's mind.

   In most contemporary societies informal social control is not
sufficient to contain deviance. Therefore, formal social controls must
be instituted. One type of formal social control is the enactment of
10 statutes, or laws, that define the actions that are prohibited to people
because they are too destructive to the society. The prohibited actions
are termed crimes and are punished by the society through its judicial
system.

   Crime, then, is any action that violates the law. Laws, in turn, are
15 passed at a variety of governmental levels: local, state, and federal. Laws
differ from the unwritten societal norms in that (1) they are put into
effect by political authority, (2) they are specific rules instead of
informal understandings, (3) they are applied uniformly, (4) they carry
specific punitive sanctions, and (5) they are administered through
20 official agencies of the society.

   Even though crimes and punishments are specifically defined,
they too are relative, varying in kinds and extent. One distinction is
made between criminal behavior on the part of adults as opposed to

juveniles under 18 years of age. The distinction is based on the belief
25   that minors are not yet fully socialized (but if they commit an especially
serious crime, juveniles may be treated as adults by the criminal justice
system). Another distinction is that between the so-called index crimes
and actions that are considered crimes by the legal codes but not by a
majority of people. The index crimes, which represent the violation of
30   mores, include murder (including homicide, voluntary manslaughter,
and involuntary manslaughter), rape, robbery, aggravated assault,
burglary, larceny, arson, and auto theft. Crimes that most people ignore
range from the prohibition in some states to serve alcohol by the glass,
although one can buy bottles, to the 55-miles-per-hour speed limit,
35   which was the law for a few years and was observed only when a police
car was in sight.

39. The last sentence in the first paragraph includes

a. only a statement of fact
b. only an opinion
c. fact and opinion

40. What leads you to believe that the following argument is invalid?
"After observing freeway traffic for one hour, the researcher
concluded that commuters observe the 55-mile-per-hour speed limit
only when a police car is in sight." (Refer to list of fallacies, page 145.)

a. faulty analogy
b. bandwagon appeal
c. argument to the person
d. hasty generalization

41. The main idea of this passage is

a. In contemporary society, crime and punishment are specifically
and absolutely defined.
b. Because of the nature of violent crime, many people have become
overly concerned with crime and criminals.
c. Though societies have specific definitions for crime and
punishment, such definitions are relative.
d. Most people cannot separate crime from deviance and thus view all
offenders in a similar light.

Passage 10-Test Copy

Hypnosis has been put to use to help treat several conditions. It has
been helpful in reducing the pain of childbirth, curing migraine
headaches, for instance. It has also been used to help people cope with
pain, quit smoking or lose weight (Wolberg, 1972).
5   Another possible use of hypnosis is to help a person recapture lost
experiences or feelings, as an aid to psychotherapy (Ferguson, 1975).
For instance, a therapist may wish to uncover a deep-seated conflict
that has its roots in the past. The patient is hypnotized, then asked to
relive the original crisis. The therapist can gain valuable information
10   from this kind of process, uncovering long-forgotten feelings and
helping the patient work through them (Hilgard, 1974). The same kind
of process can be used for reproducing unconscious dreams or
fantasies.

One of the most interesting applications of hypnosis is the use of
15 post-hypnotic suggestion. While under hypnosis, the subject is given
instructions to be acted out after he or she comes out of the hypnotic
state. For instance, subjects may be told that they will feel no pain in
an arm, that they will suddenly feel very hungry, or that they will feel
nauseous when they pick up a cigarette. Subjects may also be told that
20 they will not remember the suggestion at all. They are then brought
out of the trance, and they usually perform as expected.

42. Which of the following was not mentioned in the passage as a use for
hypnosis?

    a. curing migraines
    b. aiding childbirth
    c. recapturing lost feelings
    d. reducing stress

43. The sentence beginning in line 8, "The patient is hypnotized,
then . . . ," indicates

    a. addition
    b. time
    c. contrast
    d. clarification

44. (*For the following question, refer to the List of Fallacies.*)
If one was to argue that hypnosis could cure all migraines because
hypnosis had successfully cured migraines in a volunteered sample of
25 first-year college students, what type of fallacy would be depicted?

    a. faulty analogy
    b. circular reasoning
    c. hasty generalization
    d. argument to the people

List of Fallacies

1. Faulty cause and effect (*post hoc, etgo propter hoc*)—falsely assumes that
one event causes the second.

2. Non sequitur—conclusion not necessarily a logical result of the facts.

3. Begging the question—asserts as truth something not yet proved.

4. Circular logic—restatement of facts presented in first half of argument.

5. Hasty generalization—argument based on insufficient or
unrepresentative evidence.

6. Either/or—argument limited to two extreme choices.

7. Faulty analogy—makes inappropriate comparisons to prove a point.

8. Argument to the person (often referred to as *argumentum ad hominem,*
argument to the man)—attacks the opponent's character rather than the
issue.

9. Argument to the people (*argumentum ad populum*)—appeals to the
emotions of the audience rather than dealing with the issue.

**Posttest and
Answer Key**

10. Bandwagon appeal—asserts a truth by claiming everyone else believes or does it.

11. Red herring—introduces an irrelevant point to divert attention from the main issue.

Posttest Answer Key

Question	Answer	Skill
1.	c.	(I.B.1.)
2.	d.	(I.B.2.)
3.	b.	(I.B.7.)
4.	b.	(I.B.3.)
5.	a.	(I.B.9.)
6.	c.	(I.A.1.)
7.	b.	(I.B.3.)
8.	b.	(I.B.5.)
9.	d.	(I.A.3.)
10.	b.	(I.B.2.)
11.	c.	(I.B.8.)
12.	b.	(I.B.4.)
13.	c.	(I.B.6.)
14.	b.	(I.B.3.)
15.	c.	(I.A.1.)
16.	a.	(I.A.3.)
17.	a.	(I.B.5.)
18.	b.	(I.B.2.)
19.	a.	(I.B.1.)
20.	d.	(I.B.4.)
21.	c.	(I.A.2.)
22.	b.	(I.B.7.)
23.	c.	(I.B.7.)
24.	a.	(I.A.1.)
25.	a.	(I.A.2.)
26.	d.	(I.B.5.)
27.	a.	(I.B.1.)
28.	c.	(I.B.6.)
29.	d.	(I.B.4.)
30.	b.	(I.B.8.)
31.	b.	(I.B.1.)
32.	c.	(I.B.5.)
33.	a.	(I.B.6.)
34.	c.	(I.B.7.)
35.	d.	(I.B.9.)
36.	d.	(I.B.2.)
37.	b.	(I.A.3.)
38.	c.	(I.B.9.)
39.	c.	(I.B.3.)
40.	d.	(I.B.8.)
41.	c.	(I.A.1.)
42.	d.	(I.A.2.)
43.	a.	(I.B.6.)
44.	c.	(I.B.8.)

Posttest

Use this table to determine which of the CLAST reading skills were most difficult for you.

Question Number	CLAST Skill and Code
6, 15, 24, 41	Main idea—I.A.1
21, 25, 42	Supporting detail—I.A.2
9, 16, 37	Vocabulary in context—I.A.3
1, 19, 27, 31	Purpose—I.B.1
2, 10, 18, 36	Organizational Pattern—I.B.2
4, 7, 14, 39	Fact/Opinion—I.B.3
12, 20, 29	Bias—I.B.4
8, 17, 26, 32	Tone—I.B.5
13, 28, 33, 43	Within sentences—I.B.6
3, 23, 34	Between sentences—I.B.7
11, 30, 40, 44	Valid arguments—I.B.8
5, 35, 38, 22	Inferences and conclusions—I.B.9

Introduction

The mathematics subtest of the CLAST contains approximately 55 multiple choice questions. Except for questions on one skill, there will be 4 responses to each question. Ninety minutes are allowed for the first administration of this test.

Overview of the CLAST Mathematics Subtest

The Questions

The 55 mathematics questions will be taken from 61 skills in the subject areas of arithmetic, algebra, geometry and measurement, logical reasoning, and statistics, including probability. Only 50 of the 55 questions are scored. The other 5 questions are experimental items being tested for future use and do not count toward your score. Since you don't know which 5 are the experimental items, you should do your best on all 55 questions. Of the 50 scored questions, 13 are from arithmetic and 16 are from algebra. The remaining three areas—geometry and measurement, logical reasoning, and statistics (including probability) each have 7 questions.

The pre- and posttests included in this part of the text are very similar to the actual CLAST mathematics test. The tests and accompanying answer keys provide opportunities for needed practice and helpful diagnosis of areas where remediation might be needed. Completion of these practice tests within a 90-minute time limit will enable you to determine if you are familiar enough with the content to answer the actual CLAST mathematics questions within the specified time.

After completing your pretest you should score your responses using the answer key that follows it. Beside the correct answer is the skill code number that identifies the skill from which that question was taken. You should use these numbers to locate the instructional material included in this text for questions that you missed or felt unsure about your response. This instructional material will help you learn the necessary skills. Finally, you should take the posttest to confirm your understanding.

Special Considerations

Since the mathematics subtest is multiple choice, you can use the responses to help you answer the questions. If you work the problem given in the stimulus and don't match any of the responses, you should work backward from the answers to the question. Since there is no penalty for guessing, you should attempt every question. Your score is based on the number of correct responses. If you have no idea how to work a problem, there is still a 25%, or 1 in 4, chance that you can guess the answer. There is no chance for a correct response if you leave the answer response blank.

Test-Taking Hints

To best prepare for the mathematics section of the CLAST, you should do the following three things:

1. Become familiar with the content of all 61 mathematics skills.

2. Practice sample questions to familiarize yourself on how the questions will be asked.

3. Time yourself to make sure that you can complete 55 questions within the specified time limit.

Overview of the CLAST Mathematics Subtest

Test Wiseness

On the day that you actually take the CLAST, you should use good mathematics test-taking skills. The following hints will improve your test-wiseness skills:

1. Read each question. Immediately answer those that you know. Mark the questions that you are unsure of and return to those when you have finished reading all the questions.

2. If you are unsure of how to answer a particular question, look at all the responses and eliminate any that seem to be an unreasonable solution. Take a guess from the remaining choices.

3. Watch your time. Allow enough time to bubble a response to every question.

4. If you finished before the 90-minute time limit, go back and check your answers.

DIRECTIONS:
Read each question and select the correct response within a 90-minute time limit.

1. Sets *A*, *B*, *C*, and *U* are related as shown in the diagram.

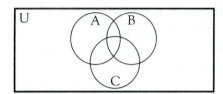

   Which of the following statement(s) is true, assuming none of the regions is empty?

   a. No element is a member of all three sets *A*, *B*, and *C*.
   b. Any element that is a member of set *B* is a member of set *C*.
   c. Any element that is a member of set *A* is a member of set *B*.
   d. None of the above statements is true.

2. Select the statement that is the negation of the statement "All highways are safe."

   a. No highway is safe.
   b. Some highways are safe.
   c. If it is not a highway, then it is not safe.
   d. Some highways are not safe.

3. Select the statement below that is <u>not</u> logically equivalent to "If the Indians win the game, then they will be the state champions."

   a. The Indians did not win the game or they are the state champions.
   b. If the Indians are not the state champions, then they did not win the game.
   c. If they are the state champions, then the Indians won the game.
   d. The Indians are the state champions or they did not win the game.

4. Given that

   i. No singers are dancers.
   ii. All dancers are agile.

   determine which conclusion can be logically deduced.

   a. No singers are agile.
   b. Some singers are agile.
   c. All singers are agile.
   d. None of the above.

5. Read the following set of premises and select the conclusions that will make a valid argument.

   "If the fruit is ripe, then we will pick it on Tuesday. If we pick the fruit on Tuesday, then we will ship it on Thursday."

   a. If the fruit is ripe, then we will ship it on Thursday.
   b. If the fruit is not ripe, then we will not pick it on Tuesday.
   c. If the fruit is not ripe, then we will not ship it on Thursday.
   d. If we ship it on Thursday, then the fruit is ripe.

6. Find the rule of logical equivalence that <u>directly</u> (in one step) <u>transforms</u> statement "i" into statement "ii."

    i. If winter is early, then heating oil is scarce.
    ii. Winter is not early or heating oil is scarce.

a. "Not (if p, then q)" is equivalent to "p and not q."
b. "Not (p and q)" is equivalent to "not p or not q."
c. "Not (p or q)" is equivalent to "not p and not q."
d. "If p, then q" is equivalent to "not p or q."

7. Study the information given below. If a logical conclusion is given, select that conclusion. If none of the conclusions given is warranted, select the option expressing this condition.

"If he grows watermelons, then he grows peanuts. He can grow watermelons or peanuts. He can grow cantaloupes and watermelons."

a. He grows peanuts.
b. He does not grow watermelons.
c. He does not grow peanuts.
d. If he grows peanuts, then he grows watermelons.

8. Round the measure 21,846 milligrams to the nearest 10 thousand milligrams.

a. 30,000 mg
b. 22,000 mg
c. 21,800 mg
d. 20,000 mg

9. Find the distance around a right triangle whose hypotenuse is 10 feet and one leg is 6 feet.

a. 22 feet
b. 24 feet
c. 30 square feet
d. 60 square feet

10. What is the area of a circular region whose radius is 3 yards?

a. 6π square yards
b. 9π square yards
c. 6π yards
d. 9π yards

11. What is the volume in liters of a container that holds 4,720 cubic centimeters?

a. 4,720 L
b. 47.2 L
c. 4.72 L
d. .472 L

12. Select the geometric figure that possesses all of the following characteristics:

    i. quadrilateral
    ii. only 2 sides are parallel

a. rectangle
b. parallelogram
c. trapezoid
d. rhombus

13. The amount of orange juice in a carton is given by which measure?

   a. square inches
   b. degrees
   c. liters
   d. meters

14. Study the information given in the figures.

  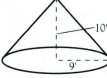

$V = 30\pi$ cu. ft. $V = 120\pi$ cu. ft. $V = 270\pi$ cu. ft.

   Calculate the volume of a cone with a radius of 12 feet and a height of 10 feet.

   a. 360π cu. ft.
   b. 480π cu. ft.
   c. 1080π cu. ft.
   d. $1,440\pi$ cu. ft.

15. The Howsers are going to wallpaper a mural on one wall of their dining room. If the wall is 9 feet by 10 feet, how many square yards of wallpaper, which costs $8.00 per roll, will they need?

   a. 10 square yards
   b. 80 square yards
   c. 90 square yards
   d. 720 square yards

16. Kelly is building a frame for his mailbox. The mailbox must be 4 feet high. If the platform on which the mailbox sits is 3 feet long, how long should the brace connecting the bottom of the post to the end of the platform be?

   a. 5 inches
   b. 7 feet
   c. 5 feet
   d. 25 feet

17. What is the <u>mean</u> of the data in the following sample?

      4, 22, 6, 4, 8, 7, 13, 4

   a. 4
   b. 6
   c. 6.5
   d. 8.5

18. Four finalists were named for the History Award. After an exam, a winner and second-, third-, and fourth-place winners will be announced. How many different ways can the finalists be ranked?

   a. 4
   b. 9
   c. 12
   d. 24

19. On a bird-watching excursion, half of the children saw 8 different types of birds. Half of the remaining children saw 10 birds, while the other half only saw 6. Which of the following statements is true about the distribution of birds?

    a. The mean is less than the mode.
    b. The median is greater than the mode.
    c. The median is equal to the mode.
    d. The mode is greater than the median.

20. A student newspaper is interested in the number of extracurricular activities in which a student participates. Which of the following procedures would be the most appropriate for obtaining a statistically unbiased sample?

    a. Print a survey in the paper that can be returned to the campus newspaper office.
    b. Have the reporter assigned to the story interview the students in his or her classes.
    c. Interview a random sample of students selected from the registrar's list.
    d. Interview every fifth student in the cafeteria line.

21. Mike has an opportunity to study abroad in Paris, Rome, London, Tokyo, or Moscow. What is the probability that he will study in London?

    a. 0
    b. 1:5
    c. 4:5
    d. 1

22. Scores on a state nursing examination were scaled so that the scores listed below correspond to the indicated percentile ranks.

Scores	Percentile Rank
400	99
350	87
300	71
250	50
200	32
150	21
100	3

What percentage of the students made below 200?

    a. 56
    b. 53
    c. 32
    d. 24

23. The following is a description of the voter registration rolls for Putnam County by sex and party affiliation.

	Republican	Democrat	Independent
Male	20%	20%	9%
Female	18%	22%	11%

What is the probability that a randomly selected voter is a female, given that the voter is Republican?

a. 1:5
b. 9:20
c. 19:50
d. 9:19

24. $-5\frac{1}{6} + 4\frac{1}{3}$

a. $\frac{5}{6}$

b. $-1\frac{1}{3}$

c. $\frac{-5}{6}$

d. $1\frac{1}{6}$

25. $\frac{-3}{4} \times \frac{7}{8}$

a. $\frac{21}{32}$

b. $\frac{7}{8}$

c. $\frac{-21}{32}$

d. $-5\frac{1}{4}$

26. $1.17 - 6.138$

a. 4.968
b. 5.048
c. −6.021
d. −4.968

27. $(-15.54) \div 3.7$

a. 4.2
b. .42
c. −4.2
d. −.42

28. If 30 is decreased to 25, what is the percent of decrease?

    a. 5%
    b. 16 2/3%
    c. 25%
    d. 83 1/3%

29. Find 18 1/4% of 360.

    a. 19.73
    b. 65.70
    c. 1973
    d. 6570

30. $5^2 + 3^3$

    a. $(5)(2) + (3)(3)$
    b. $(5 + 3)^5$
    c. $(5 + 3)^3$
    d. $(5)(5) + (3)(3)(3)$

31. Select the place value of the underlined digit.

    4̲9,362.4

    a. 10^4
    b. 10^3
    c. $\dfrac{1}{10^3}$
    d. $\dfrac{1}{10^4}$

32. At one time there were 2.7 German marks to a U.S. dollar. James gave 43.2 German marks to four friends. If each friend got an equal amount, how much money in dollars did James give each friend?

    a. $ 4.00
    b. $ 16.00
    c. $ 29.16
    d. $116.64

33. Terry takes his car to a garage. A mechanic who receives $25.00 an hour works 6 1/2 hours. The mechanic replaces $14.50 worth of parts. If the sales tax is 5%, what is Terry's total bill?

    a. $162.50
    b. $177.00
    c. $185.85
    d. $885.00

34. $2.71 =$

    a. .0271
    b. $\dfrac{271}{1000}$
    c. 27.1%
    d. $\dfrac{271}{100}$

35. $-.75 \ \square \ -.7$

    a. =
    b. >
    c. <

36. A roll of paper towels has approximately 93 individual towels on it. Which of the following values could be a reasonable estimate of the number of towels on 20 rolls?

a. 110
b. 180
c. 1,800
d. 2,000

37. Look for a quadratic relationship between the numbers in each pair. Then identify the missing term.

$(0, 0)$
$(1, 1)$
$(^3/_4, {}^9/_{16})$
$(.4, .16)$
$(-1, 1)$
$(^2/_3, \underline{\quad})$

a. $-^2/_3$
b. $^4/_9$
c. $^2/_3$
d. $-^4/_9$

38. $3\pi + 5 - 10\pi$

a. $7\pi + 5$
b. -2π
c. $-7\pi + 5$
d. 18π

39. $\sqrt{7} \times \sqrt{14}$

a. $49\sqrt{2}$
b. $7\sqrt{2}$
c. 7×14
d. 49

40. $13p - 6(4p/2 - 3)$

a. $p - 18$
b. $p - 3$
c. $p + 18$
d. $25p - 18$

41. $.07525 \div .00215$

a. 3.5×10^{-5}
b. 3.5×10^{-1}
c. 3.5×10^1
d. 3.5×10^5

42. If $4x + 3 = 3(x - 3)$, then

a. $x = -12$
b. $x = -6$
c. $x = -^6/_7$
d. $x = 0$

43. $4x + 6 < 8x + 7$

a. $x > -4$
b. $x < -^1/_4$
c. $x < -4$
d. $x > -^1/_4$

44. Given $d = t^2 - 6t$, if $t = 3$, find d:

    a. 27
    b. 0
    c. -9
    d. -12

45. Find $f(0)$, given: $f(x) = 4x^2 - 5x + 6$

    a. 0
    b. 5
    c. 6
    d. 15

46. Which is a linear factor of the following expression?

    $$8x^2 + 10x - 7$$

    a. $2x + 1$
    b. $x - 1$
    c. $4x + 7$
    d. $2x + 7$

47. Find the correct solutions to this equation:

    $$18x^2 - 9x = -1$$

    a. $\frac{1}{9}$ and $\frac{1}{2}$
    b. $\frac{1}{6}$ and $\frac{1}{3}$
    c. 6 and 3
    d. $-\frac{1}{6}$ and $-\frac{1}{3}$

48. Choose the correct solution set for the system of linear equations.

    $$5x + 2y = 7$$
    $$3x - y = 2$$

    a. $(\frac{9}{11}, \frac{31}{33})$
    b. $(1, -1)$
    c. $(1, 1)$
    d. $(3, -11)$

49. Choose the statement that is not true for all real numbers.

    a. $x + (-x) = 1$
    b. $(2x)(1) = 2x$
    c. $b(1/b) = 1$, if $b \neq 0$
    d. $7y + 0 = 7y$

50. For each of the statements below, determine whether $x = -5$ is a solution.

    i. $(x + 1)(x + 5) = 0$
    ii. $x^2 + 25 = 0$
    iii. $|x| < 4$

    a. i. only
    b. i. and ii. only
    c. i. and iii. only
    d. i., ii., and iii.

51. Suppose that x is directly proportional to the cube of y. If $x = 10$ when $y = 2$, select the correct statement to find y when $x = 50$.

    a. $y^3 = 40$
    b. $y = 10$

c. $5y = 2$

d. $y^3 = 30$

52. Identify the conditions that correspond to the graph:

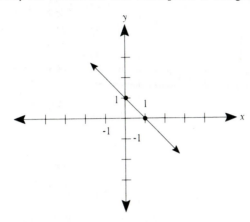

a. $x = 1$ and $y = 2$

b. $x + y = 1$

c. $x - y = 1$

d. $x + y \leq 1$

53. Choose the inequality equivalent to the following:

$$-5x > 25$$

a. $x > 5$

b. $x > -5$

c. $x < 5$

d. $x < -5$

54. The rate of flow of water under a fixed pressure emerging from a circular pipe is directly proportional to the square of the radius of the pipe. If a pipe with a 4-inch radius emits 384 cubic inches of water per second, at what rate will a pipe with a $2^1/_2$-inch radius emit water under the same pressure?

a. 150

b. 240

c. 340

d. 600

55. There are three consecutive positive integers such that the product of the first and second integers is less than the square of the third. Which inequality could be used to find n, the smallest integer?

a. $n + (n + 1) < n^2 + 2$

b. $n(n + 1) < (n + 2)^2$

c. $n + n + 2 < n^2 + 2$

d. $n(n + 2) < (n + 4)^2$

**Pretest and
Answer Key**

Pretest Answer Key

Question	Answer	Skill
1.	d.	I.E.1
2.	d.	II.E.1
3.	c.	II.E.2
4.	d.	II.E.3
5.	a.	III.E.1
6.	d.	III.E.2
7.	a.	IV.E.1
8.	d.	I.B.1
9.	b.	I.B.2a
10.	b.	I.B.2a
11.	c.	I.B.2c
12.	c.	II.B.2
13.	c.	II.B.4
14.	b.	III.B.1
15.	a.	IV.B.1
16.	c.	IV.B.2
17.	d.	I.D.2
18.	d.	I.D.3
19.	c.	II.D.1
20.	c.	II.D.2
21.	b.	II.D.3
22.	a.	IV.D.1
23.	d.	IV.D.2
24.	c.	I.A.1a
25.	c.	I.A.1b
26.	d.	I.A.2a
27.	c.	I.A.2b
28.	b.	I.A.3
29.	b.	I.A.4
30.	d.	II.A.1
31.	b.	II.A.2
32.	a.	IV.A.1
33.	c.	IV.A.2
34.	d.	II.A.3

Question	Answer	Skill
35.	c.	II.A.4
36.	c.	II.A.5
37.	b.	III.A.1
38.	c.	I.C.1a
39.	b.	I.C.1b
40.	c.	I.C.2
41.	c.	I.C.3
42.	a.	I.C.4a
43.	d.	I.C.4b
44.	c.	I.C.5
45.	c.	I.C.6
46.	c.	I.C.7
47.	b.	I.C.8
48.	c.	I.C.9
49.	a.	II.C.1
50.	a.	II.C.2
51.	a.	II.C.3
52.	b.	II.C.4
53.	d.	III.C.1
54.	a.	IV.C.1
55.	b.	IV.C.2

To add two fractions or mixed numbers, use the following steps:

Arithmetic Skills

I.A.1a.
The student will add and subtract rational numbers.

STEP 1. Find a common denominator for the fractions. (A common denominator is a number into which both denominators will divide evenly.)

STEP 2. Compute the answer using the following rules:
(a) Add if the signs are alike.
(b) Subtract if the signs are different.

STEP 3. Determine the sign by choosing the sign of the number whose absolute value is the largest. The absolute value of any number is positive. The absolute value of negative four ($|-4|$) is four (4). Also, the absolute value of four (4) ($|4|$) is four (4).

Example 1: $4\frac{3}{7} + 2\frac{5}{14}$

Solution:

$4\frac{6}{14} + 2\frac{5}{14}$ (1) Find a common denominator.

$4\frac{6}{14} + 2\frac{5}{14} = 6\frac{11}{14}$ (2) Compute.

$6\frac{11}{14}$ (3) Determine the sign.

Example 2: $-2\frac{3}{5} + -4\frac{4}{7} =$

Solution:

$-2\frac{21}{35} + -4\frac{20}{35}$ (1) Find a common denominator.

$2\frac{21}{35} + 4\frac{20}{35} =$ (2) Compute and reduce.

$\left(\frac{41}{35} = 1\frac{6}{35}\right)$

$6\frac{41}{35} = 7\frac{6}{35}$

$-7\frac{6}{35}$ (3) Determine the sign.

Arithmetic Skills

Example **3:** $-3\frac{3}{4}+2\frac{1}{3}$

Solution:		
$-3\frac{9}{12}+2\frac{4}{12}$		(1) Find a common denominator.
$3\frac{9}{12}-2\frac{4}{12}=1\frac{5}{12}$		(2) Compute.
$-1\frac{5}{12}$		(3) Determine the sign.

Example **4:** $-4+3\frac{1}{6}$

Solution:		
$-3\frac{6}{6}+3\frac{1}{6}$		(1) Find a common denominator.
$3\frac{6}{6}-3\frac{1}{6}=0\frac{5}{6}$		(2) Compute.
$-\frac{5}{6}$		(3) Determine the sign.

Example **5:** $-7\frac{1}{3}+2\frac{3}{5}$

Solution:		
$7\frac{5}{15}+2\frac{9}{15}$		(1) Find a common denominator.
$-7\frac{5}{15}-2\frac{9}{15}=$		(2) Compute
$6\frac{20}{15}-2\frac{9}{15}=4\frac{11}{15}$		Borrow $\left(7\frac{5}{15}=6+\frac{15}{15}+\frac{5}{15}\right.$
		$\left.=6\frac{20}{15}\right)$
$-4\frac{11}{15}$		(3) Determine the sign.

To subtract two factors or mixed numbers, use the following steps:

Arithmetic Skills

STEP **1.** Change the subtraction problem to an addition problem by adding the opposite of the subtrahend (the second number).

STEP **2.** Find a common denominator for the fractions. (A common denominator is a number into which both denominators will divide evenly.)

STEP **3.** Compute the answer using the following rules:
(a) Add if the signs are alike.
(b) Subtract if the signs are different.

STEP **4.** Determine the sign by choosing the sign of the number whose absolute value is the largest. (The absolute value of any number is positive.) The absolute value of negative four ($|-4|$) is four (4). Similarly, the absolute value of four ($|4|$) is four (4).

Example **6:** $-6 \frac{1}{4} - (-3 \frac{1}{2})$

Solution:		
$-6 \frac{1}{4} + 3 \frac{1}{2}$	(1)	Change to addition by adding opposite.
$-6 \frac{1}{4} + 3 \frac{2}{4}$	(2)	Find a common denominator.
$6 \frac{1}{4} - 3 \frac{2}{4} =$ $5 \frac{5}{4} - 3 \frac{2}{4} = 2 \frac{3}{4}$	(3)	Compute.
$-2 \frac{3}{4}$	(4)	Determine the sign.

Arithmetic Skills

I.A.1a.
Sample Items

1. $6 + \left(\dfrac{-7}{9}\right) =$

   a. $\dfrac{-1}{8}$

   b. $5\dfrac{2}{9}$

   c. $-6\dfrac{7}{9}$

   d. $-5\dfrac{2}{9}$

2. $2\dfrac{3}{5} + 3\dfrac{1}{8}$

   a. $5\dfrac{1}{10}$

   b. $5\dfrac{29}{40}$

   c. $4\dfrac{4}{13}$

   d. $6\dfrac{1}{10}$

3. $\left(\dfrac{-3}{4}\right) + \left(\dfrac{-6}{11}\right)$

   a. $\dfrac{-9}{15}$

   b. $\dfrac{-3}{7}$

   c. $\dfrac{-1}{4}$

   d. $-1\dfrac{13}{44}$

4. $-5\dfrac{1}{6} + 4\dfrac{1}{3}$

   a. $\dfrac{5}{6}$

   b. $-1\dfrac{1}{3}$

   c. $\dfrac{-5}{6}$

   d. $1\dfrac{1}{6}$

5. $3\dfrac{5}{7} + 4\dfrac{3}{7}$

   a. $7\dfrac{4}{7}$

   b. $7\dfrac{2}{7}$

   c. $7\dfrac{1}{7}$

   d. $8\dfrac{1}{7}$

6. $-4\,^3/_4 - 2\,^1/_2$

   a. $-2\,^1/_4$
   b. -6
   c. $-6\,^1/_4$
   d. $-7\,^1/_4$

7. $3\,^2/_3 - (-1\,^1/_3)$

   a. 5
   b. $4\,^1/_3$
   c. $2\,^1/_3$
   d. 2

ANSWERS: 1.b., 2.b., 3.d., 4.c., 5.d., 6.d., 7.a.

To multiply rational numbers in fractional form, use the following steps:

Arithmetic Skills

I.A.1b.
The student will multiply and divide rational numbers in fractional form.

STEP **1.** Change both factors to fractions.

STEP **2.** Cancel, if possible.

STEP **3.** Multiply. Change to a proper fraction, if necessary.

STEP **4.** Determine the sign by using the following rules:
(a) If the signs are alike, the answer is positive.
(b) If the signs are different, the answer is negative.

Example **1:** $1\frac{1}{3} \times \left(-\frac{1}{4}\right)$

Solution:

$\frac{4}{3} \times \frac{1}{4}$ (1) Change both factors to fractions.

$\frac{4}{3} \times \frac{1}{4}$ (2) Cancel.

$\frac{1}{3} \times \frac{1}{1} = \frac{1}{3}$ (3) Multiply.

$-\frac{1}{3}$ (4) Determine the sign.

Arithmetic Skills

Example **2:** $\left(-8\frac{2}{3}\right) \times (-15)$

Solution: $\dfrac{26}{3} \times \dfrac{15}{1}$ (1) Change both factors to fractions.

$\dfrac{26}{\underset{1}{\cancel{3}}} \times \dfrac{\cancel{15}^{\,5}}{1}$ (2) Cancel.

$\dfrac{26}{1} \times \dfrac{5}{1} = \dfrac{130}{1} = 130$ (3) Multiply and change to a proper fraction.

130   (4) Determine the sign.

To divide two rational numbers in fractional form, do the following:

STEP **1.**   Change both factors to fractions.

STEP **2.**   Multiply by the reciprocal of the second fraction.

STEP **3.**   Cancel, if possible.

STEP **4.**   Multiply and change to a proper fraction, if necessary.

STEP **5.**   Determine the sign by using the following rules:
(a) If the signs are alike, the answer is positive.
(b) If the signs are different, the answer is negative.

Example **1:** $\left(-\dfrac{3}{4}\right) \div \left(1\dfrac{1}{8}\right)$

Solution:

$\dfrac{3}{4} \div \dfrac{9}{8}$ (1) Change to fractions.

$\dfrac{3}{4} \times \dfrac{8}{9}$ (2) Multiply by the reciprocal of the second fraction.

$\dfrac{1}{1} \times \dfrac{2}{3}$ (3) Cancel.

$\dfrac{1}{1} \times \dfrac{2}{3} = \dfrac{2}{3}$ (4) Multiply.

$-\dfrac{2}{3}$ (5) Determine the sign.

Example **2:** $-2 \div -\dfrac{1}{4}$

Solution:

$\dfrac{2}{1} \div \dfrac{1}{4}$ (1) Change to fractions.

$\dfrac{2}{1} \times \dfrac{4}{1}$ (2) Multiply by the reciprocal of the second fraction.

$\dfrac{2}{1} \times \dfrac{4}{1} = \dfrac{8}{1} = 8$ (3) Multiply and reduce.

8 (4) Determine the sign.

Arithmetic Skills

| I.A.1b. |
| Sample Items |

1. $2\frac{1}{3} \times 4$

  a. $9\frac{1}{3}$

  b. $8\frac{1}{3}$

  c. $6\frac{1}{3}$

  d. $2\frac{1}{3}$

2. $\frac{-3}{4} \times \frac{7}{8}$

  a. $\frac{21}{32}$

  b. $\frac{7}{8}$

  c. $\frac{-21}{32}$

  d. $-5\frac{1}{4}$

3. $\left(-2\frac{3}{7}\right) \div \left(-3\frac{3}{4}\right)$

  a. $\frac{68}{105}$

  b. $-8\frac{4}{7}$

  c. $8\frac{4}{7}$

  d. $\frac{-68}{105}$

4. $-8 \div \frac{1}{7}$

  a. $\frac{-1}{56}$

  b. $\frac{-7}{8}$

  c. $-1\frac{1}{7}$

  d. -56

5. $\left(4\frac{2}{7}\right) \times \left(-1\frac{1}{30}\right)$

  a. $-4\frac{3}{7}$

  b. $4\frac{1}{105}$

  c. $4\frac{3}{7}$

  d. $3\frac{1}{105}$

ANSWERS: 1.a., 2.c., 3.a., 4.d., 5.a.

| I.A.2a. |
| The student will add |
| and subtract rational |
| numbers in decimal |
| form. |

To add two rational numbers in decimal form, use the following steps:

STEP 1. If the two units are different, add zeros by the last digit to the right of the decimal until there are the same number of places.

STEP 2. Compute the answer using the following rules:
(a) Add, if the signs are alike.
(b) Subtract, if the signs are different.

STEP 3. Determine the sign by choosing the sign of the number whose absolute value is the largest.

Example 1: 3.3 + (−2.012)

Solution:

3.300 + (−2.012)	(1) Add zeros.
3.300 −2.012 ‾‾‾‾‾ 1.288	(2) Subtract because the signs are different.
1.288	(3) Determine the sign.

To subtract two rational numbers in decimal form, use the following steps:

STEP 1. If the two units are different, add zeros by the last digit to the right of the decimal until there are the same number of places.

STEP 2. Change subtraction problem to an addition problem by adding the opposite of the subtrahend.

STEP 3. Compute the answer using the following rules:
(a) Add, if the signs are alike.
(b) Subtract, if the signs are different.

STEP 4. Determine the sign by choosing the sign of the number whose absolute value is the largest.

Arithmetic Skills

Example **2:** $-4.13 - .175$

Solution:	$-4.130 - .175$	(1) Add a zero.
	$-4.130 + (-.175)$	(2) Add the opposite.
	$\begin{array}{r} 4.130 \\ + \ .175 \\ \hline 4.305 \end{array}$	(3) Add because signs are alike.
	-4.305	(4) Determine the sign.

I.A.2a.
Sample Items

1. $1.17 - 6.138$

   a. 4.968
   b. 5.048
   c. −6.021
   d. −4.968

2. $-17.6 - 8.7$

   a. 26.3
   b. − 8.9
   c. 9.1
   d. −26.3

3. $3.2 + .178$

   a. 3.2178
   b. 3.378

   c. .498
   d. .3

4. $14.01 - .364$

   a. 11.37
   b. 13.654
   c. 13.646
   d. 14.646

5. $-4.68 - (-2.001)$

   a. 2.679
   b. −2.681
   c. −2.679
   d. −6.681

ANSWERS: 1.d., 2.d., 3.b., 4.c., 5.c.

I.A.2b.
The student will multiply and divide rational numbers in decimal form.

To multiply rational numbers in decimal form, use the following steps:

STEP **1.** Multiply the numbers as if the decimals were not there.

STEP **2.** Count the number of digits to the right of each decimal in both numbers.

STEP **3.** Mark off the total number of places in the product beginning on the right and counting to the left.

STEP **4.** Determine the sign by using the following rules:
(a) If the signs are alike, the answer is positive.
(b) If the signs are different, the answer is negative.

Example **1:** $(-4.2) \times .3$

Solution:		
$\begin{array}{r} 42 \\ \times\ \ 3 \\ \hline 126 \end{array}$		(1) Multiply the numbers.
$4.2 \times .3 = 2$ places		(2) Count the number of digits to the right of each decimal.
$4.2 \times .3 = 1.26$		(3) Mark off the total number of spaces.
-1.26		(4) Determine the sign.

To divide rational numbers in decimal form, do the following:

STEP **1.** Regroup the decimals so that no decimal is embedded in the divisor (the second number in the problem).

STEP **2.** Divide the numbers.

STEP **3.** Determine the sign by using the following rules:
(a) If the signs are alike, the answer is positive.
(b) If the signs are different, the answer is negative.

Arithmetic Skills

Example **2:** $14.46 \div .06$

Solution: $06.\overline{)1446.}$ (1) Regroup.

            241
        $6\overline{)1446.}$ (2) Divide.
            $\underline{12}$
            24
            $\underline{24}$
            06
            $\underline{6}$
            0

            241 (3) Determine the sign.

**I.A.2b.
Sample Items**

1. $(-0.3) \times (-.02)$

    a. .6
    b. .06
    c. .006
    d. .0006

2. $(-15.54) \div 3.7$

    a. 4.2
    b. .42
    c. −4.2
    d. − .42

3. $3.17 \times .12$

    a. 37.99
    b. 38.04

    c. .0951
    d. .3804

4. $(-.08) \div 1.6$

    a. −20
    b. −2
    c. −.5
    d. −.05

5. $(-4.1) \times (7.6)$

    a. −311.6
    b. 31.16
    c. 311.6
    d. −31.16

ANSWERS: 1.c., 2.c., 3.d., 4.d., 5.d.

**I.A.3.
The student will calculate percent increase and percent decrease.**

To find the new amount when given the original amount and percent of increase/decrease, use the following steps:

STEP **1.**   Change percent to a decimal number by moving the decimal two places to the left.

STEP 2.   Multiply the decimal times the original amount.

STEP 3.   Find the new result by:
(a) Adding new amount to the original amount if the result is an increase.
(b) Subtracting new amount from the original amount if the result is a decrease.

Example 1:   If you increase 60 by 30% of itself, what is the result?

Solution:		
$30\% = .30$	(1)	Change percent to decimal.
$60 \times .30 = 18.00$	(2)	Multiply.
$60 + 18 = 78$	(3a)	Add.

Example 2:   If you decrease 85 by 5⅕% of itself, what is the result?

Solution: $5 \frac{1}{5}\% = .05 \frac{1}{5}$ (1)   Change percent to decimal.

$$\begin{array}{r} 85 \\ \times .05\,\tfrac{1}{5} \\ \hline 17 \\ 425 \\ \hline 4.42 \end{array} \qquad \left(\frac{85}{1} \times \frac{1}{5} = 17\right)$$

(2)   Multiply.

$85 - 4.42 = 80.58$ (3b)   Subtract.

To find the percent increase or decrease, do the following:

STEP 1.   Identify the original number.

STEP 2.   Find the difference between the original number and the other number.

Arithmetic Skills

STEP **3.** Divide the original number into the difference.

STEP **4.** Change the quotient to a percent by moving the decimal two places to the right.

Example **3:** If 36 is increased to 45, what is the percent of increase?

Solution:	36 is the original number	(1) Identify original number.
	$45 - 36 = 9$	(2) Find the difference.
	$\begin{array}{r} .25 \\ 36\overline{)9.00} \\ \underline{72} \\ 180 \\ \underline{180} \\ 00 \end{array}$	(3) Divide.
	$.25 = 25\%$	(4) Change to percent.

**I.A.3.
Sample Items**

1. If you increase 48 by 25% of itself, what is the result?

   a. 12
   ' b. 36
   c. 49.12
   d. 60

2. If you decrease 120 by 75% of itself, what is the result?

   a. 30
   b. 40
   c. 80
   d. 90

3. If 30 is decreased to 25, what is the percent of decrease?

   a. 5 %
   b. 16 2/3%
   c. 25 %
   d. 83 1/3%

4. If 45 is increased to 55, what is the percent of increase?

   a. 22 2/9%
   b. 18 2/11%
   c. 122 2/9%
   d. .81 9/11%

5. If you increase 504 by 10⅙%, what is the result?

    a.   51.24
    b.   134.4
    c.   555.24
    d.   638.4

Arithmetic Skills

ANSWERS: 1.d., 2.a., 3.b., 4.a., 5.c.

To solve for a, b, or c, use the following steps:

STEP 1.   Write the formula $c = ab$.

> I.A.4.
> The student will solve the sentence $a\%$ of b is c, where values for two variables are given.

STEP 2.   Substitute numbers into the formula where:
    (a) a is the decimal form of the rate (percent).
    (b) b is the original number (it always follows the word "of").
    (c) c is the remaining number (Note: It is not the percent).

STEP 3.   Perform the necessary calculation to solve for the unknown.

Example 1:   What is 135% of 320?

Solution:		
$c = ab$	(1)	Write the formula.
$c = (1.35)(320)$	(2)	Substitute $a = 1.35$ and $b = 320$.
$c = 432$	(3)	Solve for c by multiplying.

Arithmetic Skills

Example **2:**   114 is what percent of 95?

| Solution: | $c = ab$ | (1) Write the formula. |

$114 = a(95)$ (2) Substitute $b = 95$ and $c = 114$.

$$\begin{array}{r} 1.2 = 120\% \\ 95 \overline{)114.0} \\ \underline{95} \\ 190 \\ \underline{190} \\ 0 \end{array}$$

(3) Solve for a by dividing 95 into 114 and change decimal to a percent.

Example **3:**   328 is 82% of what number?

Solution: $c = ab$ (1) Write the formula.

$328 = .82b$ (2) Substitute $c = 328$ and $a = .82$.

$$\begin{array}{r} 4\,00 \\ .82 \overline{)328.00} \\ \underline{328} \\ 000 \end{array}$$

(3) Solve for b by dividing .82 into 328.

**I.A.4.
Sample Items**

1. What is 21% of 70?

   a. 14.7
   b. 30
   c. 333 $\frac{1}{3}$
   d. 1,470

2. What percent of 50 is 80?

   a. 1.6%
   b. 60%
   c. 62.5%
   d. 160%

3. Find 18 $\frac{1}{4}$% of 360.

   a. 19.73
   b. 65.70
   c. 1973
   d. 6570

4. What is 225% of 82?

   a. .1845
   b. 18.45
   c. 184.5
   d. 1845

ANSWERS: 1.a., 2.d., 3.b., 4.c.

The expression "3^5" means that three is multiplied times itself five times, i.e., $3^5 = (3)(3)(3)(3)(3)$.

Similarly,

Arithmetic Skills

II.A.1.
The student will recognize the meaning of exponents.

Example **1:** $2^3 + 7^2 = (2)(2)(2) + (7)(7)$

Example **2:** $4^2 - 3^2 = (4)(4) - (3)(3)$

Example **3:** $(4^4)(5^2) = (4)(4)(4)(4)(5)(5)$

Example **4:** $\dfrac{7^3}{5^2} = \dfrac{(7)(7)(7)}{(5)(5)}$

Example **5:** $(4^2)^3 = (4^2)(4^2)(4^2)$

---

1. $5^2 + 3^3 =$

    a. $(5)(2) + (3)(3)$
    b. $(5 + 3)^5$
    c. $(5 + 3)^3$
    d. $(5)(5) + (3)(3)(3)$

2. $(3^4)^2 =$

    a. $(3 + 3 + 3 + 3)(3 + 3 + 3 + 3)$
    b. $(3^4)(3^4)$
    c. 3^6
    d. $(3 \times 4)^2$

3. $(4^2)(5^3) =$

    a. $(4 \times 4)(5 \times 5 \times 5)$
    b. $(4 \times 2)(5 \times 3)$
    c. $(4 + 4)(5 + 5 + 5)$
    d. $(4 \times 5)^5$

II.A.1.
Sample Items

Arithmetic Skills

4. $6^2 - 4^3$

    a. $(6 \times 6) - (4 \times 4 \times 4)$

    b. $(6 \times 2) - (4 \times 3)$

    c. $(6 \times 6)(4 \times 4 \times 4)$

    d. $(6 - 4)^5$

ANSWERS: 1.d., 2.b., 3.a., 4.a.

II.A.2.
The student will recognize the role of the base number in determining place value in the base-ten numeration system.

The following chart shows the place value of each digit in the base-ten numeration system.

$$10^6 \quad 10^5 \quad 10^4 \quad 10^3 \quad 10^2 \quad 10^1 \quad 10^0 \quad \cdot \quad \frac{1}{10} \quad \frac{1}{10^2} \quad \frac{1}{10^3} \quad \frac{1}{10^4} \quad \frac{1}{10^5} \quad \frac{1}{10^6}$$

$$\square \quad \square \quad \square \quad \square \quad \square \quad \square \quad \square \quad \cdot \quad \square \quad \square \quad \square \quad \square \quad \square \quad \square$$

This chart can be used to select the expanded notation for a numeral.

STEP 1. Align the decimal in the numeral with the decimal in the chart, placing the digits to the left and/or right of the decimal into the correct boxes.

STEP 2. Multiply the digit in the box by the power of that box.

STEP 3. Since the zero digit times a power gives zero, eliminate any zero digits.

Example 1: Select the expanded notation for 302.46

Solution: Place 302.46 in the chart in the following way:

$$10^2 \quad 10^1 \quad 10^0 \quad \cdot \quad \frac{1}{10} \quad \frac{1}{10^2}$$

$\boxed{3} \quad \boxed{0} \quad \boxed{2} \quad \cdot \quad \boxed{4} \quad \boxed{6}$ (1) Align decimals and place digits in boxes.

$302.46 = (3 \times 10^2) +$ (2) Multiply each digit by the corresponding power.

$(0 \times 10^1) + (2 \times 10^0) +$

$\left(4 \times \dfrac{1}{10}\right) + \left(6 \times \dfrac{1}{10^2}\right)$

$= (3 \times 10^2) + (2 \times 10^0) +$ (3) Eliminate any zero digits.

$\left(4 \times \dfrac{1}{10}\right) + \left(6 \times \dfrac{1}{10^2}\right)$

When given the expanded notation of a numeral, you go in the opposite direction to find the numeral.

STEP 1. Place the digit into the box with the matching power.

STEP 2. Place zeros into the remaining boxes between the digits.

Example 2: Select the numeral for $(2 \times 10^3) + \left(3 \times \dfrac{1}{10}\right)$.

Solution: $10^3 \quad 10^2 \quad 10^1 \quad 10^0 \quad \dfrac{1}{10}$

$\boxed{2} \quad \square \quad \square \quad \square \quad \cdot \quad \boxed{3}$ (1) Substitute the digit 2 into the 10^3 box and the 3 digit into the $\dfrac{1}{10}$ box.

$\boxed{2} \quad \boxed{0} \quad \boxed{0} \quad \boxed{0} \quad \cdot \quad \boxed{3}$ (2) Place zero in the remaining boxes.

Answer: 2000.3

Arithmetic Skills

To determine the place value of any specific digit, do as follows:

STEP 1. Align the decimal in the numeral with the decimal in the chart, placing the digits to the left and/or right of the decimal into the correct boxes.

STEP 2. Choose the power of the underlined digit.

Example 3: What is the place value of the underlined digit?
14.03$\underline{2}$

Solution: Place 14.032 in the chart in the following way:

$$10^1\ 10^0\ \cdot\ \frac{1}{10^1}\ \frac{1}{10^2}\ \frac{1}{10^3}$$

[1] [4] · [0] [3] [2] (1) Align the decimal.

3 has the place value   (2) Choose the power of the
of $\frac{1}{10^2}$ underlined digit.

II.A.2.
Sample Items

1. Select the place value of the underlined digit.

   4$\underline{9}$,362.4

   a. 10^4

   b. 10^3

   c. $\dfrac{1}{10^3}$

   d. $\dfrac{1}{10^4}$

2. Select the correct expanded notation for 300.4.

   a. $(3 \times 10^3) + \left(4 \times \dfrac{1}{10}\right)$

   b. $(3 \times 10^3) + \left(4 \times \dfrac{1}{10^2}\right)$

   c. $(3 \times 10^2) + \left(4 \times \dfrac{1}{10}\right)$

   d. $(3 \times 10^2) + \left(4 \times \dfrac{1}{10^2}\right)$

3. Select the numeral for

$$(5 \times 10^4) + (2 \times 10^1) + \left(7 \times \frac{1}{10}\right).$$

    a. 5,002.07
    b. 5,020.7
    c. 50,020.7
    d. 50,002.07

4. Select the place value of the underlined digit.

      38.00$\underline{1}$35

    a. 10^2

    b. $\dfrac{1}{10^2}$

    c. $\dfrac{1}{10^3}$

    d. 10^3

Arithmetic Skills

ANSWERS: 1.b., 2.c., 3.c., 4.c.

To change a fraction or mixed number to a decimal, use the following steps:

STEP **1.**   Write as a fraction.

STEP **2.**   Divide the denominator into the numerator.

Example **1:**   Change $^4/_5$ to a decimal.

Solution: $^4/_5$ is a fraction   (1) Write as a fraction.

$$5 \overline{)\,4.0}^{\textstyle .8}$$
$$\underline{4\,0}$$
$$0$$

(2) Divide.

> **II.A.3.**
> The student will identify equivalent forms of positive rational numbers involving decimals, percents, and fractions.

Arithmetic Skills

Example **2:** Change 2 ¾ to a decimal.

Solution: $2 \frac{3}{4} = \frac{11}{4}$ (1) Write as a fraction.

$$\begin{array}{r} 2.75 \\ 4 \overline{)11.0} \\ \underline{8} \\ 30 \\ \underline{28} \\ 20 \\ \underline{20} \\ 0 \end{array} = 2.75$$ (2) Divide.

To change a fraction or mixed number to a percent, use the following steps:

STEP **1.** Write as a fraction.

STEP **2.** Divide the denominator into the numerator.

STEP **3.** Move the decimal *two* places to the right.

Example **3:** Change 3 ⅕ to a percent.

Solution: $3 \frac{1}{5} = \frac{16}{5}$ (1) Write as a fraction.

$$\begin{array}{r} 3.2 \\ 5 \overline{)16.0} \\ \underline{15} \\ 10 \\ \underline{10} \\ 0 \end{array}$$ (2) Divide.

3.2 = 3.20 = 320%   (3) Move decimal two places to the right.

To change a decimal to a percent, do as follows:

Arithmetic Skills

STEP **1.**	Move the decimal two places to the left. (*Note:* If a decimal is not present, it is understood to be at the right of the number [234 = 234.].)

Example **4:**	Change 0.021 to a percent.
Solution:	$0.021 = 0.021 = 2.1\%$ (1) Move decimal and add % sign.

To change a decimal to a fraction, do the following:

STEP **1.**	Write the number without the decimal point.

STEP **2.**	(a) Count the number of places behind the decimal in the original problem. (b) Raise 10 to that number.

STEP **3.**	Write a fraction using the answer in Step 1 as the numerator and the answer in Step 2 as the denominator. Reduce if possible.

Example **5:**	Change .302 to its equivalent fractional form.

Solution:	302	(1) Write number without decimal.
	3 places behind decimal	(2a) Count the places.
	$10^3 = 1,000$	(2b) Raise 10 to that number.
	$\dfrac{302}{1000} = \dfrac{151}{500}$	(3) Write fraction and reduce.

Arithmetic Skills

To change a percent to a decimal, use the following steps:

STEP **1.** Move the decimal two places to the left.

Example **6:** Change 42% to its equivalent decimal form.

Solution: $42\% = 42.\% = .42$ (1) Move decimal.

To change a percent to a fraction, do as follows:

STEP **1.** Move the decimal two places to the left.

STEP **2.** Write the decimal as a fraction (See example 5).

Example **7:** Change 42% to its equivalent fractional form.

Solution: $42\% = 42.\% = .42$ (1) Move decimal and drop % sign.

$$\frac{42}{10^2} = \frac{42}{100} = \frac{21}{50}$$ (2) Write as fraction and reduce.

1. $^{17}/_{25} =$

   a. .68%
   b. .0068
   c. 68%
   d. 6.8

2. 1.21% =

   a. $\dfrac{121}{1000}$

   b. 12.1

   c. .0121

   d. $\dfrac{121}{100}$

3. 4.371 =

   a. 43.71%

   b. $\dfrac{4371}{10,000}$

   c. $\dfrac{4371}{100,000}$

   d. 437.1%

4. $4\,^2/_5 =$

   a. 4.4%
   b. 4.4
   c. 44%
   d. .44

5. 45% =

   a. .0045

   b. $\dfrac{9}{20}$

   c. 4.5

   d. 4500

Arithmetic Skills

II.A.3.
Sample Items

ANSWERS: 1.c., 2.c., 3.d., 4.b., 5.b.

This skill requires you to place a > (greater than), < (less than), or = (equal to) sign between two fractions or mixed numbers, two decimals, or a fraction and decimal.

To compare two fractions or mixed numbers, use the following steps:

STEP **1.** Find a common denominator.

STEP **2.** Compare the numerators of the new fractions. (The one with the largest number in the numerator is the largest.)

STEP **3.** Place the correct symbol (<, >, or =) between the two fractions or mixed numbers.

II.A.4.
The student will determine the order relation between real numbers.

Arithmetic Skills

Example **1:** $2\,^4/_5\;\square\;2\,^7/_8$

Solution: $2\,^{32}/_{40}\;\square\;2\,^{35}/_{40}$ (1) Find common denominator.

32 is less than 35   (2) Compare numerators.

$2\,^{32}/_{40}\;<\;2\,^{35}/_{40}$ (3) Place symbol.

Example **2:** $-^7/_8\;\square\;-^8/_9$

Solution: $-^{63}/_{72}\;\square\;-^{64}/_{72}$ (1) Find common denominator.

−63 is greater than −64   (2) Compare numerators.

$-^{63}/_{72}\;>\;-^{64}/_{72}$ (3) Place symbol.

To compare two decimal numbers, do the following:

STEP **1.**
(a) If the decimal terminates, add zeros until you have the same number of places in each numeral.
(b) If the decimal repeats, add the repeating digits until you have the same number of places in each numeral.

STEP **2.**   Compare the value of the numbers without the decimals.

STEP **3.**   Place the correct symbol.

Arithmetic Skills

Example **3:**   4.13 ☐ 4.131

Solution:	4.130 ☐ 4.131	(1a)	Add zeros.
	4130 is less than 4131	(2)	Compare numbers.
	4.13 < 4.131	(3)	Place symbol.

Example **4:** $4.\overline{34}$ ☐ $4.\overline{3}$

Solution:	$4.\overline{34}$ ☐ $4.\overline{33}$	(1b)	Add repeating places.
	434 is greater than 433	(2)	Compare numbers.
	$4.\overline{34} > 4.\overline{3}$	(3)	Place symbol.

To compare decimals and fractions, use the following steps:

STEP **1.**   Change the fraction to a decimal.

STEP **2.**   Compare the value of the decimal.

STEP **3.**   Place the correct symbol.

Arithmetic Skills

Example **5:** $4\frac{1}{8}\ \square\ 4.\overline{12}$

Solution:

$$8\overline{)\begin{array}{l}.125\\1.00\end{array}}\quad 4\frac{1}{8}=4.125$$

$$\begin{array}{r}8\\\hline 20\\20\\\hline 0\end{array}$$

$4.125\ \square\ 4.\overline{12}$ (1) Change fraction to a decimal.

4.1250 is greater than   (2) Add additional numbers,
4.1212 then compare the number.

$4.125 > 4.\overline{12}$ (3) Place the symbol.

To compare square roots of whole numbers that are not perfect squares, use the following steps:

STEP **1.** Square both sides.

STEP **2.** Compare the new numbers.

STEP **3.** Place the correct symbol.

Example **6:** $\sqrt{51}\ \square\ 7.3$

Solution: $(\sqrt{51})^2\ \square\ (7.3)^2$ (1) Square both sides.

51 is less than 53.29 (2) Compare the value.

$\sqrt{51} < 7.3$ (3) Place the symbol.

Arithmetic Skills

1. $4.1\overline{3}$ ☐ 4.13

   a. =
   b. <
   c. >

2. $^{17}/_{34}$ ☐ $.5$

   a. >
   b. =
   c. <

3. $8\,^2/_3$ ☐ $8\,^{17}/_{24}$

   a. <
   b. =
   c. >

4. $\sqrt{26}$ ☐ 5.4

   a. =
   b. >
   c. <

5. $-^2/_3$ ☐ $-.7$

   a. =
   b. >
   c. <

ANSWERS: 1.c., 2.b., 3.a., 4.c., 5.b.

The problems in this skill ask you to determine a reasonable estimate of a sum, the answer to an addition problem, or a product, the answer to a multiplication problem. You may also be asked to estimate an average. An average is found by finding the sum of all the items and then dividing it by the total number of items.

The first step in estimation involves rounding numbers. The rule for rounding and rounding examples are given in Skill I.B.1.

To estimate a sum, do as follows:

II.A.5.
The student will identify a reasonable estimate of a sum, average, or product of numbers.

STEP **1.** Round off each item.

STEP **2.** Add the rounded numbers.

Arithmetic Skills

Example **1:** Jane went to the bookstore to purchase some school supplies. She bought a notebook for $2.79, paper for $.99, three pens for $1.19, and a folder for $4.89. Which of the following is a reasonable estimate of her school supplies?

Solution:		
$2.79 \approx \$ 3.00$	(1) Round each price.
$.99 \approx 1.00$	
$1.19 \approx 1.00$	
$4.89 \approx \underline{5.00}$	
$\$10.00$	(2) Find the sum.

To estimate a product, do the following:

STEP **1.** Round each factor.

STEP **2.** Multiply the rounded factors.

Example **2:** To build a model, each child will need 28 building blocks. If 11 children are each going to build a model, how many pieces will the teacher need?

Solution:

Round off the number of blocks: $28 \approx 30$

Round off the number of children: $11 \approx 10$ (1) Round off each item.

$30 \times 10 = 300$ (2) Multiply.

To estimate an average when given individual items, use the following steps:

STEP **1.** Round each item.

Arithmetic Skills

STEP **2.** Find the sum of the rounded items.

STEP **3.** Divide the sum by the number of items.

Example **3:** The chart below contains a list of monthly temperatures for Florida. What could be a reasonable estimate of the average yearly temperature?

Month	Temperature
January	61
February	62
March	68
April	68
May	70
June	78
July	80
August	81
September	78
October	72
November	68
December	62

Solution:

$$61 \approx 60$$
$$62 \approx 60$$
$$68 \approx 70$$
$$68 \approx 70$$
$$70 \approx 70$$
$$78 \approx 80$$
$$80 \approx 80$$
$$81 \approx 80$$
$$78 \approx 80$$
$$72 \approx 70$$
$$68 \approx 70$$
$$62 \approx 60$$

(1) Round off each item.

$$\overline{850}$$

(2) Find the sum.

$$12\overline{)850} \approx 70$$

(3) Divide the sum by the number of items.

since $12 \times 70 = 840$.

Arithmetic Skills

To estimate an average when given a highest and lowest value, use the following steps:

STEP **1.** Look at the responses and choose the value *between* the highest and the lowest value.

Example **4:** In a physical fitness test, fifth graders had to do chin-ups. All the fifth graders did between 3 and 20 chin-ups. Which of the following values could be a reasonable estimate of the average score of the students?

  a. 2
  b. 6
  c. 20
  d. 23

Solution: Since 6 is the only number between 3 and 20, the answer is "b."

II.A.5.
Sample Items

1. Ten students competed in a high-jump competition. The highest jump was 60 inches and the lowest jump was 42 inches. Which of the following is a reasonable estimate of the students' average jump?

   a. 50 inches
   b. 61 inches
   c. 430 inches
   d. 500 inches

2. The following chart shows the growth of a laboratory plant for a period of 5 days. Based on this information, what could be a reasonable estimate of the total growth of the plant during the 5-day period?

   a. 100
   b. 85
   c. 20
   d. 15

Day	Growth in Centimeters
1	19
2	21
3	22
4	18
5	17

3. A roll of paper towels has approximately 93 individual towels on it. Which of the following values could be a reasonable estimate of the number of towels on 20 rolls?

   a. 110
   b. 180
   c. 1,800
   d. 2,000

4. Lynn made five tablecloths. The amount of fabric in each of the tablecloths was 4 1/8 yards, 3 7/8 yards, 2 1/8 yards, 5 1/4 yards, and 4 3/4

yards. Which of the following could be a reasonable estimate of the average amount of fabric per tablecloth?

a. 4 yards
b. 18 yards
c. 20 yards
d. 23 yards

Problems in this skill will be of two types:

1. Related number pairs

2. Numbers of an arithmetic, geometric, or harmonic sequence.

Arithmetic Skills

III.A.1.
The student will infer relations between numbers in general by examining particular number pairs.

   Problems of related number pairs ask for identification of the missing term of the pair. You can do this more quickly if you know whether the relationship is *linear* or *quadratic*. The stem of the question will identify the type.
   To find the missing term of a *linear* relationship, do the following:

STEP 1. Look at the first pair. Determine what number could be added to the first number to obtain the second. Second, determine what number could be multiplied by the first term to obtain the second.

STEP 2. Check the second pair to see if you can add your addend or multiply your factor to the first number to obtain the second number.

STEP 3. Eliminate the one that does not work and use the remaining addition or multiplication pattern to check the remaining pairs and find the missing term.

Arithmetic Skills

Example **1:** Look for the common linear relationship between the numbers in each pair. Then identify the missing term.
$(-3,1)$ $(7,11)$ $(4.3, 8.3)$ $(-6\frac{1}{4}, -2\frac{1}{4})$ $(-5,\underline{\quad})$

Solution: The stem identifies the number pair as linear. Therefore, look for an addend and a factor that can be used to obtain the second number from the first.

For the first pair $(-3,1)$ (1) Find addend and factor.

Find addend
$(-3,1)$: $-3 + 4 = 1$
or
Find factor
$-3 \times (-\frac{1}{3}) = 1$

$(7,11)$: Does $7 + \underline{4} = 11$ (2) Check second pair.
          (yes)
or
$\quad$ does $7 \times (-\frac{1}{3}) = 11$
$\quad\quad$ (no)

$(4.3, 8.3) \rightarrow 4.3 + \underline{4} = 8.3$ (3) Use pattern to check remaining pairs and find solution.

$(-6\frac{1}{4}, -2\frac{1}{4}) \rightarrow$
$-6\frac{1}{4} + \underline{4} = -2\frac{1}{4}$

$(-5,\underline{\quad}) \rightarrow -5 + \underline{4} = 1$

The solution is -1.

To find the missing term of a *quadratic* relationship, do as follows:

STEP **1.** Look at the first number pair to determine if the first number squared equals the second number or vice versa.

STEP **2.** Use the squaring pattern to see if squaring that particular term in the other pairs matches the other term.

STEP **3.** Use that pattern to find the missing term.

Example **2**: Look for a common quadratic relationship between the numbers in each pair.
(25, −5) (¼, ½) (1.21, 1.1) (36, 6) (.09, ___)

Solution:

Does $(25^2) = 625$? (no)   (1) Square both terms to determine that <u>second</u> term should be squared to obtain the first.
or
Does $(−5)^2 = 25$? (yes)

$(½)^2 = ¼$ (2) Check other pairs, squaring the *second* term.

$(1.1)^2 = 1.21$

$(6)^2 = 36$

$(\underline{\quad})^2 = .09$

(.3, .09)   (3) Use pattern to find missing term.

To find the missing term of a sequence, use the following steps:

STEP 1. Use the stem to determine if the sequence is arithmetic, geometric, or harmonic.

STEP 2.
(a) Arithmetic—subtract the first term from the second term to find what number you *add* to the preceding term to obtain the next term.
(b) Geometric—divide the first number into the second number to determine the number you *multiply* by the preceding term to obtain the next term.
(c) Harmonic—since the numerator will always be 1, look for a pattern in the denominators of the fractions.

STEP 3. Perform the operation identified in Step 2 to find the missing term.

Arithmetic Skills

Example **3:** Identify the missing term in the harmonic progression.
1, ⅓, ⅕, ⅐, ⅑, ____

Solution: harmonic

$$\frac{1}{1}, \frac{1}{3}, \frac{1}{5}, \frac{1}{7}, \frac{1}{9}, \underline{\quad}$$

¹⁄₁₁

(1) The stem identifies the progression as harmonic.

(2) Find a pattern for the denominators.

(3) The denominators are found by adding 2. Add 2 to 9 and write the number as a denominator of a fraction with a numerator of 1 and a denominator of 11.

III.A.1.
Sample Items

1. Look for a common linear relationship between the numbers in each pair. Then identify the missing term.

(.3, 3.3)
(6, 9)
(−1, 2)
(⅛, ²⁵⁄₈)
(−15, −12)
(⅔, ____)

   a. ⁴⁄₃
   b. ⁸⁄₁₅
   c. ¹¹⁄₃
   d. −⁸⁄₁₅

2. Identify the missing term in the following geometric progression:

27, −18, 12, −8, ¹⁶⁄₃

   a. −³²⁄₉
   b. −³²⁄₃
   c. ³²⁄₉
   d. 8

3. Look for a quadratic relationship between the numbers in each pair. Then identify the missing term.

(0, 0)
(1, 1)
(¾, ⁹⁄₁₆)
(.4, .16)
(−1, 1)
(⅔, ____)

   a. −²⁄₃
   b. ⁴⁄₉
   c. ²⁄₃
   d. −⁴⁄₉

4. Identify the missing term in the following arithmetic progression:

$$-1, -\tfrac{1}{2}, 0, \tfrac{1}{2}, 1, \underline{\quad}$$

    a. $-1\tfrac{1}{2}$
    b. $\tfrac{1}{3}$
    c. $1\tfrac{1}{2}$
    d. 2

5. Identify the missing term in the following harmonic progression:

$$\tfrac{1}{4}, \tfrac{1}{8}, \tfrac{1}{12}, \tfrac{1}{16}, \tfrac{1}{20}, \tfrac{1}{24}, \underline{\quad}$$

    a. $\tfrac{1}{8}$
    b. 28
    c. $\tfrac{1}{28}$
    d. $\tfrac{1}{48}$

ANSWERS: 1.c., 2.a., 3.b., 4.c., 5.c.

The word problems in this skill will be taken from a context of business, social studies, industry, education, economics, environmental studies, arts, physical science, sports, or consumer relations. This wide variety of problems does not lend itself to specific rules for individual types of problems. However, the following general rules for problem solving will help lead to a correct solution:

> **IV.A.1.**
> **The student will solve real-world problems that do not require the use of variables and do not involve percent.**

STEP 1.   Read the problem carefully.

STEP 2.   Underline the specific information the problem is requesting.

STEP 3.   Before performing any calculations, check the units of measurement to make sure that they are in agreement.

STEP 4.   Eliminate information that is not needed.

STEP 5.   Perform the computation and check for arithmetic mistakes.

Arithmetic Skills

STEP **6.** Once the solution is found, reread the problem to make sure the answer seems reasonable.

Example **1:** Mr. Reed conducted a survey in his music class. He found that ¾ of the students liked jazz while only ¹/₇ of the students liked folk music. If he has 28 students in class, how many more students like jazz than folk music?

Solution:	How many more students like jazz than like folk?	(2) Underline specific information.

Students that like jazz $\frac{3}{4} \times \frac{28}{1} = 21$ (5) Compute.

Students that like folk music
$\frac{1}{7} \times \frac{28}{1} = 4$

Difference between two groups:
$21 - 4 = 17$ (6) Answer.

**IV.A.1.
Sample Items**

1. At one time there were 2.7 German marks to a U.S. dollar. James gave 43.2 German marks to four friends. If each friend got an equal amount, how much money in dollars did James give each friend?

   a. $ 4.00
   b. $ 16.00
   c. $ 29.16
   d. $116.64

2. Gasoline is $1.20 a gallon. A luxury car has a 23.5-gallon tank. A compact car has a 16-gallon tank. How much more does it cost to fill the tank of the luxury car?

   a. $ 9.00
   b. $12.00
   c. $23.04
   d. $28.20

3. The Clear Telephone Company offers Mary a discount on long-distance calling. She can pay a monthly rate of $6.00 for 60 minutes of long-distance calls plus $.10 for every minute over the 60 minutes, or she can pay $.08 a minute. After reviewing her previous month's bill, she found that she had made 1 hour and 32 minutes

worth of long-distance calls. What would have been the difference between the two plans?

a. $1.36
b. $1.84
c. $7.36
d. $9.20

4. A department store sells videotape in packages of five. Each videotape can record 2 hours worth of video. If each package cost $15.00, how many hours of video can be recorded on four packages.

a. 8
b. 30
c. 40
d. 60

5. One week, Sheila ran 28 miles on a 3 ½-mile track, and the next week she ran 25 miles on a 2 ½-mile track. How many laps did she run on both tracks?

a. 6
b. 10
c. 18
d. 98

Arithmetic Skills

ANSWERS: 1.a., 2.a., 3.b., 4.c., 5.c.

The word problems in this skill are much like the problems in Skill IV.A.1. The difference between the two skills is that the problems in this skill involve the use of percent in at least one step. Remember to change a percent to a decimal before performing any computation (Skill II.A.3). Also, it will be helpful to use the formula $c = ab$ (Skill I.A.4) to solve for the unknowns.

> **IV.A.2.**
> The student solves real-world problems that do not require the use of variables but do require the use of percent.

Example **1:**	At maximum efficiency a factory can daily produce 3,000 cardboard boxes. How many boxes does the factory produce in a 5-day week if the factory is operating at an 80% efficiency level?

Solution:		
	$c = ab$	Formula for percent problem.
	$c = (.80)(3,000)$	$b = 3,000\ r = 80\%$
	$c = 2,400$	Boxes per day at 80% efficiency.
	$2,400 \times 5 = 12,000$	Boxes in a 5-day week.

Arithmetic Skills

IV.A.3.
The student solves problems that involve the structure and logic of arithmetic.

These verbal problems use the structure and logic of arithmetic rather than simple computation to find solutions. The following vocabulary is necessary for finding these solutions:

1. Whole numbers—{0, 1, 2, 3, 4, 5 . . . }.

2. Integers—{ . . . −3, −2, −1, 0, 1, 2, 3 . . . }.

3. Factors—numbers that form a product.

4. Multiple of n —product of a number and n

5. Prime—a number whose factor is itself and 1. (One is not prime.)

Use this vocabulary and the following steps to solve the problems:

STEP 1. Read the problem to identify the conditions that the solution must satisfy.

STEP 2. Test these conditions against the distractors.

Example 1: Find the smallest positive multiple of 7 that leaves a remainder of 1 when divided by 8 and a remainder of 4 when divided by 9.

    a. 35
    b. 56
    c. 49
    d. 40

Solution: Use the first condition, smallest multiple of 7, to check distractors.
a. $35 = 5 \times 7$
b. $56 = 8 \times 7$
c. $49 = 7 \times 7$
d. 40 is not a multiple of 7. Eliminate "d."

Next condition: leaves remainder of 1 when divided by 8.

$$\begin{array}{ccc} 4 & 7 & 6 \\ a.\ 8\overline{)35} & b.\ 8\overline{)56} & c.\ 8\overline{)49} \\ 32 & 56 & 48 \\ \overline{3} & \overline{0} & \overline{1} \end{array}$$

Eliminate "a." and "b."   *(Continued)*

(Cont'd.) The solution "c" can be identified since the other choices have been eliminated. However, to avoid mistakes check the last condition.

Last condition: A remainder of 4 when divided by 9.

a.
$$
\begin{array}{r}
5 \\
9\overline{)49} \\
45 \\
\hline
4
\end{array}
$$

Solution "c." is the answer.

Example **2:** How many whole numbers leave a remainder of 1 when divided into 65, and a remainder of 4 when divided into 28?

Solution: Use the first condition (leaves a remainder of 1 when divided into 65).

$$
\begin{array}{r}
\overline{)65} \\
64 \\
\hline
1
\end{array}
$$
This has to be 64.

The whole numbers must be multiples of 64:
1, 2, 4, 8, 16, 32, 64

Eliminate 1 since this term does *not* meet the first condition (leaves a remainder of 1).

There are now six possibilities. Test the second condition (leaves a remainder of 4 when divided into 28).

$$
\begin{array}{r}
\overline{)28} \\
24 \\
\hline
4
\end{array}
$$
This has to be 24.

Which numbers out of 2, 4, 8, 16, 32, 64 are multiples of 24?
2, 4, 8

The number of whole numbers is three.

Arithmetic Skills

Example **3:** What is the least common multiple of 16 and 18?

Solution: Use the first condition (must be a multiple of 16 and 18). Find the prime factor of 16 and 18.

$16 = 2 \times 8 = 2 \times 2 \times 4 = 2 \times 2 \times 2 \times 2 = 2^4$

$18 = 2 \times 9 = 2 \times 3 \times 3 = 2 \times 3^2$

Next condition: must be the least common multiple (LCM). To find the LCM, multiply all prime factors raised to the *highest power* that occurs in the factorization.

$2^4 \times 3^2 = 16 \times 9 = 154$

The least common multiple of 16 and 18 is 154.

Example **4:** What is the greatest common factor of 16 and 18?

Solution: Use the first condition, must be a factor of 16 and 18. Find the prime factors of 16 and 18:

$16 = 4 \times 4 = 2 \times 2 \times 2 \times 2 = 2^4$

$18 = 3 \times 6 = 3 \times 3 \times 2 = 2^1 \times 3^2$

Next condition: must be the greatest common factor (GCF). To find the GCF, list only the prime factors (that appear) in *both* numbers. Raise these prime factor(s) to *smallest power* that occurs in the factorization:

$2^1 = 2$

The great common factor of 16 and 18 is 2.

IV.A.3.
Sample Items

1. What is the least common multiple (LCM) of 24 and 50?

   a. 2
   b. 240
   c. 600
   d. 1,200

2. Which of the following is the greatest common factor (GCF) of 36 and 60?

   a. 6
   b. 12

c. 60
d. 180

3. Find the smallest positive multiple of 5 that leaves a remainder of 3 when divided by 8, and a remainder of 2 when divided into 72.

a. 43
b. 35
c. 128
d. 64

Arithmetic Skills

ANSWERS: 1.c., 2.b., 3.b.

Algebra Skills

> **I.C.1a.**
> **The student will add and subtract real numbers.**

To add or subtract real numbers, use the following steps:

STEP 1. Change a subtraction problem to an addition problem by adding the opposite of the subtrahend.

STEP 2. Simplify all radicals by taking the square root of perfect square factors.

STEP 3. Combine like terms by using the following rules:
(a) If the signs are alike, add like terms. Use the common sign.
(b) If the signs are different, subtract like terms. Choose the sign of the number whose absolute value is the largest.

Example 1: $\sqrt{24} + 3\sqrt{6} =$

Solution:

$2\sqrt{6} + 3\sqrt{6}$ (2) Simplify radical.
$\sqrt{24} = \sqrt{4}\,\sqrt{6} = 2\sqrt{6}$

$5\sqrt{6}$ (3a) Add and take the common sign.

Example 2: $-11\pi - 6\pi + 3 =$

Solution:

$-11\pi + (-6\pi) + 3$ (1) Change the subtraction to addition.

$-17\pi + 3$ (3a) Add and take the common sign.

Algebra Skills

Example **3:** $-\sqrt{27} + 6 + 4\sqrt{3}$

Solution: $-3\sqrt{3} + 6 + 4\sqrt{3}$ (2)   Simplify radical.
$\sqrt{27} = \sqrt{9}\,\sqrt{3} = 3\sqrt{3}$

$\sqrt{3} + 6$ (3b)   Subtract like terms.
Choose sign.

I.C.1a.
Sample Items

1. $3\pi + 5 - 10\pi$

    a. $7\pi + 5$
    b. -2π
    c. $-7\pi + 5$
    d. 18π

2. $\sqrt{18} + \sqrt{18}$

    a. 6
    b. $5\sqrt{2}$
    c. $6\sqrt{2}$
    d. $\sqrt{26}$

3. $3 - 4\sqrt{3} + \sqrt{12}$

    a. 3
    b. $3 - 2\sqrt{3}$
    c. $3 + 2\sqrt{3}$
    d. $3 - 4\sqrt{15}$

4. $-6\sqrt{2} - (-8\sqrt{2})$

    a. $-14\sqrt{2}$
    b. 2
    c. -14
    d. $2\sqrt{2}$

ANSWERS: 1.c., 2.c., 3.b., 4.d.

To multiply and divide real numbers, use the following steps:

I.C.1b.
The student will multiply and divide real numbers.

STEP **1.**   Eliminate any radical in the denominator of a fraction by multiplying the numerator and denominator of the fraction by the square root of the number in the denominator.

STEP **2.**   Multiply the numbers.

STEP **3.**   Simplify all radicals by taking the square root of perfect square factors.

STEP **4.**   Reduce fraction if necessary.

Algebra Skills

Example **1:** $\sqrt{2} \times \sqrt{6} =$

| Solution: | $\sqrt{12}$ | (2) Multiply. |
| | $2\sqrt{3}$ | (3) Simplify $\sqrt{12} =$ $\sqrt{4}\sqrt{3} = 2\sqrt{3}$ |

Example **2:** $\dfrac{6}{\sqrt{2}} =$

Solution:

$\dfrac{6}{\sqrt{2}} \cdot \dfrac{\sqrt{2}}{\sqrt{2}}$ (1) Eliminate the $\sqrt{}$ in the denominator.

$\dfrac{6\sqrt{2}}{\sqrt{4}}$ (2) Multiply.

$\dfrac{6\sqrt{2}}{2}$ (3) Simplify the $\sqrt{4} = 2$.

$3\sqrt{2}$ (4) Reduce.

I.C.1b.
Sample Items

1. $\sqrt{7} \times \sqrt{14} =$

   a. $49\sqrt{2}$
   b. $7\sqrt{2}$
   c. 7×14
   d. 49

2. $\dfrac{5}{\sqrt{3}} =$

   a. $\dfrac{\sqrt{5}}{3}$

   b. $\dfrac{5\sqrt{3}}{9}$

   c. $\dfrac{5\sqrt{3}}{3}$

   d. $5\sqrt{3}$

3. $\sqrt{6} \cdot 2\sqrt{6}$

   a. $3\sqrt{6}$
   b. $2\sqrt{6}$
   c. 12
   d. 72

4. $\dfrac{9}{\sqrt{6}}$

   a. $\dfrac{3\sqrt{6}}{2}$

   b. $\dfrac{3}{\sqrt{2}}$

   c. $\dfrac{\sqrt{6}}{2}$

   d. $\dfrac{3}{2}$

ANSWERS: 1.b., 2.c., 3.c., 4.a.

To simplify or reduce algebraic expressions, use the following steps:

Algebra Skills

I.C.2.
The student will apply the order-of-operations agreement to computations involving numbers and variables.

STEP 1. Simplify all expressions in parentheses or in the numerator or denominator of a fraction.

STEP 2. Simplify all exponents.

STEP 3. Working left to right, perform all multiplications and/or divisions in the order in which they appear.

STEP 4. Working left to right, perform all additions and subtractions in the order in which they appear.

Example 1: $\left(-\dfrac{1}{2}\right)^2 + 6\left(\dfrac{1}{8} - \dfrac{1}{4}\right) =$

Solution:

$\left(-\dfrac{1}{2}\right)^2 + 6\left(-\dfrac{1}{8}\right)$ 　　(1) Do parentheses first.

$$\dfrac{1}{8} - \dfrac{1}{4} = \left(\dfrac{1}{8}\right) + \left(-\dfrac{2}{8}\right) = -\dfrac{1}{8}$$

$\dfrac{1}{4} + 6\left(-\dfrac{1}{8}\right)$ 　　(2) Simplify the exponents.

$$\left(-\dfrac{1}{2} \times -\dfrac{1}{2}\right) = \dfrac{1}{4}$$

$\dfrac{1}{4} + \left(-\dfrac{3}{4}\right)$ 　　(3) Multiply $\left(\dfrac{\overset{3}{\cancel{6}}}{1}\right) \times \left(-\dfrac{1}{\underset{4}{\cancel{8}}}\right) = -\dfrac{3}{4}$

$-\dfrac{2}{4} = -\dfrac{1}{2}$ 　　(4) Add and reduce.

Algebra Skills

Example **2:** $\dfrac{(2x - 8y)}{3 - 1} - (3x + 6y)$

Solution: $\dfrac{2x - 8y}{2} - (3x + 6y)$ (1) Simplify the denominator.

$x - 4y - (3x + 6y)$ (3) Divide.

$x - 4y + (-3x) +$ (4) Subtract by adding the
$(-6y) = -2x - 10y$ opposite, and combine terms.

I.C.2.
Sample Items

1. $\frac{1}{2} + \frac{1}{2} \times \frac{1}{3} - \left(\frac{2}{3}\right)^2$

   a. $-\frac{1}{9}$
   b. 0
   c. $\frac{2}{9}$
   d. $\frac{1}{3}$

2. $\dfrac{3(2x - 5y)}{3} - (3x - 2y)$

   a. $-x - 3y$
   b. $\dfrac{3x - 13y}{3}$
   c. $-x - 7y$
   d. $\dfrac{-x - 17y}{3}$

3. $1 + 5^2 \cdot 4$

   a. 144
   b. 101
   c. 24
   d. 401

4. $\frac{1}{4} - \frac{1}{5} \times \frac{1}{3} \div \frac{4}{5}$

   a. $\frac{1}{3}$
   b. $\frac{1}{6}$
   c. $\frac{1}{12}$
   d. $\frac{1}{48}$

5. $13p - 6(4p/2 - 3)$

   a. $p - 18$
   b. $p - 3$
   c. $p + 18$
   d. $25p - 18$

ANSWERS: 1.c., 2.a., 3.b., 4.b., 5.c.

I.C.3.
The student will use scientific notation in calculations involving very large or very small measurements.

To multiply or divide very large numbers, use the following steps:

STEP **1.** Put the numbers in scientific notation by moving the decimal until there is one nonzero digit to the left of it and writing it in its equivalent form as a power of ten. (Count the number of places you move the decimal. If you move it to the right, the exponent is negative. If you move it to the left, the exponent is positive.)

Algebra Skills

STEP 2.
(a) To multiply, multiply the numbers not in exponential form. *Add* the exponents of the powers of ten and write that sum as a power of ten.
(b) To divide, divide the numbers not in exponential form. *Subtract* the exponents of the powers of ten and write that difference as a power of ten.

STEP 3. Write the answer in scientific notation or in standard notation.

Example **1:** $.003192 \div 1{,}520{,}000 =$

Solution:	$(3.192 \times 10^{-3}) \div$ (1.52×10^{6})	(1)	Change to scientific notation.

$$\left[\begin{array}{c} 2.1 \\ 152.\sqrt{319.2} \\ -3 - 6 = -3 + (-6) = -9 \end{array} \right]$$

(2b) Divide numbers. Subtract the exponents.

$2.1 \times 10^{-9} = .0000000021$ (3) Write the answer.

Example **2:** $(4.2 \times 10^{8}) \times (2.3 \times 10^{-5}) =$

Solution:	$(4.2 \times 10^{8}) \times (2.3 \times 10^{-5}) =$	(1)	Numbers are in scientific notation.

$$\left[\begin{array}{c} 4.2 \times 2.3 = 9.66 \\ 8 + (-5) = 3 \end{array} \right]$$

(2a) Multiply the numbers. Add the exponents.

$9.66 \times 10^{3} = 9660$ (3) Write the answer.

Algebra Skills

I.C.3.
Sample Items

1. $1,922,000 \div .0031 =$

    a. 620,000,000
    b. 620
    c. .62
    d. .00062

2. $(3.27 \times 10^8) \times (4.0 \times 10^{-10}) =$

    a. .1308
    b. −13.08
    c. 130.8
    d. 1308

3. $203,000,000 \times .00011 =$

    a. 22,330,000
    b. 22,330

    c. 2.233
    d. .0002233

4. $.07525 \div .00215 =$

    a. 3.5×10^{-5}
    b. 3.5×10^{-1}
    c. 3.5×10^{1}
    d. 3.5×10^{5}

5. $(9.1 \times 10^{-5}) \times (8.2 \times 10^8) =$

    a. 74.62×10^{-13}
    b. 7.462×10^{-3}
    c. 7.462×10^{3}
    d. 7.462×10^{4}

ANSWERS: 1.a., 2.a., 3.b., 4.c., 5.d.

I.C.4a. The student will solve linear equations.

To solve linear equations, use the following steps:

STEP **1.** Remove all parentheses by using the distributive property. Combine terms if possible.

STEP **2.** Move all the variables on one side and all constants on the other side by adding the opposite of the terms that need to be moved.

STEP **3.** Divide both sides by the coefficient (number) on the variable.

Example **1:** If $3x + 6 = 8x - 10$, then

Solution:		
$3x = 8x - 16$	(2) Add −6 to both sides.	
$-5x = -16$	Add −8x to both sides.	
$x = \dfrac{16}{5}$	(3) Divide both sides by −5.	

Algebra Skills

Example **2:**   If $x - 2(2x - 1) = 5$, then

Solution:	$x - 4x + 2 = 5$	(1) Remove the parentheses and combine like terms.
	$-3x + 2 = 5$	
	$-3x = 3$	(2) Add -2 to both sides.
	$x = -1$	(3) Divide both sides by -3.

I.C.4a.
Sample Items

1. If $4x + 3 = 3(x - 3)$, then

   a. $x = -12$
   b. $x = -6$
   c. $x = -6/7$
   d. $x = 0$

2. If $3x - (x + 6) = -8$, then

   a. $x = -7$
   b. $x = -1$
   c. $x = 1$
   d. $x = 7$

3. If $3x - 2 = 5x - 10$, then

   a. $x = -4$
   b. $x = -3/2$

   c. $x = -1$
   d. $x = 4$

4. If $6 - 4x = 10$, then

   a. $x = -4$
   b. $x = -1$
   c. $x = 1$
   d. $x = 4$

5. If $6a + 8 = 3a$, then

   a. $a = 3/8$
   b. $a = -5/6$
   c. $a = -3/8$
   d. $a = -8/3$

ANSWERS: 1.a., 2.b., 3.d., 4.b., 5.d.

Solving linear inequalities is much like solving linear *equations* (Skill I.C.4a). The following steps are the same except for an additional part in Step 3:

I.C.4b.
The student will solve linear inequalities.

STEP **1.**   Remove all parentheses by using the distributive property. Combine terms, if possible.

STEP **2.**   Move all the variables on one side and all constants on the other side by adding the opposite of the terms that need to be moved.

Algebra Skills

STEP **3.** Divide both sides by the coefficient (number) on the variable. "Flip" (less than becomes greater than and vice versa) the inequality if the number you divide by is negative.

Example **1:** $4x + 1 > 7x - 5$

Solution:

$4x > 7x - 6$	(2) Add -1 to both sides.
$-3x > -6$	Add $-7x$ to both sides.
$x < 2$	(3) Divide both sides by -3 and "flip" the inequality.

(*Note:* The solution may also be written as $2 > x$.)

Example **2:** $2(x - 3) + 3(x - 1) > 6$

Solution:

$2x - 6 + 3x - 3 > 6$	(1) Remove the parentheses and combine like terms.
$5x - 9 > 6$	
$5x > 15$	(2) Add 9 to both sides.
$x > 3$	(3) Divide both sides by 5.

(*Note:* The solution may also be written as $3 < x$.)

Algebra Skills

I.C.4b.
Sample Items

1. $4x + 6 < 8x + 7$

   a. $x > -4$
   b. $x < -\frac{1}{4}$
   c. $x < -4$
   d. $x > -\frac{1}{4}$

2. $4(2 + x) \geq 12$

   a. $x \geq 4$
   b. $x \leq 1$
   c. $x \geq 20$
   d. $x \geq 1$

3. $10 - 2(x - 4) \geq 6$

   a. $x \geq -2$
   b. $x \geq -6$
   c. $x \leq -2$
   d. $x \leq 6$

4. $2(p - 5) + 3(p + 6) \geq 8$

   a. $p \geq -4$
   b. $p \geq 0$
   c. $p \geq \frac{7}{5}$
   d. $p \geq 5$

5. $10(x + 1) - 8x \geq -1$

   a. $x \geq -1$
   b. $x \geq -\frac{11}{2}$
   c. $x \geq \frac{9}{2}$
   d. $x \leq -1$

ANSWERS: 1.d., 2.d., 3.d., 4.b., 5.b.

In this skill a formula will be given along with values for all the variables on one side of the formula. To solve for the requested variable:

I.C.5.
The student will use given formulas to compute results when geometric measurements are not involved.

STEP 1. Replace the variables with the values given in the problem.

STEP 2. To solve the requested variable, follow the order of operations given in Skill I.C.2 (1. parentheses, 2. exponents, 3. multiplication and division, and 4. addition and subtraction).

Example 1: Given $z = (2x + y)^2$, if $x = 4$ and $y = 3$ then $z =$

Solution:		
	$z = [2(4) + 3]^2$	(1) Replace the variables with the values.
	$z = [8 + 3]^2 = (11)^2$ $= 121$	(2) Simplify using the order of operations.

Example **2:** A formula for the height, h; of an object after t seconds is given by

$$h = 64t - t^2$$

What is the height of an object after 2 seconds.

Solution: $h = 64(2) - (2)^2$ (1) Replace the variables with the values.

$h = 64(2) - 4$ (2) Simplify using the order of operations.
$= 128 - 4 = 124$

I.C.5.
Sample Items

1. Given $b = 3x^2 + y$, if $x = -2$ and $y = 6$, then $b =$
   a. 18
   b. 31
   c. 42
   d. 110

2. The formula for finding the number of watts (W) of electrical power is $W = EI$. How many watts are being used when an appliance uses 120 volts (E) and 2 amperes (I).
   a. 60
   b. 122
   c. 240
   d. 1,202

3. The formula for average annual depreciation is $A = T/N$ where T is the total depreciation, N is the number of years, and A is the average annual depreciation. What is the average annual depreciation on a car with $T = \$9,000$ and $N = 5$.
   a. $45,000
   b. $1,800
   c. $180
   d. $450

4. Given $d = t^2 - 6t$, if $t = 3$, find d.
   a. 27
   b. 0
   c. −9
   d. −12

5. One study has shown that the braking distance of a car can be found by using the formula, $D = (1/10 \times \text{speed})^2 \times 5$. What braking distance (D) will the driver need in order to bring the car to a stop from a speed of 50 miles per hour?
   a. 50
   b. 125
   c. 5,000
   d. 1,000

ANSWERS: 1.a., 2.c., 3.b., 4.c., 5.b.

To find the particular value of a given function, do as follows:

Algebra Skills

STEP **1.**	Replace the independent variable with the specific domain value.

I.C.6.
The student will find particular values of a function.

STEP **2.**	Follow the order of operations given in Skill I.C.2. to solve for the dependent value.

Example **1:**	Find $f(-1)$ given: $f(x) = 3x^2 + 2x - 1$

Solution:		
	$3(-1)^2 + 2(-1) - 1$	(1) Substitute in (-1) for x.
	$3(1) + 2(-1) - 1 =$ $3 - 2 - 1 = 0$	(2) Simplify using the order of operations.

Example **2:**	Given the following function, find $f(-1/2)$: $f(x) = x^2 - 3x + 1$

Solution:		
	$(-1/2)^2 - 3(-1/2) + 1$	(1) Substitute in $(-1/2)$ for x.
		(2) Simplify using the order of operations.
	$1/4 - 3(-1/2) + 1 =$	(2a) Find the powers.
	$1/4 + 3/2 + 1 =$	(2b) Perform the multiplication.
	$1/4 + 6/4 + 4/4$	(2c) Add.
	$= \dfrac{11}{4}$	
	$= 2\dfrac{3}{4}$	

1. Find $f(0)$, given $f(x) = 4x^2 - 5x + 6$

   a. 0
   b. 5
   c. 6
   d. 15

I.C.6.
Sample Items

Algebra Skills

2. Find $f(\frac{1}{4})$, given $f(x) = 1 - 3x - x^2$

   a. $\dfrac{3}{8}$

   b. $\dfrac{5}{16}$

   c. $\dfrac{1}{8}$

   d. $\dfrac{3}{16}$

3. Find $f(-2)$, given the following function: $f(x) = 2x^3 - x^2 + 4$

   a. 12
   b. −16
   c. −8
   d. −4

4. Find $f(-1)$, given $f(x) = x^3 - x$

   a. −4
   b. −2
   c. 0
   d. 2

5. Find $f(5)$, given the following function: $f(x) = 15 - 3x - x^2$

   a. 25
   b. −10
   c. −25
   d. −55

ANSWERS: 1.c., 2.d., 3.b., 4.c., 5.c.

**I.C.7.
The student will factor
a quadratic equation.**

To factor a quadratic expression of the form $ax^2 + bx + c$, use the following steps:

STEP 1. Write two sets of parentheses ( )( ), which will be the binomial factors. Identify a, b, and c.

STEP 2. (a) If c is positive, use the sign on b in both parentheses $[(+)(+)$ or $(-)(-)]$.
(b) If c is negative, put different signs in both parentheses $[(-)(+)$ or $(+)(-)]$.

STEP 3. (a) Put factors of a in the first position of each set of parentheses.
(b) Put factors of c in the second position of each set of parentheses.

STEP **4.**
(a) Multiply the two outside terms.
(b) Multiply the two inside terms.
(c) Add these two results. Compare sum with bx term to see if they are equal. If not, change the positions of the same factors or try different factors and repeat Step 4.

STEP **5.** Match one binomial factor with the responses.

Example **1:** Find a linear factor of the following expression.
$2x^2 - x - 3$

Solution:	( )( )	(1)	$a = 2$; $b = -1$; $c = -3$.
	(+)(−)	(2)	The signs are different since c is negative.
	$(2x +)(x −)$	(3a)	Put factors of a in first position.
	$(2x + 3)(x − 1)$	(3b)	Put factors of c in second position.
	$(2x)(-1) = -2x$	(4a)	Multiply two outside terms.
	$(3)(x) \quad = \underline{\ 3x}$	(4b)	Multiply two inside terms.
	$\qquad\qquad 1x$	(4c)	Find the sum.
	$1x \ne -1x$	(4d)	Compare the sum with bx term.
	$(2x − 3)(x + 1)$	(4e)	Change the signs, since numbers matched.
	$(2x)(1) \ = \ 2x$		Repeat Step 4.
	$(-3)(x) \ =\underline{-3x}$		
	$\qquad\qquad -1x$		
	$(2x − 3)(x + 1)$	(5)	Match one of these factors.

Algebra Skills

Example **2:** Find a linear factor of the following expression.
$5x^2 - 11x + 2$

Solution:	( )( )	(1)	$a = 5; \ b = -11; \ c = 2$
	(–)(–)	(2)	The signs are alike since c is positive and both negative since b is negative.
	$(5x - \ )(x - \ )$	(3a)	Put the factors of a in first position.
	$(5x - 2)(x - 1)$	(3b)	Put the factors of c in second position.
	$(5x)(-1) = -5x$	(4a)	Multiply two outside terms.
	$(-2)(x) \ = -2x$	(4b)	Multiply two inside terms.
	$= -7x$	(4c)	Find the sum.
	$-7x \neq -11x$	(4d)	Compare the sum with bx term.
	$(5x - 1)(x - 2)$	(4e)	Change position of the factors.
	$[(5x)(-2) + (-1)(x) = -10x + (-1x) = -11x]$		Repeat Step 4.
	$(5x - 1)(x - 2)$	(5)	Match these factors.

I.C.7.
Sample Items

1. Which is a linear factor of the following expression?

   $10x^2 - 7x - 3$

   a. $5x - 3$
   b. $x - 1$
   c. $5x - 1$
   d. $10x - 7$

2. Which is a linear factor of the following expression?

   $8x^2 + 10x - 7$

   a. $2x + 1$
   b. $x - 1$
   c. $4x + 7$
   d. $2x + 7$

3. Which is a linear factor of the following expression?

$$3x^2 - 4x + 1$$

a. $x + 1$
b. $x + 2$
c. $3x + 1$
d. $3x - 1$

4. Which is a linear factor of the following expression?

$$6x^2 + 7x + 2$$

a. $3x + 2$
b. $6x + 1$
c. $2x - 1$
d. $x + 1$

Section 4-4, cont'd

Algebra Skills

ANSWERS: 1.b., 2.c., 3.d., 4.a.

To find the roots of a quadratic equation you can always use the quadratic formula. However, if the quadratic expression factors, you may find the roots by the factoring method.

Use the following steps to find the solution by the factoring method:

I.C.8.
The student will find the roots of a quadratic equation.

STEP **1.** Put equation in the form $ax^2 + bx + c = 0$.

STEP **2.** Find the linear factors (See Skill 1.C.7).

STEP **3.** Set each linear factor equal to zero.

STEP **4.** Solve each linear equation (See Skill I.C.4a).

Algebra Skills

Example **1:** Find the correct solutions to this equation:
$12x^2 - x - 1 = 0$

Solution:

$12x^2 - x - 1 = 0$	(1) Correct form.
$(4x + 1)(3x - 1) = 0$	(2) Find the linear factors.
$4x + 1 = 0 \quad 3x - 1 = 0$	(3) Set each linear factor equal to zero.
$x = -\frac{1}{4} \quad x = \frac{1}{3}$	(4) Solve each equation.

Use the following steps to find the solution by the quadratic equation:

STEP **1.** Put equation in the form $ax^2 + bx + c = 0$.

STEP **2.** Identify $a, b,$ and c.

STEP **3.** Substitute in the formula
$$x = \frac{-b \pm \sqrt{b^2 - 4ac}}{2a}$$

STEP **4.** Simplify using the order of operations.

STEP **5.** Write as two solutions.

Example **2:** Find the correct solution to this equation:
$2x^2 = 2x + 1$

Solution:

$2x^2 - 2x - 1 = 0$	(1) Write the equation in $ax^2 + bx + c = 0$ form.
$a = 2, b = -2, c = -1$	(2) Identify a, b, and c.
$x = \dfrac{-(-2) \pm \sqrt{(-2)^2 - 4(2)(-1)}}{2(2)}$	(3) Substitute in the formula.
$x = \dfrac{2 \pm \sqrt{12}}{4} = \dfrac{2 \pm 2\sqrt{3}}{4} =$	(4) Simplify.
$\dfrac{2(1 \pm \sqrt{3})}{4} = \dfrac{1 \pm \sqrt{3}}{2}$	
$x = \dfrac{1 + \sqrt{3}}{2} \qquad x = \dfrac{1 - \sqrt{3}}{2}$	(5) Write as two solutions.

I.C.8.
Sample Items

1. Find the correct solutions to this equation:

$$6p^2 - 7p + 2 = 0$$

a. $\dfrac{7 + \sqrt{29}}{2}$ and $\dfrac{7 - \sqrt{29}}{2}$

b. $^2/_3$ and $^1/_2$

c. $-^1/_6$ and 2

d. $-^2/_3$ and $-^1/_2$

2. Find the correct solutions to this equation:

$$2x^2 - x - 2 = 0$$

a. $\dfrac{1 + \sqrt{17}}{4}$ and $\dfrac{1 - \sqrt{17}}{4}$

b. $\dfrac{1 + 2\sqrt{3}}{2}$ and $\dfrac{1 - 2\sqrt{3}}{2}$

c. $\dfrac{1 + \sqrt{17}}{2}$ and $\dfrac{1 - \sqrt{17}}{2}$

d. $\dfrac{1 + \sqrt{3}}{2}$ and $\dfrac{1 - \sqrt{3}}{2}$

3. Find the correct solutions to this equation:

$$x^2 - 3 = 4x$$

a. 3 and 1

b. $-2 + \sqrt{7}$ and $-2 - \sqrt{7}$

c. 4 and -1

d. $2 + \sqrt{7}$ and $2 - \sqrt{7}$

Algebra Skills

4. Find the correct solutions to this equation:

$$18x^2 - 9x = -1$$

   a. $\frac{1}{9}$ and $\frac{1}{2}$
   b. $\frac{1}{6}$ and $\frac{1}{3}$
   c. 6 and 3
   d. $-\frac{1}{6}$ and $-\frac{1}{3}$

5. Find the correct solutions to this equation:

$$5t^2 - 5t - 1 = 0$$

   a. $\dfrac{1 + 3\sqrt{5}}{2}$ and $\dfrac{1 - 3\sqrt{5}}{2}$

   b. 2 and -1

   c. $\dfrac{5 + 3\sqrt{5}}{10}$ and $\dfrac{5 - 3\sqrt{5}}{10}$

   d. $\dfrac{5 + \sqrt{5}}{10}$ and $\dfrac{5 - \sqrt{5}}{10}$

ANSWERS: 1.b., 2.a., 3.d., 4.b., 5.c.

I.C.9.
The student will solve a system of two linear equations in two unknowns.

Solving a system of two equations in two unknowns can be done by using a method called Cramer's Rule. Since the system will always appear in the form

$$ax + by = r$$
$$cx + dy = s$$

The letters a, b, c, d, r, and s will be used to give the procedure for using Cramer's Rule.

STEP 1. Identify a, b, c, d, r, and s from their position in the problem.

STEP 2. Set up the determinants for the two solutions.

$$x = \frac{\begin{vmatrix} r & b \\ s & d \end{vmatrix}}{\begin{vmatrix} a & b \\ c & d \end{vmatrix}} \qquad y = \frac{\begin{vmatrix} a & r \\ c & s \end{vmatrix}}{\begin{vmatrix} a & b \\ c & d \end{vmatrix}}$$

Algebra Skills

STEP **3.**

Evaluate the numerators and the denominators of the fraction.

$$x = \frac{\begin{vmatrix} r & b \\ s & d \end{vmatrix}}{\begin{vmatrix} a & b \\ c & d \end{vmatrix}} = \frac{rd - bs}{ad - bc}$$

$$y = \frac{\begin{vmatrix} a & r \\ c & s \end{vmatrix}}{\begin{vmatrix} a & b \\ c & d \end{vmatrix}} = \frac{as - cr}{ad - bc}$$

STEP **4.**

Evaluate the fractions to find the solution:
(a) If denominator is not equal to zero, the solution will be two rational numbers.
(b) If the denominator is equal to zero and the numerator is *not* equal to zero, the solution is *the empty set.*
(c) If the denominator and numerator are both equal to zero, solve one of the equations for y and put in set builder notation [((x,y)|y = _____)].

Example **1:**

Choose the correct solution set for the system of linear equations.

$$3x + y = -1$$
$$-2x + 5y = 2$$

Solution:

$a = 3, b = 1, c = -2,$
$d = 5, r = -1, s = 2$

(1) Identify the variables.

$$x = \frac{\begin{vmatrix} -1 & 1 \\ 2 & 5 \end{vmatrix}}{\begin{vmatrix} 3 & 1 \\ -2 & 5 \end{vmatrix}}, \quad y = \frac{\begin{vmatrix} 3 & -1 \\ -2 & 2 \end{vmatrix}}{\begin{vmatrix} 3 & 1 \\ -2 & 5 \end{vmatrix}}$$

(2) Set up the determinants.

$$x = \frac{(-1)(5) - (2)(1)}{(3)(5) - (1)(-2)}$$

(3) Evaluate.

$$= \frac{-5 - 2}{15 - (-2)} = \frac{-7}{17}$$

(Continued)

Algebra Skills

(Cont'd) $y = \dfrac{(3)(2) - (-1)(-2)}{(5)(5) - (-2)(1)}$

$= \dfrac{6 - (2)}{15 - (-2)} = \dfrac{4}{17}$

(*Note:* The denominators will always be the same for *x* and *y*.)

Since the denominator $\neq$ zero, the solution is $(-7/17,\ 4/17)$

(4a) Find the solution.

Example **2:**   Choose the correct solution set for the system of linear equations.

$3x + y = 3$
$6x + 2y = 9$

Solution: $a = 3,\ b = 1,\ c = 6,$ (1) Identify the variables.
$d = 2,\ r = 3,\ s = 9$

$x = \dfrac{\begin{vmatrix} 3 & 1 \\ 9 & 2 \end{vmatrix}}{\begin{vmatrix} 3 & 1 \\ 6 & 2 \end{vmatrix}},\ \ y = \dfrac{\begin{vmatrix} 3 & 3 \\ 6 & 9 \end{vmatrix}}{\begin{vmatrix} 3 & 1 \\ 6 & 2 \end{vmatrix}}$ (2) Set up the determinants.

$x = \dfrac{(3)(2) - (9)(1)}{(3)(2) - (6)(1)}$ (3) Evaluate.

$= \dfrac{6 - 9}{6 - 6} = \dfrac{-3}{0}$

$y = \dfrac{(3)(9) - (3)(6)}{(3)(2) - (1)(6)}$

$= \dfrac{27 - 18}{6 - 6} = \dfrac{9}{0}$

Since the denominator is equal to zero and the numerator is not equal to zero, the answer is the empty set.

(4b) Find the solution.

Example **3:** Choose the correct solution set for the system of linear equations.

$$x + 2y = 3$$
$$2x + 4y = 6$$

Solution: $a = 1, b = 2, c = 2,$ (1)   Identify the variables.
$d = 4, r = 3, s = 6$

$$x = \frac{\begin{vmatrix} 3 & 2 \\ 6 & 4 \end{vmatrix}}{\begin{vmatrix} 1 & 2 \\ 2 & 4 \end{vmatrix}}, \quad y = \frac{\begin{vmatrix} 1 & 3 \\ 2 & 6 \end{vmatrix}}{\begin{vmatrix} 1 & 2 \\ 2 & 4 \end{vmatrix}}$$ (2)   Set up the determinants.

$$x = \frac{(3)(4) - (2)(6)}{(1)(4) - (2)(2)}$$ (3)   Evaluate.

$$= \frac{12 - 12}{4 - 4} = \frac{0}{0}$$

$$y = \frac{(1)(6) - (3)(2)}{(1)(4) - (2)(2)}$$

$$= \frac{6 - 6}{4 - 4} = \frac{0}{0}$$

Since the denominator   (4c)   Find the solution.
and numerator are
both equal to zero,
solve either equation
for y and put in set
builder notation. Taking
the first equation:

$$x + 2y = 3$$
$$2y = -x + 3$$
$$y = -\tfrac{1}{2}x + 3$$
$$((x,y) \mid y = -\tfrac{1}{2}x + 3)$$

1. Choose the correct solution set for the system of linear equations.

$$5x + 2y = 7$$
$$3x - y = 2$$

   a. $(^9/_{11}, {}^{31}/_{33})$
   b. $(1, -1)$
   c. $(1, 1)$
   d. $(3, -11)$

2. Choose the correct solution set for the system of linear equations.

$$16x + 4y = 8$$
$$4x + y = 2$$

I.C.9.
Sample Items

Algebra Skills

a. (1,2)
b. the empty set
c. ($\frac{1}{2}$, 1)
d. $\{(x,y) \mid y = -4x + 2\}$

3. Choose the correct solution set for the system of linear equations.

$$x - 3y = -3$$
$$2x + y = 1$$

a. (−6,−1)
b. (0,1)
c. ($\frac{6}{5}$,−1)
d. the empty set

4. Choose the correct solution set for the system of linear equations.

$$5x + 10y = 15$$
$$x + 2y = 8$$

a. (1,1)
b. the empty set
c. (0,4)
d. $\{(x,y) \mid y = -\frac{1}{2}x + \frac{3}{2}\}$

5. Choose the correct solution set for the system of linear equations.

$$13x + 14y = -1$$
$$7x + 3y = 4$$

a. (−1,1)
b. ($\frac{53}{59}$, $\frac{45}{59}$)
c. $\{(x,y) \mid y = -\frac{3}{7}x + \frac{4}{5}\}$
d. (1,−1)

ANSWERS: 1.c., 2.d., 3.b., 4.b., 5.d.

This skill requires the use of nine properties of real numbers. These can be divided into three categories: addition, multiplication, and both addition and multiplication. The following are instances of addition properties:

Algebra Skills

II.C.1. The student will use properties of operations correctly.

Instance	How to Recognize	What It Means
1. $2x + y = y + 2x$	The terms are reversed around the addition sign.	You can add two terms in any order and get the same sum (addition is commutative).
2. $(2x + y) + 2 = 2x + (y + 2)$	The order of the terms is the same. The parentheses are around different terms.	You may add numbers in any order and get the same sum (addition is associative).
3. $6 + 0 = 6$	Zero is added to a number.	When you add zero to a number, the sum is the original number (there exists an additive identity).
4. $x + (-x) = 0$	The sum equals zero.	Each real number has an opposite (there exists an additive inverse).

The following examples illustrate how to use these four properties to write equivalent expressions.

Example 1: Write an expression equivalent to the following:

$$x^2 + 3y =$$

Solution: $x^2 + 3y = 3y + x^2$ (1) Change the order of the terms.

Example 2: Write an expression equivalent to the following:

$$4x + 0 =$$

Solution: $4x + 0 = 0 + 4x$ (1) Change the order of the terms.

or

$4x + 0 = 4x$ (2) Add zero to the number.

Algebra Skills

Example **3:** Write an expression equivalent to the following:

$(a + b) + 0 =$

Solution: Since the operation is addition, the answer could be

$(a + b) + 0 = 0 + (a + b)$ (1) Change the order of the
$(a + b) + 0 = (b + a) + 0$ terms.

$(a + b) + 0 = a + (b + 0)$ (2) Order same ( ) changed.

$(a + b) + 0 = a + b$ (3) Zero is added to the number.

The following are instances of the multiplication properties:

Instance	How to Recognize	What It Means
5. $a^2b = ba^2$	The terms are reversed around the multiplication sign.	You can multiply in any order and get the same product (multiplication is commutative).
6. $a(bc) = (ab)c$	The order of the terms is the same. The parentheses are around different terms.	You may multiply numbers in any order and get the same product (multiplication is associative).
7. $p \times 1 = p$	One is multiplied by the number.	If you multiply a factor by 1, the product is the original factor (there exists multiplicative identity).
8. $(x)(1/x) = 1, x \neq 0$	The product is equal to 1.	Each number, except 0, has a reciprocal (there exists a multiplicative inverse).

The following examples illustrate how to use these four properties to write equivalent expressions.

Algebra Skills

Example **4:** Write an expression equivalent to the following:

$$2x(\tfrac{1}{2}x) =$$

Solution: $2x(\tfrac{1}{2}x) = (\tfrac{1}{2}x)(2x)$ (5) Switch the terms.

$(2x)(\tfrac{1}{2}x) = 1$ (8) Multiplying by the reciprocal gives 1.

Example **5:** Choose the expression equivalent to the following:

$$3x^2(yz^3) =$$

Solution: $3x^2(yz^3) = (yz^3)3x^2$ (5) Switch the order of the terms.
$= 3x^2(z^3y)$
$= x^2 3(z^3y)$

$3x^2(yz^3) = (3x^2)yz^3$ (6) Change the position of the parentheses.
$= (3x^2y)z^3$
$= 3(x^2y)z^3$

The following property is probably the most used and tested on the CLAST. This property (called the distributive property) is a number property involving multiplication and addition.

Instance	How to Recognize	What It Means
9. $3(2x + y) = 6x + 3y$	Multiply the number on the outside by each term in the parentheses.	A number times a group of addends should be multiplied by each addend.
10. $3x + 4xy = x(3 + 4y)$	A factor is taken out of each addend and placed on the outside of a parenthesis.	Expressions with common factors can be rewritten as a product.

Algebra Skills

The following examples illustrate how to use any of the properties to write equivalent expressions.

Example **6:** Choose the expression equivalent to the following:
$6x + 6y$

Solution: $6x + 6y = 6(x + y)$ (10) Take out a common factor.

$6x + 6y = 6y + 6x$ (1) Switch the order of the terms around an addition sign.

$6x + 6y = x6 + y6$ (5) Switch the order of the terms around a multiplication sign.

All of these properties can be combined in a question that asks for the statement that does *not* represent one of the real number properties.

Example **7:** Choose the statement that is *not* true for all real numbers.

a. $4(ab) = (4a)b$
b. $(2x + y)(x - y) = (x - y)(2x + y)$
c. $4(x + 3) = 4x + 3$
d. $3x + 6y = 6y + 3x$

Solution: $4(ab) = (4a)b$ True, by 6.

$(2x + y)(x - y) = (x - y)(2x + y)$ True, by 5.

$4(x + 3) = 4x + 3$ False, $4(x + 3) = 4x + 12$ by 9.

$3x + 6y = 6y + 3x$ True, by 1.

The solution is "c."

II.C.1.
Sample Items

1. Choose the expression equivalent to the following:

$$4x^2y(x + 3y^2)$$

a. $4x^2y + 12x^2y^2$
b. $4x^2y(3y^2 + x)$
c. $4x^3y + 3y^2$
d. $x(4x^2y + 3y^2)$

2. Choose the expression equivalent to the following:

$$5x^2(x^3y)$$

a. $6x^5y$
b. $5x^2(y^3x)$
c. $5x^6y$
d. $(5x^2x^3)y$

3. Choose the expression equivalent to the following:

$$14x^2 + 7x$$

a. $7x(2x + 1)$
b. $28x^3$
c. $14x(x + 2)$
d. $14x + 7x^2$

4. Choose the statement that is *not true* for all real numbers.

a. $x^2(yz) = (x^2y)z$
b. $3x + 3y = 3(x + 3y)$
c. $3y + 7x = 7x + 3y$
d. $a(1/a) = 1$, if $a \neq 0$

5. Choose the statement that is *not true* for all real numbers.

a. $x + (-x) = 1$
b. $(2x)(1) = 2x$
c. $b(1/b) = 1$, if $b \neq 0$
d. $7y + 0 = 7y$

ANSWERS: 1.b., 2.d., 3.a., 4.b., 5.a.

Algebra Skills

The mathematics necessary to master this skill is very similar to the mathematics needed for Skill I.C.6; thus, the steps will be essentially the same.

II.C.2.
The student will determine whether a particular number is among the solutions of a given equation or inequality.

STEP 1. Replace the variable in each of the three equations or inequalities with the constant given as the solution.

STEP 2. Follow the order of operations given in Skill 1.C.2 to simplify.

STEP 3. Check to see if the resulting statement is true.

STEP **4.** If it is, then the constant is a solution. If it is not, the constant is *not* a solution.

(*Note:* $|-3|$ is read "absolute value of negative 3." The absolute value of any constant is always a positive number. $|-3| = 3$ and $|3| = 3$.

Example **1:** For each of the statements below, determine whether $x = -1$ is a solution.

   i. $x^2 + 2x + 1 = 0$
  ii. $|x| < 0$
 iii. $2x + 3 = x + 2$

Solution:

i. $x^2 + 2x + 1 = 0$

$(-1)^2 + 2(-1) + 1 = 0$	(1) Replace the variable with the constant.
$[1 + (-2) + 1 = 0]$	(2) Simplify using order of operations.
Does $0 = 0$?	(3) Check to see if the statement is true.
-1 is a solution to i.	(4) Answer.

ii. $|x| < 0$

$|-1| < 0$	(1) Replace the variable with the constant.
$[|-1| = 1]$	(2) Simplify.
Does $1 < 0$?	(3) Check to see if the statement is true.
-1 is *not* a solution to ii.	(4) Answer.

iii. $2x + 3 = x + 2$

$2(-1) + 3 = -1 + 2$	(1) Replace the variable with the constant.
$[-2 + 3 = 1] \ [-1 + 2 = 1]$	(2) Simplify using order of operations.
$1 = 1$	(3) Check to see if the statement is true.
-1 is a solution to iii.	(4) Answer.

Correct response: i. and iii.

Algebra Skills

1. For each of the statements below, determine whether $x = 8$ is a solution.

       i. $x^2 - 4x + 16 = 0$
       ii. $|2x - 1| > 9$
       iii. $4x + 2 = 34$

   a. iii. only
   b. i. and iii. only
   c. ii. and iii. only
   d. i., ii., and iii.

2. For each of the statements below, determine whether $x = \frac{1}{4}$ is a solution.

       i. $4x^2 - 5x + 1 = 0$
       ii. $4x + 3 < 10 - 8x$
       iii. $|x + 2| < 3$

   a. ii. only
   b. ii. and iii. only
   c. i. and iii. only
   d. i., ii., and iii.

3. For each of the statements below, determine whether $x = -5$ is a solution.

       i. $(x + 1)(x + 5) = 0$
       ii. $x^2 + 25 = 0$
       iii. $|x| < 4$

   a. i. only
   b. i. and ii. only
   c. i. and iii. only
   d. i., ii., and iii.

4. For each of the statements below, determine whether $x = \frac{4}{5}$ is a solution.

       i. $5x + 6 > 10x + 1$
       ii. $x^2 - 2x + 6 = 6$
       iii. $15x - 16 = 4$

   a. i. only
   b. i. and ii. only
   c. i. and iii. only
   d. ii. and iii. only

5. For each of the statements below, determine whether $x = 0$ is a solution.

       i. $x^2 - 3x + 2 > 0$
       ii. $|3x - 5| = 5$
       iii. $(x + 1)(2x + 6) = 6$

   a. i. only
   b. i. and iii. only
   c. ii. and iii. only
   d. i., ii., and iii.

ANSWERS: 1.c., 2.d., 3.a., 4.a., 5.d.

Algebra Skills

II.C.3.
The student will recognize statements and conditions of proportionality and variation.

One of two types of variation will be given in each word problem. First decide what type of variation is required, then set up a ratio that mathematically represents the conditions. Listed below are the steps for solving a direct variation problem.

STEP 1. Identify as direct variation
(a) when the problem states a direct variation exists or states that a variable is directly proportional to another variable;
(b) by observing that if one quantity increases the other quantity increases or if one decreases the other quantity decreases.

STEP 2. Write one fraction with like units. Write a second fraction with the other set of like units. Be careful to put the numbers of one relationship in the numerators and the numbers in the second relationship in the denominators.

STEP 3. Set the two fractions equal to each other.

STEP 4. Check the answer with the multiple-choice responses in the problem.

STEP 5. If it does not match, find the cross product of the answer (for example, $a/b = c/d$, $ad = bc$ is the cross product).

STEP 6. Then find the cross product of the responses. Choose the response that matches.

Example **1:** Kim owns five shares of stock and receives $12 per year in dividends. If s represents the stock shares, how many shares of stock would she need to own to receive $24?

    a. $^{s}/_{5} = {}^{24}/_{12}$
    b. $^{s}/_{5} = {}^{12}/_{24}$
    c. $^{5}/_{24} = {}^{12}/_{s}$
    d. $^{5}/_{12} = {}^{24}/_{s}$

Solution:

It is a direct variation problem.

$$\frac{\text{shares}}{\text{shares}} = \frac{5}{s}$$

$$\frac{\text{dividends}}{\text{dividends}} = \frac{12}{24}$$

$$\frac{5}{s} = \frac{12}{24}$$

Answer doesn't match a, b, c, d.

Answer: $12s = 120$

Choice "a."

If $\dfrac{s}{5} = \dfrac{24}{12}$, then $12s = 120$.

Choice "a" is the solution.

(1) When the shares increase, the dividends increase.

(2) Write the fractions with like units.

(3) Set the fractions equal.

(4) Check answer with responses.

(5) Find the cross product of the answer.

(6) Find the cross product of the responses.

Example **2:** Suppose x varies directly as the square of z and $x = 5$ when $z = 4$. Select the correct statement to find x when $z = 3$.

    a. $4x = 5$
    b. $16x = 45$
    c. $3x = 20$
    d. $9x = 80$

Solution:

It is a direct variation problem (1) given in the problem.

$$\frac{x}{x} = \frac{5}{x} \qquad \frac{z^2}{z^2} = \frac{(4)^2}{(3)^2}$$ (2) Write fractions with the units.

$$\frac{5}{x} = \frac{16}{9}$$ (3) Set the fractions equal. *(Continued)*

Algebra Skills

(Cont'd)	Answers not in right form.	(4) Check the answers with the responses.
	$16x = 45$	(5) Cross multiply.
	Matches response "b."	(6) Match the responses.

The following steps can be used to solve the second type of problem, inverse variation.

STEP **1.** Identify as inverse variation
(a) when the problem specifically states an inverse variation exists;
(b) by observing that as one quantity increases the second quantity decreases, or vice versa.

STEP **2.** Write one fraction with like units. Write a second fraction with the other set of like units. Be careful to put the terms of one relationship in the numerators and the terms of the second relationship in the denominators.

STEP **3.** Set one fraction equal to the *reciprocal* of the other fraction.

STEP **4.** Check this answer with the multiple choice responses in the problem. If it does not match, find the cross product of the answer. Then find the cross product of the responses. Choose the response that matches.

Example **3:** A certain project can be completed by 5 workers in 31 days. In order to finish the project sooner, the company plans to hire additional workers. If w represents the number of workers, select the correct statement of the condition if the job needs to be finished in 28 days.

a. $\dfrac{w}{31} = \dfrac{28}{5}$

b. $\dfrac{31}{5} = \dfrac{28}{w}$

c. $\dfrac{5}{w} = \dfrac{28}{31}$

d. $\dfrac{31}{28} = \dfrac{5}{w}$

Solution:

It is an inverse variation problem.

(1) If one quantity increases, the other quantity decreases.

$\dfrac{\text{workers}}{\text{workers}} = \dfrac{5}{w}$

(2) Write the fractions with like units.

$\dfrac{\text{days}}{\text{days}} = \dfrac{31}{28}$

$\dfrac{5}{w} = \dfrac{28}{31}$

(3) Set one fraction equal to the reciprocal of the other fraction.

The answer matches "c."

(4) Check answer with the responses.

1. The speed, s, or a pulley varies inversely to its diameter. If a pulley with a 2-inch diameter runs at 15 revolutions per minute, select the correct statement of the condition when the diameter is 7 inches.

a. $\dfrac{15}{s} = \dfrac{2}{7}$

b. $7s = 30$

c. $\dfrac{s}{7} = \dfrac{2}{15}$

d. $2s = 105$

2. Last year, Mr. Jones harvested 2,000 watermelons on a 17-acre plot. Let w represent the number of watermelons that may be harvested on a 35-acre plot. Select the correct statement of the given condition.

a. $\dfrac{2000}{w} = \dfrac{17}{35}$

II.C.3.
Sample Items

Algebra Skills

b. $\dfrac{2000}{w} = \dfrac{35}{17}$

c. $\dfrac{w}{35} = \dfrac{17}{2000}$

d. $\dfrac{w}{2000} = \dfrac{17}{35}$

3. Three machines can process 9 jobs in 4 days. Let x represent the number of jobs these machines can complete in a 30-day month. Select the correct statement of the given condition.

   a. $9x = 30$

   b. $\dfrac{4}{9} = \dfrac{x}{30}$

   c. $4x = 270$

   d. $\dfrac{30}{4} = \dfrac{9}{x}$

4. Suppose that x is directly proportional to the cube of y. If $x = 10$ when $y = 2$, select the correct statement to find y when $x = 50$.

   a. $y^3 = 40$
   b. $y = 10$
   c. $5y = 2$
   d. $y^3 = 30$

5. The distance between two cities is held constant while the rate and time may change. Let r represent the rate. If the rate is 40 miles per hour when the time is 3 hours, select the correct statement of the condition when the time is 7 hours.

   a. $\dfrac{3}{40} = \dfrac{7}{r}$

   b. $\dfrac{r}{7} = \dfrac{40}{3}$

   c. $\dfrac{r}{40} = \dfrac{3}{7}$

   d. $\dfrac{40}{3} = \dfrac{7}{r}$

ANSWERS: 1.c., 2.a., 3.c., 4.a., 5.c.

Questions on this skill will ask you to identify a graph when you are given certain conditions or to identify the conditions when you are given a coordinate graph. Both types of questions require a knowledge of the Cartesian coordinate system.

The system consists of four quadrants divided by a horizontal line called the x-axis and a vertical line called the y-axis. The place where the x-axis and y-axis cross is called the origin.

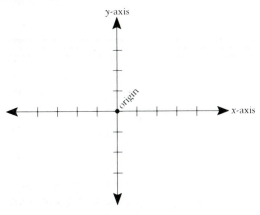

Section 4-4, cont'd

Algebra Skills

II.C.4.
The student will identify regions of the coordinate plane that correspond to specific conditions and vice versa.

An ordered pair, (x,y), is plotted by beginning at the origin. If the x coordinate is positive, move right from the origin x units. If x is negative, move left from the origin x units. From this new position, use the y coordinate to move up (positive) or down (negative) y units.

Example **1:** Graph the point (−4,3). Since the x coordinate is −4, move left four units from the origin. To graph the y coordinate of 3, move three units up from the new position.

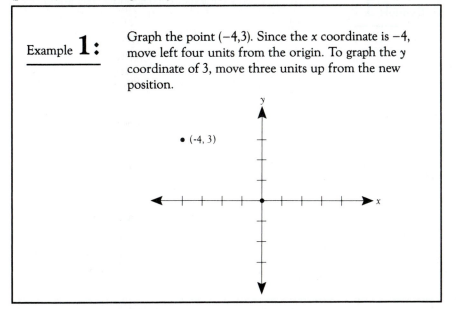

A set, or ordered pair, whose graph is a line is called a linear relation. To recognize what linear relations identify a region of the coordinate plane where there is no shaded area, do the following:

STEP **1.** Identify the number of lines that are graphed. Check responses to make sure that number of equations are listed. Eliminate any responses that do not match the number of lines.

Algebra Skills

STEP **2.** Identify the type of line(s) that is(are) graphed by

(a) vertical: $x =$ ____
(b) horizontal: $y =$ ____
(c) oblique: An equation with x and ys.

Check remaining responses and eliminate any that do not match.

STEP **3.** Identify at least two points on each line. Substitute them into the remaining responses to see if they satisfy the conditions. For example:

(a) vertical: $x = (x\text{-coordinate})$
(b) horizontal: $y = (y\text{-coordinate})$
(c) oblique: Substitute the point into the equation to see if it satisfies the equation.

Check remaining responses and eliminate any that do not match.

Example **1:** Identify the conditions that correspond to the graph.

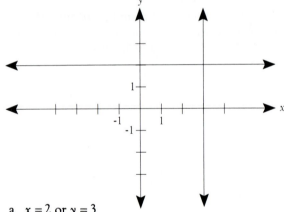

a. $x = 2$ or $y = 3$
b. $x + y = 2$
c. $x = 3$ or $y = 2$
d. $3x + y = 9$ or $y = 2$

Solution:	There are two lines.	(1) Eliminate "b."
	$x =$ \qquad $y =$	(2) One vertical, one horizontal; eliminate "d."
	$x = 3$ $y = 2$	(3) Choose (3,0) on the vertical line. Choose (3,2) on the horizontal line; eliminate "a."

The answer is "c."

Example 2: Identify the condition that corresponds to the graph.

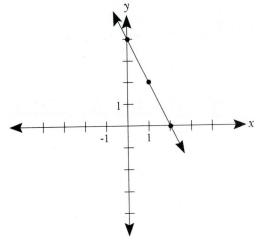

a. $y = 4$
b. $x - 2y = 4$
c. $2x + y = 4$
d. $x = 2$

Solution: There is one line.   (1) All responses are valid.

The line is oblique.   (2) Eliminate "a." and "d."

b. $x - 2y = 4$ (3) Choose $(0,4)$ and substitute
   $0 - 2(4) = 4$ into remaining responses.
   $-8 \neq 4$

c. $2x + y = 4$
   $2(0) + 4 = 4$
   $4 = 4$

The answer is "c."

Algebra Skills

To recognize what linear relations identify a *shaded* area of the coordinate plane, do as follows:

STEP **1.** Identify the number of lines that are graphed. Check responses to make sure that number of equations are listed. Eliminate any response that does not fit conditions.

STEP **2.** Identify the type of line(s) that is(are) graphed by

(a) solid vertical line $x \geq$ ____ or $x \leq$ ____;

(b) dotted vertical line $x >$ ____ or $x <$ ____;

(c) solid horizontal line $y \geq$ ____ or $y \leq$ ____;

(d) dotted horizontal line $y >$ ____ or $y <$ ____;

(e) solid oblique line. An inequality with xs and ys with $\geq$ or $\leq$.

(f) dotted oblique line. An inequality with xs and ys with $<$ or $>$.

Check responses and eliminate any that do not fit conditions.

STEP **3.** Identify a point on each line. Substitute it into the remaining responses to see if it satisfies an *equation* derived from the inequality.

Check responses and eliminate any that do not fit condition.

STEP **4.** Choose a point in the shaded region. Substitute into the remaining responses (using the inequality form). Eliminate any response that is not satisfied by this point.

Algebra Skills

Example **3**: Identify the conditions that correspond to the shaded region of the plane.

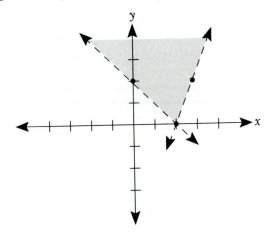

a. $x = 2$ and $y = 2$
b. $2x - y < 4$ and $x + y > 2$
c. $2x - y \leq 4$
d. $2x - y > 4$ and $x + y < 2$

Solution:

There are two lines.

(1) Eliminate "c." because only one condition.

The lines are both oblique.

(2) Eliminate "a." since those represent vertical and horizontal lines.

$2x - y = 4$ $x + y = 2$ (3) Choose the point (2,0) and
$2(2) - 0 = 4$ $2 + 0 = 2$ substitute in derived
        $4 = 4$ $2 = 2$ equation. Keep both "b."
                                           and "d."

b. $2x - y < 4$ and $x + y > 2$ (4) Choose the point (2,2) in
   $2(2) - 2 < 4$ $2 + 2 > 2$ the shaded region and
      $4 - 2 < 4$ substitute into responses
         $2 < 4$ $4 > 2$ "b." and "d."

yes

d. $2x - y > 4$ and $x + y < 2$
   $2(2) - 2 > 4$ $2 + 2 < 2$
      $4 - 2 > 4$
         $2 > 4$ $4 < 2$
no

The solution is "b."

Algebra Skills

Example **4:** Identify the conditions that correspond to the shaded region of the plane.

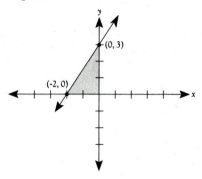

a. $2y - 3x \leq 6$ and $x \geq -2$ and $y \geq 0$
b. $2y - 3x \geq 6$
c. $2y - 3x \leq 6$
d. $2y - 3x \leq 6$ and $x \geq -2$ and $y \leq 3$

Solution: There are three lines.   (1) Eliminate "b." and "c."

(*Note*: The graph shows only one visible line, but if it were the only condition, the shading would cover *all* of one side of the line, like)

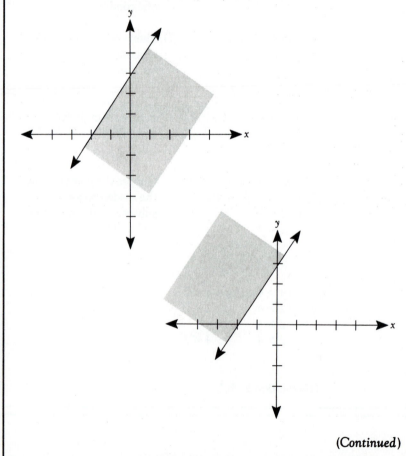

(*Continued*)

Algebra Skills

(*Cont'd.*)   Of the three lines that are bounding the shading, there is
1. one vertical:
   $x \geq$ _____ or $x \leq$ _____
2. one horizontal:
   $y \geq$ _____ or $y \leq$ _____
3. one oblique:
   x and y s $\leq$ or $\geq$

(2) Both "a." and "d." are still valid responses.

a. $\begin{array}{cc} 2y - 3x = 6 & 2y - 3x = 6 \\ 2(0) - 3(-2) = 6 & 2(0) - 3(-2) = 6 \\ 6 = 6 & 6 = 6 \end{array}$

and $\begin{array}{cc} y = 0 & \text{and} \quad y = 3 \\ 0 = 0 & 0 \neq 3 \\ (\text{Yes}) & (\text{No}) \end{array}$

(3) Choose the point $(-2,0)$ on the oblique line and horizontal line and substitute in the derived *equations* from "a." and "d."

The solution is "a."

(*Note:* The point $(0,3)$ could have also been chosen and substituted into the equations of the oblique line and the vertical line.)

To identify the graph when given the conditions, do as follows:

STEP 1.   If the conditions are inequalities, look for shaded regions. If the conditions are equations, look for lines. Eliminate any response that does not match.

STEP 2.   Choose point(s) on each line and substitute it(them) into the given equation. If the condition is an inequality, substitute the point into an *equation* derived from the inequality. Eliminate any response that does not match.

STEP 3.   If the region is shaded, choose a point in the shaded region and substitute into the inequalities. Eliminate any response that does not match the conditions.

Algebra Skills

Example **5:** Which shaded region identifies the portion of the plane that corresponds to the conditions?

$$5x - y < 10 \text{ and } x + y > -4$$

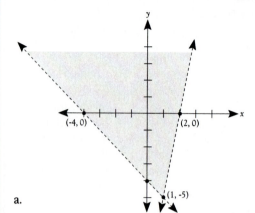

a.

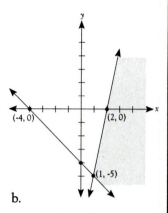

b.

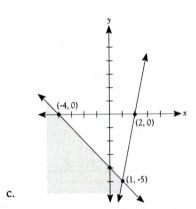

c.

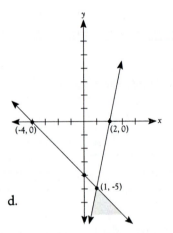

d.

Solution:

Two oblique dotted lines with shading.

(1) All the responses are valid.

$$
\begin{array}{ll}
5x - y = 10 & x + y = -4 \\
5(1) - (-5) = 10 & 1 + (-5) \\
10 = 10 & -4 = -4 \\
\text{(Yes)} & \text{(Yes)}
\end{array}
$$

(2) The point $(1, -5)$ is on both lines. All the responses are valid.

Try $(0,0)$ in Response A:

$$
\begin{array}{ll}
5x - y < 10 & x + y > -4 \\
5(0) - (0) < 10 & 0 + 0 > -4 \\
0 < 10 & 0 > -4 \\
\text{(Yes)} & \text{(Yes)}
\end{array}
$$

(3) Choose a point in the shaded area.

The solution is "a."

1. Identify the conditions that correspond to the graph.

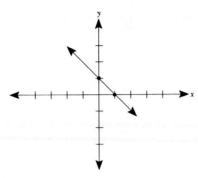

Algebra Skills

II.C.4.
Sample Items

   a. $x = 1$ and $y = 2$
   b. $x + y = 1$
   c. $x - y = 1$
   d. $x + y \leq 1$

2. Which shaded region identifies the portion of the plane that corresponds to the conditions $x \leq 4$ and $y \geq 3$?

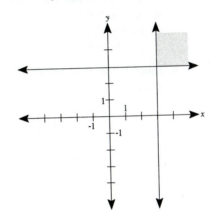

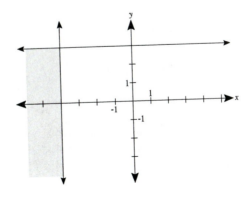

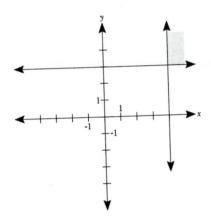

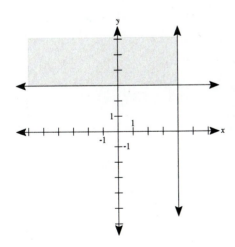

Algebra Skills

3. Identify the conditions that correspond to the graph.

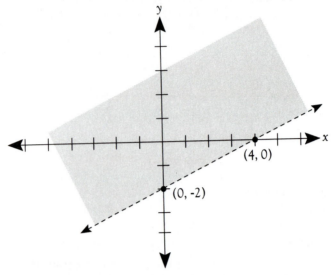

a. $x - 2y > 4$ and $x \geq 0$ and $y \geq 0$
b. $2x - y > 4$
c. $2x - y < 4$
d. $x - 2y < 4$

4. Identify the conditions that correspond to the shaded region of the plane.

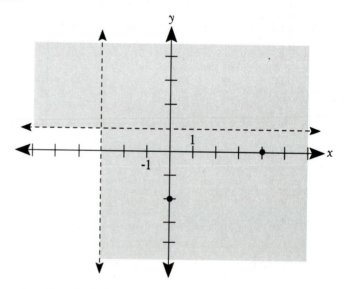

a. $x \geq -3$ and $y \geq 1$
b. $x > -3$ and $y < 1$
c. $x > -3$ or $y > 1$
d. $x \geq 1$ or $y > -3$

ANSWERS: 1.b., 2.c., 3.d., 4.c.

The stimulus will give an equation or inequality, and ask for an equivalent equation or inequality that could be derived from the original stimulus by a single operation. If the stimulus is an equation, look at each response while asking the following questions:

Algebra Skills

III.C.1.
The student will use applicable properties to select equivalent equations and inequalities.

STEP **1.** Could the same number or expression be added or subtracted to both sides of the equation to get this response?

STEP **2.** Could the same number or expression be multiplied or divided to both sides of the equation to get this response?

STEP **3.** Have two equations been combined into a single equivalent one?

STEP **4.** Are the two sides of the equation unchanged (identical) except for now being located on opposite sides.

If the answer to any of these questions is yes, that response represents an equivalent equation.

Example **1:** Choose the equation equivalent to the following:

$3x + 2 = 2x - 7$

a. $3x + 5 = 2x$
b. $6x + 2 = 4x - 7$
c. $2x - 7 = 3x + 2$
d. $2 = x - 7$

Solution:

$(3x + 2) + 3 = 2x - 7 + 3$ (1) To obtain the left side of
$3x + 5 = 2x - 4$ response "a.," add 3 to both sides.

Eliminate "a."

$(3x + 2) + 3x = (2x - 7) + 3x$ (1) To obtain the left side of
$6x + 2 = 5x - 7$ response "b.," add $3x$ to both sides.

Eliminate "b."

$3x + 2 = 2x - 7$ (4) The two sides are
$2x - 7 = 3x + 2$ switched. Change sides
                         $3x + 2 = 2x - 7$.

Choice "c." is the correct solution.

Algebra Skills

If the stimulus is an inequality, look at each response while asking the following questions:

STEP **1.** Could the same number or expression be added or subtracted to each part of the inequality to get the response?

STEP **2.** Could the same number be multiplied or divided to each part of the inequality to get the response: (*Note:* If you divide or multiply by a negative quantity, the inequality sign is "flipped".)

STEP **3.** Have two inequalities been combined into a single inequality?

Example **2:** Choose the inequality equivalent to the following:

$-4x < 16$

  a. $x < -4$
  b. $x > 4$
  c. $x > -4$
  d. $x < 4$

Solution: $-4x < 16$ (2) Look at the responses. They have been obtained by dividing both sides by -4.

$$\frac{-4x}{-4} < \frac{16}{-4}$$

$$x > -4$$

The solution is "c."

Algebra Skills

Example **3:** Choose the inequality equivalent to the following:

$$-4 < 3x - 8 < 9$$

a. $-12 < 3x < 1$
b. $4 < 3x < 17$
c. $-4 > 3x > 17$
d. $-5 < 3x - 8$

Solution:

$$
\begin{array}{ccccc}
-4 & < & 3x - 8 & < & 9 \\
+8 & & +8 & & +8 \\
\hline
4 & < & 3x & < & 17
\end{array}
$$

(1) Look at the responses. They have been obtained by adding 8 to all parts of the inequality.

The solution is "b."

---

1. Choose the inequality equivalent to the following:

$$2x + 4 > 6$$

a. $2x > 2$
b. $2x > 10$
c. $2x > -2$
d. $2x < 2$

III.C.1.
Sample Items

2. If $x > 0$, then $3x < x^2 + 4x$ is equivalent to which of the following?

a. $3 < x + 4x$
b. $3 > x + 4$
c. $x < x^2 + 4$
d. $3 < x + 4$

3. Choose the equation equivalent to the following:

$$4x + 16 = 8 - 2x$$

a. $4x = 8 - 2x$
b. $6x + 16 = 8$
c. $4x + 24 = -2x$
d. $2x + 16 = 8$

4. Choose the inequality equivalent to the following:

$$6 < 2x + 3 < 8$$

a. $9 < 2x < 11$
b. $0 < 2x - 3 < 8$
c. $3 < 2x < 5$
d. $-2 < 2x + 3$

Algebra Skills

5. Choose the inequality equivalent to the following:

$$-5x > 25$$

a. $x > 5$
b. $x > -5$
c. $x < 5$
d. $x < -5$

ANSWERS: 1.a., 2.d., 3.b., 4.c., 5.d.

IV.C.1.
The student will solve real-world problems involving the use of variables, aside from commonly used geometric variables.

The word problems in this skill will be taken from a context of business, social studies, industry, education, economics, environmental studies, arts, physical science, sports, or consumer relations. It would be impossible to list specific techniques for solving all the different types of problems that might occur. However, the general guidelines for solving word problems given in Skill IV.A.1. will help you analyze the problems in this skill.

More specifically, two types of problems that may be asked include (A) problems involving direct and inverse variation or (B) problems involving formulas.

Variation problems were already discussed in Skill II.C.3. Therefore, the text in this section will concentrate on how to solve word problems involving formulas. The following steps can be used to solve this type of problem:

STEP 1. Read the problem and write down the formula. Pay close attention to the variables.

STEP 2. Reread the problem to identify any numbers that are given for certain variables.

STEP 3. Substitute the numerical values in the formula.

STEP 4. Solve for the unknown variable.

Algebra Skills

Example **1:** If the basic structure of a rocket has mass, m; its payload has mass, p; and its fuel has mass, f; then the mass ratio, R, of the rocket is computed from the formula:

$$R = \frac{m + p + f}{m + p}$$

How much fuel must be loaded in a rocket whose basic structure and payload each has a mass of 2 tons if the mass ratio of the rocket is to be 8?

Solution:

$R = \dfrac{m + p + f}{m + p}$	(1) Write the formula.
$m = 2, p = 2, R = 8$	(2) Identify the values given for the variables.
$8 = \dfrac{2 + 2 + f}{2 + 2}$	(3) Substitute.
$8 = \dfrac{4 + f}{4}$	(4) Solve.
$32 = 4 + f$	(5) Multiply by 4.
$28 = f$	(6) Add (-4).

1. The formula $I = prt$ is used to compute simple interest. What is the amount of the principal (p) if the rate (r) is 12%, the time (t) of the loan is 4 years, and the interest (I) paid is $96?

   a. $2
   b. $48
   c. $200
   d. $4,800

   IV.C.1.
   Sample Items

2. The rate of flow of water under a fixed pressure emerging from a circular pipe is directly proportional to the square of the radius of the pipe. If a pipe with a 4-inch radius emits 384 cubic inches of water per second, at what rate will a pipe with a $2\frac{1}{2}$-inch radius emit water under the same pressure?

   a. 150
   b. 240
   c. 340
   d. 600

Algebra Skills

3. An equation for finding cost (C) of electricity for an electrical appliance is $C = \dfrac{W \times H \times A}{1000}$.

   What is the cost of operating a lamp with a 200-watt (W) bulb that burns 120 hours (H) at a rate of 8 cents (A) per kilowatt hour?

   a. $ 1.92
   b. $ 19.20
   c. $ .33
   d. $192

4. Kinetic energy is computed from the formula $KE = .5mv^2$. If you weigh 120 pounds (m) and are running at 10 feet per second (v), what is your kinetic energy in terms of foot pounds?

   a. 300
   b. 600
   c. 1,200
   d. 6,000

5. Charles's Law states that when the temperature is kept constant, the volume V of a mass of gas is proportional to the absolute temperature. If the volume is one liter when the temperature is 200°C, what is the volume when the temperature is 150°C?

   a. $\dfrac{3}{5}$ liter

   b. $\dfrac{3}{4}$ liter

   c. $\dfrac{4}{3}$ liters

   d. 1.5 liters

ANSWERS: 1.c., 2.a., 3.a., 4.d., 5.b.

IV.C.2.
The student will solve problems that involve the structure and the logic of algebra.

Writing equations or inequalities in algebraic symbols is aided by recognizing some key words. Since the variable will always be identified in the problem, the following key words will supply the symbols for translating the verbal problems into equations and inequalities:

Operation	Key Words
Addition	Sum, plus, increased by, total, more than, add
Subtraction	Difference, less than, decreased by, decrease, subtract, minus
Multiplication	Product, times, of
Division	Quotient, divided by

The equal sign (=) is written in place of such key words as "is," "was," or "equal." The key words "greater than" and "less than" are replaced by their respective symbols > and <.

To choose the algebraic description that is equivalent to the verbal description:

Algebra Skills

STEP 1. Read the problem. Identify the variable name and what it represents.

STEP 2. Identify the sentence(s) that represent the part of the problem that is to be translated.

STEP 3. Use the key words to write the equation or inequality.

Use these steps to solve the following number problems:

Example 1: The sum of a number, x, and 8 is 15. What equation could be used to find the number?

Solution:

x is the variable that represents a number.	(1) Identify the variable.
The sum (+) of a number x, and 8 is (=) 5.	(2) Identify the sentence.
$x + 8 = 5$	(3) Write the equation.

Example 2: The difference between a number, N, and three more than twice the number is eight more than the number. What equation could be used to find the number?

Solution:

N is the variable that represents a number.	(1) Identify the variable.
The difference (−) between a number (N) and 3 more than (+) twice the number (2N) is (=) 8 more than (+) the number (N).	(2) Identify the sentence.
$N - (2N + 3) = N + 8$	(3) Write the equation.

Algebra Skills

Example **3:** The square of a number, x, is greater than the sum of the number and 12. What inequality could be used to find x, the number?

Solution:		
x is the variable that represents a number.	(1) Identify the variable.	
The square of a number (x^2), x, is greater than ($>$) the sum (+) of the number (x) and 12.	(2) Identify the sentence.	
$x^2 > x + 12$	(3) Write the inequality.	

Consecutive integer problems are special types of number problems. When the problem asks for consecutive integers, let the variable represent the first consecutive integer. To find the next consecutive integer, add 1 to the previous integer until you have the correct number of integers. For example, if x were the first consecutive integer, $x + 1$ would be the second. Similarly, $x + 1 + 1$, or $x + 2$, would represent the third consecutive integer, and so on.

To find consecutive *even* or *odd* integers, let the given variable represent the first integer. Then add 2 to each previous integer to find the next one. For example, if x were the first consecutive even or odd integer, $x + 2$ would be the second and $x + 2 + 2$, or $x + 4$, would be the third consecutive integer.

Example **4:** There are three consecutive odd integers such that twice the difference of the second integer and 3 is less than the sum of the first and third. What inequality could be used to find the integers if N is the smallest integer?

Solution:		
N = smallest integer $N + 2$ = second odd integer $N + 4$ = third odd integer	(1) Identify the variable. (Add 2 to the previous integer for odds.)	
Twice (2) the difference (−) of the second integer ($N + 2$) and 3 is less than ($<$) the sum (+) of the first (N) and third ($N + 4$).	(2) Identify the sentence.	
$2(N + 2 − 3) < N + N + 4$	(3) Write the inequality.	

Another special type of verbal problem is a digit problem. For example, in the number 23 (twenty-three), the 2 is the tens digit and the 3 is the units digit. The value of this number in expanded notation is $2 \times 10 + 3 \times 1$. Similarly, problems of this type on the CLAST will contain variables that represent specific digits. For example, "Which equations should be used to find the number if the number's digits are x and y?" One method is to let x respresent the tens digit and y represent the units digit. The number would be $x \cdot 10 + y \cdot 1$ or $10x + y$. The following example illustrates how to write equations for digit problems.

Algebra Skills

Example **5:** The tens digit of a two-digit number is three more than the units digit. If the digits were reversed, the new number would be 27 less than the original number. What equation could be used to find y, the units digit?

Solution:

$y =$ units digit $y + 3 =$ tens digit	(1) Identify the variables given. (Tens digit is 3 more than units digit.)
$10(y + 3) + y =$ original number	
$10y + (y + 3) =$ number with digits reversed	
If the digits were reversed, the new number $[10y + (y + 3)]$ would be (=) 27 less (−) than the original number $[10(y + 3) + y]$.	(2) Identify the sentence.
$10y + (y + 3) =$ $10(y + 3) + y - 27$	(3) Write the equation.

---

1. The square of a number increased by 6 times the number is 27. Which equation should be used to find x, the number?

   a. $x^2 + 6x = 27$
   b. $x^2 + 6x^2 = 27$
   c. $x^2 = 6x + 27$
   d. $2x + 6x = 27$

2. Choose the algebraic equation that is equivalent to the following verbal description:

   The tens digit of a two-digit number is twice the units digit. If the number itself is 18 more than the sum of the digits, what equation could be used to find x, the units digit?

   a. $10x + 2x = x + 2x + 18$
   b. $10x + x = x + 2x + 18$

IV.C.2.
Sample Items

Algebra Skills

c. $10(2x) + x = x + 2x + 18$
d. $2x + x + 18 = x + 2x$

3. Choose the inequality that is equivalent to the following verbal description:

The quotient of a number, n, and 6 is equal to twice the number.

a. $\dfrac{6}{n} = n + 2$

b. $\dfrac{n}{6} = n$

c. $\dfrac{6}{n} = n^2$

d. $\dfrac{n}{6} = 2n$

4. There are three consecutive positive integers such that the product of the first and second integers is less than the square of the third. Which inequality could be used to find n, the smallest integer?

a. $n + (n + 1) < n^2 + 2$
b. $n(n + 1) < (n + 2)^2$
c. $n + n + 2 < n^2 + 2$
d. $n(n + 2) < (n + 4)^2$

5. Choose the algebraic description that is equivalent to the following verbal description:

The difference between three times a number, n, and seven is three more than twice that number.

a. $n - 7 = n + 3$
b. $3(n - 7) = 2(n + 3)$
c. $3n - 7 = 2n + 3$
d. $7 - 3n = 3 + 2n$

6. A two-digit positive number is equal to 12 more than the product of its digits. Which equation should be used to find the number if the number's digits are x and y?

a. $10x + y = xy + 12$
b. $x + y = xy + 12$
c. $10x + y + 12 = xy$
d. $x + y + 12 = xy$

ANSWERS: 1.a., 2.c., 3.d., 4.b., 5.c., 6.a.

To round measurements to a specific unit, use the following steps:

Geometry and Measurement Skills

I.B.1.
The student will round measurements to the nearest given unit of the measuring device used.

STEP **1.** Make sure your measurement is a decimal number. If it is not, change it to a decimal by
(a) using the following chart to identify the number of units needed to exchange units;
(b) writing a fraction using the given number as the numerator and the chart number as the denominator; and
(c) changing the fraction to a decimal.

LENGTH:	1 foot (ft.) = 12 inches (in.)
	1 yard (yd.) = 3 feet (ft.)
	1 yard (yd.) = 36 inches (in.)
WEIGHT:	1 pound (lb.) = 16 ounces (oz.)
	1 ton (t.) = 2,000 pounds (lb.)
CAPACITY:	1 pint (pt.) = 2 cups (c.)
	1 quart (qt.) = 2 pints (pt.)
	1 gallon (gal.) = 4 quarts (qt.)
TIME:	1 minute (min.) = 60 seconds (sec.)
	1 hour (hr.) = 60 minutes (min.)
	1 day (da.) = 24 hours (hr.)
	1 week (wk.) = 7 days (da.)
	1 year (yr.) = 365 days (da.)

STEP **2.** Identify the digit to be rounded.

STEP **3.**
(a) If the digit to the right is less than 5, keep the identified digit. Replace the digits to the right of it with zeros.
(b) If the digit to the right of it is 5 or greater, increase the identified digit by 1. Replace the digits to the right of it with zeros.

**Geometry and
Measurement Skills**

Example **1:**   Round 14.637 feet to the nearest hundredth.

Solution:	14.637	(1)	Measurement is in decimal form.
	14.63̱7	(2)	Identify digit.
	14.640 = 14.64	(3b)	Since 7 > 5, add 1 to 3 and replace with zeros.

Example **2:**   Round 8 yards and 2 feet to the nearest tenth.

Solution: 8 yards, 2 feet   (1)   Convert to decimal form.

(1 yard = 3 feet)   (a)   Use chart.

$8\frac{2}{3}$ (b)   Write a fraction.

8.6666   (c)   Change fraction to a decimal.

8.6̱666   (2)   Identify digit.

8.7000 = 8.7   (3b) Since 6 > 5, add 1 to 6 and replace with zeros.

Example **3:**   Round 5 hours and 15 minutes to the nearest hour.

Solution: 5 hours, 15 minutes   (1)   Convert to decimal form.

(1 hour = 60 minutes)   (a)   Use chart.

$5\frac{15}{60} = 5\frac{1}{4}$ (b)   Write a fraction.

5.25   (c)   Change to a decimal.

5̱.25   (2)   Identify digit.

5.00 = 5   (3a) Since 2 < 5, keep digit and replace with zeros.

**Geometry and
Measurement Skills**

Example **4:** Round 4,376 kilometers to the nearest thousands.

Solution:	4,376	(2)	Identify digit.
	4,000	(3a)	Since 3 < 5, keep the 4 and replace the digits with zeros.

1. Round the measure 21,846 milligrams to the nearest 10 thousand milligrams.

   a. 30,000 mg
   b. 22,000 mg
   c. 21,800 mg
   d. 20,000 mg

2. Round 16.251 milliliters to the nearest tenth milliliter.

   a. 16.25 ml
   b. 16.3 ml
   c. 15 ml
   d. 20 ml

3. Round $14\frac{3}{5}$ tons to the nearest ton.

   a. 14 tons
   b. 15 tons
   c. 20 tons
   d. 2,000 tons

4. Round 10 gallons and 1 quart to the nearest gallon.

   a. 9 gallons
   b. 10 gallons
   c. 11 gallons
   d. 20 gallons

5. Round the temperature to the nearest 10 degrees.

   a. 44°
   b. 50°
   c. 60°
   d. 45°

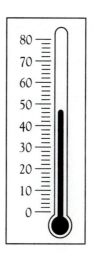

ANSWERS: 1.d., 2.b., 3.b., 4.b., 5.b.

**Geometry and
Measurement Skills**

I.B.2a.
**The student will
calculate distances.**

A polygon is a closed figure composed of line segments. To find the perimeter of a polygon, do as follows:

STEP **1.** Change all lengths to the same unit of measure.* The following chart contains some common conversions:

English	Metric
12 inches (in.) = 1 foot (ft.)	10 millimeters (mm) = 1 centimeter (cm)
3 feet (ft.) = 1 yard (yd.)	10 centimeters (cm) = 1 decimeter (dm)
36 inches (in.) = 1 yard (yd.)	10 decimeters (dm) = 1 meter (m)
5,280 feet (ft.) = 1 mile (mi)	1,000 meters (m) = 1 kilometer (km)

*Sometimes in a right triangle all the sides will not be given. Use the Pythagorean Theorem to find the missing side (see Skill IV.B.2.).

STEP **2.** If necessary, draw the figure and label each side. Add the lengths of all the sides.

3 sides—triangle
4 sides—square, rhombus, rectangle, parallelogram, trapezoid quadrilateral
5 sides—pentagon
6 sides—hexagon
7 sides—heptagon
8 sides—octagon
10 sides—decagon

Geometry and Measurement Skills

Example **1:**   What is the distance, in feet, around this polygon?

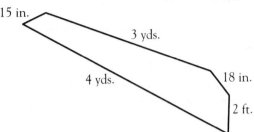

15 in.

3 yds.

4 yds.

18 in.

2 ft.

Solution:

3 yd. = 3 yd.

18 in. $=\dfrac{1}{2}$ yd.

2 ft. $=\dfrac{2}{3}$ yd.

4 yd. $= 4$ yd.

15 in. $=\dfrac{5}{12}$ yd.

$3+\dfrac{1}{2}+\dfrac{2}{3}+4+\dfrac{5}{12}$

$3+\dfrac{6}{12}+\dfrac{8}{12}+4+\dfrac{5}{12}=$

$7\dfrac{19}{12}=8\dfrac{7}{12}$

(1) Change all the lengths to yards.

$\left(\dfrac{18}{36}=\dfrac{1}{2}\quad 36\text{ in.}=1\text{ yd.}\right)$

$\left(\dfrac{2}{3}=\dfrac{2}{3}\quad 3\text{ ft.}=1\text{ yd.}\right)$

$\left(\dfrac{15}{36}=\dfrac{5}{12}\quad 36\text{ in.}=1\text{ yd.}\right)$

(2) Add the sides.

To find the distance around (*circumference*) a circular region, do as follows:

STEP **1.**   Find the radius. (The radius is the length of a segment from the center of the circle to a point on the circle. Its value is one-half the value of the diameter.)

STEP **2.**   Substitute the value of the radius for r in the formula: $C = 2\pi\, r$. If the problem gives you a value of π, substitute it into the formula also.

STEP **3.**   Multiply the value to find C, the circumference.

Example **2:** What is the distance around a circular walk that has a diameter of 8 feet?

Solution: radius $= 8 \times \frac{1}{2} = 4$ feet (1) Find the radius.

$C = 2\pi (4)$ (2) Substitute in formula.

$C = 8\pi$ feet (3) Multiply.

I.B.2a.
Sample Items

1. What is the perimeter of a rectangle whose length is 200 decimeters and whose width is 4 meters?

a. 24 meters
b. 48 meters
c. 240 decimeters
d. 480 meters

2. Find the distance around a right triangle whose hypotenuse is 10 feet and one leg is 6 feet.

a. 22 feet
b. 24 feet
c. 30 square feet
d. 60 square feet

3. What is the distance around a regular hexagon with one side of length 8 meters?

a. 40 meters
b. 48 meters
c. 56 meters
d. 64 meters

4. What is the distance around this polygon?

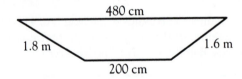

a. 71.4 m
b. 634 cm
c. 1020 cm
d. 1020 sq. cm

ANSWERS: 1.b., 2.b., 3.b., 4.c.

To find the area of a figure, use the following steps:

Geometry and Measurement Skills

STEP **1.** Write the area formula for the figure given that b = base, h = height, and r = radius.

(a) triangle: $A = \frac{1}{2}bh$

(b) rectangle: $A = bh$ or $A = lw$

(c) square: $A = bh$ or $A = S^2$

(d) circle: $A = \pi r^2$, r = radius

I.B.2b.
The student will calculate areas.

STEP **2.** Identify the given variable values and, if necessary, change to the same unit of measure.

STEP **3.** Substitute the values for the variables.

STEP **4.** Perform the computation to get solution in terms of square units.

Example **1:** What is the area of the triangle pictured below?

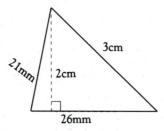

21mm · 2cm · 3cm · 26mm

Solution: $A = \frac{1}{2}bh$ (1) Write the formula.

$b = 26$ mm, $h = 2$ cm   (2) Identify the values of the
$b = 2.6$ cm   variables and change to the same units.

$A = \frac{1}{2}(2.6)(2)$ (3) Substitute in formula.

$A = 2.6$ sq. cm   (4) Multiply.

**Geometry and
Measurement Skills**

To find the surface area of a rectangular solid, use the following steps:

STEP **1.** Write the formula: $SA = 2(lw) + 2(hw) + 2(hl)$.

STEP **2.** Identify the length, width, and height of the rectangular solid. If necessary, change to the same unit of measure.

STEP **3.** Substitute the values for the variables.

STEP **4.** Perform the necessary computation to get answer in square units.

Example **2:** What is the surface area of a rectangular solid that is 2 feet long, 1 foot wide, and 4 feet high?

Solution:	$SA = 2(lw) + 2(hw) + 2(hl)$	(1) Write the formula.
	$l = 2$ ft, $w = 1$ ft, $h = 4$ ft	(2) Identify the length, width, and height.
	$SA = 2(2)(1) + 2(4)(1) + 2(4)(2)$	(3) Substitute into formula.
	$SA = 4 + 8 + 16 =$ 28 square feet	(4) Compute.

**I.B.2b.
Sample Items**

1. What is the area of a square whose side is 8 cm?

   a. 16 sq. cm
   b. 32 cm
   c. 64 cm
   d. 64 sq. cm

2. What is the surface area of the following rectangular solid?

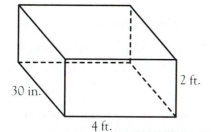

30 in.
2 ft.
4 ft.

 a. 20 sq. ft.
 b. 23 sq. ft.
 c. 46 sq. ft.
 d. 240 sq. ft.

3. What is the area of a circular region whose radius is 3 yards?

 a. 6π sq. yd.
 b. 9π sq. yd.
 c. 6π yd.
 d. 9π yd.

4. What is the area of the triangle pictured below?

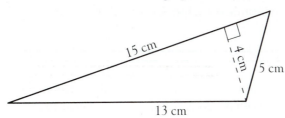

15 cm
4 cm
5 cm
13 cm

 a. 26 sq. cm
 b. 30 sq. cm
 c. 60 sq. cm
 d. 65 sq. cm

5. What is the area of a rectangle whose length is 402 centimeters and whose width is 6 meters?

 a. 2,412 sq. cm
 b. 241.2 m
 c.   24.12 sq. m
 d. 2,412 cm

ANSWERS: 1.d., 2.c., 3.b., 4.b., 5.c.

Geometry and Measurement Skills

I.B.2c.
The student calculates volumes.

To calculate the volume of a specific solid figure, use the following steps:

STEP 1. Write the appropriate formula:

(a) rectangular solid (prism): $V = lwh$

(b) right circular cylinder: $V = \pi r^2 h$

(c) right circular cone: $V = \frac{1}{3} \pi r^2 h$

(d) sphere: $V = \frac{4}{3} \pi r^3$

STEP 2. Identify the given values of the variables and, if necessary, change to the same unit of measure.

STEP 3. Substitute the values for the variables.

STEP 4. Perform the computation to get the solution in terms of *cubic* units.

Example 1: What is the volume of a right circular cylinder with a radius of 6 meters and a height of 3 meters?

Solution:

$V = \pi r^2 h$	(1) Write the formula.
$r = 6m, h = 3m$	(2) Identify the values.
$V = \pi (6)^2 (3)$	(3) Substitute into formula.
$V = \pi (36)(3) = 108\pi$ cu. m	(4) Compute.

Sometimes the volume will be given in the problem. The solution is found by performing two different types of metric-metric conversions. The following chart will help in making conversions when the volume is given in terms of liters:

Geometry and Measurement Skills

$$1 \text{ kiloliter (kL)} = 1,000 \text{ Liters (L)} \quad \text{or } L = \frac{1}{1,000} \text{ kL}$$

$$1 \text{ hectoliter (hL)} = 100 \text{ L} \quad \text{or } L = \frac{1}{100} \text{ hL}$$

$$1 \text{ dekaliter (daL)} = 10 \text{ L} \quad \text{or } L = \frac{1}{10} \text{ daL}$$

$$1 \text{ deciliter (dL)} = .1 \text{L} \quad \text{or } L = 10 \text{ dL}$$

$$1 \text{ centiliter (cL)} = .01 \text{L} \quad \text{or } L = 100 \text{ cL}$$

$$1 \text{ milliliter (mL)} = .001 \text{L} \quad \text{or } L = 1,000 \text{ mL}$$

Example 2: What is the volume in liters of a 10.5-kiloliter gasoline tank?

Solution: The volume, 10.5 kiloliters, is given.
Perform metric-metric conversion of kiloliters to liters.
$10.5 \text{ kL} = 10.5 \times 1,000 = 10,500 \text{ L}$

Other problems will require a conversion of volume in liters to volume in cubic units, or vice versa. The next chart will help in making conversions.

$$1 \text{ L} = 1,000 \text{ cm}^3 \quad \text{or } 1 \text{ cm}^3 = \frac{1}{1,000} \text{ L} = 1 \text{mL}$$

$$1 \text{ L} = 1 \text{ dm}^3 \quad \text{or } 1 \text{ dm}^3 = 1 \text{ L}$$

$$1 \text{ L} = \frac{1}{1,000} \text{ m}^3 \quad \text{or } 1 \text{ m}^3 = 1,000 \text{ L} = 1 \text{kL}$$

Example 3: What is the volume in cubic centimeters of a 2-liter bottle?

Solution: The volume, 2 liters, is given.
Perform metric-metric conversion to change liters to cubic centimeters.

By chart, $1 \text{ L} = 1,000 \text{ cm}^3$
Therefore, $2 \text{ L} = 2,000 \text{ cm}^3$

Geometry and Measurement Skills

Example 4 illustrates a problem in which you must find the volume and then use a conversion to match the equivalent solution.

Example **4:** What is the volume of a rectangular prism with length of 7 m, width of 5 m, and height of 2 m?

　　a. 70 L 　　b. 70 kL 　　c. 700 L 　　d. 700 kL

Solution: $V = lwh$ 　　　　　　(1) Write the formula.

$l = 7, w = 5, h = 2$ 　　(2) Identify the variables.

$V = (7)(5)(2)$ 　　　(3) Substitute the values.

$V = 70 \text{ m}^3$ 　　　　(4) Compute.

Since all the responses are in terms of liters, the solution, 70 m³, must be converted to its equivalent liter form.

By the chart, 1 m³ = 1,000 L
Therefore, 70 m³ = 70,000 L
Since that response is not listed, change liter to kiloliters.
By the chart, 1 kL = 1,000 liters
70,000 L = 70 kL
The answer is "b."

**I.B.2c.
Sample Items**

1. What is the volume in liters of a 485 centiliter thermos?

　a. 485 L
　b. 48.5 L
　c. 4.85 L
　d. .485 L

2. What is the volume of a sphere with a 6-foot diameter?

　a. 9 π sq. ft.
　b. 36 π sq. ft.
　c. 36 π cu. ft.
　d. 288 π cu. ft.

3. What is the volume of a right circular cone that has a radius of 4 cm and a height of 6 cm?

　a. 32 π cm³
　b. 96 π cm³
　c. 32 π cm²
　d. 96 π cm²

4. What is the volume in liters of a container that holds 4,720 cubic centimeters?

　a. 4,720 L
　b. 47.2 L

c. 4.72 L

d. .472 L

5. What is the volume of a right circular cylinder that has a radius of ½ inch and a height of 1½ inches?

a. $\dfrac{3}{8}\pi$ sq. in.

b. $\dfrac{3}{4}\pi$ sq. in.

c. 2π sq. in.

d. $\dfrac{7}{4}\pi$ sq. in.

6. What is the volume of a rectangular solid with a length of 8 dm, width of 5 dm, and a height of 3 dm?

a. 158 dm^2

b. 120 L

c. 39 dm^3

d. 1.2 L

ANSWERS: 1.c., 2.c., 3.a., 4.c., 5.a., 6.b.

This skill requires the knowledge of the relationships that exist between angle measures. These relationships will be listed below, and examples of their use will be provided.

II.B.1.
The student will identify relationships between angle measures.

RELATION **1:** The sum of the three angles of a triangle is equal to 180°.

Example **1:** In △ ABC, what is the value of x?

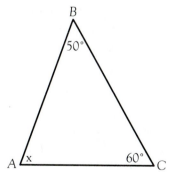

Solution: $x + 50° + 60° = 180°$ Relation 1.

$x + 110° = 180°$ Combine terms.

$x = 70°$ Solve for x.

RELATION **2:** If the base angles of a triangle are congruent, their corresponding sides are congruent. If the sides are congruent, the base angles are congruent.

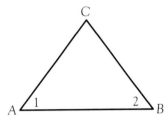

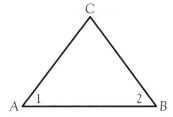

If $\overline{AC} \cong \overline{BC}$, then $\angle A \cong \angle B$ and $1 = 2$.

If $\angle A \cong \angle B$, then $\overline{AC} \cong \overline{BC}$, and $m\overline{AC} = m\overline{BC}$.

(*Note*: Congruent angles will be denoted by arcs.
Congruent sides will be denoted by slashes.)

Example **2:** In △ ABC, if $\overline{AB} \cong \overline{BC}$, what is the value of x?

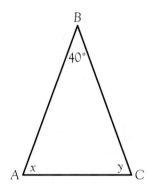

Solution:	$x + 40° + y = 180°$	Relation 1.
	$x = y$	Relation 2.
	$x + 40° + x = 180°$	Substitution.
	$2x + 40° = 180°$	Combine terms.
	$2x = 140°$	Add (−40).
	$x = 70°$	Divide by 2.

Geometry and Measurement Skills

RELATION **3:**   The angles of an equilateral triangle are congruent.

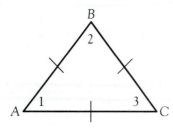

If $\overline{AB} \cong \overline{BC} \cong \overline{AC}$, then $\angle 1 \cong \angle 2 \cong \angle 3$.

Example **3:**   If $\triangle ABC$ is equilateral what is the value of x?

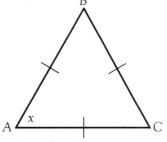

Solution:

$$m\angle BAC + m\angle ABC + m\angle BCA = 180° \quad \text{Relation 1.}$$
$$x \quad + \quad x \quad + \quad x \quad = 180° \quad \text{Relation 3.}$$
$$3x = 180° \quad \text{Combine terms.}$$
$$x = 60° \quad \text{Divide by 3.}$$

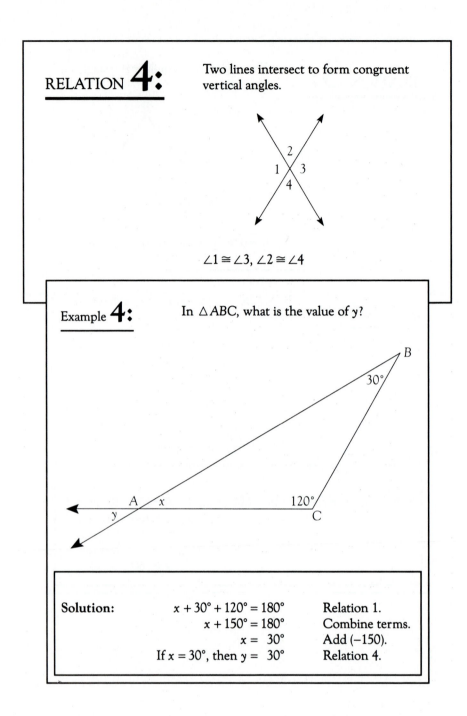

RELATION **4:**   Two lines intersect to form congruent vertical angles.

$\angle 1 \cong \angle 3,\ \angle 2 \cong \angle 4$

Example **4:**   In $\triangle ABC$, what is the value of y?

B

30°

A x

y

120°

C

Solution:	$x + 30° + 120° = 180°$	Relation 1.
	$x + 150° = 180°$	Combine terms.
	$x = 30°$	Add (-150).
	If $x = 30°$, then $y = 30°$	Relation 4.

**Geometry and
Measurement Skills**

RELATION **5:**   Two perpendicular lines form right angles.
The measure of a right angle is 90°.

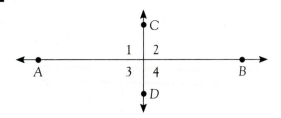

If $AB \perp CD$, then $1 = 90°$, $2 = 90°$, $3 = 90°$,
and $4 = 90°$.

(*Note:* The symbol $\perp$ means "perpendicular
to.")

Example **5:**   In $\triangle ABC$, $AB \perp BC$ and $\overline{AB} \cong \overline{BC}$, find
the value of x.

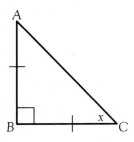

Solution: $m \angle CAB + m \angle ABC + x = 180°$ Relation 1.
$m \angle CAB + 90° + x = 180°$ Relation 5.
$x + 90° + x = 180°$ Relation 2.
$2x + 90° = 180°$ Combine terms.
$2x = 90°$ Add (-90).
$x = 45°$ Divide by 2.

**Geometry and
Measurement Skills**

RELATION **6:** Two angles, the sum of whose measures is
90°, are complementary angles.

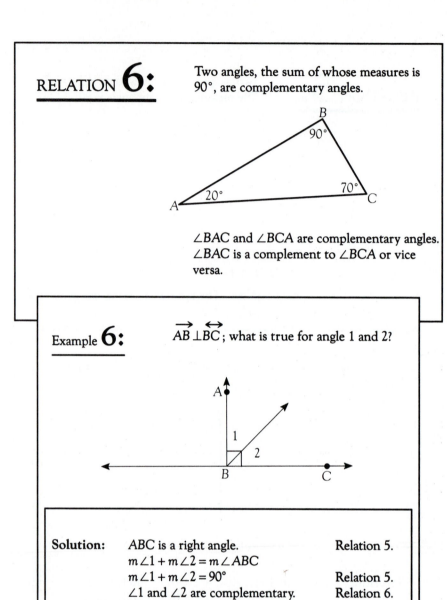

∠BAC and ∠BCA are complementary angles.
∠BAC is a complement to ∠BCA or vice
versa.

Example **6:** $\overrightarrow{AB} \perp \overleftrightarrow{BC}$; what is true for angle 1 and 2?

Solution:	ABC is a right angle.	Relation 5.
	$m\angle 1 + m\angle 2 = m\angle ABC$	
	$m\angle 1 + m\angle 2 = 90°$	Relation 5.
	∠1 and ∠2 are complementary.	Relation 6.

**Geometry and
Measurement Skills**

RELATION **7**:

Two angles, the sum of whose measures is 180°, are supplementary angles. A straight line (angle) is formed by two adjacent supplementary angles.

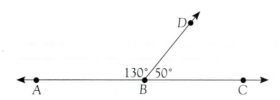

∠ABD and ∠CBD are supplementary, or ∠ABD is a supplement to ∠CBD, and vice versa.

Example **7**:

What is the value of x?

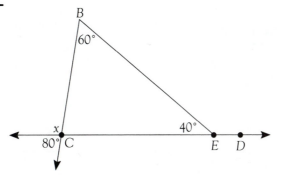

Solution:

$x + 80° = 180°$	Relation 7.
$x = 100°$	Add (−80).

Note: This can also be solved as follows:

$40° + 60° + m\angle BCE = 180°$	Relation 1.
$100° + m\angle BCE = 180°$	Combine terms.
$m\angle BCE = 80°$	Add (−100).

∠BCE and x are supplementary.   Relation 7.

$80° + x = 180°$	
$x = 100°$	Add (−80).

**Geometry and
Measurement Skills**

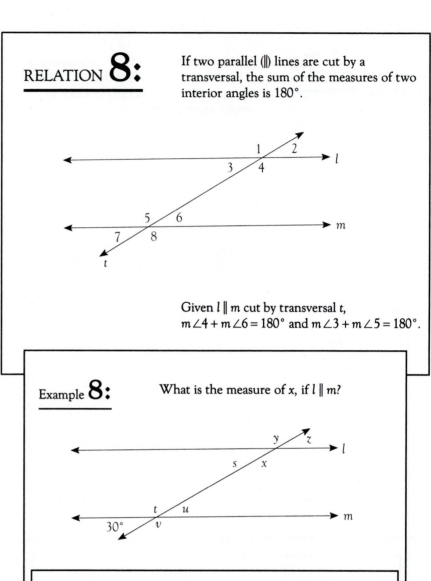

RELATION **8:** If two parallel (‖) lines are cut by a transversal, the sum of the measures of two interior angles is 180°.

Given $l \parallel m$ cut by transversal t,
$m\angle 4 + m\angle 6 = 180°$ and $m\angle 3 + m\angle 5 = 180°$.

Example **8:** What is the measure of x, if $l \parallel m$?

Solution:		
$u = 30°$	Relation 4.
$x + u = 180°$	Relation 8.
$x + 30° = 180°$	Substitution.
$x = 150°$	Add (−30).

RELATION 9: If two parallel (∥) lines are cut by a transversal, alternate interior, alternate exterior, and corresponding angles are congruent (≅).

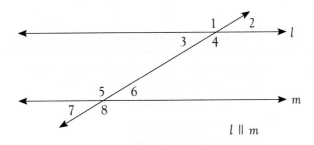

$l \parallel m$

Alternate interior angles are congruent:
∠3 ≅ ∠6, ∠4 ≅ ∠5.
Alternate exterior angles are congruent:
∠1 ≅ ∠8, ∠2 ≅ ∠7.
Corresponding angles are congruent:
∠3 ≅ ∠7, ∠4 ≅ ∠8, ∠1 ≅ ∠5, ∠2 ≅ ∠6.

Example 9: If $l \parallel m$, and $c \parallel d$, what is the measure of x?

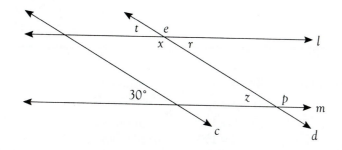

Solution:	$z = 30°$	Relation 9 (corresponding angles on c and d).
	$z = r$	Relation 9 (alternate interior angles on l and m).
	$r = 30°$	Substitution.
	$x + r = 180°$	Relation 7.
	$x + 30° = 180°$	Substitution.
	$x = 150°$	Add (−30).

Geometry and Measurement Skills

RELATION **10:** In a parallelogram, opposite angles are congruent. Adjacent angles are supplementary.

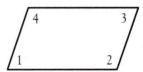

Adjacent angles:

1 and 2 are supplementary.
2 and 3 are supplementary.
3 and 4 are supplementary.
1 and 4 are supplementary.

Opposite angles:

$\angle 1 \cong \angle 3$
$\angle 2 \cong \angle 4$

Example **10:** What is the measure of s if $AB \parallel CD$ and $AC \parallel BD$?

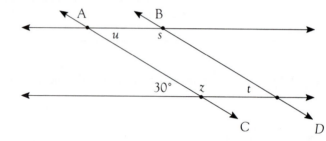

Solution:	$30° + z = 180°$	Relation 7.
	$z = s$	Relation 10.
	$30° + s = 180°$	Substitution.
	$s = 150°$	Add (-30).

To identify the relationships between angle measures, use the following steps:

STEP **1.** Read the given conditions and mark them on the diagrams. (Straight marks for congruent sides, arcs for congruent angles.)

STEP **2.** Use the relations to check the correctness of the responses.

Geometry and Measurement Skills

Example **11:** Given that $AB \parallel DC$ and $AD \parallel BC$, which of the following statements is true for the figure shown?

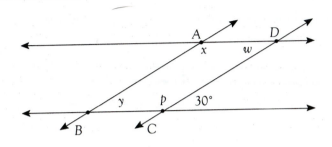

a. $p = 30°$ b. $y = 150°$
c. $w = 150°$ d. $x = 150°$

Solution: Check responses to determine which one is true.

a. $p + 30° = 180°$ Relation 7.
   $p = 150°$ Add (-30).
   Eliminate "a."

b. $p + 30° = 180°$ Relation 7.
   $p + y = 180°$ Relation 9.
   $y = 30°$ Substitution.
   Eliminate "b."

c. $p + 30° = 180°$ Relation 7.
   $p + w = 180°$ Relation 8.
   $w = 30°$ Substitution.
   Eliminate "c."

d. $p + 30° = 180°$ Relation 7.
   $p = 150°$ Substitution.
   $p = x$ Relation 10.
   $x = 150°$ Substitution.

The solution is "d."

1. In $\triangle ABC$, which of the following statements is true? (The measure of angle ABC is x.)

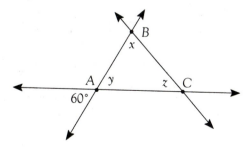

II.B.1.
Sample Items

**Geometry and
Measurement Skills**

a. $y = 60°$

b. $\overline{AB} \cong \overline{BC}$

c. $z = 120°$

d. $y > z$

2. Given that $l \parallel m$, which of the following statements is true? (The measure of angle ABC is y.)

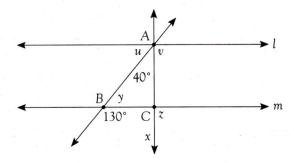

a. $x = 130°$

b. $u = 40°$

c. $u + v = 180°$

d. $AC \perp BC$

3. Given the diagram, which of the following statements is true?

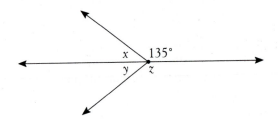

a. $z = 135°$

b. $x = 55°$

c. $x = 45°$

d. $y + z = 90°$

4. If $\overleftrightarrow{AD} \perp \overleftrightarrow{BC}$, which of the following statements is true? (The measure of angle AEB is x.)

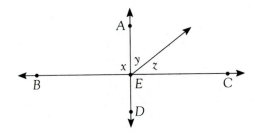

a. $y + z = 90°$
b. $y = z$
c. $x + z = 180°$
d. $x = z$

5. Given parallelogram ABCD, which of the following statements is true?

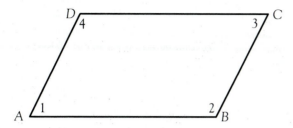

a. $\angle 1 \cong \angle 2$
b. $\angle 4 \cong \angle 2$
c. $\angle 2 \cong \angle 3$
d. $\angle 1$ and $\angle 3$ are supplementary.

Geometry and Measurement Skills

Skill II.B.1. introduced vertical, right, straight, supplementary, complementary, alternate interior, alternate exterior, interior, and corresponding angles. In this skill, those angles plus the following angles will be used to classify angles.

II.B.2.
The student will classify simple plane figures by recognizing their properties.

RELATION **11:** An acute angle has a measure greater than 0°, but less than 90°. An obtuse angle has a measure greater than 90°, but less than 180°.

Example **1:** In triangle ABC, what type of angle is $\angle ABC$?

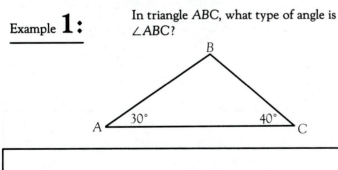

Solution:		
	$30° + 40° + m\angle ABC = 180°$	Relation 1.
	$70° + m\angle ABC = 180°$	Combine terms.
	$m\angle ABC = 110°$	Add (−70).
	$\angle ABC$ is obtuse.	Relation 11.

Geometry and Measurement Skills

Triangles can be classified by the length of their sides or the measure of their angles. The following relation classifies triangles by their sides.

RELATION **12:** A scalene triangle has no equal sides. An isosceles triangle has exactly two equal sides. An equilateral triangle has three equal sides.

Example **2:** In triangle ABC, $\angle 1 \cong \angle 2$. What type of triangle is $\triangle ABC$?

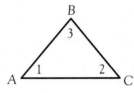

| Solution: | $\overline{AB} \cong \overline{BC}$ | Relation 2. |
| | $\triangle ABC$ is isosceles. | Relation 12. |

Relation 13 classifies triangles by angles.

RELATION **13:** A triangle with three acute angles is an acute triangle. (If the acute angles are congruent, the triangle is an equiangular triangle.) A triangle with a right angle is a right triangle. A triangle with an obtuse angle is an obtuse triangle.

Example **3:** What type of triangle is $\triangle ABC$?

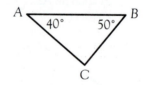

Solution:	$40° + 50° + m\angle ACB = 180°$	Relation 1.
	$90° + m\angle ACB = 180°$	Combine terms.
	$m\angle ACB = 90°$	Add (−90).
	$\angle ACB$ is a right angle.	Relation 5.
	$\triangle ACB$ is a right triangle.	Relation 13.

Quadrilaterals (four-sided figures) can also be classified by their properties. The following relations will classify quadrilaterals by their characteristics.

Geometry and Measurement Skills

RELATION **14:**

A trapezoid is a quadrilateral with only one pair of parallel sides.

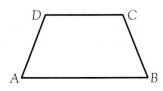

$AB \parallel DC$ $AB \parallel DC$

RELATION **15:**

A parallelogram is a quadrilateral with two pairs of parallel sides. Opposite sides are congruent. Opposite angles are congruent. Diagonals bisect each other.

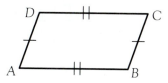

$AB \parallel DC, AD \parallel BC$

RELATION **16:**

A rhombus is a parallelogram whose adjacent sides are congruent and diagonals are perpendicular.

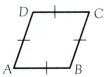

$AB \parallel DC, AD \parallel BC$

RELATION **17:** A rectangle is a parallelogram whose diagonals are congruent.

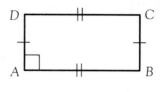

AB ‖ DC, AD ‖ BC

RELATION **18:** A square is a parallelogram whose diagonals are perpendicular and congruent. Adjacent sides are congruent.

AB ‖ DC, AD ‖ BC

Example **3:** Select the geometric figure that possesses <u>all</u> of the following characteristics:

> (i.) parallelogram
> (ii.) diagonals are congruent
> (iii.) diagonals are perpendicular

a. trapezoid
b. rectangle
c. square
d. rhombus

Solution:

(1) Eliminate "a." (trapezoid) because it is not a parallelogram (Relation 14).

(2) Eliminate "d." (rhombus) because its diagonals are not congruent (Relation 16).

(3) Eliminate "b." (rectangle) because its diagonals are not perpendicular (Relation 17).

The solution is "c."

1. Select the geometric figure that possesses all of the following characteristics:

    (i.) quadrilateral
    (ii.) Only two sides are parallel.

  a. rectangle
  b. parallelogram
  c. trapezoid
  d. rhombus

Geometry and Measurement Skills

II.B.2.
Sample Items

2. Which of the following is a right angle?

  a.

  b.

  c.

  d.

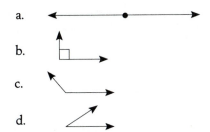

3. Select the geometric figure that possesses all of the following characteristics:

    (i.) triangle
    (ii.) All sides are equal.
    (iii.) All angles are equal.

  a. scalene triangle
  b. isosceles triangle
  c. right triangle
  d. equiangular triangle

4. What type of triangle is $\triangle BDE$?

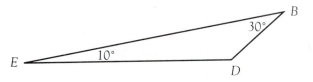

  a. isosceles triangle
  b. obtuse triangle
  c. acute triangle
  d. equilateral triangle

5. If $l \parallel m$, which of the following pairs of angles are supplementary?

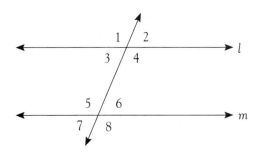

a. 4 and 6
b. 3 and 7
c. 1 and 8
d. 4 and 8

ANSWERS: 1.c., 2.b., 3.d., 4.b., 5.a.

II.B.3.
The student will
recognize similar
triangles and their
properties.

Similar triangles are triangles whose corresponding angles are congruent and whose corresponding side lengths are proportional. Given the following triangles,

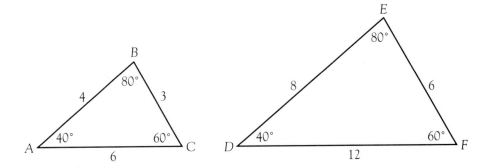

$\triangle ABC \sim \triangle DEF$ ($\triangle ABC$ is similar to $\triangle DEF$)

This notation gives a way to match corresponding angles:

$\triangle ABC \sim \triangle DEF$ $\quad \angle A \cong \angle D, \angle B \cong \angle E, \angle C \cong \angle F$

It also gives the way to match corresponding sides

$\triangle ABC \sim \triangle DEF$ $\quad \overline{AB}$ is matched with $\overline{DE}$
$\triangle ABC \sim \triangle DEF$ $\quad \overline{BC}$ is matched with $\overline{EF}$
$\triangle ABC \sim \triangle DEF$ $\quad \overline{AC}$ is matched with $\overline{DF}$

so that their lengths can be written as proportions.

One type of question in this skill asks for a specific angle measure or side length on one of two similar triangles. To find the requested information, do the following:

STEP **1.** Use the Relations in Skill II.B.1. and Skill II.B.2. to determine angle measurements.

STEP **2.** If two angles are congruent, write the notation for similar triangles. Be careful to put congruent angles in corresponding positions.

Geometry and Measurement Skills

STEP **3.**   Use this notation and the information in Step 1 and Step 2 to check the correctness of the responses.

Example **1:**   Which of the statements a–d is true for the pictured triangle if EM ∥ CF?

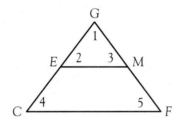

a. $\angle 1 \cong \angle 4$ b. $\dfrac{EG}{CG} = \dfrac{GM}{CF}$ c. $\angle 4 \cong \angle 5$ d. $\dfrac{GE}{GC} = \dfrac{GM}{GF}$

Solution: Since EM ∥ CF, $\angle 2 \cong \angle 4$ and $\angle 3 \cong \angle 5$

(1) Relation 9.

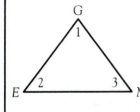   (2) Use angle measurements to set up triangles and write notation.

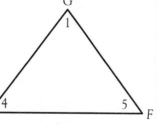

$\triangle EGM \sim \triangle CGF$

Eliminate "a." since $\angle 4 \cong \angle 2$

(3) Check responses.

Eliminate "b." since $\dfrac{EG}{CG} \neq \dfrac{GM}{CF}$

from $\triangle E\boxed{GM} \sim \triangle C\boxed{GF}$

Eliminate "c." since $\angle 4 \cong \angle 2$

The answer is "d." since $\dfrac{GE}{GC} = \dfrac{GM}{GF}$

from $\triangle \boxed{EG}M \sim \triangle \boxed{CG}F$

**Geometry and
Measurement Skills**

Example **2:** Which of the statements a–d is true for the pictured triangle?

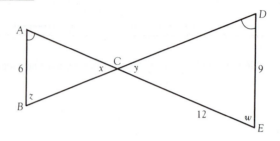

a. $x = w$ b. $BC = 8$ c. $AC = 8$ d. $\dfrac{AB}{BC} = \dfrac{DE}{DC}$

Solution: $\angle A \cong \angle D$
$\angle ACB \cong \angle DCE$

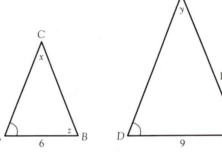

$\triangle ACB \sim \triangle DCE$

(1) Given in picture. Vertical angles (Relation 4).

(2) Use angle measurement to set up triangles and write notation.

(3) Check responses.

Eliminate "a." since $z = w$ because $x = y$ by Relation 4.

Eliminate "b." To find BC, use triangles in Step 2 to set up a proportion. Use two corresponding sides with numbers and a corresponding side with BC.

$\dfrac{AB}{DE} = \dfrac{BC}{CE}$	(1) Write proportion.
$\dfrac{6}{9} = \dfrac{BC}{12}$	(2) Substitute.
$9BC = 72$	(3) Cross multiply.
$BC = 8$	(4) Divide by 9.

The solution is "b."

(*Note:* Checking remaining responses:)

Response "c." is not
a solution:

$$\dfrac{AB}{AC} = \dfrac{DE}{DC}$$

$$\dfrac{6}{AC} = \dfrac{9}{DC} \quad \text{Can't find } AC.$$

Response "d." is not
a solution:

$$\dfrac{AB}{BC} = \dfrac{DE}{DC} \quad \text{because } \triangle ACB \sim \triangle DCE$$

(BC should match CE)

The second type of question gives four groups of triangles and asks for the group in which all triangles are similar. Triangles are similar if at least two angles are congruent or the lengths of the sides are proportional.

Use the following steps to solve these problems.

STEP **1.** If some angle measurements are given, use the Relations in Skill II.B.1. and Skill II.B.2. to determine the measurements of the remaining angles in each group of triangles. If two sets of angles are congruent, that set of triangles is similar.

STEP **2.** If the sides of a group of triangles are given, check to determine if the sides are proportional. If they are, the triangles are similar.

Example **3:** Study figures a, b, c, and d. Then select the figure in which all triangles are similar.

a.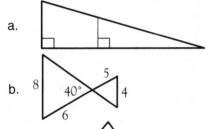

b.

c.

d.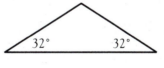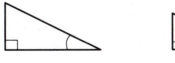

Solution:

Response a. Since angles are given, separate the two triangles.

(i.) The right angles are congruent.
(ii.) They share a common angle which is congruent to itself.

The solution is "a."   (Continued)

(Cont'd)   (Note: Check remaining responses.)

Response b. Not a solution because the sides are not proportional:

$$\frac{4}{8} = \frac{6}{5}$$

Response c. Not a solution because when the triangles are separated:

(i.) They share a common vertex angle.
(ii.) The outside triangle does not share the third angle.

Response d. Not a solution because solving for the remaining pieces gives

The first two triangles are similar, but the third one is not.

**II.B.3.
Sample Items**

1. Study figures a, b, c, d. Then select the figure in which all triangles are similar.

a.

b.

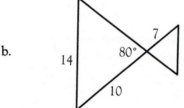

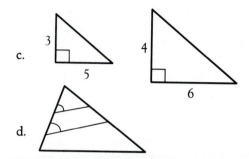

c.

d.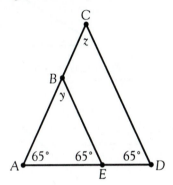

2. Which of the statements is true for the pictured triangles? (The measure of angle ACD is Z.)

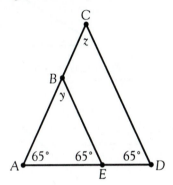

a. $y = 65°$

b. $\dfrac{AB}{AC} = \dfrac{AE}{CD}$

c. $z = 65°$

d. $\dfrac{AB}{AC} = \dfrac{BE}{CD}$

3. Study figures a, b, c, d. Then select the figure in which all the triangles are similar.

a.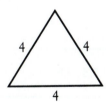

b.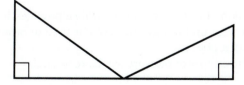

Geometry and Measurement Skills

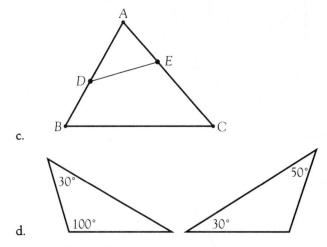

c.

d.

4. Which of the following statements is true for the pictured triangle? (The measure of angle *ACB* is *x*.)

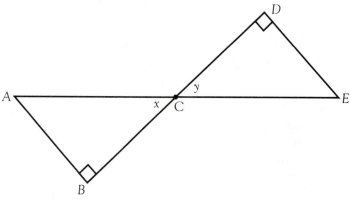

a. $\dfrac{AB}{DE} = \dfrac{BC}{CE}$

b. $\angle A \cong \angle E$

c. $\dfrac{AB}{DE} = \dfrac{CD}{BC}$

d. $x + y = 180°$

ANSWERS: 1.a., 2.d., 3.d., 4.b.

II.B.4.
The student identifies appropriate units of measurement for geometric objects.

A diagram or description of a geometric object will be provided in the stimulus. The problem will ask what unit of measure could be used to measure something involving that object.

The following three types of measure will be requested:

LINEAR — This measure is used to report the length or width of an object, the distance around the object, the height of the object, and so on. Some standard units that are used for linear measure include feet, inches, yards, meters, centimeters, and kilometers.

**Geometry and
Measurement Skills**

AREA	Square measure is used to report the surface area of a wall or floor, the amount of area on the outside of a can, etc. Some standard units that are used for square measures include square feet, square yards, square centimeters, square meters, and square kilometers.

VOLUME	Volume is the amount that an object will hold. Contents of a can, the amount of water in a tank, and the amount of milk in a carton are all examples of volume. Some standard units that are used for cubic measure are gallons, liters, cubic feet, cubic centimeters, cubic yards, cubic meters, and so forth.

To identify appropriate units of measure, use the following steps:

STEP 1. Read the problem carefully to identify what type of measure (linear, area, or volume) is being asked.

STEP 2. Choose the response that could be used for this type of measure.

Example 1: Which of the following could be used to measure the length of a couch?

a. degrees   b. meters   c. square feet   d. cubic feet

Solution:	The *length* of a couch is linear measure.	(1) Identify the type.
	The correct response is "b."	(2) Meters measure length.

Geometry and Measurement Skills

Example 2: Which of the following could be used to measure how much of the kitchen floor a floor wax will cover?

a. liters   b. feet   c. square feet   d. cubic feet

Solution:

The covering of a kitchen floor is *area*.   (1) Identify the type.

The correct response is "c."   (2) Square feet measures area.

(*Note*: Liters could be used to measure how much was in the bottle. Feet could be used to measure the height of the bottle.)

Example 3: Which of the following would *not* be used to measure the amount of gasoline in a tank?

a. liters   b. cubic feet   c. gallons   d. meters

Solution:

Amount of gasoline in a tank is *volume*.   (1) Identify the type.

Meters do *not* measure volume.   (2) Liters, cubic feet, and gallons all measure volume.

The correct response is "d."

**II.B.4.
Sample Items**

1. Which of the following could be used to measure the amount of tissue paper needed to wrap a package?

   a. liters
   b. square inches
   c. cubic feet
   d. degree

2. Which of the following could *not* be used to measure the length of a snake?

   a. feet
   b. square inches
   c. meters
   d. yards

3. The amount of orange juice in a carton is given by which measure?

   a. square inches
   b. degrees

**Geometry and
Measurement Skills**

    c. liters

    d. meters

4. Which of the following could be used to measure the height of the cylinder?

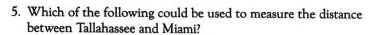

    a. gallons

    b. yards

    c. square feet

    d. cubic centimeters

5. Which of the following could be used to measure the distance between Tallahassee and Miami?

    a. kilometers

    b. cubic meters

    c. square miles

    d. cubic miles

ANSWERS: 1.b., 2.b., 3.c., 4.b., 5.a.

Each question in this skill will contain two to four geometric figures for which the same information will be given. The diagrams will be followed by a question that requires the measurement of a different, but related figure.

    To solve the generalization, do the following steps:

**III.B.1.
The student will infer formulas for measuring geometric figures.**

STEP 1. Read the problem carefully, looking at the diagrams to determine what information is given. Identify what specific measurement the problem is asking.

STEP 2. Set up a chart listing the given information and leaving a blank for the needed information.

STEP 3. Look for a pattern in the chart.

STEP 4. Fill in the missing information.

(*Note:* Since the specific measurement involves areas, volumes, surface areas, angle measures, perimeters, or circumferences, the answer could be calculated

**Geometry and
Measurement Skills**

from a formula. However, most of the problems will involve formulas infrequently used and probably not at quick recall. This choice is to encourage the use of generalization, which is what the skill tests.)

Example **1:** Study the given information. For each figure, *x* equals the measure of an exterior angle.

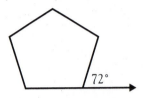

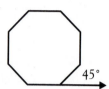

Regular pentagon   Regular hexagon   Regular octagon

What is the measure of the exterior angle of a decagon?

Solution: The diagram gives the numbers of sides and asks for the measure of the exterior angle.

(1) Identify given and unknown.

No. of Sides	Exterior Angle
5	72°
6	60°
8	45°
10	—

(2) Set up chart.

(a) As the number of sides increases, the angle decreases.

The solution is less than 45°.

(3) Look for a pattern.

(b) Is there anything you can add, subtract, multiply, or divide to get a pattern?

$$5 \times 72° = \underline{360°}$$
$$6 \times 60° = \underline{360°}$$
$$8 \times 45° = \underline{360°}$$
$$10 \times \underline{\quad} = 360°$$

$$10 \times \underline{\quad} = 360°$$

(4) Fill in the blanks.

The solution is 36°.

*There is a formula in geometry that states that the measure of an exterior angle $= \dfrac{360}{n}$ when n = number of sides.

For a decagon, $\dfrac{360°}{10} = 36°$

Example **2:**   Study the given spheres.

  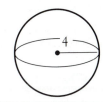

Surface area = 16π   Surface area = 36π   Surface area = 64π

Calculate the surface area for a sphere with a radius of five.

Solution:

The diagram gives the radius and asks for the surface area.

(1) Identify given and unknown.

Radius	Surface Area
2	16π
3	36π
4	64π
5	—

(2) Set up chart.

(a) As the radius increases, the surface area increases. The answer is greater than 64π.

(3) Look for a pattern.

(b) Is there anything you can add, subtract, multiply, or divide to get a pattern?

$2 \times \underline{8\pi} = 16\pi$
$3 \times \underline{12\pi} = 36\pi$
$4 \times \underline{16\pi} = 64\pi$
$5 \times \underline{} = \underline{}$

Pattern: Add 4π to middle number and multiply.
$$5 \times 20\pi = 100\pi$$

The solution is 100π.

(The formula for the surface area of a sphere is $SA = 4\pi r^2$. For a sphere with radius five, the surface area is $SA = 4\pi(5)^2 = 100\pi$.)

1. Study the information given in the figures.

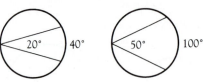 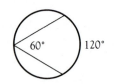 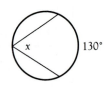

What is the measure of x?

a. 65°
b. 70°
c. 90°
d. 260°

2. Study the information given in the figures.

Area = $\sqrt{3}$ Area = $4\sqrt{3}$ Area = $9\sqrt{3}$

Calculate the area of an equilateral triangle with a side equal to eight.

a. $10\sqrt{3}$
b. $12\sqrt{3}$
c. $14\sqrt{3}$
d. $16\sqrt{3}$

3. Study the information given in the figures.

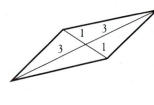 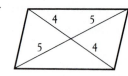 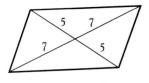

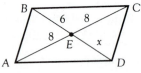

What is the measure of x, the length of segment DE?

a. 5
b. 6
c. 8
d. 9

4. Study the information given in the figures.

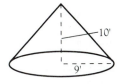

$V = 30\pi$ cu. ft.　　　　$V = 120\pi$ cu. ft.　　　　$V = 270\pi$ cu. ft.

Calculate the volume of a cone with a radius of 12 feet and a height of 10 feet.

a. 360π cu. ft.
b. 480π cu. ft.
c. 1080π cu. ft.
d. 1440π cu. ft.

5. Study the information given in the figures.

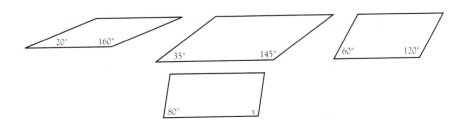

What is the measure of *x*?

a. $80°$
b. $95°$
c. $100°$
d. $145°$

Geometry and Measurement Skills

Geometry and Measurement Skills

III.B.2.
The student will select applicable formulas involving perimeters, areas, and volumes of geometric figures.

The perimeter, area, and volume formulas given in Skills I.B.2a. and I.B.2b., and I.B.2c. will also be needed in this skill. In addition, three more formulas may be needed:

(a) Circumference of a semicircle: $C = \frac{1}{2}(2\pi r) = \pi r$ (r = radius)

(b) Volume of a hemisphere: $V = \frac{1}{2}\left(\frac{4\pi r^3}{3}\right) = \frac{2\pi r^3}{3}$ (r = radius)

(c) Volume of a prism: $V = Bh$ (B = base area, h = height)

(d) Volume of a pyramid: $V = \frac{1}{3}Bh$ (B = base area, h = height)

A diagram that represents a composite of two- or three-dimensional figures will be given. To identify the correct formula for calculating a specific measure, do the following:

STEP 1. Write the formulas necessary to find the area (volume) of the individual figures.

STEP 2. Use the diagram to find the value of the variables. Use geometric properties to find any missing variable.

STEP 3. Substitute the values in the individual formulas.

STEP 4. Simplify the individual area (volume) formulas.

STEP 5. Find the sum of these areas (volumes). If the area is shaded, find the difference between the areas (volumes).

**Geometry and
Measurement Skills**

Example **1:** Study the figure showing a cube with a pyramid mounted on top. The length of a side of the cube is x. The height of the pyramid is h. Select the formula for computing the total volume.

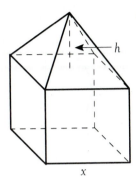

Solution:

Cube	Pyramid	
$V = lwh$	$V = \frac{1}{3}lwh$	(1) Write the volume formulas.

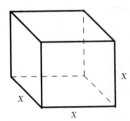 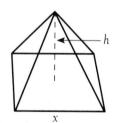

(2) Find the value of variables. (Cube—all sides are equal; Pyramid—base is a square the same size as the face of the cube; height was given.)

$V = (x)(x)(x)$ $V = \frac{1}{3}(x)(x)(h)$ (3) Substitute the values.

$V = x^3$ $V = \frac{1}{3}x^2h$ (4) Compute.

$V = x^3 + \frac{1}{3}x^2h$ (5) Find the sum.

**Geometry and
Measurement Skills**

Example **2:** Study the figure showing a square surrounded by semicircles. Then select the formula for computing the perimeter of the figure.

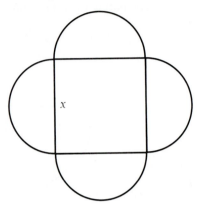

Solution:

Semicircles	Square	(1) Write the circumference formula.
$C = \pi r$	Not Needed	

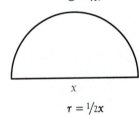

x

(2) Find the value of the variables.

$r = \frac{1}{2}x$

$C = \pi(\frac{1}{2}x)$ (3) Substitute the values.

$C = \frac{1}{2}\pi x$ (4) Compute.

$\frac{1}{2}\pi x + \frac{1}{2}\pi x + \frac{1}{2}\pi x + \frac{1}{2}\pi x = 2\pi x$ (5) Find the sum. (There are four semicircles on the outside.)

**III.B.2.
Sample Items**

1. Study the figure showing a regular octagon. Then select the formula for computing the total area of the octagon.

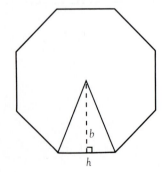

a. $TA = 4bh$
b. $TA = 8bh$
c. $TA = 4b + 4h$
d. $TA = 8(b + h)$

2. Study the figure showing the pattern that can be folded to form the square pyramid on the right. Then select the formula for computing the total surface area.

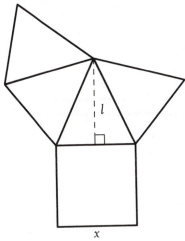

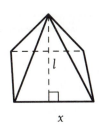

  a. $SA = x^2 + \frac{1}{2}lx$
  b. $SA = x^2 + 2lx$
  c. $SA = \frac{1}{2}lx^3$
  d. $SA = 2lx^3$

3. Study the figure showing a triangle inscribed in a circle. Then select the formula for computing the area of the shaded region.

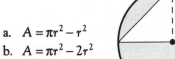

  a. $A = \pi r^2 - r^2$
  b. $A = \pi r^2 - 2r^2$
  c. $A = \pi$
  d. $A = \pi - 2$

4. Study the figure showing a rectangle surmounted by a semicircle. Then select the formula for computing the perimeter of the figure.

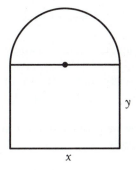

  a. $P = x + 2y + \pi x$
  b. $P = x + 2y + \frac{1}{2}\pi x$
  c. $P = 2x + y + \pi x$
  d. $P = x + 2y + \pi x^2$

5. Study the figure showing a cylinder surmounted by a hemisphere. Then select the formula for computing the volume of the figure.

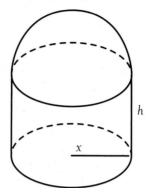

a. $V = \pi x^2 h$

b. $V = \dfrac{2}{3} \pi x^4 h$

c. $V = \pi x^2 h + \dfrac{2}{3} \pi x^3$

d. $V = \pi x^2 h + \dfrac{4}{3} \pi x^3$

ANSWERS: 1.a., 2.b., 3.a., 4.b., 5.c.

**IV.B.1.
The student will solve real-world problems involving perimeters, areas, volumes of geometric figures.**

These word problems will be taken from a wide variety of subject areas and will require the use of the perimeter, area, and volume formulas found in Skill IV 2a, 2b, and 2c. They will also include at least one simple conversion (e.g., inches to feet) within the system. Skill I.B.1 contained a chart for equivalent linear measure conversion. However, problems may contain a conversion of square or cubic units. These equivalent relations can be derived very easily from corresponding linear units.

For example, the chart states that:

$$3 \text{ feet} = 1 \text{ yard}$$

To find out how many *square* feet equal a *square* yard, square both digits:

$$(3)^2 \text{ sq. ft.} = (1)^2 \text{ sq. yd.}$$
$$9 \text{ sq. ft.} = 1 \text{ sq. yd.}$$

Likewise, to find equivalent cubic units, find the appropriate units in linear measure, then cube both digits.

$$3 \text{ ft.} = 1 \text{ yd.}$$
$$(3)^3 \text{ ft.} = (1)^3 \text{ yd.}$$
$$27 \text{ cu. ft.} = 1 \text{ cu. yd.}$$

This method will also work for metric measure.

To solve real-world problems involving perimeters, areas, volumes, use the following steps:

Geometry and Measurement Skills

STEP 1. Read the problem carefully. Identify whether the problem involves perimeter, area, or volume.

STEP 2. Write down the appropriate formula.

STEP 3. Reread the problem to find the values of the variables. Make sure the units are equivalent. Substitute these equivalent unit values in the formula.

STEP 4. Compute the answer.

STEP 5. Underline the part of the problem that identifies the solution.

STEP 6. Perform any additional computation to find the solution.

STEP 7. Re-read the problem to make sure the answer is reasonable.

**Geometry and
Measurement Skills**

Example **1:** A floor is to be covered with tiles. The length of the floor is 30 tiles and the width is 25 tiles. If the cost of each tile is $2.00, how much will it cost to cover the floor?

Solution:	Area	(1) Identify the type.
	$A = lw$	(2) Write the formula.
	$A = (30)(25)$	(3) Find the values and substitute.
	$A = 750$ sq. tiles	(4) Compute.
	How much will it cost?	(5) Underline.
	$750 \times \$2.00$	(6) Tiles $\times$ cost of one tile.
	$\$1,500.00$	(7) Cost.

Example **2:** A flower box is in the shape of a rectangular solid with a length of 4 ½ feet, a width of 3 ⅓ feet, and a height of 10 feet. How many cubic yards of potting soil will be needed to fill the box?

Solution:	Volume	(1) Identify the type.
	$V = lwh$	(2) Write the formula.
	$V = (4\,\tfrac{1}{2})(3\,\tfrac{1}{3})(10)$	(3) Find the values and substitute.
	$V = \left(\dfrac{9}{2}\right)\left(\dfrac{10}{3}\right)\left(\dfrac{10}{1}\right)$	(4) Compute.
	$= \dfrac{450}{3} = 150$ cu. ft.	
	How many cubic yards of potting soil?	(5) Underline.

$$\begin{array}{r} 16 = 16^2/_3 \\ 9\overline{)150} \\ \underline{9} \\ 60 \\ \underline{54} \\ 6 \end{array}$$

(6) Change cubic feet to cubic yards (9 cu.ft. = 1 cu.yd.).

$16\dfrac{2}{3}$ cubic yards   (7) Amount.

1. The Howsers are going to wallpaper a mural on one wall of their dining room. If the wall is 9 feet by 10 feet, how many square yards of wallpaper, which costs $8.00 per roll, will they need?

    a. 10 square yards
    b. 80 square yards
    c. 90 square yards
    d. 720 square yards

2. A mirror is in the shape of a rhombus. The length of one side of the mirror is 20 inches. How much will it cost to frame the mirror if the material costs $3.00 a foot?

    a. $ 5.00
    b. $ 10.00
    c. $ 20.00
    d. $240.00

3. In ceramics class, Kelly made a storage canister in the shape of a rectangular solid. If the canister is 10 centimeters long, 10 centimeters wide, and 20 centimeters high, how many liters will it hold?

    a. 1 liter
    b. 2 liters
    c. 1,000 liters
    d. 2,000 liters

4. A paper cup is in the shape of a circular cone. How many cubic decimeters will it hold if its diameter is 2 decimeters and its height is 30 centimeters?

    a. $\pi \, dm^3$
    b. $7\pi \, dm^3$
    c. $10\pi \, dm^3$
    d. $40\pi \, dm^3$

5. A room with a ceiling 3 m high has floor dimensions of 6 m by 80 dm. If a liter of paint covers $10m^2$ and costs $8.00 per liter, how much will it cost to paint the walls?

    a. $ 33.60
    b. $ 67.20
    c. $336.00
    d. $672.00

ANSWERS: 1.a., 2.c., 3.b., 4.a., 5.b.

Geometry and Measurement Skills

IV.B.1.
Sample Items

Geometry and Measurement Skills

> **IV.B.2.**
> **The student will solve real-world problems involving the Pythagorean property.**

The Pythagorean Theorem states: For any right triangle, the square of the length of the hypotenuse is equal to the sum of the square of the lengths of the two sides.

$$c^2 = a^2 + b^2$$

It is important to distinguish between the quantity that represents the hypotenuse and those that represent the legs. The hypotenuse is always located opposite the right angle. Its length is always the measure of the longest segment in the triangle.

To solve real-world problems that utilize the Pythagorean Theorem, do as follows:

STEP **1.**	Read the problem carefully. Write the formula: $c^2 = a^2 + b^2$

STEP **2.**	Draw a diagram of a right triangle (or use the diagram given in the problem) and label the given sides.

STEP **3.**	Check to make sure the measurement units are in equivalent units. Substitute these values into the formula.

STEP **4.**	Solve for the unknown variable.

STEP **5.**	Underline the part of the problem that identifies the solution.

STEP **6.**	Perform any additional computation to find the solution.

STEP **7.** Reread the problem to make sure the answer is reasonable.

Example **1:** A plane flies 3 miles east and then 4 miles north. How far is the plane from its starting point?

Solution: $c^2 = a^2 + b^2$ (1) Write the formula.

(2) Draw a diagram and label the sides.

c 4 miles north

3 miles east

$c^2 = (4)^2 + (3)^2$ (3) Substitute the values into the formula.

$c^2 = 16 + 9 = 25$ (4) Solve for the variable.
$\sqrt{c^2} = \sqrt{25}$
$c = 5$

How far is the plane from its starting point?   (5) Underline the requested information.

5 miles   (6) None required.

**Geometry and
Measurement Skills**

Example **2:** The Coopers bought the lot pictured below. They plan to put a sidewalk along the shortest side. The cost of the sidewalk is approximately $20 a linear foot. About how much will the walk cost?

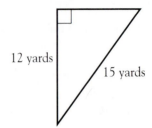

12 yards

15 yards

Solution: $c^2 = a^2 + b^2$ (1) Write the formula.

12   15

(2) Label the diagram.

15

$(15)^2 = (12)^2 + b^2$ (3) Substitute into the formula.

$225 = 144 + b^2$ (4) Solve for the unknown.

$81 = b^2$

$\sqrt{81} = \sqrt{b^2}$

$9 = b$

Approximately how much will it cost? (5) Underline the requested information.

9 yd. $\times$ 3 = 27 ft.
27 $\times$ $20 = $540 (6) Change yards to feet. Multiply times cost per linear foot.

$540 (7) Solution.

**IV.B.2.
Sample Items**

1. An attic door is 3 feet tall and 48 inches wide. What is the longest sheet of paneling that can be taken through the door?

   a. 7 feet
   b. 5 feet
   c. 14 feet
   d. 2,473 feet

2. Kelly is building a frame for his mailbox. The mailbox must be 4 feet high. If the platform on which the mailbox sits is 3 feet long, how long should the brace connecting the bottom of the post to the end of the platform be?

   a. 5 inches
   b. 7 feet

c. 5 feet
d. 25 feet

Geometry and Measurement Skills

3. The Ramoses rent bicycles and ride at an average rate of 3 miles per hour. If they ride south for 2 hours and then ride west for 2²/₃ hours, how far are they from their starting point?

   a. 4²/₃ miles
   b. 10 miles
   c. 14 miles
   d. 14¹/₃ miles

4. Kim is designing a rectangular banner that is to be 5 feet wide. If the banner is to have a 13-foot ribbon sewn down the diagonal of the rectangle, how long should the banner be?

   a. 12 feet
   b. 72 feet
   c. 144 feet
   d. 194 feet

ANSWERS: 1.b., 2.c., 3.b., 4.a.

Statistics Skills, Including Probability

I.D.1.
The student identifies information contained in bar, line, and circle graphs.

When data is displayed on a graph, it is easier to read, to look for trends, and to do comparisons. Three types of graphs will be included in this skill.

A circle graph consists of a circle divided into five to eight "pie-shaped" sections. Each section will have a category name and a numerical value. This numerical value may be a whole number that represents a frequency (how often the category occurs). The stimulus will request some of the following information about the graph. The following steps will explain how you can read a circle graph that contains frequencies to find the correct solution to the various questions.

To answer questions about circle graphs, do the following:

STEP 1. Identify the category (or categories) to which the question refers.

STEP 2. Identify the frequency(ies).

STEP 3. Use this information to answer the question:

(a) Find the frequency of a category: Choose the numerical value in the category section.
(b) Find the percent or portion of a category:
    (1) Find the sum of all the frequencies in the sections.
    (2) Divide the sum into the number of the specified category.
(c) Find the sum (or difference) of two or more categories:
    (1) Find the information for the individual sections.
    (2) Then add (or subtract) this individual information.

Example **1:** The number of people enrolled in the different fitness classes is represented by the circle graph below.

Question 1: How many people are enrolled in aerobics?

Solution: 15 (Find the number in the specific category.)

Question 2: What percent of people are enrolled in walking?

Solution: 15 + 10 + 15 + 25 + 35 = 100   (b1) Find the sum.
$^{35}/_{100}$ = .35 = 35%   (b2) Divide.

Question 3: What percent of the people are enrolled in walking or running?

Solution: Percent of walking: $^{35}/_{100}$ = .35 = 35%   (c1)
Percent of running: $^{25}/_{100}$ = .25 = 25%
25% + 35% = 60%   (c2)

Sometimes the numerical values on the circle graph represent the percent of times that the category occurs. Follow the procedures listed below for answering questions that will be asked about the circle graph:

STEP **1.** Identify the category (or categories) to which the question refers.

STEP **2.** Identify the percent(s).

STEP **3.** Use this information to answer the following questions.

(a) The frequency of a category: Multiply the decimal equivalent of the percent (proportion) times the total number of frequencies. (This whole number will be stated in the problem.)

(b) The percent (proportion) of a category: Choose the percent (proportion) given in that category.

(c) Find the sum (or difference) of two or more categories:
   (1) Find the information for the individual sections.
   (2) Then add (or subtract) this individual information.

Example **2:** The following circle graph represents the percent of the student body that participates in different student activities at Newberry College. There are 4,000 students enrolled in the school.

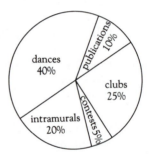

Question 1: Find the number of students who participate in intramurals.

Solution: $4,000 \times .20 = 800$ students (Multiply the proportion by the total number.)

Question 2: What percent of the students participate in contests?

Solution: 5% (Find the number associated with the category.)

Question 3: How many more students participate in clubs than in publications?

Solution: Students in clubs: $4,000 \times .25 = 1,000$ (c1)
Students in publications: $4,000 \times .10 = 400$
$1,000 - 400 = 600$ students   (c2)

Bar graphs and line graphs are located on a set of horizontal and vertical axes. The categories are usually listed on the horizontal axis. The vertical axis is labeled with whole numbers that represent the frequencies of the categories. In a bar graph, the height of the solid bar represents the frequency of the category. In the line graph, the vertical position of the point directly above the category is the frequency.

To answer questions about line and bar graphs, do the following:

STEP 1. Identify the category (or categories) to which the question refers.

STEP 2. Identify the frequency (or frequencies).

STEP 3. Use this information to answer the question:

(a) Find the frequency: Choose the number on the vertical scale.

(b) Find the difference: Subtract the values of the frequencies.

(c) Which categories are the same? Look for the two heights that are the same on the vertical scale.

Example 3: The graph below represents the number of cars sold per day during one work week. How many more cars were sold on Friday than on Tuesday?

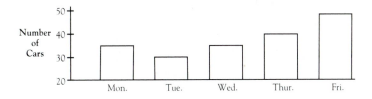

Solution:

Friday	Tuesday	
50	30	(1) Identify the categories.
		(2) Identify the frequencies.
50 − 30 = 20		(3) Difference (how many more).

Statistics Skills, Including Probability

Example **4:**   The graph below represents the Cleveland's electric bill for 6 months. Between which 2 months did the bill decrease?

Bills in $

110
100
90
80

Jan.   Feb.   Mar.   Apr.   May   June   July

Solution: February and March (Find the difference between pairs of points in which the point on the left is higher than the point on the right.)

I.D.1.
Sample Items

1. The graph below represents the percent of money spent per semester by college students. If Mary spent $6,000 in the fall semester, what is the total amount that she spent on tuition and books?

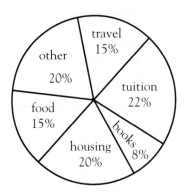

travel 15%

other 20%

tuition 22%

food 15%

books 8%

housing 20%

a. $ 480
b. $1,320
c. $ 850
d. $1,800

2. The graph below represents the favorite flavors of seventh-grade students. Which two flavors were preferred by the same number of students?

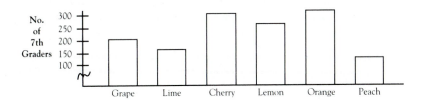

   a. lemon and grape
   b. cherry and orange
   c. lime and peach
   d. lime and lemon

3. The graph below represents the number of thunderstorms occurring each year for a 5-year period. Between which two consecutive years was there the greatest difference between the number of thunderstorms?

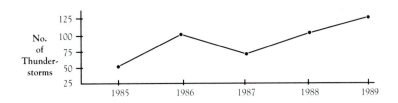

   a. 1985 and 1986
   b. 1986 and 1987
   c. 1987 and 1988
   d. 1988 and 1989

4. The graph below represents the number of people who bought dining-room suites during a special promotion sale. What percent of the buyers chose dining suites made of pine?

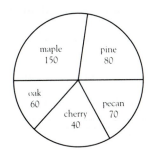

**Statistics Skills,
Including Probability**

a. 88%
b. 20%
c. 50%
d. 80%

5. The graph below represents the number of people who ordered certain drinks at a restaurant during June. How many more people preferred tea to coffee?

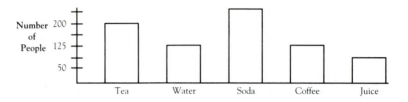

a. 75
b. 125
c. 200
d. 325

ANSWERS: 1.d., 2.b., 3.a., 4.b., 5.a.

**I.D.2.
The student will determine the mean, median, and mode of a set of numbers.**

The mean, median, and mode are called measures of central tendency. A sample of numbers will be given in the stimulus. If the question asks for the *mode*, do the following:

STEP 1. Look for the number that occurs *most frequently*.
(*Hint:* The word "mode" starts like the word "most.")

Example 1: What is the *mode* of the data in the following sample?
6, 15, 14, 8, 14, 22, 10, 14

Solution: The number 14 occurs most frequently.
6, 15, *14*, 8, *14*, 22, 10, *14*

If the question asks for the *median* of the sample, do as follows:

STEP 1. Arrange the numbers in ascending (or descending) order.

STEP 2. Mark off pairs of numbers (one on the left and one on the right) until either one or two numbers remain in the middle.

STEP 3.
(a) If one number remains, that number is the median.
(b) If two numbers remain, add them and divide by 2 to obtain the median.

(*Hint*: The word "median" looks similar to the word "middle.")

Example 2: What is the <u>median</u> of the data in the following sample?

6, 15, 12, 8, 14, 22, 10, 13

Solution: 6, 8, 10, 12 ,13, 14, 15, 22   (1) Arrange in ascending order.

6̸, 8̸, 1̸0̸, 12, 13, 1̸4̸, 1̸5̸, 2̸2̸   (2) Mark off pairs.

$$\frac{12+13}{2} = \frac{25}{2} = 12\frac{1}{2}$$ (3b) Add the remaining two and divide by 2.

Example 3: What is the <u>median</u> of the data in the following sample?

10, 9, 6, 10, 8, 7, 13, 6, 8

Solution: 6, 6, 7, 8, 8, 9, 10, 10, 13   (1) Arrange in ascending order.

6̸, 6̸, 7̸, 8̸, 8, 9̸, 1̸0̸, 10, 1̸3̸   (2) Mark off pairs.

8 is the median.   (3a) The number 8 remains.

**Statistics Skills,
Including Probability**

If the question asks for the *mean*, do the following:

STEP **1.** Find the sum of the numbers.

STEP **2.** Count the number of items in the sample.

STEP **3.** Divide the sum by that number to obtain the mean.

Example **4:** What is the <u>mean</u> of the data in the following sample?

6, 11, 7, 8, 9, 12 22, 8, 7

Solution:
$6 + 11 + 7 + 8 + 9 + 12$
$+ 22 + 8 + 7 = 90$
(1) Find the sum.

There are 9 numbers in the sample.
(2) Count the number in the sample.

$\dfrac{90}{9} = 10$
(3) Divide to find the mean.

The mean is 10.

**I.D.2.
Sample Items**

1. What is the <u>median</u> of the data in the following sample?

    22, 18, 30, 16, 22, 28, 26, 24

    a. 19
    b. 22
    c. 23
    d. 23.25

2. What is the <u>mean</u> of the data in the following sample?

    4, 22, 6, 4, 8, 7, 13, 4

    a. 4
    b. 6
    c. 6.5
    d. 8.5

3. What is the <u>mode</u> of the data in the following sample?

       11, 8, 11, 12, 11, 3, 4, 3

    a. 3.0
    b. 9.5
    c. 11.0
    d. 11.5

4. What is the <u>median</u> of the data in the following sample?

       10, 14, 4, 22, 4, 8, 16, 13, 4, 17, 9

    a. 4
    b. 8
    c. 10
    d. 11

**Statistics Skills,
Including Probability**

ANSWERS: 1.c., 2.d., 3.c., 4.c.

The fundamental counting principle is used to find the number of possible outcomes of a particular event. Events in this skill will consist of selecting *sequences of objects* or selecting *subsets of objects* from a set. Events involving selection of objects will be single events that require choices within the event. When choices are repeatedly made from the same group, then choice will be ordered. Examples of these events include choices in building a house, choosing an outfit, seating a group of people, and so on.

    To find the number of possible outcomes of an event involving selecting sequences of objects, do as follows:

> **I.D.3.
> The student will use the fundamental counting principle.**

STEP **1.** Draw a blank for each option within the event.

STEP **2.** Write the number of choices for that particular option in the blank.

STEP **3.** Multiply these numbers to obtain the solution.

**Statistics Skills,
Including Probability**

Example **1:** A restaurant offers four different sandwiches, three different chips, and five different drinks. How many different choices of meals, consisting of a sandwich, a bag of chips, and a drink, can the restaurant offer?

Solution:

___ ___ ___ (1) Three blanks for options: sandwich, chips, drink.

_4_ _3_ _5_ (2) Choices include 4 sandwiches, 3 chips, 5 drinks.

_4_ × _3_ × _5_ = 60 (3) Multiply.

Example **2:** Movie critics are asked to rank five movies from best to worst. How many different ways can the five movies be ranked?

Solution:

___ ___ ___ ___ ___ (1) Five options: 1st, 2nd, 3rd, 4th, 5th.

_5_ _4_ _3_ _2_ _1_ (2) Five choices for 1st; only four for 2nd; only three for 3rd, etc.

_5_ × _4_ × _3_ × _2_ × _1_ = 120 (3) Multiply.

The second type of problem will ask for the possible outcomes of an event that involves selecting subsets of objects. These events will always consist of a *group* from which you must select a subset. The position of the piece (what is chosen first, second, etc.) will not be important.

To find the number of possible outcomes of an event involving selecting subsets, do as follows:

STEP **1.** Identify the group or groups named in the problem.

STEP **2.** For each group write the following notation, in which n represents the number in the group and r represents the number of pieces you are taking from the group.

$_nC_r$

$_nC_r = \dfrac{n!}{r!(n-r)!}$ (If you can evaluate this notation, skip to Step 6.)

STEP **3.**　Write a fraction with r blanks in the numerator and the denominator.

STEP **4.**
(a) In the numerator, write the value of n in the first blank and the next smallest whole number in the next blank, etc., until all the blanks are filled.
(b) In the denominator, write the value of r in the first blank and the next smallest whole number in the next blank, etc., until all the blanks are filled.

STEP **5.**　Multiply the numbers in the numerator and denominator, and reduce the fraction.

STEP **6.**　If you have more than one group, multiply your individual group fractions to obtain the solution.

Example **3:**　The science club is going to choose a committee of three from its governing board to serve as a nomination committee. If the board has six members, how many different committees can be chosen?

Solution:

Governing board is the group.	(1) Identify the group.
$_6C_3{}^*$	(2) From 6 members, choose 3.
$\dfrac{-\ -\ -}{-\ -\ -}$	(3) Write the fraction with 3 blanks.
$\dfrac{6 \cdot 5 \cdot 4}{3 \cdot 2 \cdot 1}$	(4a) Write numerator. (4b) Write denominator.
$\dfrac{120}{6} = 20$	(5) Multiply and reduce.
20 committees	(6) Only one group.

$$\left(^*\text{Evaluate } _6C_3 = \frac{6!}{3!3!} = \frac{6 \cdot 5 \cdot 4 \cdot 3 \cdot 2 \cdot 1}{3 \cdot 2 \cdot 1 \cdot 3 \cdot 2 \cdot 1} = 20\right)$$

Statistics Skills, Including Probability

Example **4:** Three men and four women are applying for a mixed doubles team that consists of two women and two men. How many different teams can be chosen?

Solution:	A group of two men. A group of two women.	(1)	Identify the groups.
	$_3C_2$ $_4C_2$ *	(2)	Choose two men from three. Choose two women from four.
	$\frac{-\ -}{-\ -}$ $\frac{-\ -}{-\ -}$	(3)	Write fractions with two blanks.
	$\frac{3\cdot 2}{2\cdot 1}$ $\frac{4\cdot 3}{2\cdot 1}$	(4a) (4b)	Write numerator. Write denominator.
	$\frac{6}{2}=\frac{3}{1}=3$ $\frac{12}{2}=\frac{6}{1}=6$	(5)	Multiply and reduce.
	$3\cdot 6=18$	(6)	Multiply two answers.

(*Evaluate $_3C_2=\dfrac{3!}{2!1!}=3$, $_4C_2=\dfrac{4!}{2!2!}=6$)

**I.D.3.
Sample Items**

1. Julia has a Frequent Flyer pass that permits her to choose three flights from a list of six. How many different combinations of flights can she choose?

   a. 15
   b. 20
   c. 60
   d. 120

2. The drama director is casting a play that requires three males and two females. If five men and three women audition, how many ways can the play be cast?

   a. 10
   b. 21
   c. 30
   d. 90

3. Four finalists were named for the history award. After an exam, a winner, second-, third-, and fourth-place winners will be announced. How many different ways can the finalists be ranked?

   a. 4
   b. 9
   c. 12
   d. 24

4. A club consisting of six members is going to elect a president and vice-president. How many ways can the offices be filled?

   a. 2
   b. 12
   c. 15
   d. 30

5. John always wears a dress shirt, tie, sport coat, and slacks to work. If he has five shirts, three ties, two sport coats, and five pairs of slacks, how many different outfits does he have?

   a. 30
   b. 50
   c. 60
   d. 150

6. Mobile home buyers can choose the size, color, and floor plan of their custom-built home. If the company offers four sizes, four colors, and three floor plans, how many different mobile homes can be custom built?

   a. 11
   b. 12
   c. 16
   d. 48

Statistics Skills, Including Probability

ANSWERS: 1.b., 2.c., 3.d., 4.d., 5.d., 6.d.

The concepts of mean, median, and mode were introduced in Skill I.D.2. In that skill these measures of central tendency were calculated by recalling that mode was the most frequent item, median was the middle item, and mean was the average of all items.

In this skill, calculations of these three measures will not be possible. The stimulus will provide a diagram or description of data from which a relationship between the three can be established. Only one response will match that relationship.

To choose the interrelationship from a diagram, do the following:

> **II.D.1.**
> The student will recognize properties and interrelationships among the mean, median, and mode in a variety of distributions.

STEP **1.** Draw a blank, write the word "median," and then draw another blank.

**Statistics Skills,
Including Probability**

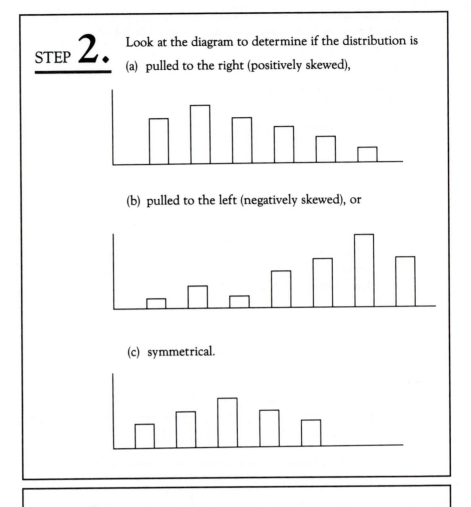

STEP **2.** Look at the diagram to determine if the distribution is

(a) pulled to the right (positively skewed),

(b) pulled to the left (negatively skewed), or

(c) symmetrical.

STEP **3.**
(a) If the graph is pulled to the right, write "mean" in the right blank.
(b) If the graph is pulled to the left, write "mean" in the left blank.
(c) If the graph is symmetrical, write "mode = median = mean." Skip Step 4 and Step 5 and do Step 6.

STEP **4.** Fill the remaining blank with the word "mode." (*Note:* Since the mode is the most frequent score, it should be written on the side with highest bars.)

STEP **5.** Place less than (<) signs between the words in the "pulled" graphs.

**Statistics Skills,
Including Probability**

STEP **6.** Check responses for the one that states the correct relationship.

Example **1:** The graph below represents the distribution of prizes, by their value, that were given away at a hardware store's grand opening. Which of the following statements is true about the distribution of prizes?

Frequency (Number of prizes worth the indicated value)

500
400
300
200
100

$10 $20 $30 $40 $50 $60

a. The median and the mean are the same.
b. The mode is greater than the mean.
c. The mode is less than the mean.
d. The median is less than the mode.

Solution:	
____ median ____	(1) Draw three blanks and write "median" in the middle blank.
It is pulled to the right.	(2) Identify type of graph.
____ median *mean*	(3) Write "mean" on the right.
mode median *mean*	(4) Write "mode" in other blank.
mode < median < mean	(5) Put < sign.
The solution is "c."	(6) Check against responses.

When a description of data is given, find the interrelationship between the measures of central tendency as follows:

STEP **1.** Read the passage. If it states that half of the sample scored a certain score, that score is the median and mode.

STEP **2.**
(a) If the remaining scores are below that score, the mean is less than the median and the mode.
(b) If the remaining scores are above that score, the mean is greater than the median and the mode.
(c) If it states that the scores are equally distributed on either side, the mean is equal to the mode and the median.

STEP **3.**
Check responses for the one that states the correct relationship.

Example **2:**
In a factory quality-control test, half of the light bulbs burned for 100 hours. Most of the remaining bulbs burned for 110 hours, while a few lasted for 120 hours. Which of the following statements is true about the distribution of scores?

a. The mode and mean are the same.
b. The mean is greater than the mode.
c. The mean is less than the median.
d. The median and the mean are the same.

Solution:

mode = median	(1)	since half of the bulbs lasted 100 hours
mean > mode mean > median	(2)	The rest of the scores were above 100.
The solution is "b."	(3)	Check the responses.

1. The graph below represents the distribution of soft drinks that are consumed weekly by teenagers. Select the statement that is true about the distribution of soft drinks.

a. The mean is greater than the mode.
b. The mean is greater than the median.
c. The mean is equal to the mode.
d. The median is less than the mean.

2. On a physical fitness test, half of the soldiers could run the obstacle course in about 20 minutes. Most of the remaining soldiers finished in 18 minutes, except for a few who finished in 15 minutes. Which of the following statements is true about the distribution of times?

a. The mean is less than the mode.
b. The mode is less than the mean.
c. The mean and mode are the same.
d. The mean and the median are the same.

3. The graph below represents the distribution of the price of a pound of tomatoes during a 5-month period. Select the statement that is true about the distribution of scores.

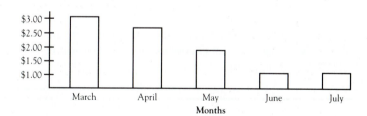

a. The mean and the mode are the same.
b. The mode is greater than the median.
c. The median and the mode are the same.
d. The mode is less than the mean.

4. On a bird-watching excursion, half of the children saw eight different types of birds. Half of the remaining children saw 10 birds, while the other half only saw 6. Which of the following statements is true about the distribution of birds?

a. The mean is less than the mode.
b. The median is greater than the mode.
c. The median is equal to the mode.
d. The mode is greater than the median.

Statistics Skills, Including Probability

5. The graph below represents the number of long-distance telephone calls made from the Smith house. Select the statement that is true about the distribution of calls.

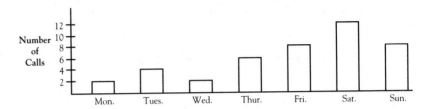

a. The mode is greater than the mean.
b. The mean is equal to the median.
c. The mode is less than the median.
d. The mode is equal to the mean.

ANSWERS: 1.c., 2.a., 3.d., 4.c., 5.a.

**II.D.2.
The student will choose the most appropriate procedure for selecting an unbiased sample from a target population.**

A random sample is a sample chosen in such a way that every member of the population has an equal chance of being selected. This sample must be chosen only from the target population. The target population is the entire group from which the sample is to be selected.

To choose the most appropriate procedure for selecting an unbiased sample, do the following:

STEP 1. Identify the target population. Eliminate any response that does not choose members of the sample from only that group.

STEP 2. Eliminate any of the remaining responses that do not permit *every* member of the population an equal chance of being chosen. For example, methods such as voluntary responses, mail-in responses, and filling out surveys in magazines are not unbiased methods.

**Statistics Skills,
Including Probability**

Example **1**: A book company wants to find out how many of its authors are considering writing another book. To do so, the company decides to conduct a survey. Which of the following procedures would be the most appropriate for selecting a statistically unbiased sample?

a. Survey a randomly selected sample of authors from the card catalog at the local library.
b. Mail a survey form to all authors on file and have them voluntarily return the survey form.
c. Survey a randomly selected sample of authors who have published in the last 3 years.
d. Survey a randomly selected sample of authors from the company's publishing records.

Solution:

The target population is the company's authors. Eliminate "a." because its population is all authors.

(1) Identify the target population and eliminate.

Eliminate "b." because voluntary mail is not random.

(2) Eliminate; not random.

Eliminate "c." because choosing only authors who published in last 3 years doesn't give *every* author a chance of being chosen.

The solution is "d."

**Statistics Skills,
Including Probability**

Example **2:** A researcher is interested in determining the support of a balanced budget among registered voters in the United States. Which of the following procedures would be most appropriate for selecting a statistically unbiased sample?

a. Randomly select regions of the country and randomly select voters from the voter registration list.
b. Survey every registered voter in California and Florida.
c. Conduct a telephone survey of people randomly chosen from the phone directory who live in New York City.
d. Pass out survey forms at the front entrance of the mall and ask people to fill them out.

Solution: The target population is voters.
Eliminate "c." and "d." because people selected may not be registered voters.

(1) Identify the target population and eliminate.

Eliminate "b." because *every* voter would not have a chance of being selected.

(2) Eliminate; not random.

The solution is "a."

Example **3**:
The owners of a resort community want to determine whether the residents would be willing to pay a yearly fee for a golf course. The owners decide to conduct a survey. Which of the following procedures would be most appropriate for selecting a statistically unbiased sample?

a. Divide the community into geographic regions, randomly select some of those regions, and then survey a randomly selected sample of people within those regions.
b. Distribute surveys to every family and have them voluntarily return the survey.
c. Select the odd-numbered houses and survey those residents.
d. Survey a random sample of residents who buy a newspaper at the community store.

Solution: The target population is residents within the community. All responses are within the target population.

(1) Identify the target population and eliminate.

Eliminate "b."—not random because of voluntary return of surveys.

(2) Eliminate any that are not random.

Eliminate "c."—not every household has chance of being selected.

Eliminate "d."—not every resident has a chance of being selected.

The solution is "a."

1. A student newspaper is interested in the number of extracurricular activities in which a student participates. Which of the following procedures would be the most appropriate for obtaining a statistically unbiased sample?

a. Print a survey in the paper that can be returned to the campus newspaper office.
b. Have the reporter assigned to the story interview the students in his or her classes.
c. Interview a randomly selected sample of students from the registrar's list.
d. Interview every fifth student in the cafeteria line.

II.D.2.
Sample Items

Statistics Skills, Including Probability

2. The high school principal wants to find out if the juniors and seniors would like to change the junior/senior dance to a junior/senior banquet and decides to conduct a survey. Which of the following procedures would be the most appropriate for obtaining a statistically unbiased sample?

   a. Survey all the students enrolled in the physical education classes.
   b. Randomly select clubs and then survey a randomly selected sample of members of those clubs.
   c. Survey a randomly selected group of seniors and juniors from a list of all juniors and seniors.
   d. Survey randomly selected junior and senior sponsors.

3. A company claims that its ice cream churner is so easy to use that even a fourth grader can make ice cream. Which of the following procedures would be the most appropriate for obtaining a statistically unbiased sample to test this claim?

   a. Have all the fourth graders enrolled in the enrichment classes use the churner to make ice cream.
   b. Let fourth-grade student volunteers use the churner to make ice cream after school.
   c. Randomly select one child from each room in the elementary school to use the churner to make ice cream.
   d. Randomly select a group of students from a list of all fourth-grade students.

4. A sample of the opinions of 120 families who live in a 10-story apartment building is needed to determine the location of a picnic area. If there are 12 families on each floor, which of the following procedures would be most appropriate for selecting a statistically unbiased sample?

   a. Survey a randomly selected sample of families with children who live in the apartment building.
   b. Survey every family on the even-numbered floors who live in odd-numbered apartments.
   c. Survey families on randomly selected floors who live in randomly selected apartments on those floors.
   d. Survey every family whose last name begins with a B., M., or T.

ANSWERS: 1.c., 2.c., 3.d., 4.c.

The probability $P(E)$ that an event will occur is

$$P(E) = \frac{\text{number of ways that the event can occur}}{\text{total number of possible outcomes}}.$$

To solve simple probability problems, use the following steps:

STEP **1.** Determine the total number of possible outcomes by listing and counting all the possibilities or using the fundamental counting principle (Skill I.D.3.).

STEP **2.** Determine the number of ways that the event can occur.

STEP **3.** Write the fraction and reduce.
(*Note:* The value of the fraction will always be greater than or equal to zero, but less than or equal to one ($0 \leq P \leq 1$). The probability equals one when the occurrence of the event is certain. The probability equals zero when the event cannot occur.)

Example **1:** Three months out of every year are considered hurricane months for Florida. If a family randomly chooses a month for a Florida vacation, what is the probability that it is a hurricane month?

Solution:
Total number of months = 12
(1) Determine the total number of outcomes.

Hurricane months = 3
(2) Determine the number of events.

$\dfrac{3}{12} = \dfrac{1}{4}$
(3) Write as a fraction and reduce.

To determine the probability that an event will *not* occur, do as follows:

STEP **1.** Find the probability that the event will occur.

**Statistics Skills,
Including Probability**

STEP **2.** Subtract that probability from 1.

Example **2:** A recent survey indicated that 6 out of 10 teenagers shop for their own clothes. How many teenagers do *not* shop for their clothes?

Solution: $P \text{ (teenager shops)} = \dfrac{6}{10} = \dfrac{3}{5}$ (1) Probability that the event will occur.

$1 - \dfrac{3}{5} = \dfrac{5}{5} - \dfrac{3}{5} = \dfrac{2}{5}$ (2) Subtract from 1.

Probabilities can also be determined for events that consist of two or more parts. These composite events may be reworded using the word "and" or "or."

Composite events are independent if the occurrence of one event has no effect on the occurrence of the other event(s).

To determine the probability of two independent events that are connected with the word "and," do the following:

STEP **1.** Reword the problem into two or more single events connected by the word "and."

STEP **2.** Find the probability of the single events.

STEP **3.** Replace the word "and" with a multiplication sign and simplify.

Example **3:** John's batting average is .350. What is the probability that he will get a hit his first two times at bat?

Solution: Event: Hit and Hit   (1) Reword the problem.

$$\frac{350}{1000} \text{ and } \frac{350}{1000}$$

(2) Find the probability of the single events.

$$\frac{\overset{7}{\cancel{350}}}{\underset{20}{\cancel{1000}}} \times \frac{\overset{7}{\cancel{350}}}{\underset{20}{\cancel{1000}}} = \frac{49}{\underset{400}{\cancel{1000}}}$$

(3) Replace "and" with $\times$ and simplify.

Dependent events occur when the occurrence of one event affects the probability of the second event. Dependent events occur when events happen simultaneously or when the total number of outcomes is affected after the first event has occurred (sampling without replacement).

To determine the probability of two dependent events connected by the word "and," do the following:

STEP **1.** Reword the problem into two or more single events connected by the word "and."

STEP **2.** Find the probability of the first event. Adjust the total number of outcomes. Then find the probability of the next event.

STEP **3.** Replace the word "and" with a multiplication sign and simplify.

**Statistics Skills,
Including Probability**

Example **4:** The U-Pick Rental Company owns 10 cars. Of the 10 cars, 2 are blue. If a business executive rents two of their cars, what is the probability that they are both blue?

Solution:	Blue and Blue	(1) Reword the problem.
	$\frac{2}{10}$ and $\frac{1}{9}$	(2) Find the probability of the first event, then the probability of the second event.
	$\frac{\overset{1}{\cancel{2}}}{\underset{5}{\cancel{10}}} \times \frac{1}{9} = \frac{1}{45}$	(3) Replace "and" and simplify.

Composite events connected by the word "and" were divided into two types, independent and dependent. Composite events that utilize the connector "or" can also be divided into two groups. One group is formed by events that are mutually exclusive. Mutually exclusive events cannot both occur at the same time.

To determine the probability of mutually exclusive events connected by the word "or," do as follows:

STEP **1.** Reword the problem into two or more single events connected by the word "or."

STEP **2.** Find the probability of the single events.

STEP **3.** Replace the word "or" with the addition sign and simplify.

Example **5:** The ABC Garage has three transmission workers, three brake workers, two front-end workers, and one manager. An employee is to be chosen at random. What is the probability that the employee is a transmission or front-end worker?

Solution: Transmission or Front-End Worker

(1) Reword the problem.

$\frac{3}{9}$ or $\frac{2}{9}$

(2) Find the probability of single events.

$\frac{3}{9} + \frac{2}{9} = \frac{5}{9}$

(3) Replace with addition and simplify.

Some composite events are not mutually exclusive. To determine the probability of nonmutually exclusive events connected by the word "or," do the following:

STEP **1.** Reword the problem into two or more single events connected by the word "or."

STEP **2.** Find the probability of the single events.

STEP **3.** Find the probability of both events "(and)" occurring.

STEP **4.** Add the two single probabilities and subtract the probability that both will occur.

Statistics Skills, Including Probability

Example **6:** Class data from a local college showed that 20 percent of the student body were enrolled in English, 15 percent were enrolled in mathematics, and 3 percent were enrolled in mathematics and English. What is the probability that a student chosen at random is enrolled in mathematics or English?

Solution: Mathematics or English (1) Reword.

$$M = \frac{15}{100} \qquad E = \frac{20}{100}$$ (2) Single probabilities.

$$M \text{ and } E = \frac{3}{100}$$ (3) Both events.

$$\frac{15}{100} + \frac{20}{100} - \frac{3}{100} = \frac{32}{100} = \frac{8}{25}$$ (4) Add single probability and subtract probability of both.

II.D.3.
Sample Items

1. Jane is looking for a full-time summer job. She has a one out of four chance of accepting a job at a clothing store and a two out of five chance of accepting a job at a bakery. What is the probability that she will *not* accept a job if she has applied only at the clothing store and bakery?

   a. $\frac{9}{10}$

   b. $\frac{13}{20}$

   c. $\frac{9}{20}$

   d. $\frac{1}{10}$

2. Five percent of the cars manufactured in the United States have a defective part. If John and Susan both buy a car, what is the probability that the cars are both defective?

   a. 10

   b. .05

   c. $\frac{1}{40}$

   d. $\frac{1}{400}$

3. James receives a shipment of 10 items, of which 2 are defective. Three items are selected at random. What is the probability that all three of the items are defective?

    a. $\dfrac{1}{125}$

    b. $\dfrac{1}{15}$

    c. $\dfrac{1}{5}$

    d. 0

4. A recent survey indicated that 2 out of 10 high school students graduate with honors. Of these, 1 out of 10 enters college and graduates with honors. What is the probability that a randomly-selected high school student will graduate from both high school and college with honors?

    a. $\dfrac{1}{50}$

    b. $\dfrac{1}{25}$

    c. $\dfrac{3}{10}$

    d. $\dfrac{1}{10}$

5. At Marion Senior High School 50 percent of the students are male and 50 percent are female. If 25 percent of the student body are seniors, what is the probability that a randomly selected student is a female senior?

    a. .50
    b. .25
    c. .125
    d. .08

6. Mike has an opportunity to study abroad in Paris, Rome, London, Tokyo, or Moscow. What is the probability that he will study in London?

    a. 0

    b. $\dfrac{1}{5}$

    c. $\dfrac{4}{5}$

    d. 1

7. The Tigers and Bengals are in two different districts. One member from each of their districts will play in the regional play-offs. The probability that the Tigers will make the play-offs is .6. The probability that the Bengals will make the play-offs is .1. What is the probability that at least one of these teams will be in the regional play-offs?

Statistics Skills, Including Probability

a. .5
b. .64
c. .7
d. .76

ANSWERS: 1.c., 2.d., 3.d., 4.a., 5.c., 6.b., 7.b.

III.D.1.
The student will infer relations and make accurate predictions from studying statistical data.

In this skill, data will be displayed in a table, histogram, broken line graph, scatter diagram, or line graph. Four types of questions will be asked about this data. In the text that follows, possible questions will be given and steps listed to obtain a solution to these questions.

Question 1: Comment on the apparent relationship between two variables.

STEP 1. Identify the values that represent each of two variables.

STEP 2. Use the values to determine the relationship between the two variables, such as

(a) There is a positive correlation between the variables. (Both variables increase or both variables decrease.)

(b) There is a negative correlation between the variables. (One variable increases while the other variable decreases.)

(*Note:* No cause-and-effect relationship can be determined from the given data.)

STEP 3. Eliminate the responses that do not match the relationships.

Statistics Skills, Including Probability

Example **1**: The number of cars on Interstate 77 and the number of reported accidents per year for a 6-year period are given below:

Year	Number of Cars	Reported Accidents
1985	46,680	234
1986	50,432	283
1987	52,861	342
1988	55,130	396
1989	58,465	456
1990	61,736	496

Which of the following best describes the relationship between the number of cars and the reported accidents?

a. Increasing the number of cars caused an increased number of accidents.
b. There appears to be a negative association between the number of cars and the number of reported accidents.
c. There appears to be a positive association between the number of cars and the number of reported accidents.
d. The number of cars does not provide information needed to predict the number of reported accidents.

Solution:

Compare cares with accidents.
46,680→234
50,432→283
52,861→342
    etc.

(1) Compare the values.

As the cars increase, the accidents increase.

(2) Determine the relationship.

Eliminate "a.," since there is not enough information to infer a cause-and-effect relationship.

(3) Check the responses.

Eliminate "b.," since both increase.

Eliminate "d.," since both increase.

The correct solution is "c."

**Statistics Skills,
Including Probability**

Question 2: Comment on the trend in a single variable.

STEP **1.** Carefully read the problem to identify the variable in question.

STEP **2.** Look for a pattern in those values, such as

(a) increasing.
(b) decreasing.
(c) remaining stable or leveling off.
(d) decreasing then leveling.
(e) increasing then stable, etc.

STEP **3.** Eliminate the responses that do not match the pattern.

**Statistics Skills,
Including Probability**

Example 2: Consider the following plot of the average price of a Telex microcomputer during the last 10 years.

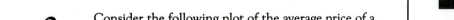
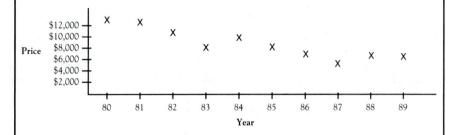

Which of the following best describes the trend in the price of the Telex?

a. The price of the Telex has been steadily decreasing for the last 10 years.
b. The price of the Telex has remained stable during the last 10 years.
c. There is no trend in the average price for any time period.
d. The price of the Telex has been steadily increasing for the last 10 years.

Solution:	Trend in price.	(1) Identify the variable.
	$12,000	(2) Price was decreasing.
	$11,000	
	$10,000	
	$8,000	
	etc.	
	The solution is "a."	(3) Match the response.

Question 3: Estimate the value of a variable within the observed range.

STEP 1. Read the problem carefully to identify the range.

STEP 2. Use the diagram to find the value that corresponds to the range (see Skill I.D.1.).

STEP **3.**   Check the responses.

Example **3:**   The following graph shows the number of new cars sold per month during 1989.

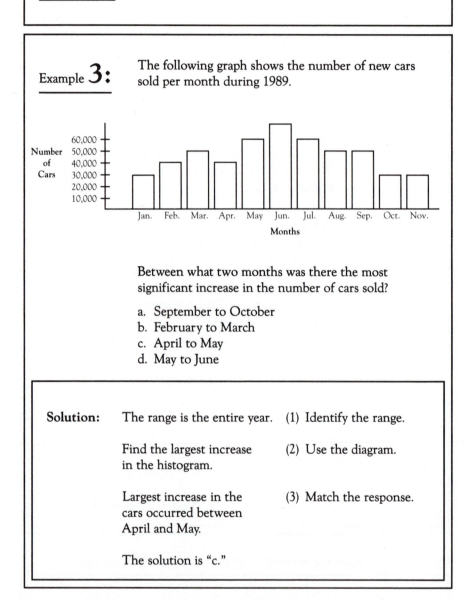

Between what two months was there the most significant increase in the number of cars sold?

a. September to October
b. February to March
c. April to May
d. May to June

Solution:	The range is the entire year.	(1) Identify the range.
	Find the largest increase in the histogram.	(2) Use the diagram.
	Largest increase in the cars occurred between April and May.	(3) Match the response.
	The solution is "c."	

Question 4: Predict beyond the range of observations.

STEP **1.**   Read the problem carefully to identify the variable about which the prediction is made.

STEP **2.**   Examine the values of the variable to see if there is a trend or pattern.

STEP **3.** Make a prediction based on the given values.

STEP **4.** Check your prediction against the responses. Make sure your prediction is obtainable, that is, physically possible.

Example **4:** The number of years of service with a company and the average salary for that number of years is given in the chart below.

Years	Salary
5	$35,000
10	$39,000
15	$43,000
20	$46,000
25	$49,000
30	$51,000

Which of the following best describes a worker's salary potential?

a. A company employee will never earn more than $51,000.
b. A company employee could someday earn $100,000.
c. The more years an employee stays with the company, the higher the average salary.
d. The salary of employees is unpredictable.

Solution:

The variable is the salary.

(1) Identify the variable.

The salary increases at least $2,000 every 5 years.

(2) Examine the values.

The salary will keep increasing at the same rate every 5 years.

(3) Make a prediction.

Both "b." and "c." say that the salary will keep increasing. However, "b." would be physically impossible since an employee would probably not be able to work that many years.

(4) Check against the responses.

Statistics Skills, Including Probability

1. Consider the following plot of the height and weight of a sample of 12 men.

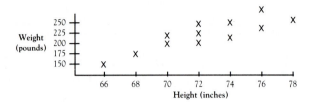

Which of the following best describes the relationship between the men's weight and height?

a. An increase in height causes an increase in weight.
b. There appears to be a positive association.
c. An increase in weight causes an increase in height.
d. There is no apparent association between weight and height.

2. The graph below depicts the base price and number of luxury (o) and compact (x) cars sold.

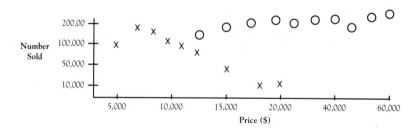

Which of the following best describes the relationship between price and the number sold?

a. The demand for compact cars is more affected by cost than the demand for luxury cars is.
b. A relationship between price and number sold exists only for luxury cars.
c. There is no apparent relationship between base price and number of cars sold.
d. A relationship between price and number sold exists only for compact cars.

3. Consider the following graph of the number of hours studied and the grade received on an exam.

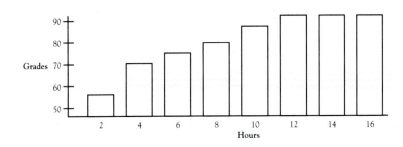

After how many hours did the grade begin to stabilize?

a. 4 hours
b. 6 hours
c. 8 hours
d. 12 hours

4. The following plot depicts the number of headaches per week experienced by women who exercise a certain number of minutes a week.

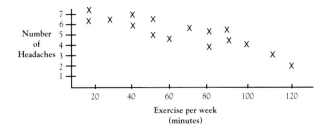

Which of the following best estimates the number of headaches a woman who exercises 70 minutes a week would have?

a. 2
b. 3
c. 5
d. 7

5. Using the chart in exercise 4, which of the following best describes the relationship between the number of headaches and the minutes a woman exercised?

a. Increased exercise caused the decrease in headaches.
b. There is no apparent association between exercise and headaches.

c. There is a negative association between the number of headaches and the number of minutes a woman exercised.
d. An increased number of headaches caused a woman to exercise less.

ANSWERS: 1.b., 2.a., 3.d., 4.c., 5.c.

IV.D.1.
The student will interpret real-world data involving frequency and cumulative frequency tables.

One of two types of tables, relative frequency and cumulative relative frequency, will be included with every question in this skill.

A relative frequency table displays data and the percent or proportion of times that it appears (relative frequency). Several types of questions will be asked about this table. In the text that follows, possible questions will be given and steps listed to obtain a solution.

Question 1: Find the mode.

STEP **1.**   Find the largest proportion (percent) in the table.

STEP **2.**   The value assigned to it by the table is the mode.

Example **1:**   The table below shows the distribution of final grades in a statistics class.

Grades	Proportion of Students
100	.05
90	.10
85	.17
80	.20
75	.13
70	.15
65	.10
60	.10

What is the mode of distribution?

Solution: The answer is 80 because .20 is the largest proportion.

Question 2: Find the median.

STEP **1.** Sum up the proportion from the lowest score to the highest score.

STEP **2.** Choose the score that lies in the sum of .50 (50%) or above.

What is the median in example 1?

Solution:

Grades	Proportion of Students
100	.05
90	.10
85	.17
80	.20
75	.13
70	.15
65	.10
60	.10

(1) Add all the proportions from the lowest grade until the sum is ≥ .50.

.20   .35   .48   .63

The median is 80.

Question 3: Find the mean.

STEP **1.** Multiply the value of the data by its proportion.

STEP **2.** Sum all entries.

What is the mean in example 1?

Solution: $(100)(.05) + (90)(.10) + (85)(.17) + (80)(.20) +$
$(75)(.13) + (70)(.15) + (65)(.10) + (60)(.10)$

$5 + 9 + 14.45 + 16 + 9.75 + 10.5 + 6.5 + 6 = 77.1$

**Statistics Skills,
Including Probability**

Question 4: What percent lies between ____ and ____?

STEP **1.** Find the two values.

STEP **2.** Add the proportion or percents between and with those values.

Example **2:** In the table in example 1, what percent of the students scored between 85 and 75?

Solution: $.17 + .20 + .13 = .50 = 50\%$

Question 5: What is the percent (proportion) above (below) it?

STEP **1.** Find the value.

STEP **2.** Add all percents or proportions below (above) it.

Example **3:** In the table in example 1, what percent of the students scored at least 85?

Solution: Add proportions for 85 and above.
$.17 + .10 + .05 = .32 = 32\%$

Question 6: Identify the value so that ____% are below it.

| STEP **1.** | Add all the proportions or percents from the smallest data up. |

| STEP **2.** | Stop at the value whose percent equals or exceeds the given percent. |
| | (To find ____ % above it, start from the largest data and add down.) |

Example 4: In the table in example 1, identify the score such that 60% of the scores are below it.

Solution:

Grades	Proportion of Students
100	.05
90	.10
85	.17
80	.20
75	.13
70	.15
65	.10
60	.10

(1) Add all the proportions from the lowest grade until the sum is ≥ .60.

.20   .35   .48   .68

The solution is 80.

A cumulative relative frequency table is founded by summing up the relative frequencies. The following is an example of a cumulative frequency table.

Scores	Percentile Rank
90	.99
80	.85
70	.65
60	.42
50	.25
40	.10

The percentile rank of .65 on the score of 70 means that 65% of the students scored below 70 on the final. The following questions might be asked about a cumulative frequency table.

**Statistics Skills,
Including Probability**

Question 7: Identify the value so that ____% are below it.

STEP **1.** Find the decimal equivalent or the next largest decimal equivalent in the chart.

STEP **2.** Write the score next to it.

Example **5:** Find the score so that 80% of the scores are below it.

Solution: .80 is not in the percentile, so go to .85. Choose the score that corresponds to it. The answer is 80.

Question 8: Identify the value so that ____% are above it.

STEP **1.** Subtract the decimal equivalent of the percentage from 1.00.

STEP **2.** Find that percentile (or next largest).

STEP **3.** Write the score next to it.

Example **6:** Identify the value so that 30% of the scores are above it.

Solution: $1.00 - .30 = .70$
Find .70 or the next largest percentile in the chart (use .85).
The score is 80.

Question 9: What percentage lies between ____ and ____?

STEP 1. Find the percentile rank of the largest score.

STEP 2. Find the percentile rank of the other score.

STEP 3. Subtract.

Example **7:** What percentage of the scores lies between 80 and 60?

Solution: $.85 - .42 = .43 = 43\%$

The table below shows the distribution by age of the percent of people treated for injuries resulting from falls.

Age Group	Percent of Age Group
0– 4	13
5–14	12
15–24	18
25–64	43
65 and older	14

1. What was the median age group of injury victims?

   a. 0–4
   b. 5–14
   c. 15–24
   d. 25–64

2. What percent of the injury victims were 24 years old and younger?

   a. 12
   b. 18
   c. 30
   d. 43

**Statistics Skills,
Including Probability**

3. If 500 people were treated at the Riverside Emergency Room for injuries resulting from falls, how many were 65 years old or older?

   a. 14
   b. 28
   c. 10
   d. 70

4. What age group was the mode of distribution?

   a. 5–14
   b. 15–24
   c. 25–64
   d. 65 and older

ANSWERS: 1.d., 2.d., 3.d., 4.c.

Scores on a state nursing examination were scaled so that the scores listed below correspond to the indicated percentile ranks.

Scores	Percentile Rank
400	99
350	87
300	71
250	50
200	32
150	21
100	3

1. What percentage of the students made below 200?

   a. 56
   b. 53
   c. 32
   d. 24

2. What was the median score on the nursing examination?

   a. 350
   b. 300
   c. 250
   d. 200

3. Identify the score so that at least 71 percent of the scores are below it.

   a. 350
   b. 300
   c. 250
   d. 200

4. What percentage of the students scored above 300?

    a. 87
    b. 71
    c. 29
    d. 21

**Statistics Skills,
Including Probability**

ANSWERS: 1.c., 2.c., 3.b., 4.c.

The table below shows the distribution of the number of books checked out per week by the members of the local library.

Number of Books	Proportion of Members
1	.31
2	.22
3	.16
4	.18
5	.13

1. What percentage of the members check out at least three books per week?

    a. 5
    b. 16
    c. 31
    d. 47

2. What is the mean number of books checked out by the members?

    a. .52
    b. 1
    c. 2
    d. 2.6

3. What percentage of the members check out less than two books per week?
    a. 9
    b. 22
    c. 31
    d. 53

4. What is the median number of books checked out by the members?

    a. 1
    b. 2
    c. 3
    d. 4

ANSWERS: 1.d., 2.d., 3.d., 4.b.

Statistics Skills, Including Probability

IV.D.2.
The student will solve real-world problems involving probabilities.

Each problem will include a table or a graph with the relative frequency in proportion (decimal) or percentage form. From this table or graph, four types of questions will be asked. In the text that follows, possible questions will be given and steps listed to obtain the solution.

Question 1: What is the probability of a specific event?

STEP **1.** Choose the proportion or percent of that event from the chart.

STEP **2.** If the value is a percent, change it to its equivalent decimal form.

STEP **3.** If the responses are in decimal form, this is the probability.

STEP **4.** If the responses are in fractional form, change the decimal to a fraction.

Example **1:** The following is a description of students in a nursery school by age and sex.

	3 Years	4 Years	5 Years
Female	13%	20%	18%
Male	10%	25%	14%

What is the probability that a randomly selected child will be a 3-year-old male?

Solution: 10%   (1) Choose percent of that solution.

10% = .10   (2) Change to a decimal.

$.10 = \dfrac{10}{100} = \dfrac{1}{10}$

Question 2: What is the probability of more than one event?

STEP **1.** Add the proportions or percent of the individual events.

STEP **2.** If the value is a percent, change to decimal form.

STEP **3.** If the responses are in decimal form, this is the probability.

STEP **4.** If the responses are in fractional form, change the decimal to a fraction.

Example **2:** Using the chart in example 1, what is the probability that a randomly selected child will be a 4-year-old?

Solution:

$20\% + 25\% = 45\%$ (1)   Add percent of 4-year-old girls and 4-year-old boys.

$45\% = .45$ (2)   Change to a decimal.

$.45 = \dfrac{45}{100} = \dfrac{9}{20}$ (3, 4)   Solution in decimal or fractional form.

Question 3: What is the probability that it was not a specific event(s)?

STEP **1.** Find the proportion or percent of the event(s).

STEP **2.** If the value is a percent, change to decimal form.

STEP **3.** Subtract the decimal from 1.00.

STEP **4.** If the responses are in decimal form, this is the probability.

STEP **5.** If the responses are in fractional form, change the decimal to a fraction.

Example **3:** Using the chart in example 1, what is the probability that a randomly selected child will *not* be a 3- or 4-year-old female?

Solution:	$13\% + 20\% = 33\%$	(1)	Add percent of 3-year-old female and 4-year-old female.
	$33\% = .33$	(2)	Change to a decimal.
	$1.00 - .33 = .67$	(3)	Subtract from 1.00.
	$67 = \dfrac{67}{100}$	(4, 5)	Solution in decimal or fractional form.

Question 4: What is the probability of an event given some prior condition?

STEP **1.** Find the total number of outcomes for the prior condition by adding all proportions or percents that meet the given condition.

STEP **2.** Change that value to a decimal.

STEP **3.** Find the proportion or percent of the specific event under the given condition.

STEP **4.** Change to a decimal.

STEP **5.** Write a fraction of the probability of the event over the total number of outcomes.

STEP **6.** Simplify.

Example **4:** Using the chart in example 1, what is the probability that a randomly selected child is 4 years old, given that the child is a male?

Solution:

$10\% + 25\% + 14\% = 49\%$	(1) Add all percents for being male (the given condition).
$49\% = .49$	(2) Change to a decimal.
25%	(3) Find the percent of 4-year-old males.
$25\% = .25$	(4) Change to decimal.
$\dfrac{.25}{.49}$	(5) Write as a fraction.
$\dfrac{.25}{.49} = \dfrac{25}{49}$	(6) Simplify.

Statistics Skills, Including Probability

Question 5: What is the expected number of occurrences of an event?

STEP **1.**   Find the probability of the event in decimal form.

STEP **2.**   Multiply the decimal value times the total number of occurrences.

Example **5:**   If the nursery school in example 1 has 80 students, how many of the students are 4 years old?

Solution: $20\% + 25\% = 45\% = .45$ (1) Find probability of being 4 years old.

          $.45 \times 80 = 36$ students   (2) Multiply probability times total enrollment.

**IV.D.2.
Sample Items**

An advertising firm provided the following distribution of the color of cars preferred by new car buyers.

Color	Percent of Buyers
Red	22
Blue	17
White	37
Black	11
Tan	8
Green	5

1. Find the probability that a buyer will prefer a black car.

   a. .08
   b. .11
   c. .37
   d. .89

2. Find the probability that a buyer will prefer a red or white car.

   a. .22
   b. .37
   c. .51
   d. .59

3. Find the probability that a buyer will *not* prefer a tan or green car.

  a. $\dfrac{2}{25}$

  b. $\dfrac{1}{20}$

  c. $\dfrac{13}{100}$

  d. $\dfrac{87}{100}$

4. If 300 people purchase a car on Saturday, how many of the cars sold would one expect to be red?

  a. 22
  b. 66
  c. 78
  d. 660

5. If it is known that a buyer would *not* purchase a black or green car, what is the probability that the car sold to that buyer is blue?

  a. $\dfrac{17}{100}$

  b. $\dfrac{4}{25}$

  c. $\dfrac{4}{21}$

  d. $\dfrac{17}{84}$

ANSWERS: 1.b., 2.d., 3.d., 4.b., 5.d.

The following is a description of the voter registration rolls for Putnam County by sex and party affiliation.

	Republican	Democrat	Independent
Male	20%	20%	9%
Female	18%	22%	11%

1. What is the probability that a randomly selected voter is an independent?

  a. $\dfrac{9}{100}$

  b. $\dfrac{11}{100}$

  c. $\dfrac{1}{5}$

  d. $\dfrac{4}{5}$

**Statistics Skills,
Including Probability**

2. What is the probability that a randomly selected voter is a female, given that the voter is Republican?

a. $\dfrac{1}{5}$

b. $\dfrac{9}{20}$

c. $\dfrac{19}{50}$

d. $\dfrac{9}{19}$

3. If 2,000 voters participated in the last election, how many would one expect to be Republican?

a. 38
b. 360
c. 400
d. 760

4. What is the probability that a randomly selected voter is *not* a Democrat?

a. .20
b. .22
c. .44
d. .58

ANSWERS: 1.c., 2.d., 3.d., 4.d.

A produce manager observed that shoppers chose the following percentages of fruit during the first week of May.

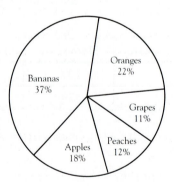

1. What is the probability that a shopper will choose a banana or apple?

a. .18
b. .37
c. .45
d. .55

2. If the produce manager has $600 to restock the produce section, how much should he spend on oranges?

   a. $132
   b. $220
   c. $660
   d. $1,320

3. If it is known that Jerry will buy only oranges, grapes, or peaches, what is the probability that he buys peaches if he chooses only one kind of fruit?

   a. $\dfrac{3}{25}$

   b. $\dfrac{4}{15}$

   c. $\dfrac{12}{23}$

   d. $\dfrac{6}{17}$

ANSWERS: 1.d., 2.a., 3.b.

Statistics Skills, Including Probability

Logical Reasoning Skills

I.E.1.
The student will deduce facts of set inclusion or set noninclusion from a diagram.

Venn diagrams will be used to picture the relationship between sets. Each Venn diagram will include a universal set, a set of all elements. The universal set will be drawn as follows:

Circles representing other sets will divide the universal set into nonempty regions. For example, given the universal set U and set A, the inside of the circle represents the region containing the *elements* or members of A.

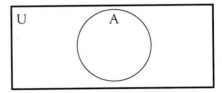

The region outside of the circle

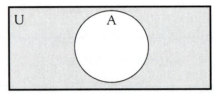

represents the region containing elements of U that are *not* in A (A'). A' is said to be the complement of A.

The following relationships occur between the universal set and at least two other given sets.

RELATION **1:** If set A and set B are subsets of U, the union of these two sets ($A \cup B$) is the set consisting of all the elements that belong to A or B.

(a) If A and B have no elements in common, the circles do not overlap. The union of A and B is the following shaded region:

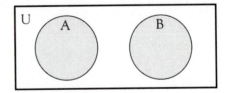

$A \cup B$ = shaded region

True statements:
    (1) Any element that is a member of A is also a member of U.
    (2) Any element that is a member of B is also a member of U.

(b) If *A* and *B* have some elements in common, their circles overlap. The union of *A* and *B* is the following shaded area:

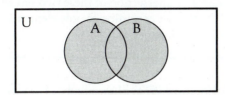

True statements:
   (1) Any element that is a member of *A* is also a member of *U*.
   (2) Any element that is a member of *B* is also a member of *U*.
   (3) Some elements of *A* are also elements of *B*.
   (4) Some elements of *B* are also elements of *A*.

(c) If all elements of one set, *A*, are members of another set, *B*, then *A* is a subset of *B* ($A \subseteq B$). The union of *A* and *B* is *B*.

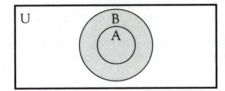

True statements:
   (1) Any element that is a member of *A* is also a member of *B*.
   (2) Any element that is a member of *A* is also a member of *U*.
   (3) Any element that is a member of *B* is also a member of *U*.
   (4) Any element that is a member of $A \cup B$ is also a member of *B*.

The complement of the union of *A* and *B* [$(A \cup B)'$] represents the region containing elements of *U* that are not in *A* or *B*.

The following Venn diagram is an example of $(A \cup B)'$.

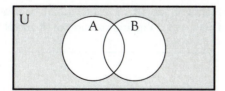

RELATION **2:** If set *A* and set *B* are subsets of *U*, the intersection of these two sets ($A \cap B$) is the set consisting of only elements that are in both *A* and *B*.

(a) If *A* and *B* have no elements in common, the set representing their intersection is the empty set ($\varnothing$).

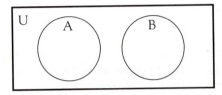

$$A \cap B = \varnothing$$

True statements:
    (1) Any element that is a member of *A* is also a member of *U*.
    (2) Any element that is a member of *B* is also a member of *U*.
    (3) No element is a member of both set *A* and set *B*.

(b) If *A* and *B* have some elements in common, the region representing $A \cap B$ will be the area common to both circles.

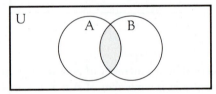

$$A \cap B = \text{shaded region}$$

True statements:
    (1) Any element that is a member of *A* is also a member of *U*.
    (2) Any element that is a member of *B* is also a member of *U*.
    (3) Some elements of *A* are also elements of *B*.
    (4) Some elements of *B* are also elements of *A*.
    (5) There is an element that is a member of $A \cap B$.

(c) If all the elements of one set, *A*, are members of another set, *B*, then *A* is a subset of *B* ($A \underline{c} B$). The intersection of *A* and *B* is *A*.

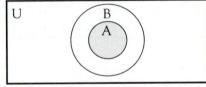

$$A \cap B = \text{shaded region}$$

True statements:
    (1) Any element that is a member of *A* is also a member of *B*.
    (2) Any element that is a member of *B* is a member of *U*.
    (3) Any element that is a member of *A* is a member of *U*.
    (4) Any element that is a member of $A \cap B$ is a member of *A*.
    (5) Any element that is a member of $A \cap B$ is a member of *B*.

The complement of the intersection of A and B [$(A \cap B)'$] represents the region containing elements of U that are not in both A and B. The following Venn diagram is one example of $(A \cap B)'$:

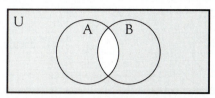

$(A \cap B)'$ = shaded region

To deduce facts when given a Venn diagram, do as follows:

STEP **1.** Look at the diagram. Read the first response.

STEP **2.** Shade the region identified first in the response.

STEP **3.** See if the shading matches the diagram given in the stimulus.

STEP **4.** Continue Steps 1 through 3 until the correct response is given.

Example **1:** Sets A, B, C, and U are related as shown in the diagram.

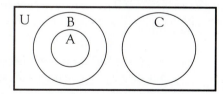

Which of the following statement(s) is/are true, assuming none of the regions is empty?

a. Any element that is a member of set C is an element of B.
b. Any element that is a member of set B is an element of A.
c. Any element that is a member of set A is an element of B.
d. There is an element that is a member of all three sets, A, B, C.   *(Continued)*

395

**Logical
Reasoning Skills**

Solution: Response "a." shading in the region that contains the element(s) of C.

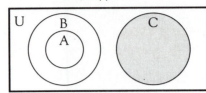

(1) Shade.

Shading shows that the member(s) is *not* an element of B.

(2) Evaluate the statement with the shading.

Response "b." Shading in the region that contains the element(s) of B.

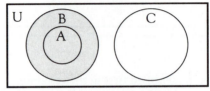

(1) Shade.

Shading shows that there is at least one member of B that is in A, but there is at least one member of B that is *not* in A.

(2) Evaluate the statement with the shading.

Response "c." Shading in the region that contains the element(s) of A.

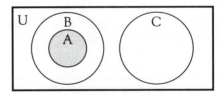

(1) Shade.

Shading shows that every member of A is an element of B.

(2) Evaluate the statement with the shading.

The solution is "c."

(*Note:* Response "d." is incorrect because C does not have any member in common with set A and set B.)

Example 1 may also be rewritten with set notation in the responses.

**Logical
Reasoning Skills**

Example **1:** Sets A, B, C, and U are related as shown in the diagram.

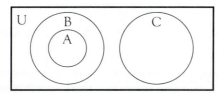

Which of the following statement(s) is true, assuming none of the regions is empty?

a. C ⊆ B.
b. B ⊆ A.
c. A ⊆ B.
d. (A ∩ B) ∩ C ≠ ∅

Solution: Using the relations given at the beginning of this section and the shading in the solution of Example 1, you can conclude that all the elements of set A are members of set B, A ⊆ B.

Example **2:** Sets A, B, C, and U are related as shown in the diagram.

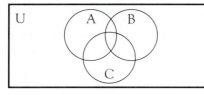

Which of the following statement(s) is true, assuming none of the regions is empty?

a. Any element that is a member of both A and B is a member of C.
b. There is an element that is a member of set A, set B, and set C.
c. Any element that is a member of U is a member of set A, set B, or set C.
d. None of the above statements is true.

(Continued)

**Logical
Reasoning Skills**

Solution: Response "a." Shading the region that contains the element(s) of both A and B.

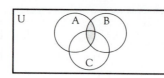

(1) Shade $A \cap B$.

Shading shows that there is at least one element of set C that is a member of set A and set B, but there is at least one member that is not in set C.

(2) Evaluate the statement with the shading.

Response "b." Shading the region that represents the element(s) that are in set A, set B, and set C.

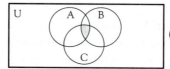

(1) Shade $A \cap B \cap C$.

Shading shows that there is an element that is a member of all three sets.

(2) Evaluate the statement with the shading.

The solution is "b."

(*Note:* Response "c." is incorrect because the shaded region shows that there are elements of U that are not in set A, set B, or set C.)

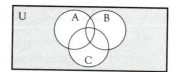

Example **3:** Sets *A*, *B*, *C*, and *U* are related as shown in the diagram.

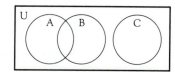

**Logical
Reasoning Skills**

Which of the following statement(s) is true, assuming none of the regions is empty?

a. $A \cup B = \varnothing$
b. $A \cap B = \varnothing$
c. $A \subseteq B$
d. $A \cap C = \varnothing$

Solution: Response "a." The region of $A \cup B$ is

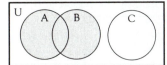 (1) Shade.

and, therefore, not empty. (2) Evaluate the statement with the shading.

Response "b." The region of $A \cap B$ is

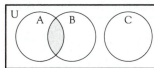 (1) Shade.

and, therefore, not empty. (2) Evaluate the statement with the shading.

Response "c." Set *A* is

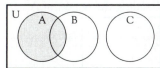 (1) Shade.

not contained in *B*. (2) Evaluate the statement
Therefore, $A \not\subseteq B$. with the shading.

(*Note:* $A \not\subseteq B$ is read "*A* is not a subset of *B*.")

Response "d." The region of $A \cap C$

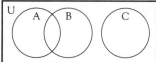 (1) Shade.

is empty since set *A* and (2) Evaluate the statement
set *C* have no element(s) with the shading.
in common.

The solution is "d."

**Logical
Reasoning Skills**

Example **4:**

Sets *A*, *B*, and *U* are related as shown in the diagram.

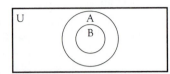

Which of the following statement(s) is *not* true, assuming none of the regions is empty?

a. Any element that is a member of set *B* is a member of set *A*.
b. $A \cup A' = U$
c. Any element that is a member of set *A* is a member of set *U*.
d. $A \cap B = A$

Solution:

Response "a." Shading the region of *B*

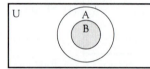

shows that they are also members of *A*.

(1) Shade.

(2) Evaluate the statement with the shading.

Response "b." Shading the region of *A* (≡) and *A'* (||||)

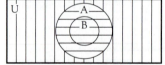

shows that the elements of both sets are the same as *U*.

(1) Shade.

(2) Evaluate the statement with the shading.

Response "c." Shading the region of *A*

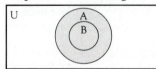

shows that they are also members of *U*.

(1) Shade.

(2) Evaluate the statement with the shading.

Response "d." Shading the region of $A \cap B$

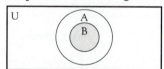

shows that the intersection is *B*, not *A*.

(1) Shade.

(2) Evaluate the statement with the shading.

The solution is "d."

1. Sets *A*, *B*, *C*, and *U* are related as shown in the diagram.

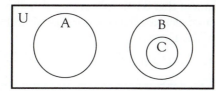

Which of the following statement(s) is true, assuming none of the regions is empty?

a. No element is a member of all three sets *A*, *B*, and *C*.
b. Any element that is a member of set *B* is a member of set *C*.
c. Any element that is a member of set *A* is a member of set *B*.
d. None of the above statements is true.

2. Sets *A*, *B*, *C*, and *U* are related as shown in the diagram.

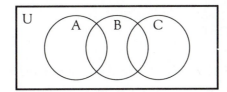

Which of the following statement(s) is true, assuming none of the regions is empty?

a. $A \cap B = \varnothing$
b. $A \cap C = \varnothing$
c. $B \cap C = \varnothing$
d. $A \cup B = \varnothing$

3. Sets *A*, *B*, *C*, and *U* are related as shown in the diagram.

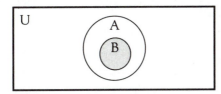

Which of the following statement(s) is *not* true, assuming none of the regions is empty?

a. Any element that is a member of set *B* is also a member of set *U*.
b. Any element that is a member of set *A* is also a member of set *B*.
c. Any element that is a member of set *B* is also a member of set *A*.
d. Any element that is a member of set *A* is also a member of set *U*.

4. Sets *A*, *B*, *C*, and *U* are related as shown in the diagram.

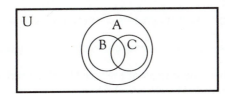

Which of the following statements is true, assuming none of the regions is empty?

**Logical
Reasoning Skills**

I.E.1.
Sample Items

a. Any element that is a member of set *A* is also a member of set *B*.
b. Any element that is a member of set *A* is also a member of set *C*.
c. There is an element that is a member of all three sets *A*, *B*, and *C*.
d. None of the above statements is true.

5. Sets *A*, *B*, *C*, and *U* are related as shown in the diagram.

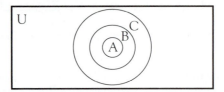

Which of the following statement(s) is *not* true, assuming none of the regions is empty?

a. $B \subseteq C$
b. $B \cap C = B$
c. $A \cup C = C$
d. $C \subseteq B$

6. Sets *A*, *B*, *C*, and *U* are related as shown in the diagram.

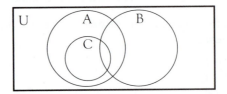

Which of the following statements is true, assuming none of the regions is empty?

a. $A \cap B = C$
b. $A \cup B = \emptyset$
c. $(A \cap B) \subseteq C$
d. $A \cup A' = U$

ANSWERS: 1.a., 2.b., 3.b., 4.c., 5.d., 6.d.

II.E.1.
The student will
identify statements
equivalent to the
negations of simple
and compound
statements.

A statement is something that can be judged true or false. Two statements can be combined together into compound statements. Three types of compound statements are

1. Conjunctions—two statements connected by the word "and" or "but."

2. Disjunctions—two statements connected by the word "or."

3. Conditionals—one statement preceded by the word "if" and one statement preceded by the word "then."

In logic, variables such as *p*, *q*, and *r* are sometimes used in place of statements. For example, instead of writing the conjunction "Today is Monday and tomorrow is Tuesday," the pattern, "*p* and *q*," can be used. The variable *p* represents the first statement, "Today is Monday," and *q* represents the second statement, "tomorrow is Tuesday."

The disjunction, "The tire is flat or the rim is bent," can be written symbolically as "*p* or *q*," where *p* represents "The tire is flat" and *q* represents "the rim is bent."

This skill asks for the negations of simple and compound statements. The symbol $\sim$ is used to indicate the negation. The word "not" is sometimes used instead of the negation sign. The negation of a statement changes it from true to false or vice versa. For example, the negation of the statement "I will run," is "I will not run." The negation of "I will not make the team" is "I will make the team."

Use the negations of simple statements and the following steps to find equivalent negations of compound statements:

STEP 1. Identify the compound statement in the stimulus as a conjunction, disjunction, or conditional. Identify the statement for *p* and the statement for *q*.

STEP 2. Identify the pattern.

(a) Conjunction: $\sim (p \text{ and } q) \equiv (\sim p) \text{ or } (\sim q)$
(b) Disjunction: $\sim (p \text{ or } q) \equiv (\sim p) \text{ and } (\sim q)$
(c) Conditional: $\sim (\text{If } p, \text{ then } q) \equiv p \text{ and } (\sim q)$

STEP 3. Write the answer using the right-hand side of the pattern.

Example 1: Find the negation of the statement "If it is cold tomorrow, then the picnic is canceled."

Solution:	Conditional	(1) Identify type and *p*
	p = It is cold tomorrow.	and *q*.
	q = The picnic is canceled.	
	$\sim (\text{If } p, \text{ then } q) \equiv p \text{ and } (\sim q)$	(2) Identify pattern.
	It is cold tomorrow and the picnic is not canceled.	(3) Write the answer.

**Logical
Reasoning Skills**

Example **2:** Find the negation of the statement "Prices are rising and inflation is climbing."

Solution:

Conjunction p = Prices are rising. q = Inflation is climbing.	(1)	Identify type and p and q.
$\sim(p \text{ and } q) \equiv (\sim p)$ or $(\sim q)$	(2)	Identify pattern.
Prices are not rising or inflation is not climbing.	(3)	Write the answer.

Example **3:** Find the negation of the statement "Jane is not at home or Bill is at school."

Solution:

Disjunction p = Jane is not at home. q = Bill is at school.	(1)	Identify type and p and q.
$\sim(p \text{ or } q) = (\sim p)$ and $(\sim q)$	(2)	Identify pattern.
Jane is at home and Bill is not at school.	(3)	Write the answer.

Negations must also be found in simple statements that begin with quantifier words, such as "all," "none," "some are," or "some are not." Use the following steps to find the negations of these statements.

STEP **1.** Draw the box.

All   Some are

None   Some are not
                                                       (one is)

**Logical
Reasoning Skills**

STEP **2.**   Identify the type of simple statement.

STEP **3.**   Start at that word in the chart and draw a diagonal line to the far opposite corner.

STEP **4.**   Rewrite the statement replacing the quantifier word(s) with the new quantifier(s).

Example **4:**   Find the negation of "All children are small."

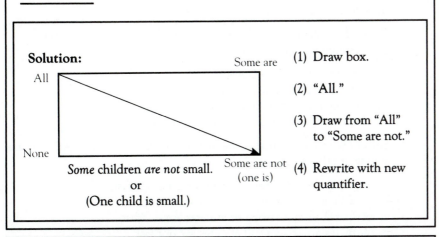

Solution:

(1) Draw box.

(2) "All."

(3) Draw from "All" to "Some are not."

(4) Rewrite with new quantifier.

Some children *are not* small.
or
(One child is small.)

Example **5:**   Find the statement that is the negation of "Some bears are tree climbers."

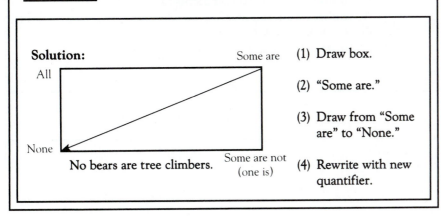

Solution:

(1) Draw box.

(2) "Some are."

(3) Draw from "Some are" to "None."

(4) Rewrite with new quantifier.

No bears are tree climbers.

Logical Reasoning Skills

II.E.1.
Sample Items

1. Select the statement that is the negation of the statement "If the stock-market prices close high, then the employees will sell."

   a. If the stock-market prices do not close high, then the employees will not sell.
   b. The stock-market prices close high and the employees do not sell.
   c. If the employees do not sell, then the stock-market prices do not close high.
   d. The stock-market prices close high and the employees do sell.

2. Select the statement that is the negation of the statement "All highways are safe."

   a. No highway is safe.
   b. Some highways are safe.
   c. If it is not a highway, then it is not safe.
   d. Some highways are not safe.

3. Select the statement that is the negation of the statement "Jane is late and the show has started."

   a. Jane isn't late and the show hasn't started.
   b. Jane is late or the show has started.
   c. Jane isn't late and the show has started.
   d. Jane isn't late or the show hasn't started.

4. Select the statement that is the negation of the statement "Some cookies contain cholesterol."

   a. No cookies contain cholesterol.
   b. If it is a cookie, then it contains cholesterol.
   c. All cookies contain cholesterol.
   d. Some cookies do not contain cholesterol.

5. Select the statement that is the negation of the statement "Athletes are strong or athletes are fast."

   a. Athletes are not strong and athletes are not fast.
   b. If athletes are fast, then athletes are strong.
   c. Athletes are not strong or athletes are not fast.
   d. Athletes are strong and athletes are not fast.

6. Select the statement that is the negation of the statement "No student works full time."

   a. If you work full time, you are a student.
   b. All students work full time.
   c. Some students work full time.
   d. If you are not a student, then you don't work full time.

ANSWERS: 1.b., 2.d., 3.d., 4.a., 5.a., 6.c.

To find the equivalence of a conditional (if _____ , then _____), do as follows:

Logical Reasoning Skills

STEP 1. Identify the statements for p and q in the stimulus.

II.E.2.
The student will determine equivalence or nonequivalence of statements.

STEP 2. Rewrite each of the responses in terms of p and q.

STEP 3. The response that matches one of the following three patterns is the solution.

(a) If $\sim q$, then $\sim p$.
(b) $\sim p$ or q.
(c) q or $\sim p$.

(*Note:* b and c are the same statements on opposite sides of the word "or.")

Example 1: Select the statement below that is logically equivalent to "If I graduate from college, then I will get a good job."

a. I graduate from college and I get a good job.
b. If I don't get a good job, then I didn't graduate from college.
c. If I get a good job, then I graduate from college.
d. If I don't graduate from college, then I won't get a good job.

Solution: $p =$ I graduate from college.   (1) Identify p and q.
$q =$ I will get a good job.

Response "a." p and q (2) Rewrite responses.
Response "b." If $\sim q$, then $\sim p$
Response "c." If q, then p
Response "d." If $\sim p$, then $\sim q$

Response "b." is the solution.   (3) Matches pattern "3a."

**Logical
Reasoning Skills**

To find the equivalence of a statement that begins "It is not true . . . ," do the following:

STEP 1. Identify p and q in the stimulus.

STEP 2. Rewrite the stimulus in terms of p and q. (*Hint*: Replace "It is not true" with the $\sim$ sign.)

STEP 3. Find the response that *matches* one of the negation patterns (Skill II.E.1.).

(a) $\sim$ (p and q) = $\sim p$ or $\sim q$
(b) $\sim$ (p or q) = $\sim p$ and $\sim q$
(c) $\sim$ (If p, then q) = p and $\sim q$
(d) $\sim$ (All p are) = Some p are not
(e) $\sim$ (No p are) = Some p are (or one p is)
(f) $\sim$ (Some p are) = No p are
(g) $\sim$ (Some p are not) = All p are

STEP 4. Replace p and q with their respective statements or negations.

Example **2:** Which of the following statements is logically equivalent to "It is not true that Terry can sing or Ruby can't dance."

a. If Terry can sing, then Ruby can't dance.
b. Terry can't sing and Ruby can dance.
c. If Ruby can dance, then Terry can't sing.
d. Terry can't sing and Ruby can't dance.

Solution:

p = Terry can sing,
q = Ruby can't dance

(1) Identify p and q.

It is not true that Terry can sing or Ruby can't dance.
~(p or q)

(2) Write the stimulus in p and q.

~(p or q) = ~p and ~q

(3) Matches 3b.

Terry can't sing and Ruby can dance.

(4) Write ~p and ~q.

The solution is "b."

Example **3:** What statement is logically equivalent to "It is not true that all trucks can carry heavy loads."

Solution:

p = all trucks can carry heavy loads

(1) Identify p.

It is not true that all trucks can carry heavy loads.

(2) Write the stimulus in p and q.

~(All p)
~(All p can) = Some p cannot

(3) Matches 3d.

Some trucks cannot carry heavy loads.

(4) Replace p.

1. Select the statement below that is logically equivalent to "If the animal is a bird, then it flies."

a. If the animal is not a bird, then it does not fly.
b. If it doesn't fly, then the animal is not a bird.
c. The animal is a bird and it flies.
d. If it flies, then the animal is a bird.

**II.E.2.
Sample Items**

**Logical
Reasoning Skills**

2. Select the statement below that is logically equivalent to "It is not true that some women are astronauts."

   a. No woman is an astronaut.
   b. If the person is an astronaut, then that person is a woman.
   c. All women are astronauts.
   d. Some women are not astronauts.

3. Select the statement below that is *not* logically equivalent to "If the Indians win the game, then they will be the state champions."

   a. The Indians did not win the game or they are the state champions.
   b. If the Indians are not the state champions, then they did not win the game.
   c. If they are the state champions, then the Indians won the game.
   d. The Indians are the state champions or they did not win the game.

4. Select the statement below that is logically equivalent to "It is not true that fish have to swim and birds have to fly."

   a. All fish have to swim.
   b. Fish don't have to swim or birds don't have to fly.
   c. If it is a bird, it has to fly.
   d. Fish don't have to swim and birds don't have to fly.

5. Select the statement below that is logically equivalent to "It is not true that no American-made cars have air bags."

   a. Mary's American-made Chevrolet has an air bag.
   b. All American made cars have air bags.
   c. If it is an American made car, it has an air bag.
   d. If the car doesn't have an air bag, it is not made in America.

ANSWERS: 1.b., 2.a., 3.c., 4.b., 5.a.

**II.E.3.
The student draws
logical conclusions
from data.**

One type of problem in this skill will present in the stimulus criteria or requirements that must be satisfied. Information will also be given about individual cases. The question will ask which of the individual cases have met these requirements. To solve problems with given conditions, do as follows:

STEP **1.** Read the problem carefully and determine what the requirements or conditions are.

STEP **2.** Record the given information for each case under the identified requirements.

STEP **3.** The individual case(s) that has/have met all the criteria will be the solution.

Example **1:** Read the requirements and each city's qualification for obtaining a new tourist attraction. Then identify which of the cities would qualify for the attraction.

To qualify for a tourist attraction, a city must have a work force population of at least 10,000 people, have 3 major highways, and be located in a climate where the average temperatures range between 50° and 90° for at least 6 months out of the year.

Del Rio City has a work force of 13,000 people, is located on the intersection of I-18 and U.S. 90, and has an average (year-round) temperature of 76°.

Star City has a work force of 11,000 people, has 3 major highways passing through it, and has an average temperature of 52° from October until April.

New Hope has a work force of 9,000 people, has 4 major highways, and has an average temperature of 70° for 9 months out of the year.

Solution: List the requirements:

	Work Force $\geq 10{,}000$	**Highways** ≥ 3	**Average Temperature for 6 Months:** $50 \leq$ temp ≤ 90
Del Rio City	wf = 13,000	Highways = 2	76°–12 months
Star City	wf = 11,000	Highways = 3	52°– 7 months
New Hope	wf = 9,000	Highways = 4	70°– 9 months

Del Rio does not have enough highways.

New Hope does not have a large enough work force.

Star City meets all requirements.

Star City is the solution.

(1) List requirements.

(2) Record given information.

(3) Check individual cases.

The second type of problem will give two premises or statements in the stimulus, with directions to choose the response that states the conclusion that can be logically deduced from the premises. One method to test the validity of each of the arguments formed by the premises and each response is by the use of Euler circles. Euler circles were developed to test syllogistic logic arguments,

**Logical
Reasoning Skills**

that is, relationships among statements that begin with all, none, some are, some are not, and so on.

Recall from Skill I.E.1. that the Venn diagram for the statement "All *A*s are *B*s" is

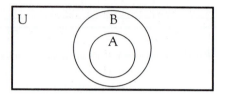

All *A*s are *B*s.

The Venn diagram for "No *A*s are *B*s" is

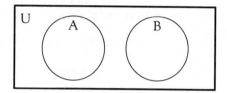

No *A*s are *B*s.

The statement "Some *A*s are *B*s" is represented as follows by the Venn diagram:

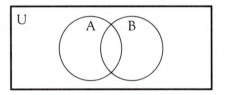

Some *A*s are *B*s.

The preceding Venn diagram also represents the statement "Some *A*s are not *B*s."

To test the validity of the argument formed by the premises and each response, do as follows:

STEP **1.**   Draw a Euler circle for each premise.

STEP **2.**   Using the diagram, test each response to determine which one necessarily follows from the set of premises.

**Logical
Reasoning Skills**

Example **1:**

Given that
  i. all Russians are friendly;
  ii. Ivan is a Russian;
determine which conclusion can be logically deduced.

a. Ivan is friendly.
b. Ivan is not a Russian.
c. Ivan is not friendly.
d. All friendly people are Russian.

Solution:

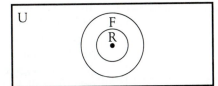

(1) Draw Euler circle for "All As and Bs" where All Russians (R) are friendly (F). Put Ivan (•) in circle A since he is Russian.

Response "a." *Ivan is friendly.* Yes, because Ivan is a member of the set of friendly people

(2) Check responses against diagram.

Response "b." *Ivan is not Russian.* No, because Ivan is a member of the set of all Russians

Response "c." *Ivan is not friendly.* No, because Ivan is a member of the set of friendly people

Response "d." *All friendly people are Russian.*

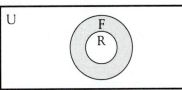

No, the shaded region represents friendly people who are not Russian.

The solution is "a."

**Logical
Reasoning Skills**

Example **2:**

Given that
  i. no animal who is a pet is wild;
  ii. all dogs are pets;
determine which conclusion can be logically deduced.

  a. All dogs are wild.
  b. Some dogs are wild.
  c. No dogs are wild.
  d. None of the above.

Solution:

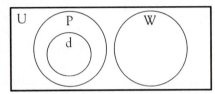

(1) Draw Euler circle for "No *A*s are *B*s," where "No animal who is a pet (*P*) is wild (*W*)." Put dogs in pets since all dogs (*d*) are pets (P).

Response "a." *All dogs are wild.* No, the set of dogs is not a subset of wild animals.

(2) Check responses.

Response "b." *Some dogs are wild.* No, the set of dogs has no member in common with the set of wild animals.

Response "c." *No dogs are wild.* Yes, the set of dogs have *no* members of the set of wild animals.

Response "d." *None of the above.* No, because response "c." is the solution.

The solution is "c."

**II.E.3.
Sample Items**

1. Read the requirements *and* each applicant's qualifications for obtaining a Charge-It card. Then identify which of the applicants would qualify for the card.

To qualify for a Charge-It card, an applicant must have a gross income of $25,000 if single ($40,000 combined if married) and have been employed with the same company for at least 5 years.

Mr. Sanchez and his wife have a combined income of $32,000. He has worked at the ABC Company for 10 years.

Dave Nichols is single. He has worked for Southern Bell for 5 years and makes $26,000.

Martha Davis is married and has worked for the same company for 8 years. She and her husband have a combined income of $45,000.

a. Mr. Sanchez
b. Dave Nichols and Martha Davis
c. All three are eligible for the card.
d. No one is eligible for the card.

2. Given that

    i. some woods are porous;
    ii. pecan is a wood;

determine which conclusion can be logically deduced.

a. Pecan is a porous wood.
b. Pecan is not a porous wood.
c. No porous wood is pecan.
d. None of the above.

3. Given that

    i. all Floridians like the beach;
    ii. Sam is a Floridian;

determine which conclusion can be logically deduced.

a. Sam doesn't like the beach.
b. Sam is not a Floridian.
c. Sam likes the beach.
d. None of the above.

4. Given that

    i. no singers are dancers;
    ii. all dancers are agile;

determine which conclusion can be logically deduced.

a. No singers are agile.
b. Some singers are agile.
c. All singers are agile.
d. None of the above.

5. Read the requirements and each applicant's qualifications for obtaining a mathematics scholarship. Then identify which of the applicants would qualify for the scholarship.

To qualify for a mathematics scholarship, an applicant must have taken four mathematics courses, have a GPA of at least 3.0, and be planning to major in applied mathematics or mathematics education.

Jean Smith has taken the following mathematics courses: Algebra I, Algebra II, Calculus, Trigonometry, and Geometry. She has a GPA of 2.6 and is planning to major in applied mathematics.

Nelson Ramos has a GPA of 3.5. He is majoring in mathematics education and has completed six mathematics courses.

Sandy Rivera is majoring in political science, has a GPA of 3.2, and has taken four mathematics courses.

**Logical
Reasoning Skills**

a. Jean Smith
b. Nelson Ramos
c. Sandy Rivera
d. All of the applicants are eligible for the scholarship.

ANSWERS: 1.b., 2.d., 3.c., 4.d., 5.b.

**II.E.4.
The student will recognize that an argument may not be valid even though its conclusion is true.**

An argument consists of two parts, a set of premises and a conclusion. The conclusion always follows the word "therefore." An argument is valid when its conclusion can be deduced from a given set of premises. The conclusion does not necessarily have to be true. In this skill, however, all the conclusions will be true statements, but one of the arguments in the responses will not be valid.

The validity of the arguments in the responses can be tested by Euler circles (See Skill II.E.3.). Use the following steps to select the argument that is not valid:

STEP 1. Draw an Euler circle for a set of premises in the first response.

STEP 2. See if the conclusion can be deduced from that set.

STEP 3. If the conclusion does follow, draw a Euler circle for another response. If the conclusion does not follow, that response is the solution.

STEP 4. Continue testing the responses until the invalid argument is found.

**Logical
Reasoning Skills**

Example **1:** All of the following arguments, "a." through "d.," have true conclusions, but one of the arguments is not valid. Select the argument that is *not* valid.

a. All peppers are hot foods and all hot foods burn my mouth. Therefore, all peppers burn my mouth.
b. All peppers are hot foods. Jalapeño is a pepper. Therefore, Jalapeños are hot foods.
c. All peppers burn my mouth and all hot foods burn my mouth. Therefore, all peppers are hot foods.
d. All peppers are hot foods. No fruits are hot foods. Therefore, peppers are not fruits.

Solution: Test Response "a."

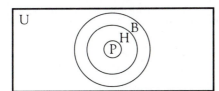

	(1) Draw Euler circle for foods. All peppers (*P*) are hot (*H*). All hot foods (*H*) burn my mouth (*B*).
All peppers burn my mouth. Yes, because peppers is a subset of hot things	(2) Test conclusion.
	(3) Conclusion does follow.

Continue testing:

Test response "b."

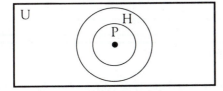

	(1) All peppers (*P*) are hot (*H*) foods. Jalapeño (•) is a pepper (*P*).
Jalapeños are hot. Yes, because Jalapeños are members of the set of hot foods	(3) Conclusion does follow.

Continue testing:

Test response "c."

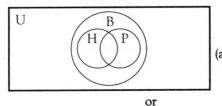

(a) (1) All peppers (*P*) burn my mouth (*B*). All hot foods (*H*) burn my mouth (*B*).

or

(Continued)

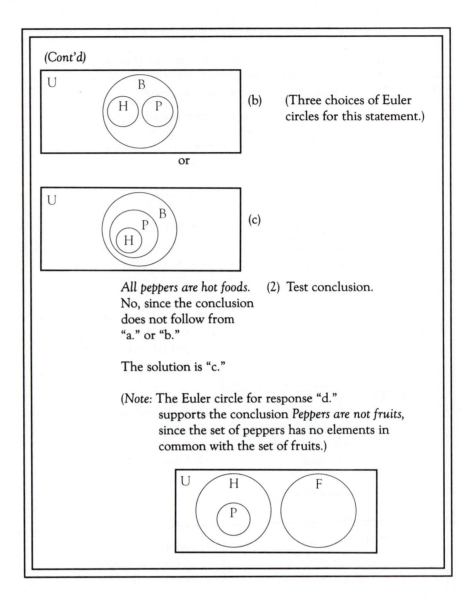

(Cont'd)

(b) (Three choices of Euler circles for this statement.)

or

(c)

All peppers are hot foods. (2) Test conclusion.
No, since the conclusion
does not follow from
"a." or "b."

The solution is "c."

(*Note:* The Euler circle for response "d."
supports the conclusion *Peppers are not fruits,*
since the set of peppers has no elements in
common with the set of fruits.)

II.E.4.
Sample Items

1. All of the following arguments, a–d, have true conclusions, but one of the arguments is not valid. Select the argument that is <u>not</u> valid.

   a. All dolphins are mammals and all mammals are warm-blooded. Therefore, all dolphins are warm-blooded.
   b. All dolphins are mammals and all dolphins are warm-blooded. Therefore, all mammals are warm-blooded.
   c. All dolphins are mammals. Flipper is a dolphin. Therefore, Flipper is a mammal.
   d. All dolphins are warm-blooded and all warm-blooded animals are mammals. Therefore, all dolphins are mammals.

2. All of the following arguments, a–d, have true conclusions, but one of the arguments is not valid. Select the argument that is <u>not</u> valid.

   a. All citizens are patriotic. John is a citizen. Therefore, John is patriotic.
   b. All elements are pure substances. Salt is not a pure substance. Therefore, salt is not an element.

c. All mosquitoes are friendly insects and all friendly insects are pests. Therefore, all mosquitoes are pests.

d. All days in April are windy. Today is windy. Therefore, today is a day in April.

3. All of the following arguments, a–d, have true conclusions, but one of the arguments is not valid. Select the argument that is <u>not</u> valid.

a. All students are smart and all students are motivated. Therefore, all smart students are motivated.

b. All cats have feet. All tigers are cats. Therefore, all tigers have feet.

c. Every human is a worker. Every worker is happy. Therefore, every human is happy.

d. All trees are plants. All plants should be preserved. Therefore, all trees should be preserved.

4. All of the following arguments, a–d, have true conclusions, but one of the arguments is not valid. Select the argument that is <u>not</u> valid.

a. All beavers are swimmers and all swimmers live in water. Therefore, all beavers live in water.

b. All beavers are swimmers. All animals are swimmers. Therefore, all beavers are animals.

c. All beavers are swimmers. All swimmers have webbed feet. Therefore, all beavers have webbed feet.

d. All beavers are swimmers. Terry's pet is a beaver. Therefore, Terry's pet is a swimmer.

5. All of the following arguments, a–d, have true conclusions, but one of the arguments is not valid. Select the argument that is <u>not</u> valid.

a. All mathematics is abstract. Humanities is not abstract. Therefore, humanities is not mathematics.

b. All mathematics is abstract. Algebra is mathematics. Therefore, algebra is abstract.

c. All algebra is mathematics. Geometry is not mathematics. Therefore, geometry is not algebra.

d. All algebra is abstract. All mathematics is abstract. Therefore, all algebra is mathematics.

ANSWERS: 1.b., 2.d., 3.a., 4.b., 5.d.

A valid argument consists of two parts, the set of premises and the conclusion. The premise set must contain at least one argument. The two parts of a valid reasoning pattern are illustrated below:

| If p, then q | Premise |
| Therefore, q | Conclusion |

This skill will give a premise of arguments, expressed in words, and ask for the conclusion that will make a valid argument. Five reasoning patterns will be used. Use the following steps to recognize valid reasoning patterns in everyday language:

> **III.E.1.**
> **The student will recognize valid reasoning patterns as illustrated by valid arguments in everyday language.**

STEP **1.** Identify p and q (and, where applicable, r).

STEP **2.** Write the statements in the premise in terms of p and q (and r).

STEP **3.** Select one of the following five patterns that matches the pattern in the premise.

    (a) If p, then q
        $\underline{p\qquad\qquad}$
            $\therefore q$

    (b) If p, then q
        $\underline{\sim q\qquad\qquad}$
            $\therefore \sim p$

    (c) If p, then q
        $\underline{\text{If } q\text{, then } r}$
        $\therefore$ If p, then r

    (d) p or q*
        $\underline{\sim p\qquad\qquad}$
            $\therefore q$

    (e) p or q*
        $\underline{\sim q\qquad\qquad}$
            $\therefore p$

    *[(d) and (e) are alternate forms of the same pattern.]

STEP **4.** Use the pattern to write the conclusion in everyday language.

Example **1:** Read the following set of premises and find the conclusion that will make a valid argument: "If I get the flu, then I will miss work. I get the flu."

Solution:	p = I get the flu, q = I will miss work	(1) Identify p and q.
	If p, then q $\underline{p\qquad\qquad}$	(2) Write premise in terms of p and q.
	Conclusion is q.	(3) Matches pattern (a).
	I will miss work.	(4) Write in everyday language.

**Logical
Reasoning Skills**

Example **2:** Read the following set of premises and find the conclusion that will make a valid argument: "If the roast is overcooked, then it will be tough. The roast is not tough."

Solution:		
p = the roast is overcooked q = it will be tough	(1) Identify p and q.
If p, then q $\sim q$	(2) Write the premise in terms of p or q.
Conclusion is $\sim p$.	(3) Matches pattern (b).
The roast is not overcooked.	(4) Write in everyday language.

Example **3:** Read the following set of premises and find the conclusion that will make a valid argument: "The heater is working or we will have to build a fire. The heater is not working."

Solution:		
p = The heater is working. q = We will have to build a fire.	(1) Identify p and q.
p or q $\sim p$	(2) Write the premise in terms of p or q.
Conclusion is q.	(3) Matches pattern (d).
We will have to build a fire.	(4) Write in everyday language.

**Logical
Reasoning Skills**

Example **4:** Read the following set of premises and find the conclusion that will make a valid argument: "If the mail arrives on time, then I will get the suit. If I get the suit, then I will go to the employment office."

Solution:		
p = the mail arrives on time q = I will get the suit r = I will go to the employment office	(1)	Identify p, q, and r.
If p, then q <u>If q, then r</u>	(2)	Write the premise in terms of p, q, and r.
The conclusion is "If p, then r."	(3)	Matches pattern (c).
If the mail arrives on time, then I will go to the employment office.	(4)	Write in everyday language.

Example **5:** Read the following set of premises and find the conclusion that will make a valid argument: "If all the fish survive, then no toxic chemicals are present. Some toxic chemicals are present."

Solution:		
p = all the fish survive q = no toxic chemicals are present	(1)	Identify p and q.
If p, then q <u>$\sim q$</u>	(2)	Write the premise in terms of p and q.
The conclusion is $\sim p$.	(3)	Matches pattern (b).
Some fish do not survive.	(4)	Write in everyday language. (Recall: $\sim$ [all are] $\equiv$ some are not.)

**III.E.1.
Sample Items**

1. Read the following set of premises and select the conclusion that will make a valid argument.

"If the fruit is ripe, then we will pick it on Tuesday. If we pick the fruit on Tuesday, then we will ship it on Thursday."

a. If the fruit is ripe, then we will ship it on Thursday.
b. If the fruit is not ripe, then we will not pick it on Tuesday.

   c. If the fruit is not ripe, then we will not ship it on Thursday.

   d. If we ship it on Thursday, then the fruit is ripe.

2. Read the following set of premises and select the conclusion that will make a valid argument.

   "If Tom's ankle heals, then he will compete in the Olympic games. Tom did not compete in the games."

   a. If Tom competed in the Olympic games, then his ankle healed.
   b. If Tom's ankle does not heal, then he will not compete in the Olympic games.
   c. Tom's ankle did not heal.
   d. Tom did compete in the games.

3. Read the following set of premises and select the conclusion that will make a valid argument.

   "Jane won the spelling bee or Ruth won the essay contest. Ruth lost the essay contest."

   a. If Ruth lost the essay contest, then Jane lost the spelling bee.
   b. Jane won the spelling bee.
   c. Jane lost the spelling bee.
   d. Ruth won the essay contest.

4. Read the following set of premises and select the conclusion that will make a valid argument.

   "If I make at least 400 on the entrance test, then I will be accepted into the school of pharmacy. I made 450 on the entrance test."

   a. I made a high score.
   b. If I don't make at least 400 on the entrance test, then I will not be accepted into the school of pharmacy.
   c. I am accepted into the school of pharmacy.
   d. If I am accepted into the school of pharmacy, then I made at least 400 on the entrance test.

5. Read the following set of premises and select the conclusion that will make a valid argument.

   "If some club member does not vote, then all election results are invalid. Francis, a club member, did not vote."

   a. All election results are valid.
   b. If all election results are invalid, then some club member did not vote.
   c. If some club member does not vote, then all election results are valid.
   d. All election results are invalid.

ANSWERS: 1.a., 2.c., 3.b., 4.c., 5.d.

Logical Reasoning Skills

III.E.2.
The student selects applicable rules for transforming statements without affecting their meaning.

To select the rule of logical equivalence that directly transforms one statement (i.) into a second statement (ii.), do as follows:

STEP 1. Identify p and q in statement "i." and write in terms of p and q.

STEP 2. Write statement "ii." in terms of p and q.

STEP 3. Write answer in Step 1 equivalent to answer in Step 2.

Example 1: Find the rule of logical equivalence that *directly* (in one step) transforms statement "i." into statement "ii."

  i. Some girls and boys are not blonde.
  ii. Not all girls and boys are blonde.

Solution:

i. *Some* girls and boys are not blonde.
Some are not p.

(1) Rewrite "i." in terms of p *and* q.

ii. *Not all* girls and boys *are* blonde.
Not all are p.

(2) Rewrite "ii."

"Some are not p" is equivalent to "not all are p."

(3) Set is equivalent.

Example **2:** Find the rule of logical equivalence that directly (in one step) transforms statement "i." into statement "ii."

    i. If I read the book, then I enjoy the movie.
    ii. If I didn't enjoy the movie, then I didn't read the book.

Solution:

  i. *If* I read the book, *then* I enjoy the movie.
    If p, then *q*.

    (1) Rewrite "i." in terms of *p* and *q*.

  ii. *If* I *don't* enjoy the movie, *then* I *don't* read the book.
    If not *q*, then not *p*.

    (2) Rewrite "ii."

"If *p*, then *q*" is equivalent to "if not *q*, then not *p*."

    (3) Set is equivalent.

III.E.2.
Sample Items

1. Find the rule of logical equivalence that directly (in one step) transforms statement "i." into statement "ii."

    i. Not all whole numbers are natural numbers.
    ii. Some whole numbers are not natural numbers.

  a. "All are not *p*" is equivalent to "none are *p*."
  b. "Not (not *p*)" is equivalent to "*p*."
  c. "Not all are *p*" is equivalent to "some are not *p*."
  d. Correct equivalence rule not given.

2. Find the rule of logical equivalence that directly (in one step) transforms statement "i." into statement "ii."

    i. It is not true that winters are cold and summers are hot.
    ii. Winters are not cold or summers are not hot.

  a. "Not (*p* and *q*)" is equivalent to "not *p* or not *q*."
  b. "If *p*, then *q*" is equivalent to "not *p* or *q*."
  c. "Not (*p* or *q*)" is equivalent to "not *p* and not *q*."
  d. "Not (not *p*)" is equivalent to "*p*."

3. Find the rule of logical equivalence that directly (in one step) transforms statement "i." into statement "ii."

    i. All art is not priceless.
    ii. No art is priceless.

  a. "Not (*p* and *q*)" is equivalent to "not *p* or not *q*."
  b. "All are not *p*" is equivalent to "none are *p*."
  c. "Not some *p*" is equivalent to "all are not *p*."
  d. "Not (not *p*)" is equivalent to "*p*."

4. Find the rule of logical equivalence that directly (in one step) transforms statement "i." into statement "ii."

      i. It is not the case that integers are real or irrational.
     ii. Integers are not real and integers are not irrational.

  a. "Not (*p* or *q*)" is equivalent to "not *p* and not *q*."
  b. "Not (*p* and *q*)" is equivalent to "not *p* or not *q*."
  c. "Not all *p*" is equivalent to "some are not *p*."
  d. "None are *p*" is equivalent to "all are not *p*."

5. Find the rule of logical equivalence that directly (in one step) transforms statement "i." into statement "ii."

      i. It is not true that if the moon is full, then the fish will bite.
     ii. The moon is full and the fish won't bite.

  a. "Not (*p* or *q*)" is equivalent to "not *p* and not *q*."
  b. "Not (*p* and *q*)" is equivalent to "not *p* or not *q*."
  c. "Not all *p*" is equivalent to "some are not *p*."
  d. "Not (if *p*, then *q*)" is equivalent to "*p* and not *q*."

6. Find the rule of logical equivalence that directly (in one step) transforms statement "i." into statement "ii."

      i. If winter is early, then heating oil is scarce.
     ii. Winter is not early or heating oil is scarce.

  a. "Not (if *p*, then *q*)" is equivalent to "*p* and not *q*."
  b. "Not (*p* and *q*)" is equivalent to "not *p* or not *q*."
  c. "Not (*p* or *q*)" is equivalent to "not *p* and not *q*."
  d. "If *p*, then *q*" is equivalent to "not *p* or *q*."

7. Find the rule of logical equivalence that directly (in one step) transforms statement "i." into statement "ii."

      i. It is not true that all dolphins are not smart.
     ii. Dolphins are smart.

  a. "Not all are *p*" is equivalent to "some are not *p*."
  b. "All are not *p*" is equivalent to "none is *p*."
  c. "Not (not *p*)" is equivalent to "*p*."
  d. "Not (if *p*, then *q*)" is equivalent to "*p* and not *q*."

ANSWERS: 1.c., 2.a., 3.b., 4.a., 5.d., 6.d., 7.c.

**IV.E.1.
The student will draw
logical conclusions
when facts warrant
them.**

In this skill the stimulus will provide premises and ask for the logical conclusion. These premises will be given in two different forms. One form will consist of statements using the connectives "if-then," "and," "or," and so on. The second form will use the words "all," "none," "some are," and "some are not."

    To select the logical conclusions when given a set of premises that use "if-then" statements, do as follows:

STEP **1.**   Read the information in the stimulus and identify statements for *p*, *q*, *r*, etc.

STEP **2.** Write each premise statement in terms of p, q, or r.

STEP **3.** Use the five valid argument patterns in Skill III.E.1.:

(a) If p, then q

$\underline{p}$

$\therefore q$

(b) If p, then q

$\underline{\sim q}$

$\therefore \sim p$

(c) If p, then q

$\underline{\text{If } q, \text{ then } r}$

$\therefore$ If p, then r

(d) p or q*

$\underline{\sim p}$

$\therefore q$

(e) p or q*

$\underline{\sim q}$

$\therefore p$

plus the equivalence statements of Skill II.E.2.:

(f) If p, then $q \equiv \sim p$ or q

(g) If p, then $q \equiv$ If $\sim q$, then $\sim p$

to deduce the conclusion.

STEP **4.** Replace p, q, or r with their statements.

Logical
Reasoning Skills

Example **1:** Study the information given below. Find the logical conclusion.

If you major in science, then you will be a researcher. If you major in mathematics, then you will be a researcher. You study science.

Solution:

p = you major in science	(1) Identify p, q, and r.
q = you will be a researcher	
r = you major in mathematics	

| a. If you major in science, then you will be a researcher. If p, then q. | (2) Rewrite premise in terms of p, q, and r. |

b. If you major in mathematics, then you will be a researcher.
If r, then q.

c. You study science.
p

| Combining (a) and (c): If p, then q p | (3) Use the argument pattern (a). |

To deduce q

| You will be a researcher. | (4) Replace q. |

Example **2:** Study the information given below. Find the logical conclusion.

If your work is not completed, then you will not pass this course. If you graduate in June, then you pass this course.

Solution:

p = your work is not complete
q = you will not pass
r = you graduate in June

(3) Identify p, q, and r.

a. If p, then q.
b. If r, then $\sim q$.

(2) Rewrite premise in terms of p, q, and r.

Since "a." and "b." do not match any pattern, use pattern (g) to rewrite "b." "If r, then $\sim q$" is the same as "If q, then $\sim r$." Now use (a) and (b):

(3) Use the argument pattern (c).

$$\text{If } p \text{, then } q$$
$$\underline{\textit{If } q \textit{, then } \sim r}$$
To deduce If p, then $\sim r$

If your work is not complete, then you will not graduate.

(4) Replace p and $\sim r$.

To select the logical conclusion when given a set of premises that use the words "all," "none," "some are," and "some are not," do as follows:

STEP **1.** Read the information in the stimulus. Draw a Euler circle to represent the conditions given (see Skill II.E.4.).

STEP **2.** Use the diagram to test each of the responses to determine which one necessarily follows from the set of premises.

**Logical
Reasoning Skills**

Example **3:** Study the information. If a logical conclusion is given, select that conclusion. If none of the conclusions given is warranted, select the option expressing this condition.

"All college professors are educators. All educators enjoy teaching. Dr. Cleveland is a college professor."

a. Dr. Cleveland enjoys teaching.
b. Dr. Cleveland is not an educator.
c. Dr. Cleveland does not enjoy teaching.
d. None of the above is warranted.

Solution:

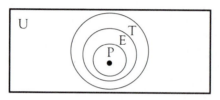

(1) Draw Euler cirlces for "All college professors (*P*) are educators (*E*). All educators (*E*) enjoy teaching (*T*). Dr. Cleveland (•) is a college professor."

Response "a." *Dr. Cleveland enjoys teaching.* Yes, because Dr. Cleveland is a member of the set of people who enjoy teaching

(2) Test responses.

Response "a." is the solution.

(*Note*: Response "b." is false because Dr. Cleveland is a member of set *E*.

Response "c." is false because Dr. Cleveland is a member of set *T*.

Response "d." is false because response "a." is the solution.)

Example **2:** Study the information given below. If a logical conclusion is given, select that conclusion, if none of the conclusions given is warranted, select the option expressing this condition.

"All hard workers win awards. All awards make people happy. Sally is happy."

a. Sally won an award.
b. Sally is a hard worker.
c. Sally did not win an award.
d. None of the above is warranted.

Solution:

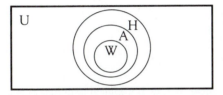

(1) Draw Euler circles for "All hard workers (*W*) win awards (*A*). All awards (*A*) make people happy (*H*).

Response "a." *Sally won an award* only if she is in set *A*. However, she could also be in shaded region below:

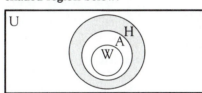

(2) Test responses.

Response "b." *Sally is a hard worker* only if she is in set *W*. However, she could also be in the shaded region below:

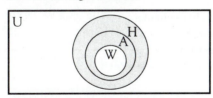

Response "c." *Sally did not win an award* only if she is not in set *A* or *W*. However, the premises leave the possibility of her being in any of the regions of set *H*.

The solution is "d."

**Logical
Reasoning Skills**

IV.E.1.
Sample Items

1. Study the information given below. If a logical conclusion is given, select that conclusion. If none of the conclusions given is warranted, select the option expressing this condition.

   "If you are an accountant, then you took business courses. If you took business courses, then you studied finance. You are an accountant."

   a. You studied finance.
   b. You own a business.
   c. You did not study finance.
   d. None of the above is warranted.

2. Study the information given below. If a logical conclusion is given, select that conclusion. If none of the conclusions given is warranted, select the option expressing this condition.

   "If the waves are high, then Sandy will go surfing. If the beach is crowded, then Sandy will not go surfing. The beach is crowded."

   a. The waves are high.
   b. Sandy will go surfing.
   c. The waves are not high.
   d. None of the above is warranted.

3. Study the information given below. If a logical conclusion is given, select that conclusion. If none of the conclusions given is warranted, select the option expressing this condition.

   "All artists are talented. All talented people are creative. John is creative."

   a. John is an artist.
   b. John is not an artist.
   c. John is talented.
   d. None of the above is warranted.

4. Study the information given below. If a logical conclusion is given, select that conclusion. If none of the conclusions given is warranted, select the option expressing this condition.

   "If I study medicine, then I will become a doctor. I will be a programmer or I will not be a doctor. I will not be a programmer."

   a. I did not study medicine.
   b. I study medicine.
   c. I will be a doctor.
   d. None of the above is warranted.

5. Study the information given below. If a logical conclusion is given, select that conclusion. If none of the conclusions given is warranted, select the option expressing this condition.

   "If the symphony comes to Atlanta, we will buy tickets. The symphony will come to Atlanta or Jacksonville. The symphony did not come to Jacksonville."

   a. We did not buy tickets.
   b. The symphony did not come to Atlanta.
   c. We did buy tickets.
   d. None of the above is warranted.

6. Study the information given below. If a logical conclusion is given, select that conclusion. If none of the conclusions given is warranted, select the option expressing this condition.

"All volunteers are conscientious workers. All conscientious workers enjoy their jobs. No security guard enjoys his job."

 a. Some security guards are volunteers.
 b. All security guards are volunteers.
 c. No security guard is a volunteer.
 d. None of the above is warranted.

7. Study the information given below. If a logical conclusion is given, select that conclusion. If none of the conclusions given is warranted, select the option expressing this condition.

"If Tom grows watermelons, then he grows peanuts. Tom grows watermelons or peanuts. Tom grows cantaloupes and watermelons."

 a. He grows peanuts.
 b. He does not grow watermelons.
 c. He does not grow peanuts.
 d. If he grows peanuts, then he grows watermelons.

ANSWERS: 1.a., 2.c., 3.d., 4.a., 5.c., 6.c., 7.a.

Posttest and
Answer Key

DIRECTIONS:
Read each question and select the correct response.

1. $(-10) \times \left(-1\frac{1}{5}\right) =$

   a. -12
   b. -10
   c. $8\frac{1}{3}$
   d. 12

2. If you decrease 20 by 15% of itself, what is the result?

   a. 3
   b. 17
   c. 18
   d. 23

3. What is the distance around the right triangle?

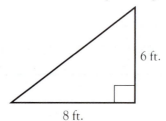

   a. 14 ft.
   b. 22 ft.
   c. 24 ft.
   d. 28 ft.

4. $\dfrac{3}{\sqrt{6}} =$

   a. $\sqrt{3}$
   b. $\dfrac{\sqrt{2}}{2}$
   c. $\dfrac{\sqrt{6}}{2}$
   d. $\dfrac{\sqrt{18}}{6}$

5. If $5a + 10 = 4a - 8$, then

   a. $a = -18$
   b. $a = -2$
   c. $a = 2$
   d. $a = 18$

6. Choose the correct solution set for the system of linear equations.

$$5x + 3y = 8$$
$$2x - y = 1$$

a. $\left\{\left(\dfrac{9}{11}, \dfrac{10}{11}\right)\right\}$

b. $\{(1, 1)\}$

c. $\left\{\left(\dfrac{10}{11}, \dfrac{9}{11}\right)\right\}$

d. the empty set

7. Mr. Diaz can purchase a microwave oven with or without the following options: turntable, seven-day timer, or temperature probe. How many different combinations of these options are available?

 a. 1
 b. 3
 c. 6
 d. 8

8. The City League is going to have a cookout for the players on the softball league. If the director allows ⅓ of a pound of meat for each person, what would be a reasonable estimate for the amount of meat that should be bought for 352 players?

 a. 12 lbs.
 b. 90 lbs.
 c. 120 lbs.
 d. 1,080 lbs.

9. Which of the statements a–d is true for the pictured triangle? (The measure of angle A is represented by the letter x.)

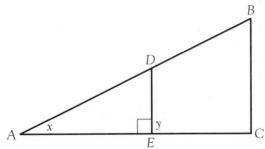

 a. $\dfrac{DE}{AE} = \dfrac{AC}{BC}$
 b. $x = 30°$
 c. $x = 60°$
 d. $\dfrac{BC}{DE} = \dfrac{AD}{AB}$

10. Choose the expression equivalent to the following:

$$8y + 10x$$

 a. $10y + 8x$
 b. $18xy$
 c. $2(4y + 5x)$
 d. $10x - 8y$

11. The graph below represents a distribution of the selling price of homes sold in April. Select the statement that is true about the distribution of homes.

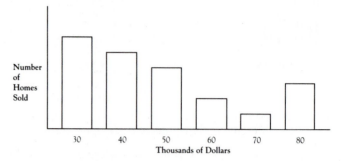

Number of Homes Sold

30   40   50   60   70   80
Thousands of Dollars

a. The mode and the median are the same.
b. The mode is less than the median.
c. The mean is less than the mode.
d. The mean is less than the median.

12. Identify the missing term in the following arithmetic progression.

$$6, 4, 2, 0, -2, \underline{\quad}$$

a. -6
b. -4
c. -3
d. 4

13. A movie-rental store has a membership fee of $10.00. Members can rent their first 3 videos for $2.00 each. Additional videos are $1.25 each. How much will it cost Pat to become a member and rent 5 movies?

a. $ 4.50
b. $ 8.50
c. $13.25
d. $18.50

14. How many whole numbers leave a remainder of 3 when divided into 48, and a remainder of 1 when divided into 16?

a. 0
b. 1
c. 2
d. 3

15. Twice the sum of a number and six is three less than seven times the number. Which equation should be used to find x, the number?

a. $2(x + 6) = 3 - 7x$
b. $2x + 6 = 7x - 3$
c. $6 + 2x = 3 - 7x$
d. $2(x + 6) = 7x - 3$

16. The following is a description of the voter registration rolls for Cliff County by age and sex.

Age	Female	Male
18–29	6%	9%
30–39	9%	9%
40–49	12%	10%
50–59	14%	11%
60 and older	13%	7%

What is the probability that a randomly selected voter will be 50 or older, given that the voter is female?

a. $\dfrac{7}{20}$

b. $\dfrac{1}{4}$

c. $\dfrac{27}{100}$

d. $\dfrac{1}{2}$

17. Given that

    i. No taxpayers are dishonest.
    ii. All Floridians pay taxes.

a. No Floridian is dishonest.
b. If you pay taxes, you are a Floridian.
c. Some Floridians are dishonest.
d. If you are not a Floridian, then you do not pay taxes.

18. All of the following arguments a–d have true conclusions, but one of the arguments is not valid. Select the argument that is *not* valid.

a. All pools are deep and all deep places are dangerous. Therefore, all pools are dangerous.
b. All pools are fun and all fun places have water. Therefore, all pools have water.
c. All pools have diving boards. All diving boards are dangerous. Therefore, all pools are dangerous.
d. All deep water has diving boards. All pools have diving boards. Therefore, all pools have deep water.

19. Select the conclusion that will make the following argument valid.

"If statistics is offered this semester, then I will graduate. If I graduate, then I will not have to sell my car."

a. If statistics is offered this semester, then I will not have to sell my car.
b. If statistics is not offered this semester, then I will have to sell my car.
c. If I graduate, then statistics was offered this semester.
d. If I do not graduate, then I will have to sell my car.

20. Study the information given below. If a logical conclusion is given, select the conclusion. If none of the conclusions given is warranted, select the option expressing this condition.

"All fossils are valuable. All valuable items need to be in a museum. Trevor's rock is valuable."

   a. Trevor's rock is a fossil.
   b. Trevor's rock needs to be in a museum.
   c. Trevor's rock is not a fossil.
   d. None of the above is warranted.

21. Which is a linear factor of the following expression?

$$2x^2 - x - 3$$

   a. $x - 1$
   b. $2x - 3$
   c. $x - 3$
   d. $2x + 3$

22. What type of triangle is $\triangle ABC$?

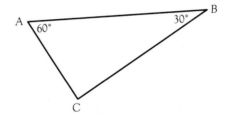

   a. equilateral
   b. right
   c. obtuse
   d. isosceles

23. $5^2 + 2^3 =$

   a. $(5 + 2)^5$
   b. $(5)(5) + (2)(2)(2)$
   c. $(5)(5)(2)(2)(2)$
   d. $(2)(2)(2)(2)(2) + (3)(3)$

24. $3.02 - (-4.121) =$

   a. -7.141
   b. -1.101
   c. 1.101
   d. 7.141

25. What is 30% of 84?

   a. .252
   b. 2.52
   c. 25.2
   d. 252

26. What is the area of a square region whose side length is 4 ft.?

   a. 16 ft.
   b. 20 ft.
   c. 16 sq. ft.
   d. 20 sq. ft.

27. $\frac{1}{4} - \frac{1}{4} \times \frac{2}{3} \div \frac{1}{3} =$

    a. $\frac{-1}{4}$

    b. 0

    c. $\frac{3}{4}$

    d. 2

28. Given $z = (x + y)^3$, if $x = 1$ and $y = -3$, then $z =$

    a. -26

    b. -8

    c. -6

    d. 6

29. The graph below represents the distribution of classes for Riverview Elementary School. Which grades have the same number of classes?

    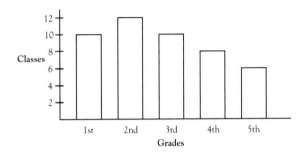

    a. 1st and 4th

    b. 1st and 3rd

    c. 3rd and 4th

    d. 2nd and 5th

30. Select the place value associated with the underlined digit.

    7.31$\underline{4}$2

    a. $\frac{1}{10^4}$

    b. $\frac{1}{10^3}$

    c. 10^2

    d. 10^3

31. In $\triangle ABC$, $x = z$. Which of the following statements is true for the figure shown? (The measure of angle A is represented by x.)

    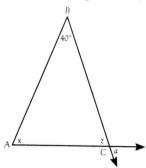

a. $a = 40°$
b. $x = 40°$
c. $z = 140°$
d. $a = 70°$

32. The amount of aluminum foil needed to cover the top of a baking dish is given by which measure?

a. quarts
b. inches
c. square inches
d. liters

33. Chris can build 4 tables in 3 days. Let t represent the number of tables Chris can complete in a 30-day month. Select the correct statement of the given condition.

a. $\dfrac{3}{4} = \dfrac{t}{30}$

b. $\dfrac{4}{t} = \dfrac{30}{3}$

c. $\dfrac{4}{3} = \dfrac{t}{30}$

d. $\dfrac{3}{t} = \dfrac{30}{4}$

34. Ten percent of the customers who have repairs made at a local garage have to return because the problem was not corrected. What is the probability that Mr. Grant will have to return twice?

a. .2
b. .1
c. .01
d. .02

35. Study the figure showing a regular octagon. Then select the formula for computing the total area of the octagon.

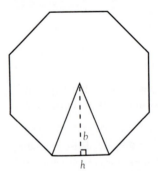

a. Area $= 4bh$
b. Area $= 8bh$
c. Area $= 8h + b$
d. Area $= 8(h + b)$

36. John was told that he could save 35% per month on his electricity bill by replacing his central heating and cooling unit. If his average monthly bill was $90, how much money could he save per year if he replaces the unit?

a. $31.50
b. $58.50

c. $378
d. $702

37. A rectangular garden measures 4 feet by 6 inches and 6 feet by 4 inches. Mrs. Walker wants to enclose it with a picket fence that costs $12 per foot. How much will the fence cost?

a. $121.00
b. $130.00
c. $230.00
d. $260.00

38. The table below shows the percent of customers ordering types of lunches at Sandy's Place.

Type of Lunch	Percent of Customers
Salad bar only	.26
Soup and salad bar	.15
Cold plate	.19
Luncheon special	.17
Sandwiches	.23

What percentage of customers order a lunch that includes an item from the salad bar?

a. .15
b. .26
c. .41
d. .60

39. Select the statement that is the negation of the statement "It is summer and it is hot."

a. It is not summer and it is not hot.
b. It is not summer and it is hot.
c. It is summer or it is not hot.
d. It is not summer or it is not hot.

40. Select the rule of logical equivalence that directly (in one step) transforms statement "i." into statement "ii."

    i. If x is even, then x is not prime.
    ii. If x is prime, then x is not even.

a. "If p, then q" is equivalent to "p or $\sim q$."
b. Not (p and q) is equivalent to "not p or not q."
c. "If p, then q" is equivalent to "If not p, then not q."
d. Correct equivalence rule is not given.

41. If $2 - 3(x - 4) \geq 1$, then

a. $x \geq -5$

b. $x \geq -\dfrac{13}{3}$

c. $x \leq -\dfrac{11}{3}$

d. $x \leq \dfrac{13}{3}$

42. What is the *mode* of the data in the following example?

$$3, 6, 3, 5, 8, 10, 12, 2$$

a. 3
b. 5.5
c. 6.125
d. 7

43. For each of the statements below, determine whether $x = -^1\!/_2$ is a solution.

i. $|x - ^1\!/_2| \leq 1$
ii. $2x^2 + x - 1 = 0$
iii. $2x - 1 = 2$

a. i only
b. ii only
c. i and ii only
d. i, ii, and iii

44. $350\% =$

a. .35
b. 3.5
c. 350
d. 35,000

45. $(-.01) \div (.5) =$

a. $-.2$
b. .02
c. .002
d. $-.02$

46. Round 3,762 pounds to the nearest 10 pounds.

a. 3,760
b. 3,770
c. 3,800
d. 4,000

47. What is the volume of a circular cone whose height is 6 inches and whose diameter is 4 inches?

a. 8π cu. in.
b. 24π cu. in.
c. 32π cu. in.
d. 96π cu. in.

48. $3,200,000 \div .00016 =$

a. $.2 \times 10^2$
b. $.2 \times 10^{10}$
c. 2×10^2
d. 2×10^{10}

49. Find f(1), given

$$f(x) = -3x^2 + 6x$$

a. 15
b. 3

    c. 0

    d. −15

50. $\dfrac{3}{4}$? $\dfrac{5}{8}$

    a. =

    b. <

    c. >

51. Choose the inequality equivalent to the following:

$$-5x < 10$$

    a. $x < -2$

    b. $x > -5$

    c. $x > -2$

    d. $x < 5$

52. Kinetic energy is computed from the formula $K = \frac{1}{2}mv^2$. If a car is traveling at a constant speed (v) of 4 m/sec and has 24,000 joules of kinetic energy (K), what is the mass (m) of the car?

    a.   750 kg

    b. 3,000 kg

    c. 12,000 kg

    d. 48,000 kg

53. Select the statement below that is <u>not</u> logically equivalent to "If the ozone layer continues to deteriorate, then our planet will become warmer."

    a. If our planet becomes warmer, then the ozone layer has deteriorated.

    b. The ozone layer will continue to deteriorate or our planet will not become warmer.

    c. If our planet does not become warmer, then the ozone layer did not continue to deteriorate.

    d. Our planet will become warmer or the ozone layer will not continue to deteriorate.

54. $8\pi - 5 + 6\pi =$

    a. $48\pi^2 - 5$

    b. 9π

    c. $14\pi - 5$

    d. $2\pi + 5$

55. Find the correct solution to this equation:

$$x^2 + 2x - 1 = 0$$

    a. −2 and 1

    b. $-1 + 2\sqrt{2}$ and $-1 - 2\sqrt{2}$

    c. −1

    d. $-1 + \sqrt{2}$ and $-1 - \sqrt{2}$

Posttest and Answer Key

Posttest Answer Key

Question	Answer	Skill
1.	d.	(I.A.1b.)
2.	b.	(I.A.3.)
3.	c.	(I.B.2a.)
4.	c.	(I.C.1b.)
5.	a.	(I.C.4a.)
6.	b.	(I.C.9.)
7.	d.	(I.D.3.)
8.	c.	(II.A.5.)
9.	c.	(II.B.3.)
10.	c.	(II.C.1.)
11.	b.	(II.D.1.)
12.	b.	(III.A.1.)
13.	d.	(IV.A.1.)
14.	c.	(IV.A.3.)
15.	d.	(IV.C.2.)
16.	d.	(IV.D.2.)
17.	a.	(II.E.3.)
18.	d.	(II.E.4.)
19.	a.	(III.E.1.)
20.	b.	(IV.E.1.)
21.	b.	(I.C.7.)
22.	b.	(II.B.2.)
23.	b.	(II.A.1.)
24.	d.	(I. A.2a.)
25.	c.	(I.A.4.)
26.	c.	(I.B.2b.)
27.	a.	(I.C.2.)
28.	b.	(I.C.5.)

Question	Answer	Skill
29.	b.	(I.D.1.)
30.	b.	(II.A.2.)
31.	d.	(II.B.6.)
32.	c.	(II.B.4.)
33.	c.	(II.C.3.)
34.	c.	(II.D.3.)
35.	a.	(III.B.2.)
36.	c.	(IV.A.2.)
37.	d.	(IV.B.1.)
38.	c.	(IV.D.1.)
39.	d.	(II.E.1.)
40.	c.	(III.E.2.)
41.	d.	(I.C.4b.)
42.	a.	(I.D.2.)
43.	a.	(II.C.2.)
44.	b.	(II.A.3.)
45.	d.	(I.A.2b.)
46.	a.	(I.B.1.)
47.	a.	(I.B.2c.)
48.	d.	(I.C.3.)
49.	b.	(I.C.6.)
50.	c.	(II.A.4.)
51.	c.	(III.C.2.)
52.	b.	(I.C.5.)
53.	c.	(II.E.2.)
54.	c.	(I.C.1a.)
55.	d.	(I.C.8.)

Acknowledgments

Isaac Asimov, from "How Easy to See the Future," in *Natural History*, April 1975. Copyright © 1975, The American Museum of Natural History. Reprinted with permission of *Natural History*.

Molly M. Bloomfield, from *Chemistry: The Living Organism*, fourth edition. Copyright © 1987 by and reprinted with permission of John Wiley and Sons Incorporated.

Mervyn Cadwallader, from "Marriage as a Wretched Institution." Copyright © 1966 by Mervyn Cadwallader as originally published by *The Atlantic Monthly*, November 1966. Reprinted by permission of *The Atlantic Monthly*.

Michael Coe, from *The Maya*, by Michael Coe. Copyright © 1987 by and reprinted with permission of Thames and Hudson.

Elliott Currie and **Jerome Skolnick**, from "Beer Wars: A Closeup of Economic Concentration," by Elliott Currie and Jerome Skolnick in *America's Problems: Social Issues and Public Policy*, Scott Foresman and Company, 1988. Reprinted by permission of HarperCollins Publishers.

Charles French, from "Money of Yesterday," by Charles French in *Hobbies Magazine*, October 1953. Reprinted by permission of *Hobbies Magazine*.

Alan Gottlieb, from "An Opposing View," by Alan Gottlieb as published in *USA Today*, May 7, 1991. Reprinted by permission of the author.

Bob Greene, from "Cut," in *Cheeseburgers*, by Bob Greene. Copyright © 1985 by John Deadline Enterprises, Incorporated. Reprinted with the permission of Atheneum Publishers, an imprint of Macmillan Publishing Company.

Robert Hickok, from "Section on Native American Songs," by Robert Hickok in *Exploring Music*, fourth edition. Copyright © 1989 by and reprinted with permission of William C. Brown Publishers.

Paul S. Kaplan and **Jean Stein**, from *Psychology of Adjustment*, by Paul S. Kaplan and Jean Stein. Copyright © 1984 by and reprinted with permission of Wadsworth, Incorporated.

Jonathan Kozol, from *Illiterate America*, by Jonathan Kozol, New American Library/Plume Books, 1986. Reprinted by permission of Doubleday, a division of Bantam, Doubleday, Dell Publishing Group, Incorporated.

Margaret Mead, from "One Vote for This Age of Anxiety," by Margaret Mead, in *The New York Times*, May 20, 1965. Copyright © 1965 by and reprinted with permission of The New York Times Company.

David G. Myers, from *Psychology*, second edition, by David G. Myers. Copyright © 1989 by and reprinted with permission of Worth Publishers, Incorporated.

John A. Perry and **Erna Perry**, from *Contemporary Society: An Introduction to Social Science*, eighth edition, by John A. Perry and Erna Perry. Copyright © 1984 by Harper & Row Publishers, Incorporated and reprinted by permission of HarperCollins Publishers.

Claude A. Villee, Jr., et al, from *Biology*, second edition, by Claude A. Villee, Jr., Elda P. Solomon, P. William Davis, Charles E. Martin, and Linda R. Berg. Copyright © 1989 by and reprinted with permission of Saunders College Publishing.

Excerpts from the Test Item Specifications for the College-level Academic Skills Test (CLAST) are reprinted by permission of the Florida Department of Education.